America's Forgotten Constitutions

America's Forgotten Constitutions

DEFIANT VISIONS OF
POWER AND COMMUNITY

ROBERT L. TSAI

Harvard University Press

Cambridge, Massachusetts, and London, England   2014

Library of Congress Cataloging-in-Publication Data

Tsai, Robert L., 1971– author.
  America's forgotten constitutions : defiant visions of power and community /
  Robert L. Tsai.
      pages cm
  Includes bibliographical references and index.
  ISBN 978-0-674-05995-5 (hardcover : alk. paper)
    1. Constitutional history—United States.   2. United States—Politics and
government.   3. United States—History—Autonomy and independence
movements.   I. Title.
  KF4541.T73 2014
  342.7302'92—dc23   2013034546

Contents

Preface

This book was conceived on the day I stumbled upon a copy of John Brown's Provisional Constitution and Ordinances for the People of the United States. Eagerly, I pored over its contents, wondering why the abolitionist's imagined community had not gained the same amount of attention as his armed assault on Harpers Ferry. The deeper I delved, the more I realized that the instrument represented the latest in the man's body of writings having political and legal significance: letters, op-eds, organizational bylaws, a declaration of independence, and then, finally, a proposal for a republican form of government. That discovery led me to wonder what other groups of Americans authored constitutions to rule themselves. The documents I collected revealed a great deal about not only substantive disagreements over law and policy but also ordinary people's divergent perceptions of political community and the constitutional process. After investigation and culling, I was left with eight experiments from generative periods in American history. What they tell us about the political tradition—its tensions, competing forms, and suppressed ideas—became the driving inquiry for this book.

Special thanks to librarians and archivists at the Center for Icarian Studies at Western Illinois University, Moorland-Spingarn Research Center Manuscript Division at Howard University, New Hampshire Historical Society, University of Chicago, and University of Nebraska.

Billie Jo Kaufman, William Ryan, and the library staff at American University provided invaluable assistance in tracking down primary and secondary materials. The *Boston College Law Review* offered an early venue to explore John Brown's constitutional theories.

A number of colleagues and friends read one or more chapters closely. Among them: Bruce Ackerman, Michael Barkun, Bethany Berger, Susan Carle, Janie Chuang, Joshua Cohen, Garrett Epps, Christian Fritz, Robert Gordon, James Henretta, Joe Lowndes, Fernanda Nicola, Jeff Powell, Kim Lane Scheppele, Howard Schweber, Mark Weiner, and Steven Wilf. Vanessa Careiro, Chris Datskos, Arija Flowers, Christine Miranda, Brian O'Connell, Brett Shields, and Gillian Thompson provided invaluable research assistance. Three anonymous reviewers for Harvard University Press pushed me to deepen the manuscript's insights, and I am grateful for their suggestions. Faculty workshops at Loyola–Los Angeles School of Law, Rutgers University Law School–Camden, Stanford Law School, University of Connecticut Law School, and University of Washington proved invaluable at crucial junctures. Other productive opportunities to sound out the book's themes took place at the D.C. Area Legal History Roundtable, University of Wisconsin Constitutional Law Discussion Group, the American Democracy Forum's Inaugural Conference on *Popular Sovereignty and American Democracy,* the Workshop on Race, Gender, and Sexuality in Law and Political Development at Ohio University, and the Charles R. Clason Lecture at Western New England School of Law. Dean Claudio Grossman's financial support of research was indispensable. Most of all, Joyce Seltzer's keen eye and commitment to the project made it possible for these American constitutions to reach a wider audience.

In America, the principle of the sovereignty of the people is not either barren or concealed, as it is with some other nations; it is recognized by the customs and proclaimed by the laws; it spreads freely, and arrives without impediment at its most remote consequences.

Alexis de Tocqueville
Democracy in America
1835–1840

America's Forgotten Constitutions

Prologue

At the close of the constitutional convention in September 1787, the men who framed the U.S. Constitution returned home believing they had designed the best possible government under trying circumstances. They were not foolish enough to think that all of a young nation's problems could be solved with the stroke of a pen, yet they pronounced themselves "satisfied that any thing nearer to perfection could not have been accomplished." First among the statesmen's objectives was the fusion of "free and independent" states into a federal republic. Unhappy with the inefficient Articles of Confederation, delegates proposed an energetic government capable of solving national problems. Perhaps most daunting, they dreamed of a single "people of America," bound by one fundamental law and a common destiny.[1]

There are many outstanding books that assess the contributions of the towering figures involved in the writing process or tell the story of ratification. More plentiful still are projects that weigh the soundness of the Constitution's original design. Instead of revisiting such questions, this study wrestles with the puzzle of ideological domination over time: how America's constitutional culture developed after the founding. Instilling a sense of self-empowerment and a belief in political possibility through the rewriting of legal texts proved essential to the experiment in self-governance. What happened next was that enough individuals took these ideas seriously and put them into practice. Multiple groups claimed the right to rule, proposing an array of legal visions. Instead of a single legal text standing intact for all time, citizens subsequently found themselves awash in competing constitutions.

Building a national legal order in the world outside the Philadelphia statehouse could never be as simple as envisioning an ideal government on paper. To the contrary, it proved infinitely challenging to bring together communities with different conceptions of the good life and understandings of their own authority. Not everyone accepted the relentless drive to create one people, the claim of national supremacy, or the prospect of sharing political power with individuals of different experiences and beliefs. Many were displeased to have their fortunes dictated by bureaucrats and judges who did not share their values. They feared the "annihilation" of not only existing governments but also distinctive ways of life. When unrest reached a perfect pitch, a group of Americans expressed their displeasure by authoring a new constitution.

If creating one people out of many was an audacious idea from the start, then the Framers' revolutionary rhetoric created as many fresh problems as it solved. Delegates to the Federal Convention invoked the people's natural right of sovereignty to justify exceeding their mandate in proposing an entirely new constitution instead of recommending modest changes. Supporters called upon the will of the people once again in defending their choice to ignore established protocols for altering the Articles of Confederation. Americans could break the rules, James Wilson explained, because "the supreme, absolute, and uncontrollable power remains in the people," with the natural consequence "that the people may change the[ir] constitutions, whenever and however they please." That argument echoed throughout the ratifying debates and eventually carried the day.[2]

In establishing the American republic, the Framers unleashed a pair of seductive ideas: popular sovereignty and written constitutionalism. One is treated as a God-given right; the other, a cherished means of ordering society. More than the brute fact of shared territory, these ideas became central to American identity and legal practice. The two principles, yoked together during a time of "great national discussion," would present a conundrum, proving to be both generative and destabilizing over time. According to their logic, the people have the right to withhold their consent to be governed. Moreover, if all share equally in that most basic right to rule, then anyone can propose a return to the drafting table. But beyond specifying a protocol for amending the 1787 Constitution, the Framers themselves left unresolved precisely when and how the twin ideas can be activated again to overthrow, transform, or subvert the legal order. Successive generations would have to determine the legitimacy of popular methods and concepts. Through trial and error, the people themselves had to decide how a new constitution could be popularly authorized and when, instead, a democratic experiment transgressed the limits of legality.

After the heady days of ratification had passed, the principles of popular sovereignty and written constitutionalism mutated in the hands of ordinary people. Americans found themselves simultaneously enchanted and repelled by what they had wrought. The prospect of starting over at any time was exhilarating, no matter how bleak one's circumstances. Indeed, the pair of ideas inspired an explosion of democratization throughout the United States and later around the world. Even so, citizens who became invested in the 1787 Constitution increasingly believed that popular sovereignty and written constitutionalism were dangerous ideas that themselves had to be reformed. The possibility that a healthy legal order could be eroded through the tools of its creation seemed positively nefarious. If the authors of new constitutions in each generation represented the imaginative, lawbreaking strain of the political tradition, then defenders of the kind of sovereignty articulated in the federal Constitution represented its order-preserving antithesis, carried out through the enforcement of ordinary law and superior force of arms.

To fully appreciate the cultural contest that characterizes the legal process in action, one must investigate the struggles of dissidents who wrote and defended their own constitutions. It requires analysis of the ideas and belief systems of groups that disagreed vehemently with the emerging national constitutional order but whose members, in their own way, remained committed to the rule of law. Many of their experiences have been neglected by academics interested in recounting the triumph of mainstream constitutionalism. But to gain an accurate sense of the tradition, it is crucial to develop a feel for the ideological periphery—or more precisely, the points of friction between conventional ideas about the American Constitution and insurgent theories of law. These points of contact, redundancy, or contradiction reveal a wealth of information about the nation's legal belief system. The primary task, then, is to chart the development of these popular legal theories and the relationships among them—whether antagonistic or complementary. These conflicts offer evidence that democratic constitutionalism ultimately entails an intellectual and spiritual struggle over ideas, values, and worldviews. Despite the common expectation that a written text can end such battles, in fact a constitution can do little more than shape how conflict unfolds.

The entire process of creating and sustaining a constitution is ideological and social in nature. To be successful, a constitution must shift allegiances, realign sources of authority, and cultivate new identities, mind-sets, and habits consistent with good citizenship. Evidence of such transformations is not found in law books alone. Differing points of view can be heard within institutions carrying the imprimatur of the 1787 Constitution, but far more antagonistic legal perspectives typically are nourished elsewhere. The sources of law can lie far beyond the control and supervision of the authorities, fostered in alternative constitutions and legal materials, popular writings, underground organizations, and the Internet. Creating an oppositional legal culture requires not only the reframing of older ideas and historical experiences but also the development of coherent and responsive theories of law, power, and community. Cogent theories of law, in turn, depend upon brave and resourceful thinkers willing to challenge legal orthodoxy.

Throughout history, a host of colorful characters—squatters and native peoples, slaveholders and abolitionists, black nationalists and white supremacists, socialists and world federalists—have felt left out of the larger project to build a single nation. Recreating life on the margins of society, popular legal theorists within these communities railed against the defects of the legal order. Convinced they would be better off under their own designs, they proposed state governments, breakaway republics, and miniature or worldwide republics not confined by physical boundaries. As resourceful Americans dreamed of the good life, they developed novel theories of community and power through a process of adaptive design, legal writing, and social resistance.

Their constitutions are forgotten in two senses. First, we have left them behind because their proponents lost crucial battles in their own time. Some ran away; others were driven underground, defeated on the battlefield, jailed, or executed. Those who did not meet a violent fate watched the implosion of their legal visions or lost the public relations war. We tend to discount the possibility that these Americans had compelling ideas, because in their own era they made a bid to rule but ultimately failed. Second, their legal theories have been for the most part rejected and suppressed by mainstream constitutionalism as perilous or wrongheaded. These rule-of-law communities have either been crushed or absorbed. In fact, the survival of the 1787 Constitution—wounded, repaired, reread, but never altogether abandoned—has diminished political possibility along the way. Its remarkable endurance has induced forgetfulness of much that has passed: failed democratic experiments, the ingenuity of alternative designs, certain tactics of direct action—even the inner workings of the ideological aspects of constitutionalism itself.

Despite our collective amnesia about these episodes, the constitutions are worth remembering, analyzed and situated within the American political tradition. Doing so tells us something about the substantive ideas, but even more it reveals the recurring forms that constitutional struggle can take. The usual approach is to study the history of American constitutional law as the creation of a single coherent tradition. From this vantage point, the law is a system of well-settled rules to be applied authoritatively, and thus it is sensible to study only a tiny set of documents. The losers in legal conflicts are relegated to the dustbin of history, their ideas presumed to be defeated for all time. But this is a mistake; defining what is suitable for study based strictly upon major legal achievements glorifies insiders at the expense of outsiders, ignores ideological rifts, and privileges technical authority over living practice. The awkward truth is that the American legal tradition is an untidy phenomenon and constitutional defeats are rarely permanent. Insurgent ideas of law can easily be nurtured in underground settings, only to reemerge in more favorable climates. By studying the U.S. Constitution's ascendance through the eyes of the discontented, it becomes possible to observe the American constitutional tradition at war with itself.[3]

There are many ways to make sense of a political tradition—one could just as easily study electoral politics, social movements, or litigation. Constitution-writing experiences are valuable because they provide windows into raging ideological battles engaged by ordinary citizens. Though discontent can surely find other outlets, Americans who dared to resist the tide of history by drafting a constitution rendered some of the most coherent and vibrant theories of sovereignty around. Unlike the typical political movement or party, whose vision might be rendered bland by an appeal to the lowest common denominator or a failure of nerve, proponents of new constitutions presented a holistic diagnosis of the American condition. These dreamers came up with comprehensive plans for a more hopeful future. And wanting desperately to be taken seriously, the people labored to integrate their critiques, experiences, and proposals with the nation's founding narrative, even as they drew sharp differences with a legal regime in place. While successful politics of all sorts must make such appeals, the founders in this volume distinguished themselves through ideological intensity, the integrity of their constitutional vision, and the intricacy of the institutions designed. Each legal experiment is explored on its own terms as a collective intellectual exercise in order to preserve what is unique about a group's behavior while emphasizing the commonalities and departures among experiences.[4]

If Americans wrote so many constitutions, why take a closer look at these eight texts? The constitutions selected for this volume appeared at historically important moments: westward expansion, industrialization and urbanization, America's reckoning with slavery, the forced integration of Indian tribes, the end of the Second World War, the ascendance of civil and human rights. Because these proved to be catalyzing experiences during America's transition from a fledgling republic to a liberal democratic nation, they generated an enormous amount of discord over fundamental values. As snapshots of ideological ferment, the constitutions that emerged from these periods expose major fault lines in our political belief system. The documents present opportunities to excavate ideas and proposals that have been defeated but remain with us, nurtured in underground settings and pockets of discontent. A number of the constitutions—such as the Icarian Constitution of 1850, the Sequoyah Constitution, or the World Constitution of 1947—allow us to contemplate moments of legal transformation often ignored by leading scholars. Significant attention has been paid to the Founding, Reconstruction, and New Deal at the expense of other generative periods, including a burst of nineteenth-century utopianism, the peak of Progressivism, and the impact of wars on a global scale. The additional episodes explored herein suggest that our constitutional past is best understood not as an explosive founding moment followed by general stability but rather as an ongoing, tumultuous social process punctuated by a succession of ideologically significant events. Other constitutions, like those of Malcolm X's followers or Aryan separatists from the Pacific Northwest, allow a different entry point into already identified moments of legal creativity, such as the black civil rights movement of the 1960s and the conservative countermobilization that took place in the aftermath of civil rights successes. In these stories, one encounters not only the breadth of societal disagreement over theories about the U.S. Constitution but also the intensity of popular defiance.

These crises yield insights about when and how disagreement boils over into concerted action. Each constitution exemplifies defiance of the substantive values of the emerging legal order, permitting investigation of the many points of friction rather than harmony. A constitution-writing event worthy of study must be motivated by the kind of outrage that would prompt vigorous reevaluation of ideas about community and power. That way, the collection of texts sheds light upon the historical development of popular sovereignty as a living practice. For this reason, though Americans wrote countless constitutions for local governments, territories, and civic organizations, most ordinary civic constitutions have been excluded from the discussion. In the main, such texts are used for private ordering and civic participation without composing an alternative theory of peoplehood or repudiating the basic precepts of the national legal order. There are always exceptions, of course, and where routine legal forms were used in transformational ways, such instances merit extended treatment.

The eight constitutions also represent legal instruments at different stages of usage and assimilation. Some, like the Icarian Constitution, were embraced by the people and fully implemented. More numerous were constitutions rejected by officials or put into practice incompletely by followers. Compiling a cross section of constitutions at different stages of legitimacy makes it possible to reach some tentative conclusions about the variety of functions that alternative legal texts might serve in a community. Doing so helps us to understand why dissidents might turn to written constitutionalism even when the odds of long-term success are infinitesimal.

Finally, the episodes illustrate a range of popular tactics in defense of a legal vision. Many subscribe to the ideal of peaceful, orderly legal change embodied in the 1787 Constitution. Yet there are always historical figures who insist upon the right to employ extralegal tactics in the defense of higher law. Revolutionaries from Robert Barnwell Rhett, a slave owner, to Imari Abubakari Obadele, a descendant of slaves, claimed that some level of force was necessary for routine resistance to unconstitutional acts as well as for order-smashing projects. In the name of the people, advocates might nullify unjust laws, organize citizen defense leagues, or forcibly liberate individuals and property. When all else failed, their theories of popular sovereignty might justify more extreme steps, such as secession or warfare.

A few caveats are in order. Not every dissident group wrote a constitution; some chose to express their unhappiness through other means. This study focuses only on transformative constitutions of the discontented. It does not try to systematically test the oft-made claim that Americans have a unique propensity to write constitutions. We would need a larger sample before it could be demonstrated, empirically, that Americans are comparatively more likely to write constitutions than the citizens of other countries. The modest goal here is to trace the contour of legal ideas and the social process by which fundamental law takes hold rather than to predict the probability of choices and outcomes. Americans have authored a variety of constitutions to resist cultural and political developments. The central lines of inquiry consist of why people wrote alternative legal texts in the face of enormous odds, how their theories diverged from the ascendant interpretation of the U.S. Constitution, and what functions these texts served for dissident communities. This is not a quantitative study of all available American constitutions but rather a case study of representative models of American constitutionalism. The chapters reveal the divergent forms of popular sovereignty as ordinary people actually practiced them and the inherent challenges faced by those theories.

Even as they present alternative readings of law, the constitutions in this volume shed light on the ideological triumph of the American Constitution. Taken together, they illustrate the broader intergenerational dynamic by which dissident legal ideas and their constituencies are created, sustained, and either integrated or marginalized. This is part and parcel of the larger process by which the U.S. Constitution has become supreme in fact: through political consolidation, the cultural policing of a national community, and extension of the rule of law as a compelling belief system. If the Constitution has prevailed as an ideal, it has been through increasingly complex strategies to match the outbursts of the discontented.

Instead of evolving as a unified tradition, popular sovereignty fragmented into competing theories of self-rule. Over time, these varying accounts of popular sovereignty acquired distinctive and recurring form. They became models, exemplars of American constitutionalism. For analytical purposes, I have divided these theories of law and politics into the *conventional, pioneer, tribal, ethical, cultural,* and *global.* Though not perfect, the categories capture the wealth of trends, origins, sources, motivations, tactics, institutions, and accounts of community reflected in post-Founding constitutions. This analytical framework underscores differences in what people believed, in the best of worlds, a constitution should accomplish. The approach better reveals how the yoked ideas of sovereignty and constitutionalism changed over time not only in the courts or in the political system, but also among the population as a whole. It allows us to observe not only ideological diversity but, more importantly, fundamental disagreements over the very aims of written constitutionalism.

The forms of popular sovereignty should be considered exemplars, prototypical models of politics and belonging. Constitutions can contain elements from different types, though it should be possible to speak of a constitution epitomizing one or another form of power. As American legal practice matured, written constitutions increasingly displayed hybrid theories of sovereignty and community.

Examining legal culture through the lens of post-Founding constitutional conflicts over popular sovereignty underscores the citizenry's disagreements over not only the good life but also who is entitled to wield power and how authority should be structured. Despite the Constitution's claim to have created a single people, Americans remained deeply divided over who actually constituted "we the people." The question had enormous implications, because the answer not only distinguished insiders from outsiders but also identified who had the rightful authority to rule. A people's basis for solidarity also mattered, for it influenced the kind of organizations one might wish to live under and justified how far the rule of law might be taken to perfect a society. Should a people be united by inclusive yet abstract political ideals, a strong moral code, or some other, more visceral, tie of affinity?

A growing conviction that the revolutionary mood should dissipate once the new legal order had been endowed with the people's sovereignty led many Americans to demand the orderly consolidation of territories, economies, and governments. The task then became one of entrenching the institutions, legal arrangements, and concepts sketched in the U.S. Constitution. According to this consensus-based vision of conventional sovereignty, one people had to be bound by broadly inclusive political beliefs, while tolerating a multiplicity of institutions and subnational communities. On this domesticated view of political power, the will of the people had to be channeled through orderly and predictable pathways once the Constitution was adopted. Short of a true revolution, there was little room for disobedience. Other forms of power soon emerged, as successive generations of Americans tested the durability of the emerging legal order. When founders wrote new constitutions, their theories of self-governance often clashed with expressions of conventional sovereignty contemplated by the federal system.

In 1832, settlers announced the formation of the independent Republic of Indian Stream in a contested area in the Northeast. Their constitution proved to be a stark instance of a broader phenomenon. Pioneer sovereignty was a disruptive form of self-organization practiced by migrants to acquire territory, extend the nation's borders, and supplant existing modes of governance. Settlers engaged in land grabbing or illegal squatting to displace occupants of the land and to discredit or reduce the scope of indigenous, non-European forms of tribal sovereignty. Their political theory, which held that true authority springs from productive use of the land, was nowhere found in the U.S. Constitution, but it dovetailed with understandings of law and power on the ground. Pioneer constitutions privileged male suffrage but otherwise tended to be welcoming at their inception, with the goals of legitimating the problematic acquisition of land, exploitation of natural resources, and disruption of boundaries. For many brave souls who transplanted the model of governance in new lands, the promise of one nation called for rewriting the terms of civic membership in ever-more inclusive terms. Pioneer sovereignty had its own difficulties, however, for it offered a vision of law that could be harnessed for nation building and economic development but also could undermine conventional sovereignty's preference for order, integrity, and gradualism.

While the denizens of Indian Stream modeled their republic after the plural city-states that had begun to dot the landscape, other settlers preferred a more perfectionist cast to their basic law and more demanding standards for citizenship. Icarians from France relocated to nineteenth-century America at a high point of communitarian experimentation. Disciples of Charles Fourier and Robert Owen could be counted among scores of "backwoods utopias" sprouting up in the New World. What distinguished Etienne Cabet's followers from so many other socialist groups was the Icarians' heavy reliance on constitutional law. Created by workers, their "community of goods" blended civic republicanism with socialism. Even more intriguing, the constitution secured the blessing of the people of Illinois, showing how a dissident legal order might survive within a dominant order that increasingly prized individualism and capitalism.

The Icarian experiment primarily represented a fascinating instance of ethical sovereignty: the conviction that a people's legal authority derives from a shared moral code. The point was not to acquire land at a breakneck pace but rather to mold ideal citizens from among those who occupied the land. Such a moral basis for a constitution could be derived from a particular religious text or a cross section of ethical traditions. The Icarians also ingeniously made use of civic constitutions for ideologically subversive ends. Ordinary citizens turned to civic constitutions to order their affairs and create organizations. Most of the time, they sprang from conventional sources of law that left the legal order unchallenged. On rare occasions, as the Icarians' creative use of agricultural constitutions attests, such texts could be used for transformative ends.

Americans who turned to ethical sovereignty after the Founding often did so out of dissatisfaction with mainstream constitutionalism, which lurched toward ideas of individual autonomy and antiauthoritarianism, and away from more demanding and exclusionary theories of community. But a central dilemma plagues all forms of ethical sovereignty: how far should a taste for reformation be indulged? Cabet would not be the last founder who treated ideological purity and moral regeneration as the ultimate ends of constitutionalism. His people's struggles with issues of sex equality, cultural change, and the orderly transfer of power from one generation to the next highlight the tensions between the aspirations of group solidarity and popular deliberation. The demise of Icaria offers insights into the limits of ethical sovereignty as well as the difficulties of pursuing transformation within the conventional legal order.

As the debate over slavery intensified and friction became commonplace among a diversifying population, ethical sovereignty became one solution to how America could be held together. Treating a constitution as a moral instrument just might bind the nation's wounds and bring spiritual renewal. Like the Icarians' basic law, John Brown's 1858 Provisional Constitution and Ordinances for the People of the United States codified a moral imperative to promote equality and dignity. Infusing the original American Constitution with Christian values, Brown wrote for a transitional community of abolitionists and freedom fighters that hoped one day to supplant a constitutional system corrupted through dependency on slave labor. In his vision of America reborn, the authentic people were national in character, committed against exclusionary limits on fellowship based on race or condition of previous servitude. More than anything, John Brown's trial and execution demonstrated the tenacity of conventional sovereignty as an ideal and the use of the courts as vehicles for ideological conquest.

The Constitution for the Confederate States of America, unveiled three years after John Brown's attempt at moral revival, provided a very different kind of answer to the questions of solidarity and power. Its framers took popular sovereignty in another direction by conceiving of a people grounded in regional and racial differences. As the slave population increased and the country's demographics changed through immigration, some Americans favored criteria for political membership that tracked cultural attributes such as sex, race, religion, or language. Whatever their contours, such expressions of cultural sovereignty are rooted in a community understood to preexist the state. Here, too, cultural theories of power involved a rejection of conventional sovereignty. Influenced by ideas of liberal egalitarianism, the law increasingly envisioned citizenship in "neutral" political terms. Racial sovereignty rejected the wisdom of agnostic notions of membership. Through the Confederate Constitution, "a slaveholding people" laid claim to a theory of white sovereignty reaching back to the nation's founding. Their unprecedented vision of a large-scale republic joined by racial and economic interests would become a model for later generations of Americans who wished to dissent from a growing national commitment to egalitarianism. Its defeat marked a turning point in the development of conventional sovereignty, which successfully defended the idea of one people and laid down new principles promoting national citizenship and civic equality.

As European settlers learned firsthand, theirs was not the only form of popular sovereignty in North America. Indian tribes, which had long governed their own affairs before contact with Europeans, continued to assert their claims to territory and protect their people against hostile policies. Tribal sovereignty, initially confronted by colonial authorities through diplomacy and war, ultimately became viewed as a form of politics to be destroyed, subordinated, or absorbed. Along the way, native theories of political power became blended with European ideas of liberty and virtuous self-rule. The story of the 1905 Sequoyah Constitution begins as Indian nations, already forcibly relocated to the Midwest and their population decimated, find themselves on the brink of legal extinction. It shows how, in a final act of desperation, the Five Tribes of Indian Territory proposed the State of Sequoyah. Along the way, Indian leaders converted their theories of tribal rule into a familiar republican one in which social groups, acting through political parties, determine the people's agenda within a conventional state. In exchange for formal power, however, native people had to adapt ancient theories of self-rule and assume a hybrid civic identity.

During the twentieth century, a heterogeneous polity was not simply tolerated but instead emerged as a cause for celebration—even a key feature of constitutional design. With the rise of pluralism, an irresistible momentum developed for international organizations, world citizenship, universal law. At the close of the Second World War, academics led by University of Chicago president Robert Maynard Hutchins drafted a constitution for the postwar order that went beyond the Charter for the United Nations. Global sovereignty of the sort exemplified in their 1947 World Constitution resembled conventional sovereignty in modern democratic nations through its endorsement of pluralism, equality, and minority rights. But world federalists' concept of power attacked the very foundations of national sovereignty, in which the people's right to rule is premised upon territorial control and shared identity. Instead, in their hands, the principles of self-rule and written constitutionalism had to be stretched to their logical ends so as to create a world community bound by mutual respect and governed through supranational institutions. Achieving one constitution for all of humanity would not only be the ultimate end of the Enlightenment project but also show off the American political tradition at its finest.

Accounts of cultural sovereignty did not disappear with conventional sovereignty's adoption of the principles of egalitarianism and pluralism. Instead, such strains of law and politics went underground. At the same time, they acquired a global dimension as proponents reached for international and foreign sources of law. With the rise of human rights discourse and the spread of decolonization, Americans welcomed sympathetic peoples beyond the nation's borders to join forces with them to preserve their ethnic or racial identity. Universalistic theories of peoplehood challenged the national, territorial notions of community endorsed by mainstream constitutionalism. Two postwar constitutions predicated on modern theories of racial sovereignty exemplify these changes. In 1968 the followers of Malcolm X demanded that the Deep South states be handed over to black Americans as reparations for slavery so they could establish the independent Republic of New Afrika. Their constitution blended African and non-African ideas and institutions. Nearly forty years later, Aryans planned for a whites-only nation in the Pacific Northwest by drawing on models of white governance from around the world. If adopted, their instrument would overturn *Brown v. Board of Education* and *Roe v. Wade*, cornerstones of the modern liberal order.

As a testament to how entrenched the U.S. legal order had become, would-be founders in both instances had to expend considerable time and resources helping the people to recover their "racial consciousness," lost through generations of education, oppression, and disappointment. Although each offered strikingly different plans for governance, they could agree on one fact now denied by defenders of conventional sovereignty: the constitution of their fathers originally authorized white power. For black nationalists, America's legal transformations did not go far enough to repudiate the past, even after the ratification of the Fourteenth Amendment and passage of civil rights laws. Conversely, these same achievements, which had become integral to the formation of the liberal order, convinced racially conscious whites that they had irrevocably lost control over their own destinies. In each situation, a constitution helped a marginalized people to recover their forgotten history and served as a beacon to despised minorities worldwide.

Through it all, the ascendance of the U.S. Constitution depended on partisans waging ideological war against threatening or inconvenient experiments in popular governance. To stabilize the fledgling republic imagined by the Framers and then transform it into a large-scale liberal order, competing forms of popular sovereignty had to be defeated, managed, or discredited. While pioneer sovereignty could be harnessed for the ends of economic development, it could also morph into a serious threat to the integrity of established governments. Experiments in pioneer rule had to be curtailed and turned into conventional states, counties, or cities. Tribal governments had to be somehow integrated into the larger order if they could not be vanquished. Socialism and other competing ideologies might be accommodated where popular pressure proved to be intense and prolonged but must otherwise be thwarted when they threatened core principles of liberty and capitalism. Racial and regional theories of self-rule deemed incompatible with the emerging pluralistic order faced marginalization. Global accounts of law threatened the nationalistic nature—and to some, the social foundations—of conventional sovereignty.

Thus, the reverence most Americans have for their Constitution has a less savory underside. Having survived well over two hundred years and counting, Americans' charter has far outlasted the typical national constitution, with an average life span of nineteen years. The extension of higher law across the continent has rested in no small part upon ideological conquest of the public imagination. All in the name of good order, defenders of conventional sovereignty have suppressed unorthodox ideas of self-rule.[5]

Whether stillborn or short-lived, each of the eight constitutions served a community struggling to define itself, attract adherents, and make authoritative law. To an impressive degree, dissenters treated their constitutions in lawlike terms even when their legitimacy was in doubt. The consensus view among experts is that a constitution serves multiple functions at once. By contrast, the interwoven stories support a "divisibility" thesis—namely, that among incompletely authorized constitutions, functions can be divided in actual practice. A constitution might serve one or more functions, but not others, at different stages of its life cycle. Iconoclasts used even imperfect constitutions for one or more of the following purposes: social protest, institution building, moral discipline, public deliberation, recruitment, resource management, legitimization of extralegal tactics, and cleansing of controversial ideologies.[6]

A desire to satisfy any of these goals in the short term could suffice to stimulate a dissident group to author a new constitution. Conversely, the long odds of some functions ever being satisfied might not stop a group from initiating the writing process. Ultimately, a constitution may be more successful in fulfilling certain functions but less successful at fulfilling others.

Social protest sits at the top of the list of valued constitutional functions. Every constitution entails a public act of defiance, inseparable from the grievances that spawned its creation. The expressive dimension of written constitutionalism alone could be tantalizing enough for desperate parties to imagine a new "people" bound by palpable despair or outrage. Not only is discontent central to written constitutionalism, its functions are carried out through the rhetoric of defiance. Inspired by Locke's formulation of sovereignty as an exercise in collective self-defense, the men of 1787 themselves characterized the stakes of constitutionalism as "nothing less than the existence of the Union" and "the fate of an empire."[7]

Successive groups of Americans adapted this survivalist rhetoric to the crises of their day. In the chapters that follow, citizens elaborated their social critique in writing. Institutional goals were often the most evident but also the hardest to accomplish by dissidents. Even where bureaucracies were not put into practice or a constitution's legitimacy remained uncertain, the text of a constitution could still be valuable to the internal relations of a community. Especially with constitutions written before a group gained control of territory or the recognition of other sovereigns, the coordinating functions of a constitution assumed great importance. Because a constitution defines a *demos,* an evocative articulation of "the people" could help draw recruits away from the dominant regime, establish new bonds, and secure crucial resources for legal transformation. A written instrument might be invoked to organize, educate, or discipline a group in the absence of formal institutions or a mature system of laws.

Deliberative reasons also motivated marginalized groups to write. Even when institutions could not be implemented right away, a constitution might prove useful in engaging fellow Americans over the meaning of the good life. Because the hallmark of a mature citizenry is the capacity to rule itself, a constitution emerged as the ultimate proof of sovereignty. Having a constitution of their own might improve the standing of people who felt marginalized or dispossessed. For groups with more extreme ideas or tactics, a constitution helped sanitize controversial ethical or political commitments or rationalize extralegal methods.

Whatever a group's complicated reasons for writing a constitution, its members labored within a legal tradition that is enthralling and dynamic, but also darker and more tumultuous than commonly admitted. Wresting legal authority from the king and church ushered in a world in which anyone could stake a claim to rule. Diffusing the locus of sovereignty set off a ferocious competition among those who dared to speak for the people, even as it promised to reward vision and initiative. Tocqueville once marveled, "In no country of the world does the law hold so absolute a language as in America; and in no country is the right of applying it vested in so many hands." Saints, demagogues, humanists, and authoritarians have all adapted the country's founding principles to remake the world. Their struggles lay bare the consequences of Americans' fateful decision to rule themselves through the written word.

The Republic of Indian Stream
1832–1835

It was a unique political establishment, one of the
smallest and most democratic in history.

—EDWIN M. BACON, *The Connecticut River,* 1907

The revolutionary fervor that culminated in the U.S. Constitution
did not dissipate after the document's ratification. Instead, as Gordon
Wood describes, an impulse to challenge authority infected "every
institution, every organization, every individual. It was as if the American Revolution had set in motion a disintegrative force that could
not be stopped." Far from arresting this dynamic, the founding generation's ingenuity ushered in an age of political development and
commercial enterprise in which higher law played increasingly elaborate functions. Americans authored state, local, and civic constitutions to liberate themselves from the past. When conventional political forms were not feasible or did not suit their needs, citizens initiated
more ambitious experiments.[1]

After ratification of the 1787 Constitution, Americans continued to
practice frontier sovereignty, a theory of self-governance predating
the Founding. This popular approach to the law entailed two contra-
dictory tendencies. One constructive tendency involved incentivizing
economic development and consolidating political power. The goal
was to make the revolutionary utterly conventional—ordinary, coherent, and efficacious. Another, more destructive tendency, involved
harnessing the spirit of experimentalism and destabilizing boundaries
and existing legal systems. This destructive dynamic proved integral
to the logic of frontier politics and necessary for its spread. It also

often led practitioners to write another round of laws to curb the theory's more corrosive features.

An early exercise in pioneer sovercignty can be discerned in the founding of the Republic of Indian Stream, in a territory of roughly 282 square miles nestled between modern-day Quebec and New Hampshire. The bucolic valley, located just above the forty-fifth parallel, is marked by three tributaries feeding into the Connecticut River. Mainly visited by American Indians and the occasional trapper or hunter, the area attracted the attention of land speculators at the turn of the nineteenth century. Within a few decades, the hopes and dreams of the settlers had merged with the land, and early forms of democratic government began to take root.[2]

This largely forgotten exercise in self-governance arose from an international dispute between England and the United States over the territory. The end of the Revolutionary War left many issues unresolved, including the boundaries between Canada and the states of New Hampshire and Maine. The Treaty of Paris had specified the border as "the northwesternmost head of the Connecticut River." England took this to be the Connecticut River itself, whereas New Hampshire interpreted the provision to mean Hall's Stream.[3] Two land companies, the Eastman Company and the Bedel Company, competed for dominion of the territory and its prospects. They lured settlers to the region and, in the process, unwittingly pushed them toward independence. Rumors spread through Indian Stream that Canada would guarantee the settlers' land claims and give them significantly larger lots if they would agree to support England's claim to the territory. Meanwhile, others hoped that New Hampshire would take steps to secure their property rights and reward their labors to extend America's westward borders.

Of the pioneer who plunged into the forests and forged democratic institutions, Tocqueville offered this telling profile:

> Everything about him is primitive and uninformed, but he is himself the result of the labor and the experience of eighteen centuries. He wears the dress, and he speaks the language of cities; he is acquainted with the past, curious of the future, and ready for argument upon the present; he is, in short, a highly civilized being, who consents, for a time, to inhabit the backwoods, and who penetrates into the wilds of a New World with the Bible, an axe, and a file of newspapers.[4]

Settlers rebelled against existing modes of life, dissatisfied with their prospects. These adventurous Americans believed that their destiny was to conquer new lands, disrupt existing political orders, and be rewarded for their industriousness and foresight. As they occupied land and worked the earth, pioneers developed new theories about law and politics. Their view of popular sovereignty was inextricably linked to territory: control of a parcel of land and productive work of it, rather than paper title, generated true authority to govern. The frontier mindset—which prized durability, self-reliance, experimentalism—discovered in natural law a compatible belief system, which could seamlessly justify efforts to gain dominion over nature and other human beings as the exercise of God-given rights.[5]

Frontier sovereignty was fueled by individual impetus to migrate, but it was also nurtured by policies favoring economic development and the lax enforcement of laws that stood in the way of settlement. Once the labor of pioneers mixed with the land, they turned to writing laws and constitutions to preserve their investment of human capital. But nation building through pioneer sovereignty necessarily entailed conflict with competing claimants, whether they were nation-states or Indian tribes. Thus, the project demanded the deliberate playing of sovereigns and other interested parties against one another, a gambit that proved ever more complicated as a constitution matured and a greater sense of order was expected. Most of the time, experiments in frontier sovereignty turned into conventional territories, counties, or states.[6]

Somewhere along the way, however, a familiar tale took a turn off the beaten path in the case of Indian Stream. Pulled in different directions, fearing a return to a lawless state of nature, residents of the territory took a stand. Instead of awaiting resolution of the boundary dispute, they announced the establishment of the Republic of Indian Stream, "a free, sovereign and independent state." Exultant on that day in June of 1832, each man solemnly swore to defend the "inviolate" constitution. For the next three years, the people of Indian Stream went their own way.[7]

Though theirs was merely one of several determinist movements during this period, it must be counted among the stronger assertions of American sovereignty. The efforts of Indian Stream's people to free themselves from their neighbors pitted them against the governments of Canada, New Hampshire, and the United States in a drama that played out through diplomacy and the actions of multiple sovereigns to enforce their own laws. The experience of these settlers, along with the responses of government officials, identified the possibilities and limitations of pioneer constitutionalism.[8]

When Pioneers Become a People

A confluence of favorable conditions led the Indian Stream migrants to turn to constitutional law to solve their problems. The boundary dispute between the United States and England created a lacuna that commercial interests and adventurous souls exploited. Authorities' efforts to encourage prospecting, exploration, and exploitation of the land served as a crucial engine of constitutional transformation. Although friction among the relevant political actors later increased in frequency and degree, states initially had a reason to look the other way as settlers seized the initiative in populating the region. While unspoiled, the area did not appear to yield essential natural resources that might have made the Upper Connecticut Valley a national priority. Neither the United States nor England hurried to resolve the boundary issue—other matters seemed more pressing between the two nations, and a certain legal ambiguity promoted the peace. Adding to the need to tread carefully, British soldiers remained in the region until 1795. American interests could be quietly promoted in the early days of the Republic through settler sovereignty until it became necessary for firmer positions to be taken.[9]

Settlers used deeds to acquire land from native peoples, even when doing so violated existing laws. In exchange for the right of heirs and "sucksessors and all Indian tribes forever" to hunt and fish on the land and for food and clothing for himself and his squaws, Chief Philip of the St. Francis tribe deeded to Thomas Eames and his friends a tract of land covering most of present-day Coos County, the territory of Indian Stream, and a portion of lower Canada. This deed served as the basis of the Eastman Company's claim on the land. Later, some members of the St. Francis tribe repudiated Philip's authority to speak on the tribe's behalf and conveyed the northern half of modern-day New Hampshire to the Bedel Company for $3,100.

Though duly recorded, these competing deeds were of dubious legality. Federal law at the time prohibited individuals from buying land from Indians. Even so, unpredictable enforcement of these laws meant that few were deterred from gaining control of desirable land or from seeking ways of improving their claims to lands seized under problematic legal circumstances. Indeed, the Eastman Company repeatedly sought legislative approval of its title from New Hampshire. Its lawyers even devised a legal strategy for getting around federal law should it ever come to that. The common law and the language of natural rights gave a veneer of legitimacy to the enterprise, lured individuals to the region, and displaced tribal sovereignty. According to the logic of frontier lawmaking, productive improvements to the land could be cited to win the state's approval of inhabitants' legal arrangements after the fact. Once New Hampshire legitimated settlers' actions, odds were good that federal authorities would defer to the state's view of land ownership.[10]

The rivalry between the speculating enterprises heated up around 1819, when Jeremiah Eames was lured away from Eastman to the Bedel Company. In the contest for the hearts and minds of settlers, the two companies surveyed the land aggressively and campaigned hard by offering inducements. The Eastman Company distributed tea, tobacco, and rum; promised to subsidize improvements to the land; and asked inhabitants to execute documents clarifying that they held title through the corporation. Elaborate bids to win the settlers' favor continued until 1830 when the two companies merged, in a last-ditch effort to pool resources and improve the proprietors' petitions to the New Hampshire legislature.

Inhabitants became accustomed to a frontier lifestyle insulated from the constant supervision of authorities. Except for intermittent enforcement actions by lawmen from nearby counties or Canada, the law was what the population of Indian Stream determined. It was in the nature of such an existence that public identities and political allegiances became more fluid. As a culture of self-governance took hold, civic identities changed. Visitors became squatters and putative landowners; surveyors and speculators began to see themselves as statesmen. To mold the place in their own political image, these New Englanders adapted civic traditions to the wilderness. Town meetings, which started as annual affairs and informal gatherings to build roads and schools, eventually gave way to regular assemblies with moderators, agendas, committees, and deliberative protocols.

So far, the same story could be told of thousands of settlements across America. In this instance, however, political forces converged to create an existential crisis that led the denizens of Indian Stream to declare independence. Early on, New Hampshire used its own courts to establish the State's jurisdiction over the contested land and to try to evict squatters. After encouragement from the New Hampshire legislature, the state's attorney general brought trespass suits against two Indian Stream residents, Ebenezer Fletcher and Abner Hyland. In 1823, the state won a judgment declaring the settlers "intruders on that ground." But obtaining judicial decrees was one thing; enforcing them would prove to be quite another.[11]

In 1824, legislative actions further spurred the inhabitants' transformation in political identity. Three measures were considered by the New Hampshire legislature. One bill rejected proprietors' title claims and incorporated into New Hampshire all land north of the forty-fifth parallel and outside of already acknowledged borders. Another resolution ended further prosecution for squatting and, in consideration of the labor performed and hardships endured by residents, quieted title to each settler in his actual possession up to two hundred acres. A third measure empowered the state to hand over the contested land to the Eastman Company alone. The first two measures were enacted into law, while the third failed.[12]

This legislative compromise, known as "the Resolve of 1824," sent mixed messages. From the perspective of New Hampshire, the inhabitants of Indian Stream would now be recognized as landowners while remaining citizens of the state. At the same time, the inhabitants understood that the state plainly had no quarrel with their presence on the land, especially as it dovetailed with officials' desires to strengthen, clarify, and perhaps extend the state's boundaries. To the extent settler sovereignty aligned with New Hampshire's efforts to consolidate its borders, settlers learned that previous illegalities could be sanctified.

Intended or not, this event accelerated the fusion of the inhabitants' sense of belonging with the land—apart from the commercial interests of squabbling companies. Pioneer sovereignty, with its emphasis on self-determination and civil rights, helped individuals break the link between corporations and land. And despite legislators' hopes, the legislation did little to increase allegiance to New Hampshire, especially among settlers whose land fell outside the terms of the Resolve. Having ratified the people's extralegal measures to occupy and work the land, the legislation gave proof that unconventional methods of pioneer sovereignty could pay off. Unlawful or questionable actions to acquire property could ripen into legal entitlements. Far from preserving the status quo, migration, land transfers, and improvements of the area continued unabated.

In 1829, the people of Indian Stream began to take steps toward independence. A five-member group selected in General Meeting on March 17, 1829, became known as the "Committee of Safety for the General Security." Led by Luther Parker, the committee submitted a petition to the New Hampshire legislature praying for a resolution of land disputes that would exclude a role for the Eastman Company. Parker, formerly a teacher in Albany and Stratford, had resettled in Indian Stream, where he operated a general store. He quickly rose to a leadership position within the independence movement.[13]

The 1829 petition offers clues that settlers had grown fond of a particular locale and were more than capable of organizing themselves for a common purpose. Parker and other members of the committee claimed to speak "on behalf of the inhabitants of Indian Stream." Originally organized to facilitate the primitive political society's mutual defense pact, the group's tasks quickly grew to encompass taking "measures to secure them in possession of their lands."[14]

The petition listed a series of grievances of "the inhabitants of Indian Stream." Members of the committee realized that it was not enough to seek a remedy from New Hampshire authorities; they also had to undermine corporate claims to speak for the people. Foremost among the complaints were unfulfilled promises by the Eastman Company to subsidize local development. In support of their request to "release the right of the title the state hath or may have to each settler," the committee's petition documented improvements made to the land by the settlers themselves. Insofar as this petition opposed the Eastman Company's efforts to gain legislative sanction of its program, this action signified something else as well: the emergence of a collective attitude and interests distinct from those of the commercial entity that had sponsored their settlement. The position staked out by the people's representatives amounted to a crucial prepolitical development in another sense, for every state must find a way to subordinate the market to the public interest.

Lawyers for the Eastman Company tried to discredit the Parker petition, proof that a move toward self-governance could be taken as a threat to corporate interests. As the years passed, "a new community spirit appeared, based upon the foundations of land hunger and opposition to the Eastman Company, to weld the factions together." A 1829 letter from Reuben Sawyer, still loyal to the Eastman Company, hinted at this independent ethos: "I take the Liberty to inform you that there is a party in this place who Stile them selves a Comity." Sawyer warned company officials that members of this group "have under taken some thing which we are not in favor nether have we authorized them to take the measures they are a taken for they are a Bout to address the Legislater in the name of the People of this Place."[15]

When the New Hampshire legislature failed to act on the Parker petition, the Indian Stream Council approved steps to record land transactions on behalf of its own citizens, under its own laws. On April 1, 1831, residents opened a land office, appointed John Haynes as examiner and recorder of deeds, and promptly began recording deeds. The residents' unity of purpose was buoyed by a decision of the king of the Netherlands in January 1831. Several boundary disputes involving the Maine and New Hampshire borders had been submitted to the king for arbitration, and in the portion of his ruling affecting Indian Stream, the king decided in favor of the British. Although the United States government did not accept the ruling, authorities exploited it to the settlers' detriment. Customs officials began collecting import duties on produce brought into New Hampshire and Vermont from Indian Stream, treating Indian Stream farmers as foreigners.

Still, settlers were slow to embrace a Canadian identity. Around this time, Canada began to conscript young men from the region for military service. These actions alienated residents who were asked to defend a country that did not afford them basic legal protections. Caught between various sovereigns, each demanding the satisfaction of obligations but extending legal benefits in uncertain fashion, should settlers perceive themselves as New Hampshirites, Canadians, or something else entirely? For many, these oppressive actions, taken without consultation, corroded any remaining sense of attachment to either political community. To the contrary, these unjust policies solidified the settlers' sense that they shared a distinctive experience and common grievances, and that they deserved to rule themselves.

Although the U.S. Senate rejected the king's arbitral decision in June 1832, the final wheels toward independence had been set in motion.

Less than a month later the settlers proclaimed themselves founders of a microrepublic.

The Constitution for a Woodland Paradise

On June 11, 1832, the inhabitants of Indian Stream met and "Voted to make [a] . . . Bill of Rights." That same day, they also designated a committee to draft a constitution to govern the people "and report as soon as con(venient) of laws for the government (of said Indian Stream) Territory as they deem neces(sary for the preservation of) order and peace."[16]

On July 9, some sixty men filed into the Center Schoolhouse. During this gathering, a draft constitution was reported, whereupon the group adjourned for a period of deliberation. When the men reconvened, they approved the constitution. In ratifying an instrument written mainly by David Mitchell and Luther Parker, the inhabitants previously known as "[t]he people inhabiting . . . Indian Stream Territory" came together to "form themselves into a body politic by the name of Indian Stream."[17]

Security and survival motivated the people's turn toward written constitutionalism. The people of Indian Stream felt they had been "left to our own resources for preserving order in society." Because legal protections did not come from expected quarters, the pioneer model had not led to greater order and safety, but rather to manipulation of their dreams by prospectors and bureaucrats. Their solution was to ordain a new constitution to ward off "Anarchy & confusion, which would destroy all the peace and happiness and pleasant prospects" of the settlers. In language reminiscent of the 1787 U.S. Constitution, the framers resolved to "preserve union among ourselves, establish Justice, ensure domestic tranquility provide for our common security and defence and secure the important Blessings of civilized society."[18]

Writing a new constitution not only stimulated the development of democratic culture but also facilitated a transformation in civic identity. Their intentions announced to the world, the inhabitants of the region completed their transformation from settlers to residents, and then to new citizens. Initially, inhabitants understood themselves as temporary workers of the land, occupying a precarious legal position. With subsistence a possibility, informal means of self-governance emerged. Once the people took steps to organize themselves under their own constitution, they conveyed to themselves the full rights and duties entailed in political liberty.

The draftsmen of the Indian Stream Constitution envisioned a people while generally avoiding cultural criteria for citizenship—with the glaring exception of sex. They accepted, without seriously interrogating, an older assumption that men alone were capable of representing their households and participating in public life. Within the male population, residency, age, and loyalty defined the boundaries of political community. Membership in the General Assembly, the usual hallmark of republican citizenship, was broadly afforded to "all male inhabitants . . . twenty-one years of age or over and who has resided in this place three months next preceding any annual session," provided he take an oath of allegiance to the constitution and laws of Indian Stream. Because settlers were constantly coming and going, in the interests of political stability anyone "absent from this place for the space of six months next preceding any session of the assembly" would have his name administratively "erased from the roll by the clerk" as if he never existed. By 1832, Indian Stream had a population of roughly four hundred, with around seventy eligible voters.[19]

By explicitly protecting a handful of familiar individual rights and generally avoiding exclusionary criteria, the constitution staked out welcoming terms of membership. Indian Stream's founders promised to tolerate a range of religious attitudes and plans for the good life, and made it relatively easy to participate in the governance of local affairs. In these and other ways, their constitution embraced the plural city-state ideal, as it had been transplanted in colonial America. An intimate republic filled with face-to-face interactions of citizens at a town meeting—the distinguishing feature of New England life— served as the drafters' working model.

Despite the preamble's cautious choice of words suggesting that the republic might last only until resolution of the border issue, the document was not, in fact, a "provisional" instrument. Citizens secured for themselves the final authority to decide whether the "boundary line has been established" on a satisfactory basis rather than conditioning the expiration of the document on some external event. The constitution imbued the government with "all the powers of a free, sovereign and independent state till such time as we can ascertain to what government we properly belong." Until that moment came, the people would rule themselves.[20]

Declaring independence from surrounding jurisdictions but treading carefully seemed wise, so as to buy time for democratic mechanisms to take root and a sovereign reputation to emerge. On this point, the drafters of the Indian Stream Constitution may have followed the example of New Hampshire, whose leading citizens had separated from England in 1776, though suggested they would "rejoice if . . . a reconciliation between us and our parent State can be effected."[21] Back then, New Hampshirites, too, had blamed their actions on the legal uncertainty caused by "the sudden and abrupt departure" of the governor and members of the council, as well as the "present unhappy and unnatural contest with Great Britain." Just as the people then had left the door open to rapprochement with England, so the denizens of Indian Stream now hedged their bets, in the event separation from New Hampshire turned out for the worse.

Beyond characterizing themselves as members of a community bound by mutual grievances, inhabitants wrote a constitution to defy the odds of survival on the frontier. In an otherwise transient and precarious existence, a new fundamental law brought a measure of psychological stability to their subsistence lifestyle. Taking the law into their own hands and designing new institutions helped them to turn their thoughts away from the selfishness that came from scrambling to survive in a world where "we are a law unto ourselves" toward the possibility of a brighter collective future.[22]

The written instrument stood as proof that settlers had moved beyond considerations of narrow self-interest. Internally, the document empowered settlers to make sacrifices to the whole, solidifying the sense of community. Externally, the constitution was meant as proof that the rule-of-law culture had matured. It signaled to prospective migrants that the place had become politically stable, where broad agreement existed to protect economic and human investments. Joining such a law-based community, in theory, should improve a family's odds of survival in the wilderness.

The Indian Stream Constitution borrowed copiously from the New Hampshire Constitution of 1784, as well as from the U.S. Constitution. Like a number of state constitutions, the Constitution of Indian Stream began with a recitation of rights. This difference reflected the Anti-federalist legacy, which held that the enumeration of rights served as a crucial means of promoting liberty, even in an age of revitalized governments. Chief among fundamental rights was that of popular sovereignty: "all government of right originates from the people, is founded in common consent and instituted for the public good." Another provision confirmed that individuals joining a society only "surrender[ed] some of their natural rights to that society." Contrasted with the idea of total alienation of sovereignty, often associated with Hobbes, Americans granted limited authority to "magistrates and officers of Government [who] are their substitutes and agents and at all times accountable to them." For the founders of Indian Stream, a cornerstone of popular sovereignty was majority rule followed by loyal acquiescence, at least when fundamental rights were not implicated: "where a large majority of the people . . . unite together . . . the minority of right ought to submit to the majority and be controlled by them."[23]

In keeping with their spare existence, the people of Indian Stream kept their list of rights short and crisply worded. They had no use for a free press clause (though New Hampshire's Constitution contained such a provision), one protecting assembly or petition, or a provision guaranteeing freedom of expression. Instead, they preferred to deal with such rights more narrowly by protecting only speech and debate "on all business before the general assembly." In their small community, vigorous debate in the legislative body would be sufficient to protect most rights.

Individuals enjoyed "equal right" to "life, liberty, and property," though consistent with the frontier ethic of shared sacrifice, each citizen was "equally bound to contribute his share in the expence of such protection, and to yield his personal service when necessary." Implementing the constitution's protection of private property, the people passed laws exempting certain property from attachment in a civil action. Such measures suggested a shared desire not to allow debt to destroy a subsistence community. To guard against such a catastrophe, citizens placed certain basic necessities beyond the destructive reach of lawsuits. This protection of a subsistence lifestyle covered:

> One Cow, one hog, one swine not over six months old, the meat of one hog, seven Sheep and the Wool of seven sheep, three tons of Hay one Bed and bedding for every two persons, all wearing apparel & all their Books

and if a farmer or mechanic twenty dollars worth tools one Gun and equipments Household furniture to the amount of twenty dollars one bushel of Grain, Meal, or flower to each person twenty five Bushels Potatoes, and two Bushels Salt.[24]

The aggrieved now expected not only legal recourse but also "prompt" justice. When facing trial, an accused could count on "face to face" confrontation of witnesses and the evidence assembled against him as well as "all proof that may be favorable to himself." Not only did the constitution demand that "all punishment" be proportional to the crime, but it also offered a justification for justice as fairness: "the true design of all punishment being to reform and not to exterminate mankind." Such a constraint on state violence (for all crimes short of murder) was essential to ensure that the rule of law would not be so harsh as to destroy already fragile communities on the edge of civilization.[25]

The institution that best embodied popular sentiment was the General Assembly. Its creation represented a significant stage in the institutionalization of frontier democracy. Originally, settlers conducted meetings in the home of David Tyler, under the auspices of the Bedel Company. With the construction of the Center Schoolhouse in 1828, policy makers moved to a civic forum that simultaneously served as a school, town hall, courtroom, and house of worship. Notices of public meetings were posted at Fletcher's and Barnes's mills, and this practice continued under the Indian Stream Constitution.[26]

New Hampshirites had found "separation of powers" important enough to put down in writing, diffusing practical authority to avoid tyranny. While the founders of Indian Stream also believed in divided government, they recoiled from overly strict understandings of separated powers for their small republic. Unlike the U.S. Constitution's grant of legislative authority to a single institution, the Indian Stream constitution conferred "supreme legislative power" upon both the General Assembly, represented by all eligible voters, and a council, a body of five citizens elected from among the General Assembly. The General Assembly was afforded "the full power . . . [to] establish all manner of wholesome and reasonable Law and regulations . . . for the benefit and welfare of this people." But in a move away from direct rule, the people denied that body power to originate legislation on its own. Instead, the Assembly could approve a bill in toto or revise the legislation presented by the council. If the council rejected an amendment, a two-thirds vote of the General Assembly could override that objection.[27]

In practice, the council possessed enormous power to shape the law. Along with the authority to "draft and present" all bills, acts, and resolves, the constitution granted to council members other powers commonly associated with that of an executive. The council had the responsibility of "watch[ing] over the general peace and safety of the inhabitants." It alone could prosecute offenders and, afterward, pardon any criminals. That body could command the militia and order the use of deadly force.

One glaring omission was the absence of a chief executive figure of the sort one would expect of a strong nation-state. Although drafters established a microrepublic, Indian Stream's multimember executive more closely resembled that of New England towns, which were run by a board of selectmen between scheduled town meetings. Such an arrangement led to discussion, horse-trading, and consensus building among equals. But it also left the council vulnerable to dissension, intrigue, and inaction. In adopting a plural executive for the republic, the people of Indian Stream ignored the advice of Alexander Hamilton, who once warned that plurality in the executive would render a nation vulnerable during "the most critical emergencies of the state" and "split the community into the violent and irreconcilable factions."[28]

After securing basic rights and designing institutions, the constitution sought to inculcate ideals "essential for the preservation of a free government." This proved necessary because the pioneer dream lured many courageous, but often shady, characters to remote locations. Besides conforming to classical republicanism, ethical norms helped to keep the peace in places the rule of law could not reach. In keeping with the overriding goal of open borders, the community sketched its civics project at a high level of abstraction. These amounted to thin civic values, intended to guide rather than exclude. The educational system and, indeed, the whole of government, ought to teach "the principles of humanity and general benevolence, public & private charity, industry & economy[,] Honesty and punctuality, sincerity & sobriety, and all social affections and generous sentiments among the people." To civilize the hardy men and women who wrestled with nature itself, literature and scientific knowledge had to be "generally diffused through [the] community."

Having established a fledgling republic, the citizens of Indian Stream immediately set about passing laws and superseding contrary laws and customs. Legislation assessed taxes for the construction and repair of highways and bridges, authorized the collection of school taxes, and recognized marriage. On the same day the people ratified a constitution, they also prohibited "Selling, vending, or giving away, distilled Liquors within one fourth part of a mile of the place where the assembly are in session on pain of forfeiting all of said liquors." This could only be a measure to ensure the soundness of the people's judgment by discouraging public inebriation or tainted deliberations. It addressed prevailing stereotypes of frontier life and encouraged various "moral virtues" within the reach of all citizens, including truthfulness and an unimpaired judgment.[29]

In addition to strengthening the powers of the sheriff for the routine enforcement of the laws, the people also formed a militia, made up of "every able bodied man within this place between the ages of eighteen and fifty." The duty fell on the captain of the militia to assemble its members once a year for inspection as well as instruction in "Military duty and tacticks." In the meantime, each member of the citizen militia was obliged to maintain arms in proper working order.[30]

Acting on the constitution's charge to create a legal system, the assembly immediately enacted a measure establishing courts of justice and "abolishing . . . all courts established before the adoption of this constitution." Every justice of the peace was granted "competent Jurisdiction for the trial of all actions Pleas & controversies," to render judgments and award remedies. Reimbursements to jurors had to be advanced by the party demanding a jury trial, and a fine was exacted from any prospective juror who failed to appear but was not "disabled by the hand of Providence."[31] Given scarce resources, the costs of confinement would be borne by each prisoner, but if that person could not pay, "reasonable expence" would be defrayed by the people.

Over the next few years, the people added intricacies to the justice system. The General Assembly enacted laws requiring a complainant to post bond sufficient to defray trial costs, compelling witnesses to appear for trial, and dealing with vexatious litigation. An 1834 law mandated the death penalty for murder. The law most resembled that of Maine, which also imposed death automatically for willful murder. But it could also be seen as a poignant assertion of pioneer sovereignty's nature. Indian Stream's death penalty stance reflected frontier justice—certain, forceful, without regret. In light of a brutal murder in the northern country in 1828, the republic's leaders wished to demonstrate they could take care of their own. A show of forceful displeasure would keep man's selfish nature and political chaos at bay.[32]

Several of the laws were designed to ameliorate the harms of economic deception that always seemed to accompany experiments in pioneer sovereignty. Elected judges operated under specific instructions to "prevent people from cheating, lying, and swindling people out of their property." Perjury so undermined settler life that a person convicted of the offense "shall be expelled from the assembly and his name stricken from the roll thereof by the Clerk." Such a violation also rendered a person legally "incapable to Give testimony in any Court."[33]

Popular Defense of the Constitution

For a brief moment in time, the Republic of Indian Stream controlled territory and held its people together. By the mid-1830s, residents of the region had, on several occasions, practiced unruly defense of their fledgling constitution. Solo acts of resistance of New Hampshire and Canadian laws became group efforts to preserve the breakaway republic. The settlers' tools of legal resistance entailed the use of sheriffs, assemblies, and posses, consistent with a small-scale vision of community. Confronted with open defiance from the settlers, neighboring jurisdictions began treating the Indian Stream affair no longer as a series of unauthorized land seizures by poorly organized "malcontents" to be handled on an individual basis, but rather as a dangerous rebellion calling for an organized military solution.

One of the galvanizing episodes over the viability of settler sovereignty occurred over taxes. Residents of Indian Stream argued that customs officials in New Hampshire lacked legal basis to levy the duties, because they relied only on their interpretation of the king of the Netherlands's arbitration order rather than a directive from

Washington. Settlers began to resist the collection of duties, which posed a serious threat to the local economy. A strategy of "passing by" the tax collectors' offices without paying duties had considerable success until tax collectors began to pay more attention and clamped down. When tax resisters were caught, officials sometimes demanded cash payment rather than the posting of a bond. If an individual could not afford to pay, items were seized. After a seizure of three wagons of goods engendered special outrage, citizens at a March 1832 meeting charged a committee of three—Luther Parker, Clark Haynes, and Nathan Judd—to formulate a plan to deal with the tax situation.

Parker drafted a complaint to Louis McLane, secretary of the treasury, on behalf of the "United Inhabitants of Indian Stream." He objected to the separate decisions of New Hampshire and Vermont tax collectors that Indian Stream was located outside of the United States and therefore subject to duties. Parker painted the settlers as law-abiding individuals who feared being caught between jurisdictions—a continuation of the frontier strategy of playing sovereigns against one another that had served the settlers well. The petition argued that forbearance on the tax question would aid the cause of international peace. Collection efforts by the United States in contested territory might lead to the aggressive invocation of Canadian law and precipitate a foreign policy crisis. The letter contained a veiled threat: if collections did not cease, residents might begin to see themselves as Canadian citizens and adjust their actions accordingly.[34]

What the citizens of Indian Stream did not know was that the deputy collector at Canaan had already written his superiors seeking clarification of U.S. policy. His letter made its way to the State Department as well as to John Weeks, the congressman representing Coos County. On March 1, the comptroller of the treasury informed Representative Weeks that customs officers would cease collections. Parker and others did not learn of the Treasury Department's decision until April, well after the committee had sent off its petition. Far from dissipating the general sense of anxiety, however, the turn of events merely strengthened the resolve of Indian Stream's leadership to make a final push toward independence.

Despite the fact that the petition arrived too late to influence the thinking of officials in Washington, preparing it nevertheless galvanized the people of the region. Now they were a duly constituted "society," citizens celebrated their most recent act of legal defiance. The position taken in the petition to escape the excise tax—that Indian Stream was not necessarily outside of the United States—coexisted with their general belief that absent a firm resolution of the boundary question, the people of Indian Stream had the prerogative to rule themselves.

The people's declaration of independence sparked other acts of disobedience. In September 1832, Moody Haynes, a citizen of Indian Stream, was arrested and held in the Court of Common Pleas in Coos County. The complainant, Melissa Thurston, claimed that Haynes had fathered her son and that state law required him to "provide for the maintenance of bastard children." Emboldened by the separatist ethos, Haynes denied that New Hampshire courts had jurisdiction over the controversy because the pregnancy itself had transpired in Indian Stream. The defense was rejected, but the argument placed New Hampshire authorities on notice of the potential legal consequences of Indian Stream's efforts at self-governance.[35]

Ironically, the successes of the unrecognized republic ultimately hastened its demise. To the extent pioneer sovereignty aligned with the priorities of existing jurisdictions, it was allowed to have its way. For a while, the democratic experiment advanced the goals of economic development and the extension of America's borders. As more individuals populated the area, it grew from a few land speculators and smugglers to a capable citizenry some four hundred persons strong in the year of the constitution's adoption.[36] But as the population increased, so did the opportunities for friction with surrounding jurisdictions. Local disputes turned into cross assertions of legal authority; eventually, these controversies pitted settlers against neighbors as well as sheriffs, courts, and policy makers. All of these factors increased the visibility of the community, made annexation of the territory desirable, and presented opportunities for other states' institutions to assert control over the people of Indian Stream and their property. For a time, neighbors tolerated low-level disobedience of their laws. Once conflict flared, states with claims to the land could no longer afford to look the other way. The clash between pioneer self-governance and the sovereignty of conventional states had to be resolved once and for all.

The end came after a series of popular and diplomatic actions to defend frontier governance sputtered and the State of New Hampshire moved forcibly to satisfy its claim on the territory and extend the rule of law over its inhabitants. Just as Virginia had quashed determinist movements by declaring it "high treason" to form separate governments, so New Hampshire now moved to destroy Indian Stream's experiment in self-rule with a show of legislative and military force. During this final phase of the constitution's cultural existence, citizens initially defended its legitimacy against external threats; then, when setbacks mounted, doubts over the future of independence sapped pioneer sovereignty of vitality. As political faith in the project faded, they began to abandon the document and their newfound civic identities.[37]

Most members of the republic toiled precariously on the edge of economic existence. Debt collectors relying on the laws of other states would occasionally try to serve process or attach property in Indian Stream to satisfy outstanding debts. To deal with perceived incursions on their sovereignty, the people came up with ways of resisting enforcement actions by more established jurisdictions. As legal conflict with neighbors increased, they enacted legislation creating a militia and strengthening the powers of Indian Stream's sheriff.

In August 1834, deputies from New Hampshire tried to confiscate the property of certain Indian Stream citizens to satisfy outstanding debts. Alarmed, the Indian Stream council wrote to Sheriff John H. White of Coos County, demanding a suspension of legal process until the boundary dispute had been settled once and for all. The council claimed to be taking "every precautionary measure to prevent any outbreak of hostilities," but warned of "an effusion of blood" if such insults to the sovereign dignity of Indian Stream continued.

That same day, the council appealed to John Forsyth, the U.S. secretary of state. Its members complained that the people's "rights are infringed upon by that part of New Hampshire claiming jurisdiction, as we think, without authority; and, should they continue to enforce their claim, even if they have no authority, resistance by force, in our present situation, would be not only difficult but disagreeable." As in previous public statements and petitions, leaders tried to stay in the federal government's good graces by reminding the secretary of state of the settlers' sacrifices in making productive use of the land. Once again, they reaffirmed that the people of Indian Stream would gladly submit to a final resolution of the boundary. Until then, however, they would pursue assistance to repel the aggression of neighbors, including by "apply[ing] to the Province of Canada." The council hastened to remind Secretary Forsyth of an earlier conflict that arose between Maine and England over comparable matters.[38]

This stunning correspondence, along with the republic's next steps, represented high-stakes diplomacy. The settlers did their best to take advantage of the principle of divided government embedded in conventional sovereignty as they searched for allies in all levels of government. In the process of trying to enlist one sovereign's aid to repel the incursions of another, the republic conducted itself as if it were a state, or at the very least, an unrecognized state. Why else send the petition to the secretary of state and appeal to the interests of American foreign policy? But Indian Stream's leaders had to solicit intervention carefully, affirming the republic's liminal status without raising the hackles of federal officials.

In response, Secretary Forsyth refused to render a decision on the legality of New Hampshire's actions, instead saying they had lodged their grievances in the wrong venue. Forsyth informed them that "if you are within the limits of the United States, as has always been maintained by this Government, it is because you are within the limits of the State of New Hampshire." He then advised "that any question arising from the exercise of the sheriff's authority, or any other questions resulting from your peculiar situation, and requiring a judicial decision should be brought before the Courts of New Hampshire."

In other words, the secretary of state ignored the people's political appeals and asserted the sovereign interests of the United States in terms of the national boundary and orderly resolution of law. He deflected specific legal questions by directing complainants' attention to the processes of conventional sovereignty, namely, state courts and elected officials. If Indian Stream officials hoped to press their claim of sovereignty upward to the highest levels, federal authorities sought to push the question downward to local governmental processes. To the extent that Indian Stream's "peculiar situation" involved challenging the Coos County sheriff's authority in contested lands, the question was more appropriately raised in judicial proceedings already under way. With this answer, the federal government simultaneously reasserted its claim on the territory and reserved its options by allowing New Hampshire's consolidation project to run its course.

In the meantime, Sheriff White consulted the chief justice of the Supreme Court and the governor of New Hampshire. Chief Justice William Richardson replied that "it will be the duty of courts to enforce the laws coextensively with the territory which the state claims" and advised that "the wisest and safest course will be to take the advice of the executive and follow that."[39]

With the courts seemingly ready to defer to the governor's office, and the executive branch increasingly active in supporting Coos County's enforcement of state laws, the processes of conventional sovereignty now aligned in an orderly way. George Sullivan, New Hampshire's attorney general, offered a legal opinion to Sheriff White. Sullivan's letter staked out positions commonly taken by those who deny the residual sovereignty of ordinary citizens. In defending the power and integrity of the conventional state, he asserted the supremacy of judges in expositing the law and the obligation of everyone else to fall in line:

> The courts of every State are bound to enforce the laws, as far as that State claims jurisdiction. The officers of the County of Coos should let the inhabitants of Indian Stream Territory understand distinctly, that if any person shall resist them, in the due *exertion* of the duties of their office he shall be punished. They can have no more right to resist officers, than the inhabitants of any other part of the State.

The attorney general chose his words carefully. He described residents as "inhabitants" of a "territory" who possessed no greater rights than "any other" citizen of New Hampshire. With both his tone and his words, Sullivan encouraged local officials to carry out their "duty" to enforce the rule of law. Whatever sovereignty settlers in Indian Stream could exercise did not encompass a "right to resist" officers of the court. Evidently, New Hampshire recognized no change in the status of Indian Stream despite its denizens' declaration of independence, treating it as an illegitimate act in a broad pattern of local defiance. In protecting the state's prerogative, Sullivan relied not only on previous precedents establishing the state's claim to the region but also the legislature's reaffirmation of such a position. Sheriff White forwarded the attorney general's letter to the Indian Stream council, signaling his resolve to enforce state law.[40]

With no allies to be found, leaders of Indian Stream did what they could to protect their right of self-rule. In March 1835, Coos County sheriff's deputies again entered Indian Stream to serve court orders but met resistance from the Indian Stream sheriff and his men. Shortly thereafter, a split emerged among the people. Acting on behalf of himself and a handful of other signatories, Parker wrote Governor William Badger requesting that New Hampshire extend its laws over the settlers. Earning the wrath of fellow citizens, Parker's petition bore the signatures of Indian Stream citizens as well as those of Stewartstown and Colebrook. The Indian Stream council fired off its own petition to the governor of New Hampshire, complaining of unauthorized efforts to serve writs within the republic's borders.

A special meeting called to order on April 18, 1835, produced a law banning unlawful service of writs in Indian Stream. This represented the community's legislative effort at self-help against outsiders. It affirmed a group sense that if popular sovereignty meant anything, it meant the capacity to resist unauthorized enforcement actions by outsiders. The law empowered the sheriff of Indian Stream and any deputies to apprehend anyone who violated the law. Offenders would be fined $100 for each infraction and jailed until the fine was paid—by far the most serious legal sanction for any offense short of murder. Officers were further "authorized & Empowered to Comand or request Such assistance as is Sufficient to arrest & keep Custody any person or persons so offending." So important was this capacity to resist the enforcement of outside legal systems that bystanders had a duty to assist in the enforcement of the law on pain of a fine "not Exceding ten dollars nor less than three dollars" or three months in jail.[41]

If a March 30 letter from Sheriff White to New Hampshire's secretary of state can be credited, leaders of the republic were growing increasingly desperate in their defiance. "They are determined to resist the officers of the State to the utmost of their ability," he reported. "They are now making preparations for repulsing any force which may be brought against them." Not only had the people began to build a jail, they had also added to "their ranks twelve or fourteen Indians, who, I am told, have engaged to assist them in case of trouble."[42]

As the search for allies began in earnest, the absence of a single chief executive giving a single voice to the republic's policies and conducting diplomacy became glaring. On July 23, 1835, sixty-four Indian Stream citizens made a bid to initiate bilateral negotiations with

Canada. Their petition, directed to the governor general of Canada, sought protection from the "invasions" of New Hampshire. The signatories stated that they were "unable to defend ourselves" against the hostile policies of that state and "pray[ed] Your Excellancy to take our case under your wise consideration, and grant us such relief as you in your wisdom shall judge proper and just." Yet a question lingered: did this group speak with the authority of the council, even in secret, or did these citizens act entirely on their own initiative?

Either way, a weak executive failed to hold the people together in a time of crisis. Madison's warnings against unrestrained factionalism became realized, as previously suppressed preferences hardened into competing constitutional visions, with each faction seeking to represent the wishes of the community. Parker, onetime founder of Indian Stream and drafter of its constitution, became leader of a group known as the "New Hampshire Boys." This faction had given up on the idea of independence and now saw absorption by New Hampshire as the only path to peace. After Parker petitioned the governor seeking the protection of New Hampshire law, he followed up with a second petition. This more specific plea turned to the matter of political reintegration, asking that Indian Stream be "classed with some town for the choice of a representative." Members of another faction, whose presence was signified by a petition to Canada, declared themselves receptive to Canadian guarantees of peace and order. The remaining faction, which remained loyal to the Indian Stream council, held out hope in the face of dwindling odds for some measure of self-governance to be retained.

Parker's actions so displeased the people that they turned him out of office on March 11, 1833, because he "threatened to do all in his power to injure the inhabitants and to destroy the constitution." Though the moderate faction seemed content to separate Parker from the reins of government for "transferr[ing] his allegiance to New Hampshire," the pro-Canada faction tried to exploit the situation by describing him as "a spy and general disturber of the peace." The people may not have seen fit to enact a law against treason, but they did take the oath seriously. In fact, one person, Jonathan C. L. Knight, swore out a complaint against Parker, which led to his arrest by Canadian authorities on a charge of disorderly conduct. Reuben Sawyer, the Sheriff of Indian Stream who by now leaned toward the British, executed the arrest warrant. According to the complaint, Parker and Knight had had an argument in the mill yard, which allegedly led Parker to brandish a knife at Knight. The discussion concerned the future of Indian Stream, with Parker supposedly promising to take up arms to help New Hampshire keep the territory. Eventually, the prosecution failed and Parker was released. But the entire episode received wide coverage in the press, stirring outrage at the "open rebellion to the laws of New Hampshire" signified by Parker's arrest under Canadian law.[43]

No longer could legal uncertainty be endured by the state. In June 1835, Governor Badger called for action in a special message to the legislature. In response, legislators resolved on June 26: "the state of New Hampshire should continue the possession of the Indian Stream Territory, and maintain the jurisdiction of the state over the same . . . and his Excellency the Governor be requested to render all necessary aid to the executive officers of the county of Coos in causing the laws of said state to be duly executed within the limits of said territory." That same day, the legislature approved a resolution classifying Indian Stream with Clarksville and Stewartstown in a single district.[44]

On July 20, Adjutant-General Low of the New Hampshire militia ordered the 24th Regiment to prepare to march on Indian Stream in support of Sheriff White. To prevent a bloody showdown, the republic's leaders tried to negotiate a face-saving denouement. The council dispatched envoys to Sheriff White. They conveyed this message: the people declined to recognize the lawman's jurisdiction over the territory, but in the interest of avoiding violence would not resist New Hampshire's display of superior force. The sheriff proposed that if the state kept the militia just outside of the territory, then inhabitants would give assurance of their submission. At a meeting at Fletcher's home, a majority of attendees assented to the negotiated agreement, though a few assembly members stormed out, including Alanson Cummings, the clerk and justice of the peace for Indian Stream. As a gesture of political integration, Richard Blanchard, a member of the council, was deputized to enforce New Hampshire law. Yet the agreement offered only a temporary respite from legal turmoil.

Canada did not give up its claim on Indian Stream without a fight. On August 5, five settlers who signed the Canadian petition wrote the governor general of Canada stating that they had given up on the possibility of that country's assistance. The civil secretary responded to this missive by asking J. Moore of the Provincial Assembly to preserve Canada's jurisdiction over Indian Stream. Acting on Moore's request, Alexander Rea, the magistrate of Hereford, contacted several leading citizens of Indian Stream presumed to be open to Canadian involvement. Appearing at a general meeting on September 26, Magistrate Rea then read the civil secretary's letter, which promised that "every legal protection will be afforded by the Magistry of the District of St. Francis as well to the Inhabitants of Indian Stream as to all others H.M. Subjects within their jurisdiction." Rea outlined a plan to bring the area under Canadian control. He recommended that the people appoint magistrates who could immediately begin enforcing Canadian law. Two names were presented to Rea, who promised to pass them along to the Canadian government.[45]

Within a few weeks, any semblance of the rule of law disintegrated, as citizens began switching allegiances. In October 1835, Coos County deputies, aided by Blanchard, arrested John Tyler. The arrest warrant cited unpaid bills at a tavern and general store in Canaan. Apparently, Tyler refused to offer any property for attachment and went with the deputies, but informed them that he believed himself a British subject and did not recognize the laws of New Hampshire. A pro–Indian Stream posse stopped the deputies and rescued Tyler, who fled to Canada and contacted Magistrate Rea. On October 21, Rea promptly issued a warrant pursuant to Canadian law to arrest the two deputies from Coos County and Blanchard. With this warrant in hand, Tyler returned to Indian Stream and, with the help of two other men, arrested Blanchard on the authority of the king of England. Blanchard, meanwhile, maintained that he was a "deputy of the sheriff of Coos County, and was at the time of my . . . abduction."[46]

Citizens friendly to Blanchard sounded the alarm. A posse led by Milton Harvey soon set out after the Tyler group. The posse succeeded in freeing Blanchard. The encounter illustrated the constitutional order's fluidity at this point. One witness recalled relying on the unsettled border as authority for demanding Blanchard's release, even describing him as one of Indian Stream's leading figures: "it evidently arose from the circumstance that the boundary line was not fully settled between the two governments, and that as the state of New Hampshire had for a long time claimed and exercised jurisdiction over the tract, . . . we felt it our duty to retake Blanchard, and to protect the officers of said settlement from arrest by officers from the Province. . . ."[47]

Several individuals offered bounties for the capture of Rea, Tyler, and others. Unwilling to let the matter go, Captain James Mooney of Stewartstown formed a second posse. This posse crossed into Canada, located Magistrate Rea, struck him with a sword, exchanged shots with him and his protectors, and chased him down. New Hampshire recovered a measure of civic pride by capturing the Canadian official who had stirred up so much cross-border trouble. There was an outstanding warrant for Tyler's arrest, but no such legal paper authorized Magistrate Rea's detention. Outraged Canadian officials complained, and diplomatic efforts later led to his release.

Residents of Indian Stream had long organized themselves spontaneously to enforce their own laws and customs. What changed now was that actions to enforce the laws of other jurisdictions put enormous pressure on the forms of justice established by local people. More than anything else, external developments spurred a reconsideration of allegiances. Under duress by more powerful outsiders, the Indian Stream legal system ceased to have any integrity of its own.

With constituent support for action at its zenith, Governor Badger called for the investigation of an apparent "rebellion" in the territory and authorized deployment of the militia. On November 13 he ordered troops to occupy Indian Stream so as to "enable the executive officers of the county of Coos to execute the laws and put down all insurrectionary movements." Although the state requested federal troops, the United States government declined to participate unless Canada escalated matters through military intervention. At all events, such assistance proved to be unnecessary. Resistance to the invasion was brief. A few individuals escaped to Canada. Those who were captured or surrendered swore fealty to New Hampshire, erasing any remaining vestiges of their Indian Stream identity. Some members of the Canadian faction later swore under oath they would not have resisted the authority of New Hampshire "had [they] not been advised to do so, and assured . . . [protection] in so doing by the government of Canada."[48]

Canada mustered a half-hearted response. Indictments were returned against all Americans who participated in the raid on Magistrate Rea.

Lord Gosford appointed a committee to venture into Indian Stream and investigate, but its members were intercepted and turned around near Fletcher's Mill by Captain Mooney. A separate effort to survey the land on behalf of Britain went nowhere. Afterward, England lodged strenuous diplomatic objections to New Hampshire's occupation of the territory, but otherwise promised not to interfere with the state's activities until the boundary was defined once and for all. An investigation conducted by the U.S. House Committee on Military Affairs considered protests by the British. Issuing the commission's report completed the transformation of the order. After reasserting New Hampshire's right to the territory, the report blamed foreigners for instigating the events at Indian Stream. External sovereigns became convenient scapegoats for the settlers' disloyalty in New Hampshire's tale of political reintegration.[49]

By this point, the land had come squarely under the military control of New Hampshire, with dissenters jailed, pacified, or run off. All that remained was recapture of the public imagination. Of course, the people themselves had to be perceived to voluntarily accept the terms of political membership. The proceedings of a joint meeting of the citizens of Stewartstown, Clarksville, and Indian Stream held on April 16, 1836, reveal an effort to repudiate the democratic experiment of Indian Stream. Luther Parker was in attendance. Among the resolutions published in the *New Hampshire Patriot,* as well as other area newspapers:

> *Resolved,* Therefore, that in the opinion of this meeting, New Hampshire has a right to exercise an unconditional control over the territory of Indian Stream.
>   *Resolved,* That our national government is bound to support the pretensions of New Hampshire in her claim to the territory of Indian Stream, inasmuch as it has in repeated instances been recognized by that government.[50]

With a people's plan for independence crushed and their thirst for stability sated, a measure of peace came to the area. Mild resistance would spring up again. For instance, some men living in Indian Stream refused to appear for militia duty as required by New Hampshire law. None of these incidents threatened the status quo. In December 1840, individuals of the region, their desire for self-governance awakened but disciplined, petitioned to be incorporated as the township of

Pittsburg. The legislature acted on the petition swiftly, and the first town meeting was conducted on March 9, 1841. Indian Stream's borders continued to be disputed by diplomats until being resolved by treaty in 1842, which established America's border at the head of Hall's Stream. But this matter no longer concerned the locals. The federal government reimbursed New Hampshire for expenditures related to its handling of the Indian Stream affair, proof that the interests of conventional sovereignty had been more than adequately protected.

For a number of years, settlers in the region had successfully governed themselves. After declaring independence, they ruled for another three years. Because the citizens of Indian Stream reused familiar local forms of self-governance (council, sheriff, judges), they were able to implement their institutions to a significant degree at very little cost. Until New Hampshire raised the stakes by aggressively enforcing its laws, Indian Stream laws had every bit of the integrity and force one would expect in the rule of law. The people successfully publicized their grievances, and to the extent they wished to raise the profile of a set of issues affecting the region, that, too, must be a counted as a victory for the constitution.

Why, in the final analysis, did this exercise in frontier constitutionalism fail? Some commentators direct their condemnation at the avaricious land speculators. Roger Brown, for one, contends that the Eastman Company's drive to win legislative confirmation of its claim forced New Hampshire's hand. Moreover, he faults the competition between rival firms, which "planted the seeds of unrest and dissatisfaction among the settlers." According to this way of thinking, it became "a matter of honor for New Hampshire and duty to keep them."[51]

But Brown's thesis leaves too much at one party's door. It presumes that the fate of the people could have turned out differently, if only the Eastman Company had behaved better. This seems doubtful given the larger political and legal forces at work. The capitalist drive to accumulate profits certainly played a crucial part in setting a chain of events in motion. Even more important, however, was the cohesiveness of community sentiment. The spirit of independence had so pervaded the populace that when Parker began to rethink New Hampshire's claim, he found himself ostracized from the council and its business because he had "lost the confidence of the people." By authoring a new constitution, the people had made a show of popular solidarity. That citizens of Indian Stream would defend their sovereignty to the brink of war turned out to be the real surprise, for they went further than most determinists dared.[52]

Ultimately, pioneer sovereignty could be no more than a transitional form of politics. Structurally, it had to contend with the broader constitutional project to create a single legal order. As a legalized strategy for economic development, the model proved effective in encouraging the migration of people and investment in the land. It mobilized settlers to assault existing borders and indigenous ways of life. But Indian Stream had to ripen into an independent nation (recognized or otherwise), become a conventional state as part of the United States, or be integrated into another jurisdiction (Canada or New Hampshire). As America's frontiers continued to shift, so the fledgling democracies littering the landscape had to assume a more domesticated form. Without allies, the people of Indian Stream had neither the resources nor the will to resist the intervention of their neighbors.

Lasting independence had always been the least likely outcome. Unlike Hawaii or Puerto Rico, or even the several Indian tribes, Indian Stream did not comprise a native people whose long tradition of self-governance might have merited a more nuanced arrangement with jurisdictions that had a claim on the land. Neither the United States nor Canada could abide a tiny independent nation on its borders. The small population and territory, too, worked against the possibility that Indian Stream might become one of the several states such as Vermont—a congressional strategy that determinist movements pursued in other contexts but the inhabitants of Indian Stream never considered a serious option.

Eschewing state constitutionalism, the republic's hope for survival turned into an effort to gain the recognition of an established nation-state, coupled with a protective alliance. Entreaties to Canada, New Hampshire, and the U.S. government to forge such a relationship were not reciprocated. Initially, each nation played to settle its own claim to the territory while devoting the minimal resources necessary to preserve its claim. Once it became apparent that no country wished to force the action by seizing physical control of the territory or clearing it of settlers, the only question was which nation would absorb Indian Stream without leading to its depopulation and destruction. Ironically, the same strategies that made democratic experimentation possible hastened its end. Juggling multiple sovereigns and holding them at bay proved to be too difficult for the settlers. The crisis of 1835 intensified divisions within the society, as each faction invited external intervention. As two nations dawdled, a nearby state stepped into the breach.

New Hampshire, the best-placed actor, took decisive action when the opportunity arose to divide and conquer. Civic pride may have played some role, but proximity, resources, and self-interest had larger roles in New Hampshire's push for an integrative resolution when it did. Canada's sudden and rather clumsy actions to preserve its claim on the territory, coupled with evidence of Canadian sympathizers among the populace, told New Hampshire that frontier democracy had gone on long enough at this site. The state found itself in a position to capitalize on the moment. When New Hampshire officials realized that no reprisals would come from its forcible integration of Indian Stream and that the federal government would back its display of military might, so ended the only other possible outcome—that Indian Stream might be recognized as its own state as part of a rapidly expanding nation.

This episode would later be eclipsed by the Dorr Rebellion, which featured dueling governors each armed with a constitution and, like the Indian Stream experiment, prompted authorities to use military force to reintegrate the polity. Through public relations and the legal integration of the land and inhabitants, New Hampshire successfully altered the people's collective memory, to the point that Indian Stream is today considered a part of official state history, with wilder memories of the experiment left to local lore. And yet the demise of the Indian Stream republic showed that pioneer sovereignty had its limits after the Founding. The episode dramatized the weaknesses in that model of politics, especially where an enclave is surrounded by the irresistible forces of political consolidation. When authorities put down the "Indian Stream rebellion" and converted the republic into one New Hampshire county among many, they sent a message to all Americans that acts of popular sovereignty would have to conform to the priorities of an emerging national order. Meanwhile, the logic of pioneer sovereignty—emphasizing openness and a thin vision of civic equality—facilitated massive demographic and economic changes. Ironically, the model's successes stimulated reactive theories of law and politics to emerge, ones that would turn more sharply toward moral reformation and cultural exclusivity.

CHAPTER TWO

The Icarian Nation
1848–1895

We shall, from this time, accustom ourselves to a
language still more moderate, kindly, and fraternal;
and increase our efforts to command the esteem of our
adversaries.

—ETIENNE CABET, ADDRESS, 1847, REPRINTED IN *Community of Icarie*, 1903

Pioneer dreams inspired Americans to try their hand at creating ever
more perfect societies, though not all such experiments were cut from
the same cloth. After decades of rapid economic development, the
first half of the nineteenth century emerged as a high point of socialist
utopianism. It was the age of Robert Owen and Charles Fourier, and
countless others who founded small-scale cooperatives around the
world. These visionaries idolized labor and the shared ownership of
property, sang the virtues of loving one's neighbor, and railed against
constitutional orders that degraded humanity for the sake of economic advancement. As they interacted with American legal ideas,
their visions of community and power helped to reshape the constitutional tradition.

An intriguing figure fitting this mold was Etienne Cabet, a socialist
lawyer and politician who antagonized French authorities during the
reign of Louis Philippe through his orations and writings. As a public
figure, he navigated both insider and outsider personas. He held a
leadership position in the Carbonari and served as attorney-general
of Corsica. Later, he won admiration as a populist critic of the king's
policies. Among his complaints: unequal suffrage, an onerous tax
system, unhealthy industrial working conditions, and the absence of
nationalized health care and education.

To address such social ills, Cabet proposed the establishment of a
socialist republic, which he called "Icaria." At first, he felt confident

that such a legal order could be formed in France, adopted wholesale if the moment arose and piecemeal if regime-shaking conditions did not materialize. As Cabet grew disillusioned with the progress of revolutionary change in France, he turned his attention to laying the foundations of a socialist state in the United States. The people of France still clung to the tradition of constitutional monarchy while Americans' rejection of kingship invited new modes of popular governance. These French immigrants discovered a country in transition, a people still mobilized for the relentless expansion of western borders yet tolerant of communitarian experimentation. The Icarians' perfectionist orientation toward society and humanity fit comfortably with the revolutionary tradition of their adopted country. At the same time, the Icarians offered an ethical alternative to the growing American order, which prized rapid economic development and increasingly professed neutrality as to competing conceptions of the good life. Citizens who had grown more skeptical of rampant individualism and the ravages of industrialization found the Icarian message of social harmony intriguing.[1]

Efforts to found Icaria in Texas failed miserably, owing to poor advance planning and the impossibility of developing land in compliance with state law. The remnants of the first colony eventually joined with a second expedition, with the combined group resettling in Nauvoo, Illinois. There the community prospered after authoring a constitution and gaining the endorsement of the state government to farm the land as an agricultural society. Through these efforts, a people adapted agrarian socialism to the democratic culture of America. By turning to constitutional mechanisms, the Icarians distinguished themselves from the typical civic association, or even the usual cooperative. Examining their unorthodox legal order, Carol Weisbrod finds that Icarians believed that "[s]overeignty was in the state" and that "[w]hat the community did by way of contract it did because the state allowed it that freedom." In reality, that was true in only the most formal sense, for the Icarians had a far more ambitious and subversive theory of politics in mind. These pioneers took strategic advantage of federalism, finding spaces for democratic trial and error within the larger American legal order where a unity of interests between their dissident political community and one conventional state could be achieved. In designing the federalist system, the Framers of the U.S. Constitution had mentioned the power of the states to resist the assimilating effects of time, creating "a nation whose affairs are in the highest degree diversified and complicated." A single state, exercising what Louis Brandeis once called "the right to experiment," could license "novel and social experiments without risk to the rest of the country." The Icarians exploited federalism's experimentalist rationale by creatively using state laws to advance their social project. Yet the fact that ordinary laws could be enforced against them was an unpleasant fact to be avoided rather than the basis of their theory of popular authority.[2]

If exploitation of federalism was primarily a tactical calculation, then the foundations of Icarian self-rule lay elsewhere: a secularized vision of Christian charity formulated in Europe and adapted to Americans' experiences. These founders would offer a worker-governed alternative to a liberal society dominated by rapacious owners and manufacturers. In fact, the history of Icaria in America entailed a novel variation on popular sovereignty. While retaining a separatist orientation usually associated with pioneer governance, a people took strategic advantage of state laws to nurture their distinctive way of life while deflecting the concerns of Illinois authorities about disloyalty and disorder. Obedience to state law was largely instrumental and based on convenience; the people's true theory of sovereignty was grounded in the socialist values articulated in their own constitution. Conventional sovereignty became merely a means of placating outside authorities and gaining recognition, with the core of the people's authority underwritten by the morality of mutual interdependence.

The Icarians' socialist ideology therefore added a third element to the mix: ethical sovereignty, in which a strong moral code imbued every institution and every relationship in a constitutional order. Not only did the Icarian creed depart from the plural model of the frontier community, but it also turned the pioneer model on its head through its opposition to economic development based on radical individualism. The very existence of Icaria subverted national economic policy and the values of the dominant constitutional order.

The hybrid nature of the Icarian system would solve some problems while creating others. The Icarian approach facilitated the peaceful and legal acquisition of land and successfully warded off external threats to the integrity of their own laws. In fact, the strategy helped Icaria to outlast many of its socialist counterparts. Even so, the legal order faced enormous challenges from within, as the community struggled to remain faithful to its ideological foundations under the pressures of cultural changes. Along the way, the Icarians also made a difficult transition from charismatic leadership to democratic self-rule.

Journey to Icaria: A Theory of Law

Conflict with the French order gave rise to Cabet's political maturation, as well as his plan to resettle in America. Alarmed by Louis Philippe's consolidation of authority after overthrowing Charles X and his suppression of popular criticism, Cabet took up the pen. His book *Histoire de la révolution de 1830* accused the king of betraying the principles and aims of the revolution. Emboldened by the success of his book, Cabet founded the newspaper *Le Populaire* and published articles criticizing social policy. This led to Cabet's arrest and trial for printing pamphlets judged "an affront to the king." The Assize Court of Seine sentenced him to two years in prison, a fine, and forfeiture of all voting and publishing rights for a period of four years. Alternatively, he was offered the option of five years in exile. Rather than accede to the state's desire to silence him, Cabet chose banishment.

While in exile in England, Cabet studied philosophy and political theory. He read Thomas More for the first time and became acquainted with the work of Robert Owen, a prominent socialist. Owen founded New Harmony, a commune in the United States that had achieved worldwide renown. Cabet became convinced that democracy could not persist in its current form, with material excess and class-based interests strangling the promises of social equality. In place of private property and the free market, he advocated the creation of *la communauté de biens,* or the "community of goods." Following Owen's lead, Cabet increasingly looked toward America as providing the best environment in which to establish a more perfect legal order.

Abjuring violence, Cabet endorsed "primitive Christianity" as the means of establishing a more benevolent legal order. Taking Jesus of Nazareth as a practitioner of early socialism, Cabet "exhorted the people to renounce secret societies, plots, mutiny and insurrection" in favor of "persuasion, conviction, and the free consent of the individual." Engaging others through reason and righteous example, rather than force, would lead to the triumphal creation of Icaria. Internalization of republican precepts through "self-improvement and moral reflection" would be sufficient to "graft a new state of society upon the old one."

Voyage en Icarie emerged during this period of intense intellectual growth. Like Thomas More's *Utopia* or Plato's *Republic,* the book is an extended meditation on the structure and workings of the ideal state. Though perhaps not as beautifully executed as the other works, it is similarly an exercise in political fiction and a blueprint for a just society. A reader is instantly struck by the notion that linguistic discipline—through the formation and preservation of an egalitarian language—would be essential to a nation's identity and its long-term prospects. Cabet depicts the travels of Lord Carisdall, a believer in an aristocratic monarchy, who brings older views into contact with the new and dramatizes the possibility of political conversion to democratic socialism. Upon his arrival in Icaria, Carisdall is handed a handsome volume "whose binding was as strange as it was beautiful," used to educate people on the Icarian language. The nation's tongue is described as a "perfectly rational, regular, simple language . . . whose rules are very few in number and without exception . . . whose words have a perfectly defined meaning; . . . and the study of which is so easy that the average person can learn it in four or five months."[3]

The formation of a universal discourse of governance would overcome the obstacles to political justice posed by the "multiplicity and imperfection of languages" found in the world. Perusing the book for several days inspires Carisdall to tour Icaria for himself. The rest of the book consists of the visitor's journal, with the observations of others occasionally copied into his account. What he notices is a republic characterized by good order: "[T]he perfection of Icarian cultivation and the striking beauty of the countryside," matched with "charming farms and villages." Money has been abolished; poverty has been eradicated through public ownership of property and the sacrificial labor of all. Wherever one turns, there is evidence of the success of legalized socialism. As the citizens like to warn visitors, "the air we breathe here is deadly for the aristocracy." Living among the citizens is joyously called a process of "de-aristocratiz[ing]" some-one "from head to foot."[4]

Socialism is simultaneously the product of popular governance and its most idealized incarnation. The principles of popular sovereignty and nationhood—rule by citizens who imagine themselves as a distinctive people—are interwoven with the community's substantive socialist policies. That is to say, republicanism and socialism are understood as compatible bodies of knowledge rather than direct competitors. Envisioned as a perfect harmonization of these traditions, "[t]he community is a Democracy and a Republic."[5]

As one of the visitor's hosts explains, "the People consists of the totality of all Icarians without exception." To "the people alone belongs, with sovereignty, the power to draft, or cause to be drafted, their social contract, their constitution, their laws." How, then, is one to treat public officials? All public servants "are the trustees of the people . . . elected, temporary, responsible for their actions, and removable, and, to prevent ambitious encroachment, no one person may exercise both a legislative and executive function."[6] This brand of self-rule not only resonated with nineteenth-century Europeans yearning for freedom, it also would have sounded familiar to Americans raised on ideas of indirect rule and divided government.

More troubling for lovers of art or individual expression, majoritarian rule also paves the way to cultural control: "Because the people are sovereign, they have the right to regulate, by their constitution and laws, everything pertaining to their persons, actions, goods, food, clothing, lodging, education, their work, and even their amusements." In the ideal state, music and art abound, though as in Plato's imaginary republic, "every work of art is created with a utilitarian goal." Nothing should distract from the fundamental tenets of the community. As Lord Carisdall notes, "There is nothing useless and, above all, nothing harmful. . . . There is nothing in support of fanaticism and superstition." All art serves "liberty and its martyrs" or inveighs "against its former tyrants and their followers." One would "never see any of those nudes or voluptuous paintings that hang in our capital cities to please the powerful libertines."[7]

Modesty, reason, and the public good must overcome extravagance, vice, and selfishness. Some variety of expression could exist, but not for its own sake, and artistic works have to be justified according to the republic's organizing values. One of the country's most treasured objects is a national printing shop, which serves to educate the citizens and inform them of daily events.

The justice system in Icaria is predicated on popular judgment, leading to the possibility of two very different reactions on the part of observers. One, that of a society "where no one need lock a door, and where there are no drunkards, no thieves, and no policeman." The other reaction: "Nowhere on earth are there more policemen" than in Icaria, for "all our citizens, are required to oversee law enforcement and to pursue or denounce the persons whose misdemeanors they witness." It is beside the point which characterization is more accurate, for all Icarians are expected to police the community's values.[8]

Ideally, the adjudication of offenses occurs within particular institutions, thereby enlisting the collective wisdom of peers and experts. "Every school is a court for judging the misdemeanors committed in the school. Every workshop judges the offenses that occur there. . . . Each family constitutes itself as a court of justice to judge family misdemeanors." Not only does the approach produce specialized law, but the Icarian's theory of law also allows the rule of law to extend to every facet of social existence. "[T]here is no area where courts and justice are not in existence," according to the story, "and that there is no other land where delinquents can boast that they are judged by their peers to this extent."[9]

Voyage en Icarie appeared in 1840 and captured the attention of revolutionary France. It instantly became one of the most successful books of its kind, satisfying widespread desire for democratic governance, renewed virtue, and shared ownership of the means of production. Cabet's newspaper attracted thousands of subscribers, mainly from among the working class.[10] For some, readership would evolve into followership, as Icarian communities began to be organized throughout Europe.

From Colony to Republic

In 1847, as the new regime cracked down on socialists instead of implementing their proposals, Cabet announced his plan to establish an Icarian state in America. Quoting Jesus of Nazareth, he said, "If they persecute you in one city, go you into another." Although France no longer seemed hospitable to the working class, America's idyllic environs and democratic openness beckoned. With a flourish, Cabet declared to the people of Europe, "Travailleurs, allons en Icarie!"[11]

He called on "Icarians of all countries, who are well acquainted with our Icarian system and our Icarian doctrine, who adopt them completely," to devote themselves to "the cause of the People and of Humanity." All would labor "to bring about the triumph of our system of Fraternity and Community, Equality and Liberty, of Democracy and of the Republic." Offering his own twist on Americans' theory of pioneer sovereignty, Cabet beseeched followers to "aid us to establish in the wilderness an Icarian Commune and afterward a State."[12]

The response proved overwhelming. From among thousands of volunteers, Cabet handpicked an initial group to travel to the United States. On February 3, 1848, an advance guard composed of sixty-nine men set off for Texas, a location recommended by Owen. Cabet himself did not make the trip but promised to join the colony when he could. As the ship left the dock at Le Havre, the travelers sang:

> Arise, workers bent down in the dust.
> The hour of awakening has sounded.
> On the American shores,
> See the flag of the Holy community waving.
> No more vice, no more suffering,
> No more crime, no more pain.
> Hallowed Equality advances.[13]

Expectations were sky high. In a pamphlet, Cabet later explained how his followers fulfilled their dreams of creating the ideal state in the American backwoods: "The Icarian Colony in America was founded for the purpose of clearing, cultivating and subduing the wilderness, while establishing there all useful industries for the production and manufacture of all that is needed for a people." Their strategy for "creating a State" entailed "creating first one Commune, then others successively."[14]

Far from disengaging from the world, the group hoped to commence a bold democratic experiment. Founders described themselves as "a people . . . creating a State" who aspired to have "the best system of political and social organization" seen yet on the earth. The world ought to see the community as a "little democratic Republic," with its system of governance embodying the principles of "radical and pure Democracy." Because of their ambitions, the Icarians did not form a common civic association in the United States. Rather, these transplants practiced a more sophisticated kind of constitutional development by using creative legal techniques to construct a competing political order within a recognized nation-state. According to this type of interstitial resistance, dissidents exploit lacunae in existing legal systems to create an alternative political order. The Icarians exploited American federalism by finding common ground with the policies of one state to establish a community whose values opposed the cultural values of the nation-state as a whole. By taking care not to repudiate all claims made on them by other jurisdictions, they tried to reduce friction with the authorities and neighbors while alternative institutions were built, communal practices took hold, and political beliefs spread. One ought not take their pacific ethics at face value and underestimate the extent to which such a society can exist in opposition to dominant political systems.[15]

The size of the republic was the subject of much discussion. In *Voyage en Icarie*, Cabet agreed with Plato that the city offered the ideal site for virtuous interaction. In practical terms, that meant either that one gained control of an existing legal order or established a new order beyond anyone's jurisdiction. To adapt his ideas to the reality of existing nation-states, Cabet treated "[t]he Icarian Commune [a]s the foundation of the Icarian State which is composed of many communes."

Cabet believed, as many republicans through the ages have believed, that there was a strong correlation between the size of a deliberative body and the quality of its deliberations. For this reason, he set limits on the size of any particular community: "The population of the Commune must not exceed the number of citizens who can unite in a single Assembly, about 1,000 or 1,200, with their wives and children, about 4 or 5,000 souls." Because such alternative forms of self-rule would necessarily be located within recognized nation-states and scattered across jurisdictions, the Icarian nation had both local and transnational dimensions. Fellow citizens shared principles, identities, and outlooks, even if they did not always share the same patch of land. And Icarians would offer "asylum" or safe harbor to republican refugees from around the world.

Icaria resembled the microrepublic of Indian Stream in that both drew heavily from the small republic tradition. At the same time, given Icarianism's stronger ideological cast—its class consciousness and dedication to workers worldwide—the republic viewed itself as part of a larger moral-legal order. Some of the Icarians' preference for small-scale organization was due to strategic calculations, borne out of a desire to appear unthreatening to the authorities and their neighbors. Their later efforts to expand the republic by adding new colonies confirm that they never surrendered their universalist orientation. Thus Icarianism straddled the tensions in the American political tradition, at once imagining a single, worldwide community while subscribing to the view that face-to-face interactions in each colony produced the best policies.

The Icarians were also pioneers in the sense that they, too, saw themselves to be settling America and working the land. But their theory of power and community derived from membership in a broader idea of the working class, along with the economic interests and ethical norms that bound that group. Unfortunately, the group's initial plunge into the American frontier without their leader proved to be a disaster. What the Icarians assumed would be 1,000,000 acres of Texas farmland near the water turned out to be 100,000 acres of wilderness some 250 miles from the Red River. Instead of a contiguous territory, they gained title to only every other plot of land, allocated in chessboard fashion. To take rightful possession, they had to build a home on each parcel of land within an impossibly short period of time. As news of the French Revolution of 1848 reached the dispirited advance party, some wished to return home to carry on the struggle. Disease, hunger, and fatigue joined demoralization in ravaging the settlement. A second advance party of nineteen left for Texas, but only ten made it. The community broke up rapidly after that, with the bulk of the group setting off for New Orleans.

Meanwhile, cheered by the turn of events in France, Cabet posted notices throughout Paris urging his countrymen to support the provisional government and postpone implementation of the Icarian system. It did not take long for his mind to change. On December 13, 1848, unhappy with the establishment of a "bourgeois republic" in France instead of a "popular or democratic republic," and persecuted anew for his socialist criticisms, Cabet departed for America.

He arrived in New Orleans in January 1849 accompanied by some 450 followers. There, Cabet convened a meeting of the Assembly made up of the remnant of the original expeditions and the group accompanying Cabet. After learning of the advance parties' misfortunes, he proposed that anyone who wished to return to Paris could do so. The majority—some 280 persons—opted to soldier on. This group sailed for Nauvoo, Illinois, by riverboat up the Mississippi River. By March 1849, the Icarian community had secured a permanent home and began eking out a modest lifestyle.

After the disaster of Texas, the Icarians became more legal scavengers than disruptors of borders, gravitating to a location that had already been settled and gaining lawful control of land. They scoured the remains of previous settlements, turning discarded structures to new ends. Nauvoo had been settled by Joseph Smith and his followers after being driven from Missouri. The Mormons migrated westward when spiraling conflict with local inhabitants culminated in Smith's murder at the hands of a mob in 1844. Cabet and his disciples leased some 1,500 acres containing structures built by Mormon hands, including a forty-room dwelling house, farms, and workshops. They purchased houses, a mill and distillery, as well as the remains of the Mormon temple, which had burned to the ground. Taking stones from the temple, they constructed a schoolhouse. The Icarian strategy of adapting existing materials for new ends extended to the law, where they found ways to use state laws to subvert the dominant moral-legal order. A key component of the plan entailed making a foreign vision of power and community palatable under the terms of the American political tradition.

Popular sovereignty and written constitutionalism gave meaning to their adventure from the start. Before members of the advance party departed for the New World, they had executed a social contract drafted by Cabet. According to this provisional constitution, published in an issue of *Le Populaire,* Cabet would be installed as director-in-chief of the community for the first ten years. In a ritualized call and response, Cabet had members of the advance guard orally affirm their commitment to the social contract in front of hundreds of observers along the dock. Before the ship departed, he asked whether the pilgrims had sincerely devoted themselves to the principles of socialism and whether they were willing to endure hardship to establish the republic. The provisional constitution was renewed during the crisis of faith in New Orleans and again in Nauvoo.[16]

Within a year of making Nauvoo home, Cabet vowed to cede power back to the people. Instead of being governed by one man who alone dictated communal norms, the Icarians would rule themselves according to a written charter. On February 21, 1850, a convention of Icarians at Nauvoo ratified a constitution. Deliberations spanned nine meetings. Cabet confessed that the exercise was a crucial phase of a concerted effort "to put the Social Contract in harmony with the law and the republican sentiment of the Americans." In writing the constitution, they sought to "profit" from their recent experience governing themselves and interacting with neighbors. The document's length and detail can be explained in part because of the intended audience: The Icarians' new neighbors and the Illinois legislature. From the former, they hoped to enjoy peaceful relations; from the latter, formal recognition of Icaria as a lawful entity. Consistent with their moral vision and pacific tactics, Icarians would implement a constitution through reason, self-improvement, and ethical modeling. Like the Pauline communities that had to exist within the Greco-Roman world, Icarian communities would coexist with a rotting industrial order. At the same time, legal force did not disappear entirely from their existence. Instead, a constitution redirected violence away from external enemies toward internal dangers posed by citizens failing to live up to Icarian values.

On February 1, 1851, the Illinois legislature passed *An Act to incorporate the Icarian Community*. The state law declared Cabet, his associates, and their successors to be "constituted a body politic and corporate," with the power to own property, and to sue and be sued. It authorized the Icarian Community to pass bylaws concerning "the government of the property and business" and "regulating its internal policy." The Icarians were empowered to make their own laws so long as they were "not inconsistent with the Constitution and Laws of this State." Legislators promised to construe the act "liberally" for the benefit of the Icarian experiment. By enacting the law, the people of Illinois gave their blessing to the Icarians' social democratic project. Formally, the state chartered the community to operate as an agricultural society; its activities had to remain compatible with the policies of the state. Such treatment dovetailed with Illinois's policy of encouraging productive use of arable land. But informally, the alternative microrepublic had gained a measure of credibility that accompanied conditional recognition—a legal status of which few dissident communities could ever boast.[17]

The Icarian Constitution underwent revision and reratification on May 4, 1851, once the bill of incorporation became law. A series of exchanges between the Icarians and state officials produced a sanctioned form of socialism, adapted to the political culture of the times. According to the letter of the law, the republic satisfied the conventional rules of federalism. Yet the Icarians' social and economic ethics undermined the values extolled by the program of national development, as well as the origins and supremacy of higher law. Moreover, the Icarian Constitution had a mixed heritage. According to Cabet, the government of Icaria did not reflect a single nation-state's heritage, but rather an amalgamation of traditions: "It is planned that it shall be neither exclusively French nor German, American nor English."[18]

The Icarian pilgrims calculated that by accommodating the American political tradition, they would make foreign ideas palatable to local authorities as well as to neighbors. They agreed to be bound by a constitution and democratically enacted laws to show the world what legal socialism could accomplish. The Icarians also embraced popular sovereignty and written constitutionalism to distinguish themselves from the Mormons, a group that had been perceived as aloof, foreign, and dangerous. An extensive system of laws satisfied Illinois politicians who "wanted no more one-man-controlled communities in the Prairie State." In this sense, outsiders treated the Icarian Constitution as a written promise to abide by American rule-of-law principles. Upon the constitution's unanimous approval by the Icarian people, it was sent along to the Illinois secretary of state, who duly recorded it.[19]

A complicated political dance ensued as the nation within a nation-state sought to become self-sustaining. Outwardly, the Icarian republic professed obedience to American laws and customs, sometimes going to great lengths to celebrate national holidays. Cabet even presided over a mass ceremony where Nauvoo colonists were sworn as U.S. citizens. Privately, however, the feeling was that "American laws . . . cannot be called upon by Icarians. For these People, between them, there are no other laws than Icarian laws, no other Courts and no other Juges [*sic*] than their General Assembly, their Sovereign to all." In other words, while they respected the laws of existing nation-states as a practical matter, Icarian law was superior as a matter of theory. If and when conflict arose between the duty to obey the conventional sovereign and the duty to obey Icarian law, Icarian forms of sovereignty must enjoy the primary claim on the people's allegiance. The Icarian theory of law proved to be indispensable to its longevity. It gestured toward the state's power and allayed the suspicions of neighbors, while securing the state's blessing for Icarians to govern their own.[20]

The Icarian Constitution: Fraternity, Labor, and Judgment

The 1850 Icarian Constitution contained an extensive discussion of the Icarians' social and ethical system, crafted to render it "appealing to the approbation of the average legislator by expressing many of the glittering political maxims of the American Declaration of Independence." Icarians did not disparage the U.S. Constitution directly but rather found inspiration in its promises. Co-opting the vernacular of their new country, they argued that true "liberty" and "equality" required moving to a more advanced form of democratic rule and a repudiation of rapacious capitalism. Thus, instead of rejecting the American Constitution openly, the Icarian Constitution subverted its design by rejecting the economic and cultural values that had become closely associated with the national order as Americans pursued rapid economic advancement and political consolidation.[21]

The constitution balanced the Icarians' political aspirations with the legal realities they faced as a nascent republic. One provision established the principle that "the number of its members is unlimited." What the rest of the world saw would be more unassuming. Inasmuch as the society wished its true ambitions known without provoking open conflict with existing authorities, the constitution predicted, "It is destined to become a City and a State obedient to the general laws of the United States," while conceding that "[i]n the meantime it is obedient to the laws of the State of Illinois."[22]

At 183 separate provisions, the Icarian Constitution found a place among the longest charters written on American soil. When compared to the plans of governance of other utopian societies, it was distinguished by its detail, complexity, and aspirations. The closest analogue would be the community of New Harmony, which adopted seven constitutions over the course of its brief existence. Most other such perfectionist societies relied on general statements of principles or simple charters of incorporation dealing with the disposition of property. Few, if any, sought to create dispute-resolution mechanisms or other law-based institutions on the scale of Icaria.[23]

Despite the many ideas articulated, the constitution treated some matters at length, even repetitively, while giving cursory attention to others. Out of practicality the Icarian nation had to deal with the laws of existing sovereigns, yet the community nevertheless behaved internally as though it were a nation unto itself. In a statement of motives, the people affirmed the existence of the Icarian nation and concluded that its democratic principles compared favorably with those of other countries. They boasted that their constitution and laws were "perhaps the most liberal, the most democratic and the most popular that exist." The 1850 Constitution extended "universal suffrage" to all men, and guaranteed "the right of each citizen to propose laws, to discuss and vote upon them." Although it denied women a vote, the constitution accorded them restricted deliberative rights, including "the right to assist in the Assemblies and to take part in all discussions, to express their minds and defend their interests."[24]

The people of Icaria touted their laws for going "the farthest" in taking democracy seriously, by "declar[ing] that taking part in the General Assemblies is not alone a right, but a duty; and this principle, that participation is a duty, is a great step in the practice and organization of the Democracy." This more robust approach to political membership departed from the plan of most conventional states in America, which tended to treat voting as part of the bundle of rights of citizenship rather than as an obligation. Besides the principle of compulsory participation, members of the community referred to one another as not only brothers and sisters but also more formally as *citoyens* and *citoyennes*.

Equality served as a foundational principle, with the Icarian Constitution recognizing "all to be equals in law and duty." Servitude "is done away with," putting the community in line with the people of Illinois. The Illinois Constitution of 1818 had banned the introduction of involuntary servitude and slavery but left existing practices intact; in 1848, a new state constitution finally banned slavery outright, except as punishment for crime. Not only was the Icarians' position forward-looking when compared to the rest of America, but the Icarians' ban on servitude was also comprehensive, confronting the problem in all of its incarnations.[25]

Still, the Icarians held a complicated view of equality. Instead of merely professing a general idea as the U.S. Constitution had done and leaving it to interpreters to carve out exceptions and extenuating circumstances, the Icarian document expressly acknowledged that "[e]quality is *relative* and *proportional.*" A person's share in the political community's benefits and burdens depended on his needs and abilities. This confession of complexity rendered the Icarian concept of equality more realistic but also vulnerable to arguments that individuals of varying backgrounds might be entitled to differential treatment.[26]

The concept of liberty was divided into three types: natural liberty, social or civil liberty, and political liberty. Natural liberty encompassed freedom from force and the right to "defence against all attack," but could be constrained by any agreements freely entered, including the basic law of a community. Social or civil liberty was characterized by a citizen's relationship to others as delineated by law. Reflecting both the instrumental and reformative qualities of the law, social liberty permitted the people to make policy and discipline the community in order to prevent "all that is injurious" and "ordering all that is useful." Finally, the people defined political liberty as "the exercise of Sovereignty and in the making of the Constitution and laws."

The political liberty created by the 1850 Constitution proved to be highly majoritarian. Procedural rules permitted constitutional amendments only every other year. This design choice, which put the Icarians at odds with a number of pioneer and state constitutions, implied a desire to settle as many issues as possible in writing rather than leave their basic law subject to cultural or generational disruptions. Whether by design or accident, the Icarians' devotion for written law also increased the majoritarian nature of everyday decisions. The General Assembly—and to a large extent the president as guardian—would be a perfect manifestation of the people's values, unassailable until the next textually authorized moment for making changes to the constitution. Until such a moment, the Icarian vision of ethically in-flected power and community would be maintained through majority rule and popular judgment against individual citizens.

At its core, the Icarian Constitution represented a collective renun-ciation of "the old Society" based on radical individualism. The people turned away from not only the crumbling European order but also the American laissez-faire system that caused an explosion of eco-nomic development while shredding the moral fabric of a nation. Ethical labor helped forge the political bonds among the people. Un-der the basic law, "[t]he Community provides each one with all he needs, the only condition being that he work according to his strength." According to the Icarian motto, the "First Right is to live; First Duty is to Work."[27]

Consistent with their moral views on economic liberty, property was held in common and subject to collective control. The Icarians abolished taxes and found private insurance no longer necessary be-cause the community provided "mutual and universal *assurance* against all accidents, disasters and misfortunes." Once servitude, "money for internal use," and wages had been outlawed, gone too were laws gov-erning master and servant. Similarly, a blanket prohibition on "buying and selling, trafficking, and bargaining" obviated any need for laws dealing with the undesirable by-products of commerce initiated by self-interest, such as fraud or breach of contract.

Because of their ethical commitments and the fact that so many entitlements accompanied the grant of Icarian citizenship, the repub-lic erected higher barriers to entry than the conventional state and rigorously policed them. Initially, an applicant had to pay in six hun-dred francs, though this amount would be reduced over time as ap-plicants dwindled. A newcomer could expect provisional citizenship status for a period of four months, at the end of which time the Gérance, or board of managers, would interview the candidate to ensure the applicant was suited to the Icarian lifestyle. The General Assembly would then separately consider the case for admission. Each applicant had to gain the favorable vote of three-fourths of the Assembly to secure "definitive admission."

The Icarians' strong turn toward the law exerted a gravitational pull on communal relations. Their penchant for aggressive lawmaking was exacerbated by their peculiar blend of socialism, republicanism, and popular sovereignty. More social and economic questions became resolved as a matter of fundamental law rather than ordinary law or practice—hence, the code-like quality of the Icarian charter. Theirs was not a pluralistic order that tolerated disagreements over the good life but rather a legal system conceived with the goal of maximizing ideological coherence. Additionally, questions of justice in individual cases would be handled not by professional judges but by the people themselves meeting in appropriate contexts. Formally, the constitution "d[id] away with . . . the pay of public officers; . . . the budget and taxes; . . . *legal processes* and the courts, with their employees of all kinds." Adjudicatory power remained but became absorbed by other institutions.

Because the constitution outlawed prominent features of nineteenth-century capitalism and guarded against extreme poverty and degradation, the necessity of a sophisticated criminal law was not as dire as it had become in urban communities. The Icarians practiced institution-specific justice, with a strong preference that allegations of lawbreaking should be adjudicated within the workplace. The combination of these factors—a propensity toward formality and decisive resolutions—ensured that the law became the primary means of conducting communal relations, with all of its friction and coerciveness. Few matters escaped the judgment of the Icarian people, but without the usual procedural and rights-based safeguards expected in American courts.

Implementing the criminal justice system foreshadowed in *Voyage en Icarie,* the constitution required each workshop director to report possible violations in the workplace and establish a general "duty of each citizen to make known, in the interest of the Community, the offenses committed against it." Once offenses were reported, it became the responsibility of the Gérance "to investigate offenses and demand against the offenders the execution of the laws." Offenses "against workshop regulations" would be "judged by the workshop," ensuring expertise, fairness, and representativeness in peer judgment. The General Assembly served as the court of final resort, hearing "cases of appeal on all criminal acts which have taken place out of the Assembly and which have been previously judged by a Jury." By contrast, "Common offenses against the Community" could be directly "judged by the General Assembly or by a jury."[28]

Icarian law authorized two types of punishment, consistent with its policy of nonconfrontation vis-à-vis the state. The first kind of sanction consisted of public censure. The quality and duration of this shaming mechanism could be tailored as a workplace sanction or one effectuated by the General Assembly, accompanied "with more or less of publicity." An alternative sentence involved physical "exclusion," which could take the form of separation from the workshop (likely accompanied by job reassignment), the General Assembly (presumably along with loss of deliberative and voting rights), or the community as a whole (banishment). The republic did not authorize detention or any other kind of physical punishment, which would have put the community at greater risk of being perceived as usurping the function of state and local authorities.[29]

Everyday authority was distributed to institutions that roughly resembled those found among the Icarians' neighbors. Such sovereignty, which ultimately "belongs to the Community," had to be "exercised concurrently in the name of the Community through the General Assembly and the Managership." The people lodged legislative authority in the General Assembly, with the power to propose laws left to either the Gérance or the citizens themselves. One provision, which hinted at the possibility of a worldwide assembly, offered a taste of what the future might hold if Icaria grew to match its citizens' ambitions. "When the membership becomes too great," founders expected the General Assembly to be "replaced by the Popular Assemblies and by a representative or national Assembly," with legislative and judicial powers to be distributed by "a special constitutional law."[30]

Like a number of towns following the small republic tradition, Icarianism experimented with a multimember executive branch. The Gérance, an elected six-person body, was "charged with the execution of the laws." The president served as a member of the Gérance, and all members were elected to one-year terms. Half of the board turned over every six months to ensure a measure of continuity. To facilitate a mild version of separation of powers, members of the board were forbidden from "presiding over the General Assembly."[31]

Officially, the president of the Icarian Community occupied the same position as any other member of the board, though he labored under the overarching charge of "supervision and general direction." At the same time, other provisions suggested that the officeholder was first among his peers. If the board became divided over a policy matter, the president held "the deciding voice." Like a head of state, he alone represented the community "in all of its external relations." The president could "act, correspond, negotiate, treat and appear in courts" on Icaria's behalf.[32]

The constitution urged "respect for law," which not only entailed obedience to principles and judgments but also acquiescence in majority rule. In a wrinkle that would be repeatedly invoked to quell defeated dissenters, fundamental Icarian law demanded "[s]ubmission of the minority to the majority." This feature of Icaria's form of governance arguably departed most from the substantive ideals of the American constitutional tradition, which prized conscience and dissent. Each citizen of Icaria had "the right of expressing, in all freedom, his opinion . . . in debate," tracking the ideal of political and especially legislative speech, but such a right to disagree dissolved once the legislative body acted on an issue. By criminalizing "falsehood and slander," as well as "[i]nsulting, criticizing and speaking ill of the General Assembly," Icaria followed America's early tradition of suppressing seditious libel and falsity rather than blazing a path toward expressive liberty. The general orientation of Icarian sovereignty was majoritarian decision making within the bounds of socialist ethics, but without the limits on government despotism and protection of individual liberty commonly associated with J. S. Mill.

Those who found themselves in the minority on a public question were instructed that they "must give way to the majority, and carry out its decision without resistance, without complaint, without criticism, until the formal revision in the form laid down by the Constitution and Laws." The command that dissent had an expiration date was restated in the January 30, 1850, law governing the General Assembly, which warned: "After a free and regular discussion, all criticism particularly in private is forbidden as anarchical and anti-social." By blending strict majoritarianism with socialism and closing down informal opportunities of dissent, the Icarians' charter embraced popular sovereignty in a highly authoritarian incarnation. This basic principle would be cited time and time again—initially by Cabet and then by leading figures in the reform movement—to end social disputes by admonishing defeated members to submit or withdraw from Icaria peacefully in the name of fraternity.[33]

The people became obsessed with law as a tool for resolving disputes and molding the perfect citizen. The constitution defined five categories of offenses that regulated nearly all spheres of Icarian life: the state or "society" itself; the nation's "principles, laws or regulations"; common objects; care and economy of citizens; and the family. All told, some forty-eight articles regulated the admission of new members, sixteen laws governed visitors, twenty-one articles addressed education, and twenty-two articles regulated the Assembly's affairs.[34]

Each household was required to keep a library of Icarian reading materials. When citizens skipped meetings of the Assembly or tried to abstain from voting, supplementary laws addressed such derelictions of duty. A law banned fishing and hunting; another forbade children from throwing rocks or climbing fences. As Jules Prudhommeaux observed wryly, "Not a month or even a week goes by that does not see a new law or regulation to blossom."[35]

The children of Icaria felt the brunt of the law, "contain[ing] about 30 articles of which the first lays on the child 23 different obligations: not to eat green fruit . . . ; not to eat or drink anything between meals; not to eat or drink too much; an order to eat everything without dislike for any food. . . ." Under Cabet's educational plan, young children would be housed in a separate boarding school, with parental contact restricted to a few weekend hours. His educational system was reminiscent of ancient Sparta's method of inculcating republican virtue among the young, shorn of its militaristic emphasis. Nevertheless, extensive regulation of the family generated a certain amount of opposition among the people, pitting mothers and fathers against their leader's vision of ethics inculcated from birth.[36]

The constitutional status of women would be far more contentious, given a clash between the law's promise of equality and its preference for strict social order. On this question, Icarian laws and practices proved to be more progressive than some communities of the day and less egalitarian than others. The constitution walked a line between "recogniz[ing] all to be equals in law and duty" and accounting for natural differences between men and women that, in the view of Cabet and some citizens, ought to limit the role of women in public life. This uncertainty in the political and legal status of women was reflected in the constitution, whose wording suggested that wives and children were admitted as adjuncts to men.

Formally, all citizens would receive the same education and be expected to labor on behalf of the community. Work was declared "a public function," with "[a]ll kinds of work . . . equally esteemed and honored." In practice, the range of occupations varied because Cabet jealously guarded the power to assign citizens to perform tasks. In a polity founded on labor, work assignments conferred a functional, if not formal, legal status. Traditional sex roles, along with the skills each member brought to the colony, had a way of defining the jobs performed on behalf of the republic. Women bore primary responsibility for the cooking and laundry. The men operated printing presses, made shoes and other goods for the outside world, worked farmland, and baked bread and pastries.[37]

Unlike the Shakers, who mandated celibacy, or the Oneidans, who favored "complex marriage" over simple marriage, every Icarian was expected to find a suitable spouse of the opposite sex and raise a family. Cabet "consider[ed] marriage, rendered perfect, as the best means to guarantee the happiness of Women which would result in the happiness of Men, Society and Humanity." To improve the institution of marriage, the constitution abolished dowries and proclaimed, "The choice of a spouse must be perfectly free." Yet once again, equality only existed within a republican regime founded on a well-ordered household. Equality between husband and wife would be honored in a system of compulsory marriage. The law guaranteed a right to divorce, but anyone who dissolved the bonds of marriage "will and must marry another."[38]

By defining the Assembly as constituted by "all men who have been definitely admitted and who are twenty years of age," the 1850 Constitution excluded women from the franchise. Instead, *Icariennes* were "admitted to a separated place, with consultative voice." There seemed to be some discomfort with denying women a role in the very activity that defined citizenship in a republic, so drafters added that women "are expected to give their advice on all questions which particularly concern them." A similar practice of consulting the Icarian youth later emerged for those occasions when the community's affairs concerned them specially.

Despite reservations Cabet harbored about the wisdom of sex equality, a number of women found themselves energized by Icarianism's emancipatory agenda. In France, Cabet gave speeches calling attention to the plight of women. Madame Cabet contributed to rising expectations that Icaria in America would advance the cause of women worldwide. As the advance guard prepared to depart France, she had pronounced: "Soon the women will equally be called to vote. . . . Women will be instructed, informed, given responsibilities. They will develop their energies and capabilities. They will know the dignity, the liberty, and the joy of totally participating in the life of the Icarian nation."[39]

These words expressed the hope of greater gains among women who threw in their lot with the founders of Icaria. Women heard that if they sold off their jewels and gave up their taste for fine things, true equality awaited in the new world. In fact, a number of European women wrote to Cabet expressing disappointment at being left out of the advance guard.

After the settlement of America, Cabet's preference for chivalry and modesty remained at war with his professed commitment to gender equality. Over time, sexual propriety became a major focus of the community's legal proceedings. Although Icarian law did not try to interdict the mixing of the sexes as the laws of the perfectionist Amana community did, chaste behavior became a major subject of communal policing. The General Assembly tried citizens on charges of fornication and banished offenders from Icaria. Mounting concerns about drinking and smoking led Cabet to propose, and the Assembly to approve, moral reforms codified in the Forty-Eight Articles. These laws aimed at fostering "temperate, frugal, simple" behavior called on citizens to remain silent in the workshops, prohibited hunting and fishing for pleasure, and admonished the people to accept the rule of law "without criticism and without muttering." All personal property had to be surrendered to the Gérance, a new rule directed at some women who had kept jewelry and fine things upon entering Icaria. After passage of reforms, Cabet relied on a network of allies and informants to police his vision of social order.[40]

From the very start, Icarian women voiced their opposition to certain policies, leading Cabet to complain constantly about "obstinate" women. Early objections were levied against Cabet's method of assigning workers' roles and his rule requiring that children be given up entirely to the community from the moment of birth. Later, dissident *Icariennes* formed groups to resist being "silenced by a sentiment of equality." In letters to supporters in Europe, Cabet would caustically refer to such women as the "Mariannes" who believed in "unlimited liberty, absolute equality"—an outcome that was not only practically impossible but also at odds with the ideals of republicanism and fraternity. Cabet disparaged them as "women who called themselves Icarians but who were not, who by no means understood our doctrines, who had only egotism and vainty [*sic*] with ignorance, without social qualities and without judgment." The bubbling conflict over sex equality, among other issues, illustrated the difficulties the republic had with its transition away from the ideas of a single visionary and toward a political direction determined by the many. It also dramatized the growing pains an alternative legal order can experience when it rejects pluralism and individualism, values abundant in American society at large.[41]

A Constitution Fractures

A perfect subsistence society had been imagined, with laws of every sort designed to ensure its moral integrity. But constitutional survival is ultimately a social phenomenon, one that depends on a unity of beliefs, perceptions, and expectations of the citizenry. On this level, Icaria did admirably well, but its brand of ethical sovereignty ultimately succumbed to internal strife worsened by a harsh vision of the law.

Although the 1850 Constitution demanded obedience to settled law, experience teaches that no text can eradicate dissent by decree. Cabet's ramped-up efforts at social control, coupled with plans to extend the reach of his office, provoked resistance among the populace. Escalating conflict not only led to an erosion of support for the spiritual leader of Icaria in America but eventually unraveled the social foundations of the legal order itself. The legal order faced an intergenerational crisis, where younger and newer members found themselves pitted against older members of Icaria. This crisis was worsened by the community's struggles in making a clean transition from charismatic leadership to democratic rule. Finally, given the highly legalistic nature of constitutions characterized by ethical sovereignty, policy disagreements consistently turned into zero-sum brawls over basic values, with each side believing the future of the enterprise would be compromised by even the smallest setback.

Each thread of crisis eventually focused on Cabet himself, who became viewed as either a savior or a traitor. The people's exposure to American culture and ideas of radical democracy ushered in by the 1850 Constitution proved to be Cabet's downfall, as some believed he had betrayed the original tenets of equality, fraternity, and liberty. In large part because of the thickness of the constitutional regime—fidelity to ideological values was paramount, and dissent could not be brooked—defeat of one party could only result in one of two options: surrender or separation.

Defense of the original constitution against a return to charismatic leadership initially took the form of petitions. On April 1, 1850, twelve male and four female citizens published a protest against the "suppression of liberties" and "intolerance of opinion." Angers flared, families took sides. In February of the following year, twenty Icarians left the community, accusing Cabet of "inequality, servility, spying, and treachery." Ideological disputes spilled into the workplaces and dining halls as each side believed it represented the true interpretation of the Icarian Constitution. Marches, counterdemonstrations, fistfights, and even a riot or two broke out as the social consensus underwriting the original constitution deteriorated.[42]

Adding fuel to the fire was Cabet's December 1855 proposal to amend the constitution to strengthen the chief executive. He sought the creation of a four-year term for the presidency along with exclusive authority over policy making and execution of the laws. In the name of moral restoration, Cabet called for greater centralization of power. Declaring the republic on the verge of collapse, he demanded the authority to reorganize the entire system by which social goods were created and distributed, along with the power to replace any officer at will. Finally, Cabet insisted upon emergency powers so he could suspend the operation of any ordinary law for six months if he deemed it "dangerous to the society." After Cabet's lengthy tirade against dissidents, two members of the board of directors, J. B. Gérard and Alexis Marchand, resigned. Within a week, workers could be seen marching around the refectory singing, "the blood flag of tyranny is raised against us."

Those who urged the people to resist a return to one-man rule comprised certain elite men of Icaria, past and present members of the Gérance, and workshop foremen. They had the backing of unskilled laborers who experienced the worst of work and living conditions, as well as men and women stung by Cabet's moral directives and unhappy about his business decisions.

Defenders of the democratic regime pointed out that the changes were out of order because the procedures laid down in the 1850 Constitution allowed amendments only every other year. They further argued that such changes violated the terms of the charter granted by the State of Illinois. Ultimately, they insisted that under the rule of law Cabet himself must yield to the will of the people. When Cabet refused to withdraw the unpopular amendments and persisted with a program of moral restoration, he was soundly defeated for president by Gérard at the next election. The cagey Cabet then relented and became the beneficiary of a momentary spirit of rapprochement. Gérard pronounced himself satisfied with a seemingly chastened Cabet, the two men embraced publicly, and Gérard resigned the presidency. Afterward, Cabet was once again elected president, but for a single year.[43]

Immediate breakdown may have been averted, but hostilities would multiply, playing out through the institutions devised in the original constitution. Factions had crystallized, one identified with Cabet's cult of personality and strict moral vision, and another that worried about his leadership style and increasingly destabilizing proposals. Already monopolizing the printing press, the *Cabetistes* gained control of the Gérance, while the dissenters held sway in the General Assembly. Their ideological battles were fought in the dining hall, in the Assembly, and in the press. Writing from Paris, Cabet's daughter bemoaned the "infamy and ingratitude" of her father's opponents. They emulated "Judas" and "want the Community divided in order to be free to live their own way," but she predicted that if it happened, "they will cut each other's throats, for they will have to live with their own resources, not one Icarian will give them assistance."[44]

Besides poisoning relations, disunity took a toll on membership. On February 17, 1856, fifty-seven Icarians decided to leave for good. Then, on May 12, Cabet declared that his opponents had revolted against the original constitution and social compact, and that because the polity had crumbled, individuals "had returned to their natural rights." He asked dissenters to relocate to Iowa, the site of another colony. This proposal was rejected.

Things came to a head in August 1856, when the anti-Cabet faction gained a preponderance of votes in the Gérance. Outgoing members refused to give up their offices, and new directors had to be installed by civil authorities in Nauvoo. The infighting had spilled into the larger legal order, with neighbors increasingly paying attention. In protest, supporters of Cabet stopped working in the shops, fields, and mills. A legal order founded on labor and communal resources was challenged on this very basis. Faced with a general strike, the new majority then issued a warning: Those who refused to work would not eat. Outraged *Cabetistes* retaliated by storming the refectory and assaulting Gérard in the process. Though violence had erupted, it did not change the fact that political power had shifted decisively. Having gained the upper hand, the dissenters—now describing themselves as the Majority—replaced pro-Cabet teachers with those not allied with the deposed leader.[45]

Cabet then ordered an ally to file a lawsuit in state court seeking formal dissolution of Icaria (this legal action would finally be rejected by the slow, grinding legal system on March 16, 1857, long after the community had fractured). The *Cabetistes* also petitioned the Illinois legislature to repeal the Act of Incorporation, declaring "an entire failure" of the plan "to create a better state of Society" once boldly sanctioned by Illinois. They cited the "lawless, turbulent character" of the body politic and argued that Icaria no longer "advance[d] the public good." A motion to repeal the act failed, 55–9. By now, factions had so hardened that few hesitated to resort to the laws of outsiders to advance their positions.[46]

On September 27, 1856, eighty-four men and forty-nine women signed a document laying out formal charges against Cabet. In their judgment, the founder had preached civil war, sabotaged the community's credit worthiness, and used "all the resources of trickery, hypocrisy, and lies to achieve his goal: the annihilation of the community." Thereafter, Cabet and his supporters were excluded from the General Assembly. In a last-ditch appeal for popular support, Cabet published a document titled *Declaration of Rights of the Icarians*, setting forth thirteen conditions for his continued leadership. One hundred and fifteen citizens signed the document, praising Cabet for "never deviating from his democratic and Icarian principles" and an embodiment of "true Icaria."[47] It would be the visionary's last stand.

A month later, on October 25, the General Assembly indicted Cabet for affronts to Icaria's constitution and laws. The legislature claimed he had incited "violent demonstrations of the men of his party" and "endeavored to bring forth a financial crisis in the community." Cabet had "induced the men of his party to refuse to perform their daily labor" and "stirr[ed] up a kind of civil war." In a remarkable turn of events, the people's interpretation of the original constitution had prevailed over that of the republic's founder. Icaria's visionary leader was expelled by democratic vote for having usurped his lawful authority under the community's basic charter.[48]

Because every constitutional crisis turned into all-out battles, it was wise to keep a packed bag before wading into the questions of the day. At the start of November, nearly 180 persons led by Cabet departed Nauvoo for St. Louis, Missouri, leaving some 209 individuals behind. But not before taking a parting shot. In *Farewell of Mr. Cabet and the True Icarians to the Inhabitants of Nauvoo,* Cabet appealed to Icarians' shared experience in becoming "naturalized American citizens." But he complained bitterly that the victors had violated the Icarian Constitution and, through an illegitimate election, "pretended to be the Gérance of the community." Members of the new minority, Cabet argued, had been oppressed mercilessly. However, in the name of fraternity, his followers chose separation and further hardship over total war to defend liberty. A week after arriving in St. Louis, Cabet died suddenly from natural causes.

By 1860, the Nauvoo colony had disbanded. Icarians now lived mostly in Cheltenham, Missouri, where the pro-Cabet forces relocated, and Corning, Iowa, where a slow trickle of migrants became the remnants of the Nauvoo commune. Less than two decades after the schism, the community faced another series of internal crises. The conflict produced two factions: the reformers and the conservatives. In the eyes of the younger generation, Icaria had become too insular and stagnant. They longed to engage the social debates spreading across the country and turn Icaria into a magnet for communists worldwide. They believed that the republic should extend the vote to women and lower the barriers to entry, so as to diversify the community and attract the next generation of socialists. For the conservatives who transplanted European socialism in American soil, a simple democratic lifestyle needed to be preserved against the vagaries of social experimentation.[49]

The reformers drew first blood. On April 17, 1876, during a meeting of the Assembly, they read aloud a document protesting the repressive policies of the majority and expressing a desire to split from the rest of the community. They "reproached [conservatives] for the lack of regard for the rights and opinions of women, their hostility to propagandism, their persecution of the progressives, etc." In doing so, they accused their opponents of betraying not only the goals of socialism but also its transformative mission. Reformers portrayed their own actions as an effort to achieve more perfect rule "according to the writings of Citizen Etienne Cabet." But Icarian ideals had to be grounded in scientific demonstration and discussion, not blind adherence to Cabet's teachings.[50]

Their petition listed fourteen grievances. Among the reformers' specific complaints was a "[l]ack of Fraternity and tolerance" and a "[l]ack of liberty of discussion in the general Assembly, which keeps the truth from having its day." In particular, conservatives had engaged in "[s]ystematic persecutions against all the promoters of progressive ideas." They decried the insularity of the Icarian leadership, demanding access to "cosmopolitan ideas" and an "introduction to the ideas of rights of nationalities." Despite a promise of sex equality, conservatives had shown an "[a]bsolute lack of regard for the opinions of *citoyennes*."

The widening dispute took a toll on family structure. Reformers accused conservatives of "attempts to divide families" and "[e]fforts to demoralize the young and continually depreciate them." Conservatives had set unmarried people against those with families. Taking issue with the educational system, the petition sought greater "liberality in instruction" out of fear that the next generation would be left behind.[51]

Jules Leroux, a proponent of sex equality and resident of the colony by special arrangement, influenced progressives with his attacks on the principle of majority rule. "Majority Icarianism," he wrote, amounted to nothing more than a "miserable doctrine condemned by its own fruit." He found this constitutional defect to exacerbate strife among the people, by "ruining not only the less strong voters, but their women, children, [and] lay-brothers." To Leroux's mind, majoritarian Icarianism mistakenly made the "principle of authority synonymous with the principle of equality," leading to the oppression of the individual at every turn.[52]

Emile Péron, a newcomer from New York, emerged as a leader of the progressives over the summer. On September 26, 1877, the reformers announced a plan to withdraw and establish an autonomous commune on land that would remain jointly owned. They advocated that "a division of land and stock be made *pro rata*, each stockholder, man, woman, and child, to be given ten acres of land; that henceforth we carry on our affairs, agricultural, industrial, and financial, as two distinct branches of one community; [and] that the land be held on both sides in usufruct only." The proposal to introduce elements of individual land ownership was defeated, as was a measure to extend suffrage to women.[53]

Undeterred, progressives embarked on a general strike as positions hardened. They also enlisted state law by filing suit in Adams County Circuit Court, arguing that managers had fraudulently exceeded the mission of the joint-stock "agriculture society." Their handwritten complaint claimed that the corporate form had been chiefly used for "the establishment of Communism" rather than legitimate business purposes. This move was particularly damaging to morale, for it suggested that some citizens would do and say anything to win, including characterizing well-established socialist practices as inconsistent with outsiders' law.

Demoralized members of the community not only turned the narrow form of corporate law against the republic, they also employed American constitutional rights to argue that intractable tension had emerged between Icarian law and the laws of other jurisdictions. Plaintiffs accused the board of "exercis[ing] powers not conferred by the law, by assuming in their corporate capacity to control the stockholders of said Company, socially, and in every other way, in their person, liberty of action." Appealing to the ethics of the dominant legal culture, they argued that Icaria's leaders had "refuse[d] the right to individuals to control their own property." Progressives pointed out that the corporation sought to "take charge, control and dispose of the children of the individual members, regulating their education, . . . and exercise that control paramount to the parents." They further raised the specter of Icarian law as a threat to American law nationwide. Their legal brief stated that the managers "claim and exercise judicial power in corporate capacity, and have and do try parties guilty of offenses against the law of the land, thereby abrogating so far as in their power the courts of the land." In this way, unhappy citizens appealed to conventional sovereigns to perceive Icarianism as a danger to order and justice. No longer loyal to Icarian law, they promoted the worst characterization possible.[54]

For their part, conservatives emphasized that stockholders "freely, voluntarily, and knowingly signed the articles of incorporation and bylaws" when they joined. They stressed that each stockholder had "perfect and complete liberty" when it came to religious belief, philosophy, or politics. Alas, conservatives' effort to cast Icaria as merely the product of liberty of contract failed. The State of Illinois would insist on having the final say. By court order dated August 17, 1878, the Adams County Circuit Court declared the charter void, finding that the group had exceeded its authority as a chartered business corporation by engaging in manufacturing. Trustees appointed by the court undertook an equitable division of the property. The younger faction paid for the dining hall, while the older faction agreed to relocate one mile from the previous site.[55]

Stung by their experience with American law, the faction representing the older generation of pioneers continued to downscale their use of the law. Instead of drafting a new constitution, they authored an instrument titled *Contract of the New Icarian Community*. Eschewing the authoritative, nationalistic language of American constitutionalism, they instead reverted to the atomistic vernacular of contract. In this public statement, the group described itself as an "association" rather than a nation, with each signatory "promising" or "agreeing" to abide by certain terms. To distinguish itself from Icarian competitors, New Icaria's founding papers clarified that each member "shall labor at all times according to their strength and capacity" and be compensated through lodging, food, clothing, and care, "but no other compensation of any sort." The language was spare, bereft of any pretense to universal socialist governance.

Among other improvements, the internecine struggle had produced a codification of the subjects on which women could count on the vote, leading to a liberalization of Icarian practices, even among the older set. The new social contract provided: "The adult members of the 'sex féminine' have the right to vote upon all admissions and exclusions; they are both electors and eligible for all committees and for the office of the Director Clothing. They have the right to vote upon the revision of the contract, upon the dissolution of the society, and in general upon all matters of moral and intellectual interest, such as education, propaganda, and amusements." In all other situations, a "majority vote of the adult men" would govern.[56]

Now mostly separated from elders, the younger faction reorganized by writing another constitution, confidently declaring its members the heirs of revolutionary liberty and equality. Their document, almost certainly drafted by Péron, "overthrows the demi-gods and their Jacobin notions of political infallibility" and "formulates the Icarian creed according to rationalism founded on observation." Among the innovations of *Jeune Icarie* was the abolition of the presidency and board of directors in favor of rule by four trustees. This reform codified a lesson about how the rule of law must discourage demagogues and tyrants, learned first hand from the people's earlier encounters with their visionary leader turned dictator.[57]

Additional provisions extended suffrage to women without qualification and provided for payment to anyone who withdrew from the community "the amount of property actually paid in by them, less a proportion of the indebtedness of the society" plus any "sums for years of service." Reflecting the group's thirst for engaging the world around them, another measure specified that moneys be set aside for "the propagation of principles which tend to the political, philosophical, and economic emancipation of mankind." Pamphlets containing the constitution and laws of Icaria were printed for the benefit of interested members of the public, including prospective members.

After only a few years, Young Icaria folded. Having won the ideological battle, reformers nevertheless had difficulty holding together the community. A clutch of members relocated to California to establish Icaria-Speranza while others, like Péron, drifted away from Icarianism entirely. The Cheltenham community, particularly hard hit by the death of Cabet, continuing divisions, and losses from the Civil War, was dissolved in 1864. On August 3, 1886, an Adams County court dissolved Icaria-Speranza and ordered what remained of its property to be liquidated. Outstanding debts were paid and leftover sums distributed among members. New Icaria disbanded by unanimous vote on February 3, 1895, with its eight remaining elderly citizens reintegrating themselves into nearby towns.[58]

By the end of the nineteenth century, a reversal of the constitutional process had become complete. A socialist republic established with a state's imprimatur had now, at the invitation of its own membership, become systematically disassembled according to state law. These immigrants who once understood themselves as dual citizens watched their status transformed so that all that remained was a single status under conventional law, along with their own lingering memories of the socialist experiment. In truth, ordinary law merely ratified an unraveling of the body politic already long underway. The American plan for political consolidation had stressed individualism and laissez-faire economics, putting enormous strain on dissident communities such as Icaria. The Icarian people increasingly questioned the extent of socialist planning, demanded a greater individual voice in political affairs, and yearned for a greater interaction with their neighbors. All of these complaints were fostered by the pressures of conventional sovereignty, which always laid a dormant claim to the Icarians' allegiance.

Unable to cope with cultural and generational changes, an alternative community lost its ability to resist the priorities and values of the national legal order. The original Icarian Constitution had declared individualism to be the great enemy of happiness, leading to "fractions and pieces [that] are infinite, which produce . . . weakness." It was not naked self-interest but a citizenry activated by fundamental disputes over policy and values that led to Cabet's fall from favor and the eventual schisms. At the same time, Icaria's constitutional design exacerbated rather than ameliorated social conflict. During disputes, each side appealed to original principles underwriting the constitution. Even within a community organized according to a basic law of equality, questions inevitably lingered over just how far the principle would extend and who should decide. Icarian law offered no satisfying answer and only a harsh procedure for maintaining social consensus, to the point that conventional authority—and the sovereignty of others—came as a welcome salve to the pain of social turmoil. The Icarian legal process encouraged groups to push for total victory over ideological adversaries, a dynamic that led to escalating cycles of antagonism.[59]

In their answer to the problems of insularity and tyranny, the Icarians parted ways from defenders of conventional sovereignty, who above all believed in the inherent selfishness of man and prized separation of powers. Icaria's primary approach to social conflict was to expand rights in collective terms in an effort to eradicate ideological tension. Instead of strengthening the principle of divided government by creating new institutions to counteract self-interest, the people's commitment to ethical sovereignty pushed them to separate from opponents, scale down the size of the community, and obscure their theory of law.

Although one-man rule gave way to competing versions of popular rule among the people, constitutional conflict took a toll on democratic faith. The people's overthrow of the founder of Icaria produced a leadership vacuum, and as much anxiety as relief. Doubts crept in about the entire project, a situation that invited a routine but decisive exercise of conventional sovereignty to end the experiment. The lifestyle of sacrificial subsistence offered by the Icarians already made recruitment challenging. A dedication to ideological purity, crucial to visions of ethical sovereignty, made reconciliation and growth even more difficult. As a people repeatedly turned to separation as a solution, an already small community became atomized ever more, until the smallest disagreements could no longer be overcome by resort to shared ambitions or ethics—or anything that resembled law.

CHAPTER THREE

John Brown's America
1856–1859

I want to have the enquiry everywhere raised—Who
are the men that are undermining our truly republican
and democratic institutions at their very foundations?

—JOHN BROWN TO FREDERICK DOUGLASS, JAN. 9, 1854

If Americans' original sin was slavery, the precarious compromise
crafted by the men of 1787 merely delayed the Day of Judgment. The
federal Constitution never used the term "slavery" much less enshrined it as a practice. Rather, speaking obliquely on the subject, the
document treated slaves as less than full persons for representation
purposes and required states to "deliver up" any "Person held to Service or Labour in one State" who had escaped. It allowed Congress to
tax but not prohibit the importation or migration of slaves until
1808. Though satisfactory to no one, this effort to manage the problem allowed each side to see what it wanted. Abolitionists believed
that if the hated institution did not wither on its own, then Congress
could finish the job once the cooling off period had elapsed. Slaveholders, on the other hand, saw in the founding text an endorsement
of their way of life, or at least a commitment to permit each state to
decide its own course.[1]

Slavery not only served as a focal point of constitutional conflict, it
also inspired new theories of politics and self-organization. As the midway point of the nineteenth century approached, Americans' thirst for
land had not yet been slaked. In due course, their drive to expand the
nation's westward borders became enmeshed in the slavery dispute.
The populace battled over slavery not only in legislatures but also on
the ground, square mile by square mile. After the Kansas-Nebraska Act

authorized squatter sovereignty to determine the fate of slavery in these new territories, thousands of proslavery and free-state settlers descended on the region. Armed forces clashed as Kansas erupted in a bloody constitutional battleground. In the fall of 1855 John Brown, who would later become infamous for his attack on Harpers Ferry, led a company of men to defend the city of Lawrence against border ruffians from Missouri who had designs to "wipe out the abolition town."

On March 6, 1857, the Supreme Court's ruling in *Dred Scott* shattered any lingering hope for incremental change. Instead of lauding the original compromise, Chief Justice Roger Taney's opinion advanced a robust theory of racial sovereignty to settle the slavery question once and for all. Slaves were not, and could never be, "constituent members of th[e] sovereignty" that authorized the U.S. Constitution because they belonged to a race that had "for more than a century before been regarded as beings of an inferior order, . . . bought and sold, and treated as an ordinary article of merchandise and traffic, whenever a profit could be made by it." Precious little could stand in the way of this "fixed and universal" principle supposedly favored by "the civilized portion of the white race": neither the Northwest Ordinance of 1787, which tried to confer citizenship on nonwhites in the Northwest Territory, nor the Missouri Compromise of 1820, which excluded slavery in northern lands acquired in the Louisiana Purchase. Not only could slaves never be made "citizens" in a fundamental sense, but even political solutions interfered with each slave owner's right to dispose of his "property" as he saw fit. The authors of *Dred Scott* envisioned a single community of white citizens capable of self-governance, whose boundaries could never be altered through ordinary law.[2]

Thus, two theories of self-governance emerged as potent alternatives to the pragmatic consensus originally espoused in the 1787 Constitution. One was the idea of racial sovereignty, articulated by prominent slaveholders and endorsed by the Supreme Court in *Dred Scott*. According to this theory of politics, only white Americans, descended from European stock and steeped in a culture of republican governance, rightfully ruled through law. Another path, traveled by John Brown and certain abolitionists, led to the development of visions of ethical sovereignty to redeem a people corrupted by slavery. Since

Brown had given up hope that the original Constitution could be wrestled from the clutches of the Slave Power, he chose to start over. By letters dated April 29, 1858, Brown politely invited several "true friends of freedom" to attend "a quiet convention" to deliberate on a new moral vision. A new constitution under discussion outlawed slavery, emphasized equal labor, family, and religion, and imposed stronger democratic controls over public officials and the rule of law. Ideally, the document would rival, and then eventually replace, the decayed remains of the 1787 Constitution.[3]

The convention took place in Chatham, Canada, a haven for freed slaves. Brown's symbolic choice of location for America's refounding cannot be overstated, with tens of thousands of fugitive slaves living in the region. Slavery caused one of the first American diasporas, and Brown believed that a lasting solution had to reconnect former slaves with former masters, blacks who had been degraded as well as whites who benefited from the fruits of bondage. At the appointed hour the morning of May 8, 1858, invitees filed into the British Methodist Episcopal Church. After the convention was called to order, participants learned of Brown's shocking plans to liberate Southern slaves through guerrilla warfare. After the administration of an oath of secrecy to the attendees, the proposed constitution was read, debated, and approved.[4]

Thirty-four black men and Brown's twelve white recruits participated in the convention. Most free blacks came from the Chatham area, though a handful crossed the border from as far away as Ohio and Michigan. The process of meeting clandestinely, hashing out the nation's problems, and declaring one's allegiance to ageless principles had been carried out before by virtuous men. These abolitionists imagined themselves following in the footsteps of the revolutionary generation. Their deliberations took place in secret, after which each man signed the Provisional Constitution and Ordinances for the People of the United States. That evening, delegates selected Brown as commander in chief and J. H. Kagi as secretary of war. In a testament to their commitment to equality, they elected two black men—Alfred Ellsworth and Osborne P. Anderson—as congressmen for the new government-in-waiting.[5]

Besides presenting an ethical alternative to a slave-owning republic, the Provisional Constitution fulfilled other functions in John Brown's "war against slavery." Within the antislavery movement, the constitution played a role in recruiting and disciplining followers, sanctifying the group's resort to violence as a political weapon, and securing the support of Northern financiers. But the group's outspoken willingness to use violence as an instrument of the people's will posed an enormous challenge to its ethical commitments and attracted determined opponents. This militant orientation not only made it difficult for John Brown's men to reach their goals for recruitment and creating stable institutions but also gave multiple jurisdictions openings to crush their exercise of popular sovereignty by enforcing ordinary criminal laws.

From Military Bylaws to Liberation Texts

The genesis of the group's theory of ethical sovereignty could be found in Brown's evaluation of slavery. Brown awakened to the horrors of slavery in his youth, when he befriended a slave boy during his travels. Brown recoiled at his host's mistreatment of the boy, who was "beaten before his eyes with Iron Shovels or any other thing that came first to hand." Witnessing this brutality firsthand led young Brown to "reflect on the wretched, hopeless condition, of . . . slave children . . . who have neither Fathers nor Mothers to protect & provide for them." His initial foray into abolitionism consisted of sheltering runaway slaves, but over the course of this life he turned increasingly toward legal separatism and armed resistance. Brown's decision to engage slaveholders directly, even violently, distinguished him from other practitioners of ethical sovereignty such as Etienne Cabet. If Cabet's inspiration had been the persecuted Christ who shepherded others to justice through his own suffering, then Brown's model was the prophetic Jesus who furiously overturned the money changers' tables and reminded his disciples, "It is not peace that I have come to bring, but a sword." A loving vision of community would be matched with a righteous fury unleashed against external opponents of legal justice. "Hung be the Heavens in Scarlet," Brown famously warned slaveholders and their friends.[6]

Surviving texts reveal John Brown's attraction to written constitutionalism and, more broadly, the stirrings of a theory of ethical sovereignty. In the summer of 1856, thirty-five men gathered with Brown in the forests of Kansas and adopted a covenant, pledging themselves and their "sacred honor" to "the maintenance of the rights and liberties of the Free State citizens of Kansas."[7] Bylaws were added to the covenant, providing for the election of officers, the handling and disposal of booty, the prosecution of the laws, and the barring of profane, uncivil, drunken, or disorderly conduct, as well as theft and waste. The covenant ensured "the benefit of an impartial trial" to any person who surrendered. Violators of the law would be tried by a twelve-person jury, which would be drawn from the company to which the accused belonged.[8]

At first, "a strict an[d] thorough military discipline" proved to be the major organizing principle, while other features of political community remained little addressed. For example, the organization, known as "the Kansas regulars," was open to anyone who could be trusted to join the volunteer force and "agreed to be governed" by the covenant and bylaws. Those who did so swore to "faithfully and punctually perform our duty." The general tenor of the substantive laws—refraining from "disorderly attack or charge," the maintenance of arms in proper working order, and even the ban on alcohol and profane language—reinforced the primary concern of the laws to create an effective, morally responsible fighting force. Despite the group's commitment to defending the "rights and liberties" of ordinary people ravaged by the scourge of slavery, few specific liberties were spelled out.

Already, majority rule could be discerned as a principle for self-governance. Military offices and jurors were chosen according to majority vote, with an accused tried by fellow members. A supermajority (two-thirds) of the association had to give its assent to alterations of the bylaws. Beyond fashioning a rudimentary legal process and military code, however, the covenant showed no interest in sketching a policy-making process or creating additional political institutions. This was not surprising, since these nascent rules were made for a small group on the move. Policy in this context could not be separated from military strategy, leaving most discretion to Captain Brown.[9]

During the same time period, John Brown authored an analogue to the Declaration of Independence. Drafted sometime in the summer of 1859, this document was styled, "A DECLARATION OF LIBERTY: By the Representatives of the Slave Population of the United States of

America." Where the Kansas Regulars' covenant existed primarily for internal consumption, the declaration proclaimed the group's state-building intentions to the world. In it, the undersigned parroted the natural-law language of the founding generation, and "assert[ed] their Natural Rights, as Human Beings, as Native and Mutual Citizens of a free Republic," to "break that odious yoke of oppression, which is so unjustly laid upon them by their fellow countrymen." Invoking the people's right to begin again, the document recounted injustices wrought not by an external government but rather by American lawmakers and judges who had jointly perverted the legal order by entrenching slavery.[10]

Despite these substantive differences, the declaration copied the classic terminology popularized by previous generations. It criticized corrupt officials for their "unjust rule," treating them as temporary "servants of the people." At the same time, the signatories professed fidelity to more enduring American ideals. They tendered past petitions for redress at "every stage of these oppressions ... answered only by repeated Injury" as proof of the breakdown of the political order. The theory and practice of conventional sovereignty, in failing to solve the slavery problem decisively, had instead been hopelessly disfigured by the practice. A new moral-legal order had to be birthed upon the ashes of the old.

Raised in a strict Calvinist home, John Brown comfortably fused Christian ethics with the abstract expressions of freedom and equality in America's governing texts. He "believe[d] in the Golden Rule, ... and the Declaration of Independence ... think[ing] they both mean the same thing." A new covenant had to be made before God because the promises of the Declaration of Independence and U.S. Constitution were broken by politicians and judges addicted to the economic and political fruits of slavery. In his reading of those documents, liberty and equality had been extended to all. But the Supreme Court in *Dred Scott* "declared [slaves] to have no rights which the white man is bound to respect." That judicial ruling was void and unworthy of respect because it amounted to nothing more than man's perversion of inviolable truths. The eternal inhumanity of slavery stripped official actions of any pretense of sovereign authority, for "[o]ur servants, or Law makers are totally unworthy [of] the name of Half civilized men."[11]

The group's theory of legal change was rooted in desperation. No one could credibly claim that John Brown's constitution reflected the preferences of the median voter living in mid-nineteenth-century America. No reasonable person could have expected the document to garner the backing of elected officials necessary to get it to a vote under the terms of the 1787 Constitution, much less secure a supermajority of votes in the statehouses or conventions. In fact, the Chatham convention returned to first principles precisely because radical abolitionists had given up any hope for constitutional transformation through conventional means.

Facing long odds, proponents of legal change could continue to urge elected national politicians to take up their cause, though likely in vain, or give up the fight completely. This was the proposition perceived by most opponents of slavery willing to work within the framework of the original Constitution, from Abraham Lincoln to Frederick Douglass. Alternatively, revolutionaries could do what the founding generation itself did: forsake the rules for securing amendments to the existing Constitution, come up with new rules for approving a new national constitution that abolished slavery, and appeal directly to the people of the United States. This approach best described John Brown's actions. With no real hope that their constitution could survive formal review according to the rules set forth in 1787, members of the Chatham convention invoked their natural right to self-governance in order to bypass the process outlined in the U.S. Constitution.

A major difference, however, was that the Framers of the original U.S. Constitution crafted a public ratification protocol that matched their desire to stake a claim to the consent of a national community. John Brown's group, by contrast, found it unnecessary to reach beyond a community of partisans to authorize a provisional constitution. Until word leaked out about the charter, the group labored under an oath of secrecy. Participants believed that certain formalities ought to be observed to both legitimate their procedural break and repair the breach, but they ignored this aspect of the Framers' experience, at least for the time being. Their actions show that the expressive, deliberative, and disciplinary objectives of constitution writing won out over any goal of implementing formal institutions. They wanted a constitution right away, one they could show off to former slaves, recruits, and financiers, and one that could set the terms for moral reform.[12]

The fact that a new republic had not yet achieved legitimacy in the eyes of outsiders did not frustrate the legality or efficacy of the Chatham constitution for Brown and his underground community. Instead of waiting until territory had been acquired or recognition was granted from other sovereigns, they proceeded to observe the constitution's dictates. The group merely needed to create protocols and organizational structure such that rule of law norms might be predictably enforced. One of the great advantages of a morally grounded constitution is that even if institutions cannot be implemented in the foreseeable future, the text can still fulfill a disciplinary function. John Brown's men could maintain a dissident constitutional order within a corrupt legal order simply through a threefold strategy: authoring a charter, ratifying it, and heeding the principles expressed in the document. Self-discipline could then, in turn, enhance a new constitution's deliberative and community-building effects. To the extent that fellow Americans perceived an alternative polity to be authentically motivated by higher law, a constitution could shape public debate and generate supporters.[13]

This general approach made Brown's vision of law less like the separatism of Indian Stream and closer to the complex resistance of the Icarians. In each situation, a group of Americans sought to establish a shining City on the Hill. Where the settlers' republic sought independence from existing sovereigns, Brown's republic, like Cabet's, envisioned multiple political communities inhabiting the same space for the foreseeable future. Brown and his men resembled the Icarians in another sense: they believed that the political order's legitimacy did not depend on control of any particular parcel of land. So long as their brand of ethical self-governance could be practiced, even in a rudimentary way, one could find a thriving republic.

In one crucial respect, however, Brown's theory of law differed from Icarian law: it did not depend one iota on ordinary law, even out of practicality. Rather, its entire legitimacy depended on a compelling vision of legal justice. The gap between the present and future would be filled by the group's practices in modeling ethical self-rule. Perhaps some supplementary ratification process could be undertaken down the road, but for now, democratic change would occur primarily through the group's own righteous example. If the group succeeded in establishing a radically egalitarian community, then by modeling an alternative democratic existence, perhaps others would appreciate both the wisdom and viability of such a course of action. At some point, the dominant regime might be weakened sufficiently that reform or revolution would come. And if not, a dissident legal order would continue to grow steadily by adding converts. Either way, they might make progress toward the ultimate goal of revitalizing the republic.

A Moral Revival: Equality, Industry, Moderation

If Brown grew increasingly frustrated with the depths of human depravity under the guise of law enforcement, the Provisional Constitution answered the questions Brown worked to have "everywhere raised." The text also reflected a maturation of Brown's political thought, representing the final stage of his own evolution in identity from itinerant farmer to guerrilla fighter to nation builder.

Drafted in the Rochester home of Frederick Douglass, the Provisional Constitution had been the subject of secret discussion among close allies before being unveiled in Chatham. Brown was the principal architect, though Frederick Douglass apparently made suggestions and corrections, and it is possible that others' views were considered, though little record remains of anything but the Chatham proceedings. "When [Brown] was not writing letters," Douglass reports, "he was writing and revising a constitution which he meant to put into operation by the men who would go with him into the mountains."[14]

As an expression of political sentiment, the document enjoyed its greatest success. The constitution represented a public defiance of slavery and the theory of racial sovereignty created to defend the institution. In many instances its language is more direct than the U.S. Constitution. Drafters could afford to be less ambiguous because they did not yet need to worry about the mechanics of ratification. But they also chose their words differently due to their overriding preference for achieving moral clarity as to ideas of liberty and equality over broad consensus. Rather than paper over disagreements over human dignity and political power, as the federal Constitution had done, the constitution articulated unambiguous philosophical positions.

Drafters pronounced slavery utterly incompatible with universal ideals expressed in the Declaration of Independence, a vice that "degraded" everyone it touched. The constitution's preamble lamented the nation's addiction to slave labor, which had commenced "a most barbarous, unprovoked, and unjustifiable war of one portion of its citizens upon another portion." Members of the Chatham convention had been motivated to act by "a recent decision of the Supreme Court," which "declared [slaves] to have no rights which the white man is bound to respect." This new constitution repudiated *Dred Scott* and served to "protect our persons, property, lives, and liberties." In their generous usage of the inclusive "we" and the vocabulary of American liberty, the delegates conducted themselves as a freshly constituted assembly of "citizens of the United States and the oppressed people."[15]

The directness with which the constitution addressed the national problem of slavery, embraced large-scale republicanism, and employed the American Constitution's institutions and titles, distinguished the text from earlier constitutions. If the Indian Stream Constitution presented its independence in qualified and localist terms, and the Icarian Constitution obscured its ambitions through reliance on state law, then John Brown's constitution appeared as an open and notorious competitor to the 1787 Constitution.

The Provisional Constitution was not a work of pure fantasy but rather a sober governing document that tried to manage the problems of an uncertain future and the imperatives of here and now. Despite repeated references to an already constituted "organization," many of the provisions expressed principles of governance that would morally bind the future citizens of a revitalized republic. The "organization," in this sense, could be seen as a temporary and incomplete representation of "the people" who simultaneously authorized a break in historical time and who, from that moment onward, will constitute a community of the righteous.

One of the more striking aspects of the constitution was its utter silence about states; nowhere can be found a reservation of the state's authority or even whether states would survive in the new republic. There is no hint that the national government should be constrained to exercise only those powers enumerated in the constitution. In this respect, the group's dedication to the idea of a single, national people authorized to make all laws in the name of good order distinguished it from utopian societies that had no use for a national identity or for such legal ideals. Rather than retreat to a set of parochial norms or modes of existence in the face of manifest injustice, Brown's followers hoped to recreate the nation's founding experience, without making the mistakes of their predecessors. Still, in rejecting regional power and states' rights, their approach to legal power also set the constitution apart from both *Dred Scott*'s vision of cultural sovereignty and the federal structure established by the men of 1787.

A society purged of ideas of racial solidarity and power would be a radically egalitarian community, separated by neither race nor condition of servitude. "All persons of mature age, whether proscribed, oppressed, and enslaved citizens, or of the proscribed and oppressed races of the United States . . . together with all minor children of such persons" shall enjoy constitutional protections. The Chatham delegates thus approved the idea of a single, diverse people living in harmony. Overall, the drafters' goal was not "expatriation" of slaves, as even many leading abolitionists preferred, but rather social "integration." Hence, the community's aspirations set its theory of self-rule apart from those espousing white supremacy, on the one hand, and those advocating early strains of black nationalism, on the other.[16]

At the same time, like Cabet before him, Brown's vision descended from the prophetic tradition. The constitution arose mostly from one man's imagination and emerged from debate intact, which not only facilitated ideological coherence but also demonstrated that moral regeneration of the people was more important than institutional reorganization or territorial control. Although Madison, Hamilton, and Jay, too, had talked about inculcating civic virtue, they left it chiefly to institutional designs and private organizations to do so. Brown shared these men's interest in large-scale community and their concern for civic virtue, but not their fears about ethical hegemony. John Brown's republic actively sought "men of integrity, intelligence, and good business habits." Officeholders had to demonstrate "first-rate moral and religious character."[17]

Brown often stated that "all great reforms, like the Christian religion, were based on broad, generous, self-sacrificing principles." The foundations of the people's authority likewise arose from a shared moral code. His band of antislavery freedom fighters, as well as the transitional form of government, were self-consciously "organized on a less selfish basis" than prevailing forms of civic life. Yet they would not go so far as to follow the socialists into utopia by requiring the joint ownership of property. Instead, Brown's group was content to emphasize the priority of work—honest labor, shared by all, for the good of all. In exchange for the protections afforded by the state, each citizen assumed a duty to "labor in some way for the general good" or risk sanction. Moreover, to conserve scarce resources as much as to encourage living modestly, the constitution outlawed the "needless waste or destruction of any useful property" or unnecessary killing of animals. While members of the group could hardly be called environmentalists in any modern sense, they found it important to convert private notions of frugality into civic values.[18]

Reformation of civil society entailed a corresponding reformation of the citizen and family life. Republican virtues and Christian ethics became mutually reinforcing. Like the Icarians, Brown's group believed in a basic relationship between work and freedom. The Provisional Constitution's emphasis on subsistence living and individual responsibility for labor served a liberation ideology. A society in which each person consumed primarily what he produced and what he required would not be tempted to enslave human beings or mistreat them. On this view of the causes and nature of inequality, profit motive and intemperance engendered institutions that traded on human degradation. The Chatham Constitution appeared to endorse the "Free Labor" critique of the laissez-faire order, which dehumanized slaves and working-class Americans alike.

The constitution's overriding concern for establishing norms of behavior spilled over to the topic of rights. It did not use the term "rights" or separately enumerate them, preferring instead to characterize duties or explain the scope of constitutional protections. The instrument eschewed a general commitment to freedom of speech, instead emphasizing that "[p]rofane swearing, filthy conversation," and quarreling are all prohibited. A preference for civilized, Christian discourse underscored the socially conservative strain of group life. Intoxication, indecent behavior, and "unlawful intercourse between the sexes" were put strictly off limits.[19]

This general approach to rights also applied to gun use, which characterized it less as an entitlement than as an admonition that citizens be "encouraged to carry arms openly." The Provisional Constitu-tion's protection of gun rights went further than the Second Amend-ment to the U.S. Constitution and many state constitutions in that it neither tied the right to bear arms to the existence of a "militia" nor limited the right to "self defense." Even so, a gun owner had to dem-onstrate "good character and . . . sound mind and suitable age." A handful of high officials enjoyed the exclusive right to carry con-cealed weapons. Even a radical defender of gun possession such as John Brown envisioned that the right would not be unlimited.[20]

To restore just rule and weld together disparate communities, reli-gious and family life would be made a national priority. The repeated mention of marriage, family, and religion in the Provisional Constitu-tion stood in sharp relief from the U.S. Constitution, which made no general commitment to marriage or family (these being judge-read rights), barred the establishment of religion, and guaranteed its free exercise (including one's refusal to worship). In comparison, under John Brown's constitution, marriage would have to be "respected" and "families kept together, as far as possible." To reverse the disas-trous effect of slavery on the black community through a continua-tion of the Underground Railroad strategy, "broken families [were] encouraged to reunite, and intelligence offices established for that purpose." Brushing aside any concerns about unifying church and state or trampling the rights of nonbelievers, the constitution required the entire nation to observe the Sabbath. This time should be devoted not to ordinary labor but rather to religious instruction, the educa-tion of the less fortunate, or some other personal improvement.[21]

These features of the Provisional Constitution were reminiscent of Haiti's 1801 and 1805 constitutions. The original constitution, writ-ten by the slave leader Toussaint L'Ouverture, established a free soci-ety based on Catholicism and marriage, a "civil and religious institu-tion . . . distinguished and specially protected by the government." The version approved four years later affirmed "freedom of worship" and renounced a "predominant religion" within the nation, while as-serting that a "Haitian" must be "a good father, good son, a good husband, and especially a good soldier." John Brown, reportedly im-pressed with L'Ouverture's successful slave revolt, may well have been influenced by Haiti's rebirth through an exercise of ethical sovereignty.[22]

If relocating family and church to the center of written constitutionalism proved to be the hallmark of Brown's political revival, the rest of his institutional innovations seemed less ingenious by comparison. Design choices seemed motivated less by a desire to maintain rigid social control than to offer a plan that might eventually appeal to a broad cross section of society. Unlike the Icarian constitution, which dramatically remade existing institutions to foster ideological consistency and local governance, Brown's constitution retained a familiar national character. Organizationally, he hewed to the general contours of the 1787 Constitution instead of experimenting with entirely new institutions. The Provisional Constitution carried over the principle of divided government and used titles and terminology taken from that text, ensuring that the new constitution would be recognizable by the common man.

Here and there, however, certain fanciful modifications could be discerned. For example, drastic limitations on the size of Congress—restricting that body to "at least five but no more than ten members"—seemed idiosyncratic and possibly counterproductive. It is uncertain whether this cap on the legislature was born out of a transitional need to maintain secretive deliberations by the provisional government, but if it instead represented a lasting effort to recapture small, pastoral government, this design choice conflicted with the group's large-scale ambitions.

Enhancing popular control over the law, Brown and his followers installed strict term limits for nonjudicial officers. The president and vice president were elected to three-year terms, selected not by an electoral college but directly by "the citizens or members of this organization." The Chatham delegates abolished the Senate in favor of a single "Congress or House of Representatives." Rounding out the theme of popular rule, the members of the Supreme Court (five total, including a chief justice) would be elected by the citizenry rather than appointed, and no measure guaranteed life tenure based on good behavior. All of these departures from the 1787 Constitution reflected suspicions among abolitionists, which Brown shared, that certain aristocratic features of the Constitution had aided the growth of slavery, even though the original document never enshrined the institution. The overall thrust of the legal design, however, was majoritarian without a demand for acquiescence that can come with more demanding forms of ethical sovereignty.[23]

In establishing the judiciary, drafters avoided the cumbersome language of the U.S. Constitution in favor of a single statement conferring general jurisdiction on federal courts except in cases involving "the rules of war." Once all judges were anchored firmly to the electoral process, concerns about judicial overreaching waned. Moreover, since ethical commitments had been clarified, the possibilities for judicial misadventure presumably shrank. Brown's response to *Dred Scott*, then, proved to be more nuanced and institutionally conservative than one might expect. Instead of abolishing the judicial branch, turning its power over to another institution, or severely curtailing its jurisdiction, the group remained committed to judicial review. If judges disappointed the populace, they could be impeached as before.[24]

Although ostensibly a holy war, the battle against slavery would be waged according to rules of necessity, fair play, and temperance. The Provisional Constitution called for the humane treatment of prisoners, one of several measures that codified the Golden Rule. "No person . . . shall afterward be put to death, or be subject to any corporeal punishment, without first having had the benefit of a fair and impartial trial." No one should be "treated with any kind of cruelty, disrespect, insult, or needless severity." Each citizen, including members of the Provisional Army, labored under a duty to treat prisoners "with every degree of respect and kindness that the nature of the circumstances will admit of, and to insist on a like course of conduct from all others, as in the fear of Almighty God, to whose care and keeping we commit our cause." Exemplifying an Old Testament approach to retributive justice, serious violations merited the gravest sanctions. The "forcible violation" of female prisoners incurred the death penalty, one of a handful of death-eligible crimes mentioned. In comparison, the Eighth Amendment of the U.S. Constitution bars only "cruel and unusual punishment," and makes no mention of the death penalty. For lesser, noncapital offenses, John Brown's constitution punished offenders through "hard labor on the public works."[25]

Certain procedures effectuated the orderly disposition of confiscated property, fair treatment of "neutrals," and expeditious court martials. Deserters would be treated harshly, along with individuals who took up arms against the abolitionist cause after receiving a "parole of honor." All of these features, which grew out of the group's covenant and military bylaws, confirmed the community's sense that it was engaged in a "war" against slavery. Members of the Chatham convention could imagine a new world without human subjugation, but for the moment it existed mostly in embryonic form. That nascent community had to be defended vigorously, but without ever forgetting the ethical revival at the heart of the people's efforts at self-governance.

Constitutional Functionality: Recruitment, Outreach, Discipline

By all accounts, John Brown's men took the constitution's political theory seriously and followed protocol assiduously. As the community grew, its values became more integrated and refined. The group's covenant and bylaws reflected nascent rule of law principles embraced by the guerrilla fighters, which were taught, discussed, and internalized. The Provisional Constitution systematically outlined the legal values the group already embraced. It mattered little that John Brown's men failed to acquire land to call their own. They waited for no one else to acknowledge the legitimacy of their enterprise. Though never fully institutionalized, the Provisional Constitution still served the goals of planning, recruitment, stirring public debate, and fostering internal discipline. Their legal code, an amalgamation of liberal and religious ethics, was enforced at campfires and on the open road, and in everyday life at Kennedy Farm.

Constitutional ideals and vocabulary shaped post-Chatham planning. A document created for the Harpers Ferry assault sketched the organization of the War Department: "A company will consist of 56 privates, 12 non-commissioned officers (8 corporals, 4 sergeants), 3 com. off. (2 Lieutenants, a Captain), and a surgeon." The privates would be organized into bands and led by a corporal. Every two bands would compose a section; every two sections would compose a platoon and be commanded by a lieutenant. From there, four companies would make a battalion, four battalions a regiment, and four regiments a brigade. The movement had big ideas: it envisioned a free republic in the future large enough to sustain 4,600 troops. Brown and Kagi issued written military commissions in their official capacities of "commander in chief" and "secretary of war." As far as they were concerned, a government-in-waiting was entitled to protect the people. As they developed plans for communal self-defense, the group drew on ideas of popularly sanctioned violence and the constitutional terminology of institutions to lend their guerrilla tactics a patina of legality.[26]

Once Brown had a constitution in hand, blessed by freedmen and abolitionists, the document aided recruitment and fundraising. Brown may have eschewed conventional politics, but he proved adept at managing public sentiment through the exercise of charismatic leadership. He was a master at writing letters to the editor, cultivating sympathetic news accounts, and spreading his religiously inflected constitutional vision in salons and open meetings alike. He curried support among prominent black intellectuals, less educated freedmen, and white abolitionists and artists. Brown had the personality of a preacher, the mind of a military tactician, and the instincts of a trained advocate.[27]

Ideas of racial sovereignty had inflicted untold damage on the population. In his writings, Brown saved most of his scorn for "the extreme wickedness of persons who use their influence to bring law and order and good government, and courts of justice into disrespect and contempt of mankind" by protecting slavery. He accused adherents of white superiority of "destroy[ing] confidence in legislative bodies, and to bring magistrates, justices, and other officers of the law into disrespect amongst men." Brown hoped that his words and deeds, while "utterly incapable of doing the subject any possible degree of justice," might nevertheless empower friends of justice. Though he might fail in his mission, others might "take it up and clothe it in the suitable language to be noticed and felt."[28]

The Provisional Constitution was strategically unveiled to help raise finances for his efforts to topple the Slave Power. In February 1858, Brown met with Franklin Benjamin Sanborn, a member of the Secret Six who often funded Brown's operations. Huddled in the home of Gerrit Smith, Brown presented his plan to "beat up a slave quarter" in the South, raid a federal arsenal to replenish their weapons, and then escape with willing slaves into the mountains. During this meeting, Brown presented the Provisional Constitution to demonstrate the seriousness of his scheme. Another meeting took place in March in Boston with other supporters. Before this audience, Brown praised the "highly moral" men he had with him and again displayed the constitution that would govern his mountain community.[29]

The charter no doubt appealed to these abolitionists, who had long hoped that slaves be not only freed but also integrated into the polity.

Brown tried to sell the entire daring plan—raiding slave quarters, arming the liberated, and then establishing a self-regulating society—as part of a systematic effort at "slave improvement." Several of Brown's backers looked to him to lead the acculturation of freedmen. They came to believe that, by winning their own liberty during a raid, slaves would themselves start the process of becoming virtuous citizens. Gerrit Smith felt that black "self-respect" and manhood were implicated in such political violence. Likewise, Thomas Wentworth Higginson and Samuel Gridley Howe found resistance by the oppressed to be a "morally uplifting" stride into the "normal community."[30]

John Brown encouraged these expectations of his democratic experiment. The Provisional Constitution presented reformers with a glimpse of the end goal: a society repopulated by formerly kidnapped and dehumanized individuals molded into citizens capable of self-governance. Taking matters into their own hands would put slaves "on the road to perfectibility." A republic governed by former slaves and lovers of equality would demonstrate to the world the falsity of the argument—implicit in the logic of racial sovereignty—that slaves could never achieve the temperance and reason desired of full citizens.

Besides appealing to white financiers, the Provisional Constitution played a role in the group's labors to win black support. Some black abolitionists, including Frederick Douglass and Henry Highland Garnet, believed Brown's course of action to be foolhardy. In a series of meetings, Brown tried to convince Douglass of the virtues of the plan. He dangled the presidency in front of Douglass, arguing, "If we can hold a stated area for a month at least, I am sure our northern friends will alter the whole fabric of the present government." Eager to have the former slave and electrifying speaker symbolize the rebirth of the American people, Brown urged Douglass to "take power, be the first president of the new provisional government."[31]

Although Douglass refused the position and declined to accompany Brown and his men to Harpers Ferry, this exchange reveals that the legal instrument was designed with an eye toward securing the blessings and participation of prominent black leaders. Brown shrewdly understood that an alternative republic could not long last if freedmen and slaves remained suspicious of his motives. The Provisional Constitution would serve a deliberative function as news of its existence spread among abolitionists and slaves. Even as Brown inched toward new beginnings, public perception of the new constitution's viability could nevertheless impact "the fabric of the present government."

Brown almost certainly carried the draft constitution with him to see Harriet Tubman in St. Catharines, Canada, in April 1858. There, he secured her promise to help recruit freed slaves for the raid on Harpers Ferry. A delay in the timing of the raid and news of a turncoat in their midst (the mercenary Hugh Forbes) probably depressed turnout, though a number of former slaves did attend the Chatham convention in May.[32]

On July 4, 1859, John Brown arrived at Kennedy Farm, some five miles north of Harpers Ferry. Under the assumed name Isaac Smith, Brown began to prepare for the assault with John E. Cook, who along with Brown's sons had scouted the town. Despite praying for greater participation, the community at Kennedy Farm grew no larger than twenty-one, sixteen whites and five blacks. Thirteen had fought by Brown's side in Kansas. For a time, Brown's daughter Annie and his daughter-in-law Martha joined the group.[33]

Just as the group's theory of ethical sovereignty informed the wording of its liberation documents, so the ideals endorsed in the community's legal canon appeared to have been incorporated seamlessly into life on Kennedy Farm. As they prepared for the assault on the armory, the political values of the whole became fused with the religious values of each member. At the close of the Chatham convention, copies of the constitution had been printed, with the original kept in Brown's possession along with his Bible.[34]

Though never tested to the same degree as the Icarian Constitution, the precepts of the Provisional Constitution still informed the group's actions at the level of social discipline and legal ritual. Under a general injunction to labor on equal terms, members of the group engaged in "cooking, washing, and other domestic work . . . no one being exempt, because of age or official grade in the organization." To pass the time, they sang, discussed Thomas Paine, and maintained their weapons in working order. They prayed each day for divine guidance, and from time to time rededicated themselves to the new constitution. The Bible and their political texts inspired even the smallest of decisions, amplified military discipline, and infused their dealings with one another. They may have lacked land or a capital they could call their own and had few tangible signs of sovereignty. But in the ways that mattered most to an ethical theory of the law, they behaved as a self-governing people.[35]

On Sunday morning, October 16, 1859, the members of the group gathered for Bible study. Together, they analyzed selections of Christian texts on the obligation of men to free others from bondage. Before the men departed for Harpers Ferry that evening, they assembled a final time to renew their oaths to one another other and to the Provisional Constitution. After the religious service, Brown appointed Anderson chairman of the Revolutionary Council. Anderson, in turn, asked Aaron Stevens to read the constitution aloud to the men as a sentry stood guard outside the room. Brown interrupted the performance only to stress Article 32's Golden Rule, which required all members of the group to treat those they encountered with "every degree of kindness and respect" and avoid "cruelty, insult, or needless severity." Though they planned to use force, they had to do so in a way that could be justified according to the American legal tradition.[36]

This final ritual act solidified their political bonds even as it helped them to muster the courage to put their lives on the line. Right before the men launched themselves at the Southern order, their constitution served the ultimate disciplinary function: focusing their minds on the task at hand, giving advance meaning to the lives they might have to take and the lives of compatriots that could be lost, and reminding them of the military hierarchy necessary for success. After administering the oaths, Adjutant General Kagi presented each officer with his military commission. At the close of the proceedings, John Brown traveled to nearby Dunkers to preach to a small congregation of citizens as he often did, leaving his men to make final preparations.

That evening, Brown gave the order to begin the attack on Harpers Ferry. Without firing a single shot, the group seized the armory. Holding it was a different matter. Some men guarded the armory, while the rest fanned out, freeing slaves and taking hostages. Shots were exchanged when they encountered resistance from Virginians willing to defend the rights of slaveholders and the rule of law. As the encounter dragged on until daybreak, citizens began to awaken to news of the assault. Angry townspeople armed themselves, took up strategic positions, and fired on Brown and his men. They surrounded the engine house where the raiders held hostages.[37]

The raiders' encounter with a train that had stopped near the armory allowed the conductor to alert the authorities that a party of men had come "to free the slaves." Militiamen from nearby towns began to pour into the area, and a detachment of U.S. Marines led by Robert E. Lee was dispatched to Harpers Ferry. After Brown rejected Lee's demand for unconditional surrender, the military stormed the engine house. By Tuesday morning, it was all over. Ten members of the Provisional Army had been killed, including two of Brown's sons. The mayor of Harpers Ferry and a U.S. Marine were among the dead. Slaves who had not escaped or joined Brown's party were returned to their masters. The decisive conclusion to the raid ended any possibility of state-building by members of John Brown's party.[38]

Trial and Execution: Constitutionalism by Other Means

Remarkably, the significance of John Brown's constitution did not dissipate with his capture. It continued to serve the cause of public reason in other ways as its proponents faced their own popular judgment. The defeat of the Harpers Ferry raid ended the group's experiment in democratic self-governance, but not its message. To defenders of the conventional order, John Brown's constitution was unauthorized and his actions lawless. In fact, its mere existence should be taken as evidence of malice. Through the criminal process, the state tried to discredit the Chatham convention's exercise of ethical sovereignty and deter others from employing violence as a tool of constitutional change. In the war over constitutional ideals, a question lingered: could insurgent legal ideas survive this formalized reaction from the state? Only if a defendant could successfully put state authorities (along with the U.S. Constitution) on trial in the court of public opinion.

Both the United States and Virginia had jurisdiction to try the captured men. But Virginia insisted on going first, and the Buchanan administration did not object. The Commonwealth of Virginia charged Brown and four others with insurrection, murder, and treason. The State's response put immense pressure on the movement's claim to know the best interests of the people. Through the criminal process, the State employed criminal law to parry the radical abolitionist's argument that targeted violence could ever be justified in fostering constitutional change.[39]

The political stakes were most visibly dramatized in Charlestown, where the Provisional Constitution assumed a central role during Brown's trial. When the governor of Virginia assured Brown would be given a fair trial, Brown lashed out in response, decrying the proceedings as a "mockery of a trial," the kind of façade "cowardly barbarians" would perpetuate to hold on to power. The trial began on October 25, barely a week after his capture. Each participant in the criminal proceedings had occasion to interpret the constitution through oral argument and the testimony of witnesses. The Commonwealth put on a string of witnesses who described firsthand Brown's objective to incite a slave rebellion. To make out treason, the indictment charged the defendants with forming their own unrecognized government. At this point, the fact that the Provisional Constitution resembled the U.S. Constitution, employing similar institutions and terminology, put the defendants in serious legal jeopardy. If anything, the text's aspiration to create a single national order, abolishing slavery and states' powers along the way, appeared especially threatening. As the prosecutor explained, "The prisoner had attempted to break down the existing Government of the Commonwealth, and establish on its ruins a new Government: he had usurped the office of Commander-in-Chief of this new government, and, together with his whole band, professed allegiance and fidelity to it." At trial, prosecutors introduced the document into evidence, arguing that the "Provisional government was a real thing, and no debating society." They repeatedly pointed to the constitution as proof of a plan to subvert Virginia's existing form of government. For their crimes, Brown and his men ought to be treated as despicable criminals rather than virtuous revolutionaries.

Brown's lawyers also wished to lean on the Provisional Constitution, but for a different reason. They wanted to argue that their client was insane at the time of the raid, but Brown refused to allow "any attempt to interfere in my behalf on this score," disparaging such a strategy as "a miserable artifice and pretext." This left his attorneys to suggest, weakly, that the "pamphlet," taken from his body, was proof only of a "harmless organization . . . a mere imaginary government to govern themselves, and nobody else." Hemmed in by their client's preferences, defense lawyers argued that the constitution lacked features one would expect of a serious charter and instead resembled an internal policy document for a common civic association. While admitting that Brown had stirred citizens against slavery, they played down the charter's real-world significance. American society was overrun with clubs that debated political matters and published polemics against state officials, Brown's lawyers reminded the jury, but no one would seriously consider them "miniature government[s]." If the constitution opposed any sovereign, it "allud[ed] to the government of the whole United States in general, and not to this state or any other in particular." The argument would be a difficult sell. Because the Chatham convention had designed a plan for large-scale government in direct competition with the existing legal order, the defense sounded evasive and too clever by half.[40]

In a stunning turn of events, then, both parties to the criminal action debated the legal and political significance of the raiders' exercise in constitution writing. Formally, there may have been legal questions of culpability and punishment involved, but in actuality the very fate of the movement was on trial: its goals, methods, and legacy. Was the political community described in the document real or purely fictive? And if the constitution involved more than fantasy, did it constitute proof of an intention, as Virginia prosecutors argued, "to take possession of commonwealth and make it another Hayti?" The document betrayed the traitorous designs of Brown and his men, the prosecution argued: "The 46th section [of the Provisional Constitution] has been referred to, as showing it was not treasonable, but [t]he whole document must be taken together. . . . When you put pikes in the hands of slaves, and have their masters captive, that is advice to slaves to rebel, and punishable with death." Brown had entered the state "for the nefarious purpose of rallying forces into this Commonwealth, and establishing himself at Harper's Ferry as a starting point for a new government." Rather than levying war against Virginia, the defense replied, the constitution proved the defendants' goal was "simply resisting with a high hand the constituted authorities of the land." They had merely organized to release the slaves, not to destroy state government.

Given the group's belief that writing the constitution entailed forming a sacred compact, it should be no surprise that John Brown refused to allow his lawyers to point to this document as evidence of insanity. After cool reflection on the matter in the jailhouse, he rejected the invitation to participate in the public denunciation of his political enterprise. To claim insanity—and to discredit the document in the process—would by his own hand render the Provisional Constitution the scribbles of a single man rather than the considered judgment of many virtuous citizens gathering out-of-doors. It would turn legal ideals into incoherent, mad babbling instead of a communal exercise of public reason. Opting for that trial strategy would destroy any impact the document might have in shaping the beliefs of Americans. This tactical choice, then, was pregnant with constitutional significance, at the very moment the dissident community's credibility was tried along with its leader.[41]

The legal document continued to serve the goal of outreach in other ways upon Brown's capture. At trial, the defense strategy reinforced his message that extreme measures were morally justified against certain targets, so long as they were taken to reform the political order and constrained by the principle of moderation. Brown demanded that the trial be continued so his lawyers could locate witnesses who would testify to his instructions to observe "The Golden Rule," a principle of temperance derived from Jesus's example and codified in the constitution. Consistent with this injunction, Brown urged his men repeatedly not to fire unless fired upon, and demanded that prisoners be treated well. Over objections by the prosecution, jurors heard testimony that Brown "gave frequent orders not to fire on unarmed citizens." Slave owners were to be taken as hostages only to safeguard the escape of slaves.[42]

One of the major points of emphasis by the defense was a difference between liberating slaves and violating the law. Brown repeatedly insisted, "I never had any design against the life of any person, nor any disposition to commit treason, or excite slaves to rebel, or make any general insurrection." On this view, Brown lacked the mens rea to commit the crimes of which he was accused. At all events, the general litigation approach accorded with Brown's long-standing constitutional theory, namely, that he was motivated by principles of higher law, not selfish goals one typically associated with the violation of ordinary criminal law. Because God's law trumped man's law, Brown could not be held responsible for helping to bring man's law in line with the divine. By underscoring his community's ethical precepts, Brown hoped the jury would nullify the proceedings by approving his use of justifiable force to right a moral wrong.

During his interrogation and trial, Brown consistently stated his design "to free the slaves, and only that." His lawyers asked jurors to bear in mind that "there is a great difference between levying war and resisting authority. . . . A man may resist authority with ever so much violence, and bloodshed may ensue from such resistance, but that is not treason." This position accorded with Article 46 of the constitution, which disavows any purpose to "encourage the overthrow of any State government, or of the general government of the United States." Instead, the document's signatories "look to no dissolution of the Union, but simply to amendment and repeal." This surprising disclaimer was the only provision that had generated significant debate at Chatham, with Brown speaking out strongly in favor of its adoption. Some members of the convention in Canada surely hoped for revolt or the outbreak of general hostilities over slavery, and may have been far more disillusioned than others about American ideals. By insisting upon the provision, the new commander in chief demanded a group commitment to work within the American tradition to secure creative "amendment and repeal" of the constitution and laws rather than levy war against the United States or proslavery states. The group did not attack the rule of law or particular governments. Instead, it levied war against the institution of slavery and a theory of cultural authority that made it possible.[43]

Virginians called to pass judgment on Brown refused to absolve him or endorse his approach to legal change. After deliberating for forty-five minutes, the jury convicted Brown on all charges. Judge Richard Parker sentenced him to death by hanging for his "attempt to subvert by force the institution of slavery as established in this state" and "advising slaves in rebellion against the authority of their owners." Judge Parker, himself a slave owner, held up Brown's sentence as "a warning" to any abolitionist who might turn to extralegal violence: "In mercy to our own people—to protect them against similar invasions upon their rights—in mercy and by way of warning to the infatuated men of other States who, like you, may attempt to free our negroes by forcing weapons in their hands, the judgment of the law must be enforced against you." Conventional sovereignty, as expressed through the laws and judgments of Virginia, ultimately had a strong hand in the questions of when and how the people might debate the slavery question.[44]

John Brown's words at sentencing confirmed the broad contours of his original plan. They did so without destroying his prophesy of a body politic cleansed of slavery. Upon hearing the verdict he declared: "I deny everything but what I have all along admitted, the design on my part to free the slaves." He then mentioned his harrowing liberation of slaves from Missouri, saying, "I designed to have done the same thing again on a larger scale." On that occasion, Brown had published an editorial justifying his ordeal as "forcibly restor[ing] [eleven persons] to their natural & inalienable rights." Now, as then, he invoked natural law as a basis for absolving him from punishment. In God's eyes, it was "unjust" to punish him because he had intervened not "on behalf of the rich, the powerful, the intelligent, the so-called great," but "on behalf of His despised poor." His paramount goal had always been vindication of the rights of those "disregarded by wicked, cruel, and unjust enactments." He had merely served "the ends of justice" by enforcing the New Testament's injunction to treat others as one might wish to be treated. Until his dying breath, Brown believed himself to be an instrument of the law, "raised up by Providence to break the jaws of the wicked."[45]

From beginning to end, Brown's efforts to restrict violence against morally justified targets were calculated to not simply maximize his constitution's influence on public debate but also preserve each citizen's capacity to participate as a member of the political community. No doubt many law-abiding Americans would recoil at violence, but John Brown's followers gambled that adhering to a principle of moderation would prove their democratic commitment and allow their tactics to be overlooked. The assault on Harpers Ferry—which Brown described as "a discriminating blow at Slavery . . . in accordance with my settled policy"—would clarify the moral and legal stakes, empower the oppressed, and pressure citizens to choose sides.[46]

The Tactics of Legal Change: Modeling and Violence

Importantly, then, Brown did not turn his back on democratic dialogue even as he wandered further down the dark path of violence. Rather, over time, he became convinced that bolder action was needed to stir average Americans to do away with slavery. Yet he continued to feel the need to conform his actions to the American political tradition. His own thoughts began with modest ideas that later flowered into a constitutional vision implemented through extralegal tactics. In a letter to his brother Frederick, dated November 21, 1834, John Brown conveyed his desire to "do something in a practical way for my poor fellow-men who are in bondage." He mentioned his personal plan to raise and educate a slave child "as we do our own." In this way, he planned to educate others on the importance of egalitarianism by modeling such virtues in his own life.

Sensing the limits of private action to end slavery, he then hinted at a more ambitious undertaking that entailed educating and organizing slaves. "Perhaps we might, under God, in that way do more towards breaking their yoke effectually than in any other." The enlightenment of young blacks "would most assuredly operate on slavery like firing powder confined in rock, and all slaveholders know it well." If "the Christians in the free States" would get to work teaching blacks, the people "would find themselves constitutionally driven to set about the work of emancipation immediately." Thus, John Brown's constitution can be understood as the culmination of two separate strategies of legal change: first, ethical modeling, and second, extralegal violence. For some time, each of these approaches developed somewhat separately, but upon maturation became a benevolent constitutional vision backed by the use of targeted force. Because Brown and his men possessed no formal authority to secede or curtail the Slave Power, the constructive part of their plan for legal change entailed political disaffiliation coupled with ethical modeling. Former slaves and masters might one day be reunited, but only through bullets, a renunciation of slavery, and a more lasting basis for political community.[47]

Brown's turn toward militancy began with small acts of illegality that grew in scope with every blow that failed to turn the tide against slavery. On January 15, 1851, he formed a Springfield branch of the U.S. League of Gileadites in response to the passage of the Fugitive Slave Act. Forty-four members of the secret group resolved "as citizens of the United States of America" to resist slave catchers and local authorities who tried to enforce the federal law. Officers would be elected after "some trial of the[ir] courage and talents." Brown recommended the use of weapons and lassos once Gileadites "collect together as quickly as possible," and to make no confession if captured.[48]

Brown's armed force in Kansas and Virginia represented the accumulation of his experience in guerrilla warfare. And yet, far from being a final burst of aggression or a suicide plan, Brown's Harpers Ferry plan appeared to be an extension of a broader effort to spur democratic change. Some commentators have pointed out the fact that few slaves could be found in the area as evidence of other motives or poor planning, but in fact a diffuse population in the area enhanced the prospects of guerrilla warfare. Brown's past efforts at targeted liberations and the conversion of slave-owning property involved relatively small, mobile groups that might have a chance of eluding pursuers. Thus, the plan would seem to be a logical, if risky, step toward the fulfillment of their state-building ambitions.

Though his ideas about sanctioned violence departed from the precepts of conventional sovereignty, Brown was not alone in his belief that forceful resistance to unjust practices had its place in the American constitutional tradition. Lysander Spooner, another abolitionist with whom Brown shared ties, argued that because slaves had a natural right to liberty, they also had "the right to take it by stratagem or force." Spooner's self-defense theory extended to others who might come to the aid of a vulnerable member of the political community. He rooted the right to use force on behalf of slaves in a "duty of the bystanders to go to his or her rescue, by force, if need, be," when "a human being is set upon by a robber, ravisher, murderer, or tyrant of any kind." Spooner claimed, as did Brown, that "[t]he state of Slavery is a state of war. In this case it is a just war, on the part of the negroes—a war for liberty, and the recompense of injuries; and necessity justifies them in carrying it on by the only means their oppressors have left to them." While Spooner cautioned against a "general insurrection, or any taking of life, until we of the North go down to take part in it," he heartily advised the targeted use of force against slave owners, including "the flogging of individual Slave-holders" and "compelling them . . . to execute deeds of emancipation, and conveyances of their properties, to their slaves."[49]

Resistance of usurpations of government "is a strictly constitutional right," Spooner insisted. "And the exercise of a right is neither rebellion against the constitution, nor revolution—it is a maintenance of the constitution itself, by keeping the government within the constitution." This perspective joined the principle of written constitutionalism with the claim that popular sovereignty authorized a broad range of direct actions to resist unjust laws. Spooner's endorsement of violence shocked even abolitionists who preferred that constitutional change unfold in more orderly and peaceful terms.[50]

Spooner's writings developed older received wisdom as to when extralegal tactics might be justified by higher-law principles. The act of breaking a constitution or forcefully resisting its usurpation is as much a part of the American political tradition as making, amending, or construing a constitution. Under Lockean principles of consent, sovereignty and self-defense are intimately connected and treated as inviolable rights. Colonialists took up arms against the king in the name of their God-given liberty, clothing their break in natural-law principles. American revolutionaries' use of force was subordinated to and constrained by their legal arguments rather than substituting for them.[51]

Leveraging this tradition, John Brown and his men dramatized the ambiguities in the 1787 Constitution exploited by slaveholders. Portraying themselves as faithful interpreters of the original Constitution, they labored to illustrate how its provisions could be avoided, defied, and where necessary, rewritten. They couched their plans in the American idioms of political renewal—what a surviving member of the movement called "language every where understood by the haters of tyranny." Radical abolitionists argued that the natural-law right of self-defense extended to the protection of fellow human beings threatened with violence. John Brown's program to populate his community by "free[ing] the slaves" but not necessarily to provoke a "revolt" or general war was compatible with this ideology. He and his supporters understood themselves to be levying war against an entrenched industry rather than against particular sovereigns. They used war as a metaphor to symbolize the force required to remedy a grave legal violation and to rally the people to their cause. Brown took up arms when ordinary politics and less forceful methods, such as the Underground Railroad and slave stealing, did little to change the basic political, legal, and economic structure that enabled the persistence of slavery.[52]

John Brown's exercise in written constitutionalism occurred after his participation in the fight over slavery in Kansas, a bloody affair that threatened to rend the antislavery coalition. The timing of these events suggests that the Declaration of Liberty and Provisional Constitution may have been aimed in part at this audience: sympathizers who feared a backlash and observers who might yet join the antislavery cause but wondered about the ultimate ends of extralegal agitation.

On May 24, 1856, Brown's men dragged several unarmed proslavery settlers at Pottawatomie out of their beds and killed them in brutal fashion. The murders stunned opponents and supporters alike. They appeared to be acts of reprisal for the assault on Lawrence by proslavery forces. Although Brown was not one to voice regret, the writing of political liberation documents following the bloody days of Kansas might have been an effort to back away from the brink of unrestrained violence, to place the extreme events of Kansas in context, and, if possible, to reconfirm the goals of constitutionalism. If this is correct, the band's resort to legal text can be understood as an attempt to erase the horrific memory of bloodshed, and, after the chaos of Kansas, a promise to return to the rule of law.

Unlike most slave revolt leaders who preceded him, Brown spent considerable efforts to articulate the contours of the next constitutional order. Such differences in vision and tactics were stressed during Brown's life and continued after his death. Osborne P. Anderson, the only surviving member of the party that raided Harpers Ferry, explained:

> Hark and another [slave] met Nat Turner in secret places, after the fatigues of a toilsome day were ended; Gabriel promulged his treason in the silence of the dense forest; but John Brown reasoned of liberty and equality in broad daylight, in a modernized building, in conventions with closed doors, in meetings governed by the elaborate regulations laid down by Jefferson, and used as their guides by Congresses and Legislatures.[53]

This passage suggests that in death, as in life, the movement remained cognizant of the need for authorization according to the American political tradition. According to the author, slave revolts were lawbreaking affairs—arguably meriting punishment as "treason." By contrast, the Brown group's activities constituted the exercise of democratic "reason" in the pursuit of "liberty and equality." It is not merely one's goals but also one's methods that distinguish a constitutional actor from the typical lawbreaker. Emulating Jefferson's "elaborate regulations" for assemblies transformed the legal quality

of their antislavery crusade. Even Anderson's use of America's founding iconography reinforced the point. The orderly meetings convened
by Chatham's virtuous delegates "in broad daylight, in a modernized
building," was set against slaves' impromptu schemes formulated "in
the silence of the dense forest." By calling a convention, Brown had
avoided creating a "skulking, fearful, cabal" and instead turned a citizens' gathering into an "indispensable institution for the security of
freedom." Invoking the Anglo-American custom of meeting out-of-
doors when conventional government broke down, the group staked
a legitimate claim to know the best interests of the people. And having taken such steps, they believed their extralegal tactics to have been
sanctified by higher law.

When told about John Brown's plan, Frederick Douglass reportedly
said that the plan "had much to commend it." Although "a general rising among the slaves, and a general slaughter of the slave-masters"
would be counterproductive, Brown's plan to create "an armed force
which should act in the very heart of the South" might have some salu-
tary benefits. Brown argued, and Douglass apparently agreed, that
"the practice of carrying arms would be a good one for the colored
people to adopt, as it would give them a sense of their manhood."
Arming blacks would have a civilizing effect, for "No people . . . could
have self-respect, or be respected, who would not fight for their freedom." Once an antislavery regime had been fashioned, freedmen could
be assimilated into the dominant political culture, regain their "manhood," and take up the hard task of self-governance.[54]

How, then, did Harpers Ferry figure in a plan to reestablish self-
governance in egalitarian terms? Brown could have hidden in the
Blue Ridge Mountains and established a utopian society without
launching this particular assault. The group could have continued its
practice of ethical modeling, occasionally repopulating itself through
isolated acts of liberation. Why attack federal property if one did not
have designs to levy war against the federal government? It was certainly possible to expand the slave-stealing enterprise from a fortified
position without such a grandiose statement.

Brown's "true object" through his raid was to "destroy the money
value of slavery property" by "rendering such property insecure." His
plan involved creating groups of armed men and "begin[ning] on a
small scale." These roving bands, containing his "most persuasive and

judicious" freedom fighters "shall go down to the fields from time to time, as opportunity offers, and induce the slaves to join them, seeking and selecting the most restless and daring."[55] The project to disrupt slavery as an industry (in the words of Spooner, to "make slavery unprofitable" and "make slaveholders objects of derision and contempt") would take years, and even then, there was no guarantee that the underground community could long survive. Having been part of several secret societies, the idea of organizing a law-based community became increasingly attractive. Slave stealing, never more than an interim tactic of desperation, matured into a plan to turn degraded human beings into full citizens.

John Brown and his men planned to escape into the Blue Ridge Mountains with whatever slaves joined them, and hold their ground "despite all efforts of Virginia to dislodge them." Complicated calculations favored the assault on the armory as a way of initiating their plan to establish a republic. Explanations that focus on Harpers Ferry in isolation fail to appreciate the logic of popular violence, which involves, above all else, manipulating political perceptions in the face of inadequate resources. No doubt Brown sought a galvanizing statement to prove that transformation was possible and urgently required. Located in Mr. Jefferson's Virginia, the home of outspoken critics of slavery and the state with the largest slave population, the Harpers Ferry armory presented a tantalizing opportunity to jumpstart the national debate over slavery.

Douglass recoiled from the planned attack for fear it would "array the whole country against us." He offered instead, "Why don't you forget about this Harper's Ferry attack and resume the policy we have agreed on of gradually and unaccountably drawing off the slaves to the mountains?" Brown's answer underscored both the group's national ambitions and his own pragmatic calculations that withdrawal from society alone could not succeed: "[G]radually and unaccountably the slaveholders will surround us and slaughter us and the world will know nothing about it until we are dead." To foster a full-scale movement for renewal, they needed to show the world that fighting for liberty "should be the noblest task an American can perform." Absent a bold move to embolden slaves and broader support from right-thinking people, the group's state-building plans would never succeed.[56]

Even if the group did not wish to levy war against the United States, its members certainly believed the federal government to be morally implicated in the entrenchment of slavery. Armed with Sharps rifles acquired from Northeastern benefactors and pikes for the slaves, Brown anticipated that the group would quickly run out of munitions. Each man "had forty rounds a piece when [they] went to the Ferry," and two men were sent to secure a local rifle factory. If taxpayers' dollars were being utilized on behalf of proslavery forces, then why not secure some of these resources for antislavery advocates while making a grand gesture? "And as far as the U.S. arsenal is concerned," Brown asserted, "there is nothing sacred about it—it is as much ours as it is theirs." They had been "using the arms to suppress other Americans; we have the same right to use those guns to free them." That the property was federal in nature was therefore not as important as "show[ing] the slaves how to do something as well as their oppressors."[57]

Anderson makes a revealing admission in recounting the events at Harpers Ferry: "It was no part of the original plan to hold on to the Ferry, or to parley with prisoners; but by doing so, time was afforded to carry the news of its capture to several points, and forces were thrown into the place, which surrounded us." Brown ordered three men to stay behind at the farm as sentinels, under instructions to guard arms and supplies, and to move them to a nearby schoolhouse when rejoined by men from the assault company. Holding the town temporarily was consistent with the group's plan to make a symbolic statement with the raid, replenish supplies, and liberate nearby slaves. Survivors of the raid were to meet up with their comrades and freed slaves before moving on. Tactical mistakes during its execution made escape and further implementation of the group's constitutional vision impossible.[58]

At one of their meetings, Brown showed Douglass drawings that illustrated a "plan of fortification" of various forts in the mountains, which might be connected by "secret passages." Through the creation of a free state in the mountains, perhaps others tainted by participation in a thoroughly corrupt system would see reason to join the community and thereby become educated in a new life. As he reportedly explained: "If the slaves could in this way be driven out of one county, the whole system would be weakened in that State." Organized according to the rule of law and a familiar political iconography, a nation within a nation could serve as an inspiration to others. Brown's repeated disavowal of treasonous intentions, coupled with his turn toward constitutional methods, suggest a general strategy to contest the meaning of the U.S. Constitution—even to break it symbolically—so others might see that the time had come for renewal.[59]

Members of the group hoped to recreate life at Kennedy Farm on a grander scale "in a mountainous region," though out of necessity they left many details unexplored. The Provisional Constitution envisioned that "Schools and churches [would be] established, as soon as may be, for the purpose of religious and other instructions."[60] Other forms of institution building and civic education would eventually follow, adapted to the fledgling community's environment. The flag of the people "shall be the same that our fathers fought under in the Revolution." One day, the republic might grow to its full scale, but until slaves were liberated and political conditions stabilized, it would have to remain a roving, hidden community.

Authorities interdicted the plan to establish a free republic before institution building could begin in earnest.[61] Brown was executed on the morning of December 2, with military forces arrayed impressively around him. One will never learn whether through their strategy of modeling and targeted violence, the community might have won new converts from among those inclined to disaffiliate from the prevailing political regime. Brown and his followers imagined a temporal community that could, for a time, survive within a decaying republic. Indeed, they understood themselves bringing the community into existence by living out its terms. Most important, they believed that this transformation could take place from within the American political tradition.

John Brown had come to believe that the emancipatory rhetoric of national leaders had become cynical and empty. He eyed the rise of the Republican Party suspiciously, predicting that politicians took antislavery positions for partisan gain but would never act to rid the country of the evil behavior. Conventional politics, which depended on polite discourse, moral compromise, and incremental change, seemed futile in the face of manifest injustice. Only concerted, armed action had a chance to awaken the conscience of the people and cause a genuine change in the status of the oppressed.

Brown adopted democratic idioms, giving them a less forgiving and more urgent cast than his contemporaries. Unlike the pioneers, territorial control was tangential to his group's conception of political authority. At the same time, their theory of politics and community—imagining a single national people governed by institutions and a moral code—directly challenged the legitimacy of the conventional legal order. Their focus on moral regeneration, in turn, fostered a sense of missionary urgency and spurred a greater reliance on armed conflict. But like the denizens of Indian Stream, the group's tactics (which went significantly beyond the pioneers' limited forms of resistance) rendered the dissident community highly visible and vulnerable. What is more, Brown's single-minded attempt to foster ethical sovereignty left the group inattentive to practical details that might have helped them acquire land and hold it, or to formulate contingency plans. Critically, the nascent republic never grew much larger than the members of the fighting force themselves.

Such a magnificent legal vision could only prevail or collapse absolutely. Brown was right about one thing—their dissident order would either supplant the slaveholding polity or become utterly absorbed by it. Crushing the raid and executing its charismatic leader under Virginia law meant, for all practical purposes, ending a democratic experiment before it could be fully implemented. When the Harpers Ferry attack failed spectacularly, little remained but to hope that the values expressed in the Provisional Constitution might outlast Southerners' efforts to hold on to slavery with all of their might.

CHAPTER FOUR

Confederate Anxieties
1860–1865

The South must control her own destinies or perish.

—ROBERT BARNWELL RHETT, *Charleston Mercury,* NOV. 1, 1859

As the midway point of the nineteenth century approached, Americans' hopes dimmed for a satisfactory solution to the dispute over slavery. Conventional sovereignty, as it developed, seemed to yield polarization and gridlock rather than principled answers; the ideal of one national people frayed under this duress. For their part, Southerners felt vindicated by *Dred Scott,* which celebrated racial power and the rights of slaveholders, even if the ruling did not eliminate their sense of siege. To the dismay of slave owners, abolitionists refused to abide by the decision. Instead, galvanized by what they believed to be an erroneous and unjust outcome, they pressed more urgently for the eradication of a cherished institution. Northern politicians, led by Abraham Lincoln, warned that the Supreme Court would inevitably deprive states of the power to outlaw slavery. Unless "the power of the present political dynasty shall be met and overthrown," Lincoln thundered, "we shall *awake* to the *reality,* . . . that the *Supreme* Court has made *Illinois* a *slave* State." More and more, as representatives of the conventional legal order inched toward racial egalitarianism, Southerners felt that saving their agrarian civilization required taking matters into their own hands.[1]

If ethical sovereignty like the sort advocated by John Brown represented one kind of response to the problem of slavery, cultural sovereignty soon emerged as another. Proponents of Southern independence articulated a theory of popular sovereignty in regional and racial terms, proposed the codification of proslavery principles, and commended the "constant recognition & assertion of a *Southern Nationality.*"[2] Moral renewal was not the driving force behind the Confederate experiment. Instead, the Southern account of self-rule blended ideas and institutions from conventional and cultural sovereignty. Confederate statesmen envisioned a large-scale republic based on shared territory, as well as the organizing structure and many of the ideals of the revolutionary generation. At the same time, they also emphasized the social distinctiveness of one area of America from the rest, along with ineradicable racial differences. A "slaveholding people" would reset the clock on America's democratic experiment, resorting to higher law to shield their agrarian civilization against the destructive forces of pluralism and individualism.

Another salient point of departure involved resources and tactics. Unlike many separatists of the past, disunionists were men of standing. Many held elective or appointed office in the U.S. government or their states of residence. They were property owners and slaveholders; they enjoyed political influence and access to government resources. These material advantages shaped not only their tactics but also their legal theories, from their notion of regional peoplehood to the right of secession. Where the founders of Indian Stream and John Brown's men could only wage guerilla warfare, secessionist leaders had sufficient manpower and arms to defend their legal vision through full-scale war. The Confederate theory of separation was informed by greater access to formal political power. It revolved around states' rights rather than the right of individuals or social groups to withdraw from the Union. Seceding states hoped other slaveholding states would emulate them, but they abandoned further dialogue with opponents over fundamental matters of law.

Longtime proponents of secession earned the moniker "fire-eaters," which captured a subset of activists within Southern radicalism. These figures found themselves connected through a network of common politicians, teachers, advisors, and opinion makers interested in honing Southern complaints into secessionist ideology. They prodded mainstream politicians toward a final breach, warning that compromises with the "rapacious" North amounted to dangerous accommodation and merely delayed the inevitable.

Among the best-known fire-eaters, Robert Barnwell Rhett hailed from South Carolina. He earned his early reputation by assailing federal tariff policy as part of a plot to make Southerners "vassals and slaves of a consolidated empire." Rhett's mentor John C. Calhoun secretly authored *The South Carolina Exposition and Protest,* which defended the prerogative of states to nullify federal laws believed to be unconstitutional. Writing in protest of the Tariff of 1828, Calhoun asserted the right of South Carolina to secede if the law were not repealed. Following Calhoun, Rhett had urged the people to resist the tariff, saying he "prefer[red] disunion to such a Government."[3] Aware that such open displays of defiance could earn reprisals, he embraced the label "traitor" as proof of his commitment.

In one form or another, Rhett had advocated "revolution" or "a Confederacy of the Southern States" since the 1830s. To him, it seemed obvious that each encroachment of the federal government brought it closer to the elimination of slavery. Whereas Calhoun urged compromise over specific disputes, Rhett continued to galvanize the people for Southern independence. "A people, owning slaves, are mad, or worse than mad, who do not hold their destinies in their own hands," the fire-eater diagnosed. He often closed his orations with an injunction that slaveholding people "must rule themselves or perish."[4]

Rhett served in the South Carolina statehouse before serving briefly as the state's attorney general. A six-term U.S. Representative, he was also elected to the U.S. Senate but resigned abruptly to protest South Carolina's refusal to secede from the Union in 1852. Whether holding office, giving speeches as a citizen, or turning the *Charleston Mercury* into a platform for anti-Union essays, Rhett helped complete the intellectual and political groundwork for South Carolina's decision as the first state to break from the Union based on ideas of cultural sovereignty.

Developing a Southern Identity

A theory of cultural sovereignty is predicated on the uniqueness of a people's heritage, group characteristics, demographic makeup, or beliefs. On this view, the right to rule does not inhere in every human being who happens to occupy territory but arises from, and can only be exercised by, those who display certain cultural attributes. Geography can serve as a way of marking the boundaries of community, but only if it is plausible that a people living in a particular location might be said to have physical traits or social attitudes in common. When ideas of cultural difference harden into a right to govern, law itself can emerge as an implement to preserve identity, political power, and influence over social and economic policy. More often than not, cultural power is restorative, a collective effort to regain control over important social institutions or to prevent further erosion of cherished ways of life.

A theory of cultural power can only arise in opposition to other cultural systems, real or perceived: other mind sets, goals, entities, demographics, social practices. The Confederate theory of self-governance was built in opposition to the North, the Republican party, radical abolitionists and egalitarians, and eventually the national government as enemies of a Southern lifestyle. The complaints of secessionists ran from the concentration of federal authority, to the admission of new states upsetting the balance of power in Congress, and to tariffs laid on the production of goods sold overseas. Whatever the issue, fire-eaters seized every opportunity to emphasize the abject failure of the national government to protect Southern interests, the corrupted condition of the U.S. Constitution, and the vision of Southerners as a people destined to rule themselves. Above all, slavery knitted together the strands of Southern defiance of the federal government. In a society where the planter class comprised an influential minority, enormous efforts had to be undertaken to convince citizens of the indispensable nature of slavery. As intellectuals labored to defend slavery, they honed a striking theory of cultural sovereignty. The people's claim to rule was grounded in two precepts: regional distinctiveness and the superiority of white civilization.[5]

Antebellum writings depicted slaveholding as a practice bestowed by Providence and "inherited from ancestors," a linchpin of the region's political economy. The slave-master relationship represented the prototypical model of a well-ordered society. Calhoun explained how the plantation, not individuals or families, served as the building block of society:

> The Southern States are an aggregate, in fact, of communities, not individuals. Every plantation is a little community, with the master at its head,

who concentrates in himself the united interests of capital and labor, of which he is the common representative. These small communities aggregated make the State in all, whose action, labor, and capital is equally represented and perfectly harmonized.[6]

By grounding political authority in the plantation, the Confederate theory of politics departed from classical approaches as well as the atomistic model of politics based on individuals and cities found in the urban North. The model made hierarchy and agricultural production essential to politics. Only whites who appreciated the benefits and sacrifices of this system had the right to self-determination.

Beyond reimagining the foundations of government, the principle of equality played a crucial role in secessionist arguments. Repeatedly, Southern leaders complained of "a disparaging discrimination" practiced by abolitionists who infiltrated conventional government. Instead of human equality, however, disunionists claimed that their foes had destroyed the structure of the Constitution and harmed the civil rights of white Americans. Whereas abolitionists stressed the equality of man to enlarge the boundaries of community, fire-eaters argued that slavery ensured the political equality of states, especially states whose populations dissented from fashionable sentiments. In their view, northern states and "Black Republicans" had conspired to violate the Fugitive Slave Clause of the U.S. Constitution and guarantees of due process of law by refusing to return slaves to their rightful owners.

Legislation admitting new states to the Union diminished the political influence of slaveholding states, exacerbating structural inequality. As Calhoun's many resolutions on the matter put it: "the union of these States rests on an equality of rights and advantages among its members; and that whatever destroys that equality, tends to destroy the Union itself." Planters chafed against an onerous tangle of federal and state laws restricting their ability to migrate with slaves and dispose of their human "property" as they wished. They clamored for the right to "equal enjoyment of the common Territories of the Republic." These restrictions assumed especially ominous tones in the cotton states. Surrounded by the disfranchised and confined by egalitarian policies they found dangerous, white citizens felt a profound loss of control over their destinies. If the slave population increased without an outlet, William Lowndes Yancey predicted, slave labor would eventually drive out free labor, decimating the Southern economy as well as causing "our political destruction."[7]

If the Constitution of their fathers no longer commanded the unquestioned allegiance of slaveholding citizens, it was because they no longer saw the instrument as "framed by Southern talent and understanding." Casting themselves as a subjugated people, disunionists sought to recapture the rhetoric of civic equality from their adversaries. "What a sad comment on the condition of the South!" Yancey roared. "Manacled and robbed, she is exhorted to be quiet, for lost rights are but spilt milk!"[8] To liberate the slaves, the North would happily force an entire region's population into political "submission." The American people did not face a choice between freedom and slavery, but rather between the "White Slave Trade," which exploited workers and abandoned them to starve, and the "Black Slave Trade," which fostered interdependence.

Defenders of slavery realized that more profound modifications to political theory might be necessary to meet the relentless but wrongheaded logic of racial equality. Thomas Jefferson served as an important foil for theories of white power because Jefferson's eloquent words in the Declaration of Independence had inspired all manner of liberation movements. A beloved and influential Virginian, his doubts about the morality of slavery had to be isolated and discredited as unrepresentative of Southern thought. Fire-eaters assailed Jefferson's antislavery views as "fundamentally wrong" and a "mental poison spread through our political sphere."[9]

A number of intellectuals favored Aristotle's formulation of a state based on "man's social nature" over Locke's social contract theory upon which a free society must be founded. Published after Calhoun's death, *Disquisition on Government* defended white equality as a political principle. Calhoun argued that "great and dangerous errors [in public debates] have their origins in the prevalent opinion that all men are born free and equal." The state of nature "never did, nor can exist; as it is inconsistent with the preservation and perpetuation of the race." Because perfect equality was incompatible with liberty, it followed that men, "instead of being born free and equal, are born subject, not only to parental authority, but to the laws and institutions of the country where born and under whose protection they draw their first breath." In this way, white sovereignty entailed the belief that the right to rule arose from social differences.[10]

Instrumental concerns also drove theoretical development. Some pamphlets circulating among the populace yoked the African slave to the white pioneer as the exultant engine of manifest destiny. One such pamphlet observed, "The African has gone with the pioneer of the forest, over rivers, mountains, hills, and valleys, from State to State, until his arrival at the present boundary." But the slave's "destiny is not yet fulfilled, his career of usefulness not yet completed." A vast unmeasured wilderness lay untouched, and the African must "make room again, as he has done before, for the white man" who desires to relocate. The slave must "go into new territories, open new cotton, sugar, and tobacco fields."[11]

In fact, those who made slave ownership a symbol of prosperity adapted pioneer sovereignty to the needs of Southern existence.[12] The continued subjugation of Africans was necessary to conquer new lands, exploit natural resources, and grow the national economy. Allowed to flourish, slavery would guarantee America's orderly ascension into the ranks of great civilizations. Anyone who wished to dismantle the institution therefore stood in the way of political destiny.

At its core, abolitionism interfered with the slaveholding states' right to determine the boundaries of political membership, an essential feature of sovereignty. In their view, the people of the Southern states had in regulating slavery merely fashioned a "form of civil government instituted for a class of people not fit to govern themselves." Emancipation attacked the people's right to define and regulate themselves. The rhetoric of equality was effective in creating solidarity, for in an honor-bound society citizens felt keenly that compromises forbidding slavery's growth "dishonored" Southerners and "degraded" their way of life. Disagreement over the wisdom and morality of slavery amounted to little more than sectional "hostility" and "discrimination." Leading figures recoiled at abolitionist descriptions of them as "barbarians" and "criminals." Citizen memorials to Congress urging the emancipation of slaves were perceived as "insulting petitions" rather than legitimate grievances. If Northern encroachments caused "a degradation no other free people than the people of the South ever endured," then failure to defy the corruption of conventional sovereignty would reveal free whites to be "a weak and conquered race."[13]

For all of these reasons, the defense of slavery through a society's fundamental laws emerged as an indispensable component of the Southern theory of agrarian republicanism. On the Senate floor Calhoun in

1837 extolled slavery as "a positive good" rather than an unfortunate practice.[14] He began by asserting, "there never has yet existed a wealthy and civilized society in which one portion of the community did not live on the labor of the other." Turning to the achievements of American slavery he pronounced: "Never before has the black race of Central Africa, from the dawn of history to the present day, attained a condition so civilized and so improved, not only physically, but morally and intellectually."

Not only did many Southern intellectuals justify slavery as a method of improving the moral and economic conditions of the people; some went so far as to argue that the institution promoted peace and happiness. As Calhoun argued, the slaveholding states' facility with a "patriarchal mode" of extracting African labor "exempts us from the disorders and dangers" resulting from the inevitable conflict between labor and capital in an advanced society.

As socialist experiments became all the rage, George Fitzhugh even suggested that "[a] Southern farm is the beau ideal of Communism." In this way, the Southern version of cultural sovereignty incorporated a critique of industrial democracy, without embracing any of the major tenets of socialism. Though suspicious of socialism's utopian tendency toward "Free Love" and "No-Government," Fitzhugh did not shy away from claiming that black slavery possessed features that attracted some reformers to socialism. He noticed that "[o]ne of the wildest sects in France proposes not only to hold all property in common, but to divide the profits, not according to each man's input and labor, but according to each man's wants." He then boasted, "this is precisely the system of domestic slavery with us." The slave is taken care of "in old age and in infancy, in sickness and in health, not according to his labor, but according to his wants." Of course, "the master's wants are more costly and refined, and he therefore gets a larger share of the profits."[15]

Despite the slave's inability to own the means of production or the goods, he nevertheless "exhibits all the pride of ownership" when he "boasts of 'our' crops, horses, fields, and cattle," and "enjoys as much of the fruits of the farm as he is capable of doing." Contrasting the Southern way of life with Northern existence, Fitzhugh described a system of "reciprocal affection": "Love for others is the organic law of our society, as self-love is of theirs." Instead of a system of "free competition or liberty" promoting self-regard and oppression of workers by manufacturers, Fitzhugh claimed that domestic slavery encouraged "joint participation" in the production of goods and a mutuality of interests. Thus, slavery insulated Southern society from the ravages of radical individualism and the excesses of the laissez-faire system. But it did so without abandoning capitalism.

To charges that black slavery harmed white laborers, slaveholders insisted that the institution "raises white men to the same general level, . . . dignifies and exalts every white man by the presence of a lower race." As Jefferson Davis explained in the U.S. Senate, "It is the presence of this lower caste, those lower by their mental and physical organization, controlled by the higher intellect of the white man, that gives this superiority to the white laborer." As an instrument of hierarchy and control, slavery ensured the equality and prestige enjoyed by free whites.

Edwin Ruffin, an ardent spokesperson for secession and agricultural reformer, elaborated the case for slavery as a mechanism for advancing white civilization. In an address before the Virginia State Agricultural Society, Ruffin described the North as a society of unwashed immigrants and ignorant wage slaves "unacquainted with the principles of free government and unused to freedom in any form." Because this population could effortlessly "be directed, governed, and enslaved by a few master-minds," the changing demographics of America posed a serious danger to the long-term health of popular sovereignty. From this perspective, free labor and unchecked migration were antithetical to civic republicanism. Preserving slavery meant localizing the incidences and sources of disorder in one part of the economy, an area of the United States, and a segment of the population. At the same time, by confining "the drudgery and brutalizing effects of continued toil to the inferior races," the "superior race" was free to "improve mind, taste, and manners." If a choice had to be made, many Southerners preferred enduring the consequences of racial separation over exacerbating class differences among poor whites. As another secessionist argued, "In the North, social distinctions are defined by the rich and the poor. In the South, color draws the ineffaceable line of separation."[16]

Behind the ardent defense of slavery lay not only fears of economic ruin from emancipation but also the dread of racial mixing. The loss of political and cultural control could manifest in violent, sexualized fantasy. Some warned that radical equality would expose the Southern man's "wives and daughters to pollution and violation, to gratify the lust of half-civilized Africans." A fear of violence and miscegenation ran especially strong in cotton-growing states, where "the slave outnumber[ed] the white population ten to one." Opinion makers foresaw two possibilities if abolitionism ran its course: whites "degraded to a position of equality with free negroes, . . . fraterniz[ing] in all the social relations of life; or else there will be an eternal war of races, desolating the land with blood, and utterly wasting and destroying all the resources of the country."[17] Through techniques of racial and regional solidarity, intellectuals made slavery the linchpin of their imagined community. This cultural conception of power gained such vitality that it flourished apart from, and even became understood to preexist, the law. All that remained was to find popular tools to bring the law back into alignment with this theory of politics.

Secession: A People's Remedy within Each State

The final piece of the puzzle involved settling on secession as a remedy and a written constitution as the means of securing a new cultural order. Secessionists described withdrawal from the 1787 Constitution as "the right of self-preservation," governed by "the law of necessity and of right." Though described as a measure of desperation, the right of the people to self-determination did not include the power to "resist" duly elected public officials, which "would be rebellion and treason," nor did it involve "the right to injure others." Rather, as Yancey put it, secession "is the right to save ourselves from despotism and destruction—the right to withdraw ourselves from a government which endeavors to crush us."

Proponents of secession admitted to the friction inherent in the remedy. Secession, like nullification, amounted to an "antagonistic" tactic resting "on the basis that the States are sovereign."[18] Its very rationale undermined the project of creating one American people. Yet advocates tried to minimize secession's potential for undermining the rule of law by locating the remedy in the people of each state. Procedurally, one would expect the right to withdraw to be exercised only in the gravest of circumstances. Secession was different from ordinary lawbreaking or even low-level political resistance, whether undertaken by individuals living in remote regions or organized groups like John Brown's men.

A concordance in social beliefs and economic interests gave Southerners hope that a final political division could succeed. Separatist leaders calculated that, if they struck a blow at the right moment, the states of the Deep South might add border states, making it a formidable nation. Then, European demand for a steady supply of cotton might lead diplomats to pressure Washington to let the South go its own way.

Lincoln's election in November 1860 hastened the slaveholding states' decision to make a final break. Fire-eaters felt that, despite Lincoln's rhetoric of unity, upon taking office he would merely accelerate Republican plans to dominate the South and eradicate slavery. Though duly elected as president, Lincoln was seen as a "traitor" to the original understanding of the U.S. Constitution. The Republican Party's 1860 platform denounced proposals to reopen the African slave trade, "under cover of our national flag, aided by perversions of judicial power, as a crime against humanity and a burning shame to our country and age." Declaring "the normal condition of all the territory of the United States is that of freedom," the party committed itself to defending liberty "against all attempts to violate it." Lincoln himself predicted that "this government cannot endure, permanently half *slave* and half *free*" and he disparaged the policy of settler sovereignty as the way to handle slavery in the territories as a dangerous façade. Disunionists would seize upon these pronouncements as evidence that the incoming president's "opinions and purposes are hostile to slavery" and that he would work to achieve its "ultimate extinction."[19]

A few weeks after the election of a "Black Republican President" without the support of a single southern state, conventions organized by slaveholding states began announcing plans to secede from the Union. South Carolina would be the first to go. On December 24, 1860, delegates acting on behalf of the people declared their independence and invited other states to "join us in forming a Confederacy of Slaveholding States." Two documents publicized South Carolina's decision "to act or be disgraced": Charles G. Memminger's *Declaration of the Immediate Causes Which Induce and Justify the Secession of*

South Carolina from the Federal Union and Robert Barnwell Rhett's *Address to the People of the Slaveholding States*. The convention proceeded to determine the rights of "every free white person" now that the people of the state had reclaimed power delegated to the federal government.[20]

Mimicking the structure of the 1776 Declaration of Independence, South Carolina's declaration of secession cited "frequent violations" of the U.S. Constitution by Northern states as cause for withdrawing the people's consent. Representatives then laid claim to two principles: "the right of a state to govern itself" and "the right of a people to abolish a Government when it becomes destructive of the ends for which it was instituted." Repudiating the founding goal of creating a single people who wielded singular power, the statement characterized the original 1787 Constitution as nothing more than a compact between states:

> We maintain that in every compact between two or more parties, the failure of one of the contracting parties to perform a material part of the agreement, entirely releases the obligation of the other; and that where no arbiter is provided, each party is remitted to his own judgment to determine the fact of failure, with all its consequences.

Through this statement, representatives of South Carolina declared conventional sovereignty as it had developed to be a failure and turned their backs on the national narrative of shared destiny. Instead of endorsing a perpetual union, secessionists reached back to the legal theory underwriting the Articles of Confederation, in which the people of each state retained ultimate power over their own destiny.

In reclaiming that power, South Carolina clarified that the preservation of slavery was essential to its citizens' consent to join the Union as well their decision now to leave it. The Fugitive Slave Clause "was so material to the compact, that without it that compact would not have been made." Because the fight over slavery imperiled its future, South Carolina now "dissolved" the bonds between the states and "resumed her position among the nations of the world, as a separate and independent state; with full power to levy war, conclude peace, contract alliances, establish commerce, and to do all other acts and things which independent States may of right do."

Rhett, a convention delegate and chairman of the Committee with the Slaveholding States, began his accompanying address by staking out themes of cultural preservation. He described the original U.S. Constitution as a fragile compromise protecting Southern existence. But radical egalitarians had subverted this agreement. Among the "aggressions and unconstitutional wrongs perpetrated by the people of the North on the people of the South," Rhett argued, "[t]he one great evil from which all other evils have flowed, is the overthrow of the Constitution of the United States." He charged Northerners with transforming the Framers' original design from a "confederate republic" into a "consolidated democracy." Thus, "[t]he Southern States now stand exactly in the same position toward the Northern States that our ancestors in the colonies did toward Great Britain." Having made this historical analogy, Rhett argued that "the people of the Southern States are compelled to meet the very despotism their fathers threw off in the Revolution of 1776." The fire-eater cast separationists in noble terms, describing their work as faithfully "imitat[ing] the policy of our fathers."[21]

Rhett pronounced the original basis for union dead and buried. The 1787 democratic experiment "failed" because Northern empire building, fueled by "negro fanaticism," had caused the original Constitution to be gradually "abolished by constructions" of it. Over time judges and politicians, swayed by advocates, had destroyed the instrument's intended meanings. As a result, "the most civilized and prosperous communities have been impoverished and ruined by Anti-Slavery fanaticism." As the North pursued "sectional predominance," he continued, "[a]ll fraternity of feeling between the North and the South is lost, or has been converted into hate." Whatever "identity of feeling, interests and institutions which once existed is gone. . . . [North and South] are now divided, between agricultural—and manufacturing and commercial States; between slaveholding, and nonslaveholding States." Southern "institutions and industrial pursuits have made them totally different peoples." The 1787 Constitution could no longer command respect. It was "now too late to reform or restore the Government of the United States" because "[a]ll confidence in the North is lost in the South."

This theory of popular sovereignty was several steps removed from the lawless idea that an unhappy individual citizen could refuse to obey any law believed to be unconstitutional or morally bankrupt. Additionally, the implementation of any plans for withdrawal had to be tempered by two "moral obligations or restrictions": "not to break up the partnership without good and sufficient cause" and "avoid[ing] the infliction of loss or damage upon any [parties]"—conditions believed to be amply satisfied on this occasion.[22]

According to Rhett and other subscribers to the compact theory of constitutionalism, the will of the people could be executed only through each state, not the people themselves apart from state processes. At the founding "separate, independent States" entered into the Union without parting with their sovereignty. Only through erroneous interpretations of fundamental law did Northern judges and politicians accomplish the "annihilation of the sovereignty of the states."

Rhett moved from the principle of states' rights to the idea of a new political community based on regional and cultural similarities, announcing South Carolina's intention to help form "a great Slave-holding Confederacy." Instead of lingering over "the shattered remains of a broken Constitution," Rhett demanded the Southern people's right "to be let alone to work our own high destinies." If slaveholding states could chart their own path, the future would be magnificent:

> [O]ur population doubles every twenty years; . . . starvation is unknown, and abundance crowns the land; . . . order is preserved by unpaid police, and the most fertile regions of the world where the white man cannot labor are brought into usefulness by the labor of the African, and the whole world is blessed by our own productions.

He asked the people of other states to imagine "a great Slaveholding Confederacy, stretching its arms over a territory larger than any power in Europe possesses—with a population four times greater than that of the whole United States when they achieved their independence of the British Empire."

In both theory and practice, then, the Confederate approach to withdrawal differed from approaches to popular sovereignty that came before. Secessionists' desire to separate completely from the Union signaled they cared neither for further dialogue nor rapprochement with opponents. The absence of any strong ethical program, moreover, indicated no interest in the strategy of modeling practiced by John Brown's men or the Icarians. The only parties worth engaging now were other states with analogous cultural configurations. Racial and economic congruence, rather than moral revival, served as the organizing principles.

Florida, Mississippi, and Alabama answered South Carolina's call in the new year, followed by Georgia, Louisiana, and Texas. After the formation of the Confederate States of America, they would add Virginia, Tennessee, North Carolina, and Arkansas. Replicating South Carolina's characterization of the Union, each convention dissolved the "compact" between sovereign states. Based on this shared theory of constitutional usurpation, every convention reclaimed for the citizenry all the rights and powers of a "free, sovereign, and independent state." Co-opting the rhetoric of enslavement, Southerners announced they would prefer to "die free men than live as slaves." Each seceding state seized the moment to embrace the theory of racial and regional self-determination articulated by fire-eaters.[23]

Georgia's declaration of independence cited "numerous and serious causes of complaint" against Northern conduct concerning "the subject of African slavery." The people of Georgia announced their intention to resist "not only . . . the loss of our property, but the destruction of ourselves, our wives, and our children, and the desolation of our homes, our altars, and our firesides." Mississippi's secession statement, too, made plain that its "position is thoroughly identified with the institution of slavery." The "schemes of emancipation" pursued by the North "tramples the original equality of the South," and government policies revealed a "design to ruin our agriculture, to prostrate our industrial pursuits and to destroy our social system." Independence would be the antidote to perpetual "degradation."[24]

Drawing on their pioneer origins, the people of Texas pleaded the case for "the beneficent and patriarchal" institution of negro slavery as "a relation that had existed from the first settlement of her wilderness by the white race, and which her people intended should exist in all future time." Equality meant government by "all white men," Texas delegates insisted, and the "servitude of the African race" was "abundantly authorized and justified by the experience of mankind, and the revealed will of the Almighty Creator, as recognized by all Christian nations." Each of the seceding states seized upon John Brown's assault on Harpers Ferry, directly or obliquely, as proof that Northern hatred of slavery knew no bounds.

Seceding states dispatched commissioners to the remaining slave-holding states to spread the good news of independence. These missionaries described separation as a last-ditch effort to save their way of life. Extending the principle of equality to nonwhites would unravel the fabric of Southern existence by diminishing the political status of whites and exposing women and children to dangerous kinds of social intercourse. Sent to Georgia, Judge William L. Harris of Mississippi stated that the people "had rather see the last of her race, men, women, and children, immolated in one common funeral pile [pyre], than see them subjected to the degradation of civil, political, and social equality with the negro race." Speaking before assembled delegates in Alabama, Andrew Pickens Calhoun prophesied that any slaveholding state that remained in the Union would face "degradation and annihilation."[25]

Those who spread the gospel of separation warned that impending emancipation would also unleash a cycle of retribution and crime by freedmen, the "drones and pests of society." Steven Fowler Hale, sent by the people of Alabama to Kentucky, argued that where "the two races would be pressing together, amalgamation or the extermination of the one or the other would be inevitable."[26] He raised the specter of white civilization unraveled by the principle of individual equality:

> [A]ll [will] be degraded to a position of equality with free negroes, stand side by side with them at the polls, and fraternize in all the social relations of life, or else there will be an eternal war of races, desolating the land with blood, and utterly wasting and destroying all resources of the country. Who can look upon such a picture without a shudder?

Remaining in the Union, commissioners predicted, would spell the end of white society. At best, interbreeding might eviscerate white culture. At worst, open black-white conflict, long suppressed through slavery, would lay waste to the rule of law.

Pamphlets from religious and civic leaders during this period echoed these themes of racial sovereignty. Defenders of Southern rights ridiculed any suggestion that the profession of equality in the Declaration of Independence encompassed blacks or that the 1787 Constitution's appeal to "We the people" meant to overturn an institution that "informs all our habits of thought, lies at the basis of our political faith and of our social existence." Fusing law and culture, they insisted that the only path forward would be "the formation of an independent nation" by "a homogenous people, governed by the same sentiment and acting upon the same interests."[27]

Within a few months, the Southern independence movement had reached the point where collective action could be taken. As each state broke the bonds of union, secessionists seized federal arsenals, customs houses, garrisons, and other resources. A constitutional convention was scheduled for February 3, 1861, to form a new government. Rhett set off for Montgomery, Alabama, clutching a copy of the U.S. Constitution and proposed amendments.[28]

The sessions of the Montgomery Convention took place at the Alabama statehouse. Delegates elected Howell Cobb convention president and Johnson J. Hooper secretary. The Montgomery Convention appointed a Committee of Twelve to draft a provisional constitution. Headed by Memminger, the committee labored under an injunction of secrecy. On February 8, delegates approved the provisional constitution. After signatories swore to support the Provisional Constitution, the Congress proceeded to elect Jefferson Davis and Alexander Hamilton Stephens as president and vice president. Davis, who traveled to Montgomery from Brierfield Plantation for his inauguration, called on loyal citizens to defend the new constitution "to the last extremity with Southern blood and Southern steel."[29]

The day after the signing of the Provisional Constitution, the convention appointed a second Committee of Twelve to craft a permanent constitution. Rhett maneuvered himself onto the Second Committee of Twelve and secured the chairmanship. After Rhett's presentation, delegates debated the draft constitution in secret session for ten days. Lincoln's inauguration became overshadowed by news that the Confederate Constitution had been approved on March 11.[30]

During this time, the convention designed a new flag to convey the people's dedication to racial sovereignty. Members retained the stars and stripes, as well as the colors red, white, and blue—"true republican colors." Those charged with the task of designing a flag were determined to not "'keep,' copy or imitate" the U.S. flag, especially after discovering that the Republic of Liberia and the Sandwich Islands had adopted it. In the end they settled on a design that signified the purity of the Confederate cause but did not resemble the Yankee flag that had been "pilfered and appropriated by a free negro community and a race of savages." Even at the level of symbolic politics, race mattered. The final design of the constitution would leave no doubt of the people's plan for a perpetual white empire based on the plantation system.[31]

Cultural Sovereignty in Conventional Form

Although the Confederate Constitution invoked the Creator to show that Southerners were a God-fearing people, it signaled no grand project of ethical transformation. The constitution neither engaged in a major redesign of national bureaucracies nor challenged the standard approach to divided powers. Instead, drafters employed the 1787 Constitution as their blueprint, copying the bulk of it word for word and incorporating the Bill of Rights. This could not have been altogether surprising, given the Confederate theory of constitutional usurpation and the narrow range of deal-breaking issues. On the verge of secession, the Columbia *South Carolinian* had expressed this sentiment: "No one can demonstrate that the present Constitution never worked for good. It is only the construction put upon it, and a few erroneous sentences within it, that have done the whole mischief." Architects of the Confederate Constitution perceived their work as "more a matter of restoration, than of innovation." The lack of bureaucratic innovation underscored the fact that the dispute was not over failed institutions so much as a desire to reestablish racial power and regional influence. Once slave states withdrew from the Union, many believed that the sources of cultural conflict had been extirpated.[32]

The new constitution no longer aspired "to form a more perfect Union." Though states' rights rhetoric had helped organize Southern rage against the Union, the final design of the Confederacy retained its commitment to large-scale republicanism, albeit one founded on the political economy of the plantation. The constitution's protection of slavery betrayed the people's belief in a white man's republic. Of the twelve million inhabitants of the Confederate states, roughly two-thirds of the population (women and slaves) were ruled by the remaining one-third (white men). As a general proposition, however, racial supremacy was not completely worked out in the constitution. Instead, the protection of chattel slavery, constraints on the federal government, and widely shared expectations of proper social roles together sufficed to save white civilization.[33]

Key elements preserved slavery for as long as a state determined to keep it. If the 1787 Constitution assiduously avoided the word *slave*, the Confederate Constitution used the phrase openly. It carried over the Three-Fifths Clause for apportionment purposes, pausing only to proudly substitute "three fifths of all slaves" for "three fifths of all other Persons" as distinguished from "free persons." To the delight of slaveholders, the convention codified the *Dred Scott* decision. Entirely new provisions preserved a slave master's economic interests as matters of fundamental right. No law "denying or impairing the right of property in negro slaves shall be passed." In any new territories, "the institution of negro slavery . . . shall be recognized and protected by Congress and by the territorial government." Clarifying the consequences of travel, an issue raised in *Dred Scott,* a slave owner now could count on "the right of transit and sojourn in any State of this Confederacy, with their slaves and other property; and the right of property in said slaves shall not be thereby impaired."

Alexander Stephens, speaking extemporaneously in Savannah a week after approval of the permanent constitution, discussed these "improvements on the old Constitution." After recounting changes to the presidency and congressional power, he came to the proslavery features: "The new Constitution puts at rest, *forever,* all agitating questions relating to our peculiar institution—African slavery as it exists among us—the proper *status* of the negro in our form of civilization." Leaving little doubt as to the cultural causes of the split, he called the dispute "the immediate cause of the late rupture and present revolution." He then denounced "the assumption of the equality of the races," advanced by luminaries such as Jefferson, as a fundamental error. The Confederate Constitution rejected this belief and, as Stephens proudly announced, established the first nation-state organized on the principle of white sovereignty:

> Our new government is founded upon exactly the opposite idea; its foundations re-laid, its cornerstone rests upon the great truth that the negro is not equal to the white man. That slavery—subordination to the superior race—is his natural and moral condition. . . . This, our new government, is the first in the history of the world based upon this great physical, philosophical, and moral truth. . . . It is upon this, as I have stated, our social fabric is firmly planted.[34]

Although this principle of racial superiority was not inscribed in the Confederate Constitution as explicitly as it might have been, protecting slavery meant reaffirming not only "the firm convictions of the framers of the new constitution" but also "public sentiment." Certainly no one in Montgomery had risen to defend black equality during the proceedings. In Savannah, Stephens reiterated what he had said days before in Atlanta: the people had made "African *inequality* and subordination, and *equality* of white men, the chief cornerstone of the Southern Republic." While the Confederate Constitution helped the people hold the line against the forces of radical egalitarianism and urbanization, "the process of disintegration in the old Union may be expected to go on with absolute certainty."[35]

As much as these provisions brought the original Constitution in line with planters' theory of cultural sovereignty, some members of the convention wanted to go further. More exacting slave-trading protections, such as requiring compensation from states that failed to comply with the Fugitive Slave Clause, went down in defeat. Rhett originally hoped to preserve Congress's power to reopen the foreign slave trade, but acquiesced to protectionist sentiment and fears that European countries might hesitate to deal fairly with a slave-trading nation. His plan to exclude from the Confederacy any state "which does not authorize the institution of slavery within its limits" did not garner sufficient support, nor did related efforts to bar admission of states and territories that failed to ensure slavery. How to deal with additional states proved a sore point for fire-eaters, as they feared "being dragged back eventually into the old political affiliation with the States and peoples from whom we have just cut loose."[36]

Debate on the last point was especially keen. In a close vote, the convention adopted a two-thirds threshold for the admission of new states. This supermajority threshold gave some assurance that slaveholding states could deny entry to states hostile to slavery, without drastically limiting the Confederacy's growth by making slavery an absolute condition of admission. The procedural mechanism allowed slave states to police the terms of cultural sovereignty at the heart of the legal order.[37]

Stronger principles of racial supremacy could have been enunciated, but most founders pronounced themselves satisfied. Robert Smith, a delegate from Alabama, lauded the openness with which the new constitution resolved the slavery question once and for all. "We have dissolved the Union chiefly because of the negro quarrel," he pointed out. "We have now placed our domestic institution, and secured its rights unmistakably, in the Constitution; we have sought by no euphony to hide its name—we have called our negroes 'slaves,' and we have recognized and protected them as persons and our rights to them as property." Renouncing radical egalitarianism, the Confederate Constitution resisted the "[w]ild, impractical and false notions, as to the equality of the human race, got abroad both here and in Europe." Although the document did not define citizenship, leaving the matter mostly to the states, each seceding state quickly amended its own constitution reserving citizenship for "free white persons."[38]

Though preserving a slaveholding existence provided the major impetus for a new charter, other concerns bubbled to the surface when the opportunity finally arose to contemplate ideal rule. None of the modifications altered the fundamental nature of the Confederate Constitution as an expression of cultural self-governance. Delegates made a few changes to restrain the Confederate Congress. In a series of rulings in the early days of the American republic, the U.S. Supreme Court had relied on broad terms in the 1787 Constitution to expand the power of the national government. Disunionists had expressed horror that "[t]he whole Constitution by the constructions of the Northern people, has been swallowed up by a few words in its preamble." To prevent history from repeating itself, drafters kept the Necessary and Proper Clause, but refused to carry over the elastic phrase "to promote the general welfare" from the original Constitution. An amendment offered by Rhett, and accepted by the convention, barred Congress from levying "duties or taxes on importations from foreign nations." Another limitation advanced by the fire-eater ensured that Congress's power of appropriations to "facilitate interstate commerce" did not extend beyond certain "internal improvements." By severely restricting the spending power, no appropriation could be made unless two-thirds of both houses agreed with the president.[39]

Confederates proved more wary of presidential power than their forebears. Acting on Rhett's proposal, the convention settled on a six-year term for the president without the possibility of reelection, so as to "remove from the incumbent all temptation to use his office or exert the powers confided in him for any objects of personal ambition." In Rhett's view, the abuse of presidential patronage had become a "great evil" under the original Constitution, reminiscent of how "the re-eligibility of the Consuls of Rome opened the way to the Roman

Empire."[40] Another modification stripped the president of the power to make recess appointments when a candidate has been rejected by the Senate.

The founders' concerns about presidential overreaching did not mean they wished to turn the president into a figurehead. In perhaps the most significant change, drafters gave the president a line-item veto. To improve accountability within the executive branch, the constitution clarified that all principal officers and anyone acting in a diplomatic capacity "may be removed at the pleasure of the President"; "[a]ll other civil officers . . . may be removed at any time" upon notice to the Senate. An innovation that would have allowed cabinet members to hold office in Congress—favored by Stephens and Robert Toombs—failed to make the final cut. Instead, cabinet members could, upon the action of Congress, enjoy a seat in either house "with the privilege of discussing any measures appertaining to his department."[41]

With a few notable departures, Confederate statesmen retained the federal judiciary. Instead of the judicial power extending to "all cases in law and equity," drafters limited judges to controversies sounding in "law" alone, allowing Congress alone to establish the scope of legal remedies. They deleted language in the original Constitution that conferred jurisdiction over matters "between citizens of different States," leaving such disputes in state courts. To protect each state's public fisc, the convention incorporated the U.S. Supreme Court's interpretation that the Eleventh Amendment barred suits against states without their consent. Beyond these measures, the Confederate Constitution retained the national character of the 1787 design. Stronger state sovereignty measures were repeatedly turned aside, including a proposal to explicitly reserve each state's right to secede from the Confederacy. Rhett's motion to permit any state in peacetime to demand the removal of Confederate troops from its territory was tabled, and his proposal to deny the Supreme Court jurisdiction over state court decisions also failed.[42]

In keeping with their desire to ensure the constitution would be responsive to the will of the people, drafters reworked the amendment process. They denied Congress any role in proposing substantive changes, leaving the body only the technical duty of calling a national convention of states when enough states proposed a change.

Architects made it easier for states to propose an amendment, whenever demanded by "any three States, legally assembled in their several conventions." The three-fourths threshold for approval in the 1787 Constitution became a two-thirds standard in the Confederate charter. In these procedural changes one could detect an indictment of the original document, which allowed mistaken interpretations to become entrenched and grievances to fester. Had it been easier to repudiate the false understandings put on the Constitution, Rhett insisted, "the vast discontent which preceded the war, and made it inevitable, would have been easily arrested and allayed; and the States assembled in convention would have settled amicably all their differences."[43]

As the Montgomery Convention finished its work, delegates agreed that ratification by five state conventions would cause the permanent constitution to go into legal effect. After recording the ayes, each delegate signed the document, kissed the Bible, and "perfected [his] rebellion." The Confederate Constitution was then enrolled on parchment, printed, and sent on for consideration by each state.[44]

Debates in the state conventions mostly centered on the need for swift action weighted against the necessary deliberation to produce loyalty and affection on the part of citizens. Delegates to conventions in Alabama and Louisiana moved that the constitution be submitted to the people as a whole, but when such motions were defeated, they joined colleagues to urge immediate ratification in convention. The desire to foster unity among the populace, secure foreign allies, and shore up the new nation's credit won the day. A permanent constitution, they believed, would help them achieve these goals. Commissioners who traveled to London and Paris to win formal recognition and alliances took copies of the constitution along. Alabama became the first to ratify the Confederate Constitution, on March 12. Georgia, Louisiana, and Texas gave their assent in short order. Mississippi's approval on March 29 caused the constitution to go into effect. After the outbreak of war, conventions in Virginia, Arkansas, Tennessee, and North Carolina consented to Confederate rule.[45]

In the meantime, Rhett and the South Carolina delegation returned home. Already worried about the potential for dilution of cultural authority, proslavery forces revisited provisions that had not been accepted in Montgomery. Fire-eaters' goals for the state ratifying convention included protecting the principle of racial sovereignty from attack by external sources and permanently entrenching the Slave Power. Rhett himself proposed an ordinance requiring the governor of South Carolina to call a convention in the event any nonslaveholding state were ever admitted to the Confederacy. He insisted that "the slaveholding and non-slaveholding States cannot live in peace under the same government." Rhett later proposed that South Carolina "does not consider itself bound to enter to continue in confederation with any State not tolerating the institution of slavery." This measure went down in defeat, 41–89. Once it became clear that delegates preferred an imperfect constitution to continued debate, Rhett and other fire-eaters threw their support in favor of ratification.

South Carolina's leaders remained unhappy with certain features of the Confederate Constitution. They believed the Montgomery Convention should have gone further to entrench the plantation system, ensure the clout of larger slaveholding states, and reinvigorate the slave trade. Despite ratifying the document, the state convention remained in session for an additional two days. Eventually, delegates passed a resolution calling for a national convention to discuss constitutional amendments after formation of the permanent government. The convention overwhelmingly supported four amendments. These measures demanded that the Confederacy repeal the Three-Fifths Clause and instead count negroes in full; prohibit the admission of any nonslaveholding state except through unanimous consent; repeal the ban on the foreign slave trade; and prohibit Congress from contracting any debt except for war purposes. None of these proposals went any further, as war soon dominated the entire field of action. Still, they demonstrated the depths of the people's thirst for cultural sovereignty.[46]

Warfare to Preserve Racial Independence

With the enormous task of political re-creation completed, the Confederate Congress set about doing the people's work. But every exercise in cultural sovereignty faces unique challenges. From within, the state must navigate between the demands of people who want greater cultural purity and those who would be content with less ideologically strident stances when balancing other priorities. To outsiders, a new nation-state founded on racial and regional power will almost certainly be identified as a threat to some sovereigns' visions of community. Thus, the Confederate theory of self-rule not only challenged the prevailing understandings of the 1787 Constitution but also threatened to disrupt American relations with other countries. In fact, other nation-states treated the Confederacy at arm's length, as the United States made clear to its allies that they should not interfere with internal matters.

Confederate leaders hoped to "commence our new national life, unmolested." Their dream of being let alone was quickly shattered. With shots fired at Fort Sumter, and failed peace talks in Washington a distant memory, armed conflict became the primary means of defending the legal vision of a slaveholding society. Their legal transformation complete, Confederate officials described the Union now as "a foreign power" bent on "subverting [the new nation's] independence." In this light, the South was guilty of no more than taking up arms "in defense of an inherent, unalienable right" of sovereignty.

Organized violence thus served as the means for preserving a theory of cultural self-governance. Because secessionists dreamed of a large-scale republic on the same continent as the United States, total war and mass casualties had to be expected. There remained no room for nuances in one's justifications such as those engaged by John Brown, who claimed he had levied war against an immoral practice rather than against particular sovereigns. Brute power and military strategy dominated the penultimate stage of the constitutional process, but debate over the legality of each side's tactics and ends continued.

To motivate troops, officials issued a clarion call to wage "the second great war of independence," which history would record as "a great and holy war of self defense" and "civil liberty." Speakers hailed Roger Taney, author of *Dred Scott,* as a hero who tried in vain to "interpose . . . the unspotted arm of justice between the rights of the South and the malignant usurpation of power by the North." As fighting broke out, Henry Wise, former governor of Virginia, called on citizens to defend their rights against those who have "abolitionized your border" and "undertaken to teach you what should be the moral duties of men." Wise invoked the notorious liberator's reputation for resourcefulness and zeal: "Take a lesson from John Brown" by recycling whatever was handy in defense of constitutional ideals. "Manufacture your blades from old iron, even though it be the tires of your cart-wheels."[47]

Lincoln's administration vigorously contested the Confederate theory of popular sovereignty. Lincoln drew a hard line against secession to preserve the principle that the American Constitution had formed one people. The Union created in 1787 was "perpetual," the president declared, something implied in universal law as well as the U.S. Constitution. Though he rejected Southerners' compact theory, for the sake of argument he entertained the idea of state-by-state consent and found it wanting on its own terms: "If the United States be not a government proper, but an association of States in the nature of contract merely, can it, as a contract, be peaceably unmade by less than all the parties who made it? One party may violate it—break it, so to speak— but does it not require all to lawfully rescind it?" Slaveholding states had not gained the consent of the remaining states to secede, and the agreement inherent in the original Constitution simply could not be revoked by any single state. The president dismissed out of hand the legality of expressing popular discontent through withdrawal: "Plainly the central idea of secession is the essence of anarchy." Instead, while recognizing the people's collective right to amend the Constitution or their "revolutionary right to dismember or overthrow it," Lincoln suggested that sovereignty belonged to all of "the people who inhabit" the country. Individual states could not unmake the Union without subverting the expectations of the American people.[48]

In defense of the 1787 Constitution, Lincoln tried to turn the language of popular self-rule against the Confederacy by charging that secessionists had levied "war upon the first principle of popular government—the right of the people." This was true in two senses: defying the will of the majority to make policy under the terms of the original Constitution and insisting, contrary to the purpose and design of the American Constitution, that "large control of the people in government is the source of all political evil." In other words, secessionists had subverted the rule of law through their outrageous legal theories.

When Lincoln called out the militia to reestablish the boundaries of the national community, he described the seceding states as "insurrectionary combinations" pursuing a "rebellion." Stripping Confederates of any legitimate claim to higher law, Lincoln indicated that Southern troops should be treated as no different from John Brown's men: a "disloyal portion of the American people" or "insurgents" whose actions were unauthorized by the political tradition. Convinced of the rightness of his theory of self-rule, President Davis reacted with outrage that the South "is declared to be guilty of insurrection" and moaned that "its citizens are stigmatized as 'rebels,' as if they had revolted against a master."[49]

Lincoln placed the U.S. Constitution firmly on the side of racial egalitarianism when he announced the Emancipation Proclamation days after bloody Antietam. In doing so, he broadened the plural model of conventional sovereignty to include the enslaved. By liberating slaves in the seceding states, the executive order struck at the heart of the dissident legal order, battle by battle. This presidential act heightened the Southern sense of siege. It enjoined freedmen to "abstain from all violence, unless in necessary self defense," and to "labor faithfully for reasonable wages," seeking to ameliorate concerns that emancipation would unleash chaos while winning new converts to the emerging pluralistic order. That the administration had now openly committed itself to abolition was not lost on slaveholders. The Confederate president rebuked Lincoln for his audacity: "It affords to our people the complete and crowning proof of the true nature of the designs of the party" that elevated Lincoln to power and usurped the mechanisms of conventional sovereignty. Turning the tables, Davis warned that any slaves found to abet Northern troops would be punished as criminals under Confederate law for "exciting servile insurrections."[50]

As alternative designs go, the Confederacy was implemented on a substantial scale. The Confederate Congress remained active throughout much of the Civil War, pivoting from designing a constitution to making new laws and evaluating which former U.S. laws would be retained. Founders contemplated a Supreme Court, but never established it. Only the Senate passed a bill to create a Supreme Court, though denying it the power to review state court judgments; the House never took action on the measure.[51]

Why, ultimately, did the Confederate experiment in cultural sovereignty unravel? Stephanie McCurry, emphasizing demographic realities, contends that white women and slaves helped bring the Confederacy to its knees. She analyzes how women aided draft dodgers and deserters, rioted to feed the families of soldiers, and opposed impressment and taxes. Internal factors indeed played a significant role in weakening a political community already under stress. These protests by women contributed to the depletion of resources and faith in the project, yet they did not seem to be agitations *on the basis of sex*. This difference is important, for such resistance apparently did not force a fundamental rethinking of ideals of racial or regional sovereignty, and there seems little evidence of a sustained effort to reorient ideas of patriarchy or whiteness. No lasting burst of sex-based egalitarianism emerged from their protests. Instead, the acts of defiance by female planters were couched in terms of military duty, family subsistence, and states' rights. For all of these reasons, their agitation contributed to the general sense of disorder instead of directly challenging the precepts of the constitutional order itself.[52]

The actions of slaves presented a somewhat different story. The ideology of racial authority worked primarily to promote white solidarity but faced challenges in keeping slaves in line. Once conventional authorities warmed to emancipation as federal policy, they began to successfully erode slaves' allegiance to their masters and to local forms of authority. Taking advantage of the sudden proliferation of sovereigns, slaves decided to help dismantle a legal order that dehumanized them. With news of approaching Union troops, slave uprisings and escapes became more frequent, as did efforts to take up arms for the North. It is difficult to imagine how the Confederate Constitution could have survived with its keystone institution under siege.[53]

All of this transpired against a field of armed conflict, which opened existing fissures among the Southern people. From its inception, their theory of politics had been ambitious and exclusionary. As a direct and open challenge to conventional sovereignty, its legal vision was always likely to generate the strongest reaction that could be mustered by defenders of the 1787 Constitution. Ultimately, the Confederate order collapsed due to a precipitous decline in political faith among all classes, punctuated by decisive military defeats. In the face of enormous outside challenges, white solidarity could not overcome internal divisions based on class, state citizenship, and personality. As war ravaged the Southern economy, the Confederate theory of politics proved incapable of keeping the people together, even at the level of shared economic interests. Born on the eve of war, the Confederate Constitution's best hope lay in surviving the conflict and sustaining feelings of cultural attachment. But as battlefield losses mounted, the Confederate army experienced demoralized troops and desertions. Despite some notable victories, by the spring of 1862 President Davis openly discussed the necessity to "reform and recruit our scattered and shattered forces." States balked at raising taxes to fund the war. Dwindling resources led Davis to propose changes to the law in the name of "absolute necessity" that would allow officers to impress private property based only a promise of future payment.

Impressment officers proved wildly unpopular, with local newspapers "advis[ing] the people to resist them." The rhetoric of popular sovereignty, states' rights, and property rights unleashed by secessionists now eluded official control as the language of liberty became turned against the Confederate project itself. The dire situation regarding manpower caused the administration to enact a series of conscription laws that provoked even more resistance. A number of state officials chafed at the very proposal, complaining that the law violated state sovereignty. The governors of Texas and Georgia, in particular, accused the federal government of decimating the stable of able-bodied militia members necessary to defend their borders. At that point, each state began to make plans for its own survival at the expense of the Confederacy.[54]

The degree to which conscription laws bred class resentment can hardly be overstated. Because the conscription laws exempted any white person who could provide a substitute as well as one white man for every twenty slaves owned, yeoman farmers and the working class felt that they bore the brunt of the sacrifices to save the republic. Class divisions began to overcome feelings of racial solidarity. Expressing his constituents' anger to President Davis, Mississippi senator James Phelan declared, "Never did a law meet with universal odium than the exemption of slave owners. . . . It has aroused a spirit of rebellion . . . and bodies of men have banded together to resist." A patriotic desire to defend the glorious legal order disintegrated into rampant grousing that the conflict had become a "rich man's war, poor man's fight." Already suspicious that secession had been driven by slaveholding elites, some plain folk swore "they will 'fight for no rich man's slaves.'" Despite the predictions of leading theorists, slavery failed to ensure the survival of white community. To the contrary, toward the end the institution turned into a source of social division among whites.

Protests broke out over the draft, aided by soldiers' wives and local officials suspicious of central authority. Congress had designated exemptions for those occupying jobs crucial to the home front, such as civil servants, railroad and river workers, miners, druggists, and teachers. Officials helped people avoid military service by adding them to civil service and state militia rolls. Sparing no effort in whipping up citizens' disgust at the administration, Georgia's governor said, "no act of the Government of the United States prior to Georgia's secession struck a blow at constitutional liberty so fell as has been struck by the conscription act." He called the law a "palpable violation of the Constitution" that approached "military despotism." In defying the draft, the people put the principles of state autonomy and personal liberty above the very survival of the legal order. The bonds of community would continue to unravel from within, as battlefield losses mounted.

Rhett's own journey from visionary to dissident tracked the rise and fall of Confederate constitutionalism. More and more, Rhett felt that the Confederacy resembled the hated Union. He accused President Davis of marginalizing true believers like himself, being thirsty for power, and mismanaging the war. Day after day the pages of the *Mercury* accused the administration of betraying the principles of Southern independence. The legal order for which Rhett and others had toiled faced impending destruction due to "a series of the most matchless blunders." Even though Rhett argued for a stronger Congress to better handle the war, his own constituents disowned him in 1863. He experienced defeat at the hands of a younger man who characterized Rhett's criticisms as a declaration of war against the legal experiment in a time of crisis. Rhett saw his ouster as a referendum on secession, which had brought not prosperity but ruin. Yet he remained a critic of the Confederacy until its last days. Amid calls to impeach President Davis, Rhett's frustrations led him to recommend to Stephens that Davis be ousted and replaced by Robert E. Lee.[55]

President Davis's November 1864 proposal to emancipate slaves agreeing to fight for the Confederacy earned perhaps the strongest rebuke. Congress had already authorized the impressment of slaves to cook, work in hospitals, or improve fortifications. As the situation grew dire, Davis raised the idea of allowing black soldiers to earn their way to freedom. The outcry echoed throughout the states. What was left to fight for, Rhett complained, if the Confederacy gave up the very institution that had prompted independence in the first place? Aghast at the plan to arm slaves, the aging fire-eater could not shake the feeling that the administration was willing to forsake "Southern civilization" and the principle of white sovereignty for a measure of peace. To Rhett, this "third stage of usurpations" on the part of the new government should be regarded as the ultimate treachery.[56]

At that point, even the most ardent defenders of race-based sovereignty abandoned the Confederate experiment. Many joined Rhett in condemning the proposal, despite impassioned pleas of military necessity from General Robert E. Lee and Secretary of State Benjamin Judah. To detractors, the legislation not only seemed to exceed the powers of Congress and interfere with property rights, it also undermined the organizing ethos of a slaveholding nation. Infuriated, Representative Henry S. Foote compared Davis to Lincoln for thinking that the federal government could free slaves without the consent of the several states. "The South went to war to defeat the designs of the abolitionists," Senator Robert M. T. Hunter observed caustically, "and behold! in the midst of the war, we turn abolitionists ourselves!" Others looked upon the idea as "the death knell of [the] cause." Cobb put it thus: "If slaves will make soldiers our whole theory of slavery is wrong." On March 18, 1865, in one of its final legislative acts, Congress approved Davis's proposal to arm slaves. But in an effort to meet constitutional objections, the law conditioned postservice emancipation upon the consent of slave owners and capped the number of such soldiers at no more than 25 percent of the eligible male slaves in any state. The war ended before the policy could be fully implemented. But the damage had been done: once high officials showed themselves willing to betray the principles of their own revolution, they could no longer count upon the loyalty of ardent practitioners of cultural sovereignty.[57]

On June 15, 1864, members of the Confederate Congress published a final manifesto. Crafted as an appeal to "the public opinion of the world," the document expressed a people's "desire to stand acquitted before the tribunal of the world, as well as in the eyes of omniscient justice." In it, leaders recapitulated their cultural theory of self-rule, described the war as "wholly one of aggression" on the part of Union forces, and announced their "sincere desire for peace, on terms consistent with our honor and the permanent security of our rights."[58]

Confederate leaders who refused to recognize the ominous signs had looked to the 1864 election. If the troops could just hold out until then, perhaps the Union, exhausted from fighting the war, would oust the abolitionist president. Lincoln's reelection dashed any residual hope for a negotiated peace. Despite efforts to win recognition from Great Britain and France, neither country ever had formal dealings with the Confederacy. Foreign dependency on Southern cotton failed to move other nations from a policy of neutrality, as they searched elsewhere for the commodity.

Ultimately, major battlefield defeats sealed the fate of the Confederate order. When news of Lee's surrender at Appomattox reached Richmond, Davis escaped with members of his cabinet. He issued a final proclamation on the run, hinting at signs of impending defeat: "The General-in-Chief found it necessary to make such movements of his troops as to uncover the capital." Trying to put a positive face on dire circumstances, he stated that the people had "now entered upon a new phase of the struggle." He urged his countrymen to "not despond," but rather, "relying on God, meet the foe with fresh defiance, and with unconquered and unconquerable hearts."[59]

With the fall of Richmond came an extended period of military occupation. Reconstructive measures now had to be taken to confirm the victors' more limited conception of popular sovereignty, the Union as "perpetual," and Confederate statesmen as outlaws. Whichever side one had taken during the Civil War, something could be gained from believing that the Southern people's theory of cultural sovereignty had been judged wanting in a trial by ordeal. A return to unsupervised self-governance would come at a cost. Though left out of the terms of surrender, it soon became apparent that the price to be paid for Southern defiance would be support of constitutional amendments repudiating core features of Confederate rule. Once approved, the Thirteenth, Fourteenth, and Fifteenth Amendments abolished slavery and involuntary servitude, extended federal authority over states where the constitutional virtues of liberty, due process, and equality may be at stake, and guaranteed black suffrage. The most strident theories of state sovereignty, regional distinctiveness, and racial superiority had been subdued.

In their place, the revised Constitution more firmly protected the rights of individual citizens, regardless of race or previous condition of servitude. The amended constitution strengthened the instrumentalities of ordinary government to effectuate these unifying principles, even against recalcitrant states. In the end, the Civil War led not to two American empires side by side but the further consolidation of a single, pluralistic legal order. As Jefferson Davis himself recognized, these "new relations required a complete revolution in the principle of the government of the United States."[60]

The American people had to be reconstituted by a respect for the major principles of this reconstructed legal order. Federal officials extended amnesty and clemency to eligible citizens willing to renounce their allegiance to the Confederate order and swear to uphold the U.S. Constitution, laws, and proclamations related to slavery. Not only were the losers in the struggle expected to embrace egalitarianism, individualism, and nationalism as constitutive principles, but they also had to deny the validity of their own legal theories.[61]

The Slave Power might have been vanquished, but dreams of Southern self-rule would live on. Though slavery no longer could be countenanced, the revised constitution remained an object of scorn. Rhett advocated ongoing resistance to the Fourteenth and Fifteenth Amendments, which "if carried out according to their manifest intent," would lead to "Constitutional despotism." Under these new powers, Rhett observed, "[t]he states are constitutionally annihilated." Until his last breath, he disputed the legitimacy of these provisions that had been secured "by fraud or force."[62] Rhett predicted these measures would never gain the true assent of the people:

> Union, between Free Peoples, must exist from *free-will* and *consent*—created by mutual respect and esteem. Force may subject, but it cannot unite; and as long as it is the instrument of a connexion, antagonism will prevail. No Free Peoples autonomy can come from authority—it must arise from within, and if it does not, future contests are inevitable.

The Confederate theory of popular governance had been bested on the battlefield and its lands reclaimed by Union forces, but "[h]ow the Southern People will fare, in the future struggles, should they arise, will depend upon themselves." Their insurgent legal order may have been dismantled, but it might still enjoy a second life in the hearts of the people, as they "labor in chains," biding their time. An inner constitution could be constructed while Southerners awaited their opportunity to regain "greatness and freedom." It would be nurtured, safe and largely undetected, if citizens bore "persecutions [as] our greatest blessings." Even if the day of reckoning was some time off, they should "cherish the hot antagonism, which seethes and boils over in our hearts, still beating with the blood of our children—fathers—brothers—friends—fallen in battle in defense of their Country."

CHAPTER FIVE

The Sequoyah Convention
1905

When his Nation has a place,
His name shall live in history's page,
The grandest of his race.

—J. S. HOLDEN, "SEQUOYAH," 1898

As important as the slavery controversy had been for the advancement of legal ideas, the fractious relationship between Indian nations and agents of the political order, too, left an indelible mark on the political tradition. The presence of Indian nations scattered across the continent complicated the project of economic and political development licensed by conventional law and executed by pioneers in unruly ways. European settlers learned firsthand that the indigenous population had their own worldviews and ancient forms of self-governance; land would not be ceded without a fight. Friction between different peoples and political systems became a fact of life, played out against the backdrop of ever-shifting boundaries. As the ideology of manifest destiny infused American politics, law became a weapon among those who desired to destroy tribal self-rule or tame its potency. Tribal sovereignty was perceived as a threat to the goals of creating an American empire and constituting one people. Native theories of power and community had to be wrestled to the ground and subordinated to the U.S. Constitution. At the same time, the practices of written constitutionalism and popular sovereignty appeared in the arsenal of the oppressed, means of resisting the demands of the majority or the imperatives of legal consolidation.

The indigenous peoples of the Americas began practicing their own form of constitutionalism well before Europeans arrived, around A.D.

1142. Known as the "Great Binding Law," the Constitution of the Iroquois Nations established a federal framework for tribal governance. Originally recorded on wampum belts and transmitted orally, its terms were later recorded in writing. After contact with European settlers, Indian legal traditions began to take on outside influences.

As early as 1827, the Cherokee had a constitution establishing a republican form of government. Other tribal constitutions soon followed, penned by the Choctaw, Creeks, Seminole, Chickasaw, and Osage. Principal chiefs or governors worked with councils to conduct the people's business, while light horsemen enforced the decisions of tribal courts. By the mid-nineteenth century, with the consolidation of the American constitutional order well under way, "small red republics" and openly defiant tribes existed within more conventional states.[1]

These constitutions served several conflicting functions for their makers: battling the tide of assimilation, preserving a measure of tribal sovereignty, satisfying external political pressures, and embracing selected rule-of-law mechanisms favored by white Americans. Yet the price to be paid to retain a measure of sovereign respect was high: changes to theories of Indian self-rule, obedience to the U.S. Constitution and laws. As tribal sovereignty became domesticated, it became subject to the pressures of ordinary politics within the national legal order.

The Cherokee Nation was the largest of the Five Civilized Tribes, a term used by whites to refer to a set of tribes amenable to adopting the ways of settlers. The 1827 Cherokee Constitution bore all the hallmarks of the American political tradition, a hybrid legal culture nurtured by European, native, and colonial ideas. Invoking a multiplicity of sources, from the "sovereign ruler of the Universe" to treaties with the United States, "the people of the Cherokee Nation" asserted their right to govern lands whose boundaries shall remain "unalterably the same." To resist white encroachments, they designated tribal lands the "common property of the nation" and forbade Cherokee citizens from disposing of land improvements to outsiders. Drafters borrowed individual rights from the Anglo-American tradition, such as trial by jury, "free exercise of religious worship," and protection against "unreasonable seizures and searches."[2]

Designed while the federal government careened toward the removal of native peoples from ancestral lands, the Cherokee Constitution represented a concerted effort to stave off dominion by the state and eradication of the Indian way of life. Some felt that the strategy amounted to capitulation to white norms rather than shrewd state-craft. But another conviction had won out: better to selectively adopt some of the white man's methods where they did not violate native beliefs rather than be overwhelmed by his priorities. This pattern would be repeated as tribes clashed with states and the federal government. A defiant bout of constitution writing would occur, involving some amount of political and cultural adaptation, only to be followed by another round of attacks upon tribal sovereignty.

A raft of broken promises by federal authorities, the passage of the Indian Removal Act of 1830, and the forced migration of native peoples to Indian Territory under President Andrew Jackson set the stage for a more urgent phase of resistance and reorganization. The conclusion of the Civil War led the federal government to impose restrictions on tribal affairs as punishment for siding with the Confederacy. Afterward, an independence movement emerged to improve the political status of the inhabitants of Indian Territory, those who had been forcibly relocated as well as those who had wandered to the region. In 1905, leaders of the movement unveiled a constitution for a proposed State of Sequoyah—named after the beloved Cherokee who invented a practical writing system.[3]

Through the years, the clash of sovereigns had gradually eroded and transformed tribal rule. Despite the independent genesis of tribal sovereignty, proponents of conventional politics increasingly perceived Indian rule in cultural terms. If anything, the Confederate experiment taught agents of ordinary law they had to be on guard against theories of self-rule that challenge the idea of one American people, as a way to ward off violence and disorder. That experience also hastened the view that Indian tribes resembled practitioners of racial sovereignty. The more that Indians asserted the right to rule themselves, the more that officials perceived tribal sovereignty as a major threat to the U.S. Constitution's claim on all people. To satisfy pioneer demand for new lands, federal and state authorities levied war against Indian governance, isolating tribes and then breaking them down through restrictions on tribal rule. By the end of the nineteenth century, the fusion and destruction of competing legal orders had reached the point that any pretense about respecting tribal sovereignty came to an end. A pluralistic American order came to mean citizenship for Indians grounded in property ownership rather than group rights founded on decision making by native populations. In a series of laws seeking to fashion political community on these terms, Congress abolished tribal governments and alloted Indian lands on an individual basis. No longer would native peoples be allowed to resist national policies by living in enclaves beyond the reach of the law.

Facing legalized extinction, the Sequoyah movement's leaders turned away altogether from tribal sovereignty, which they believed to be doomed, and resorted to state constitutionalism as the best hope for Indian survival. They justified their shift in aspirations as a matter of natural rights and treaties guaranteeing Indian self-rule. Despite the rhetoric of Indian survival by movement leaders and white Americans' perceptions of the enterprise, the final design of the Sequoyah Constitution eschewed forms of cultural sovereignty. Substantively, the instrument did not embody the values or priorities of Indians alone, but rather it encompassed the interests of all inhabitants who desired an integrated political community. Nor did the document express a powerful theory of ethical sovereignty. Progressivism's moral reform project did have an impact on the constitution's design. But instead of prizing ideological purity, the constitution reflected the crosscurrents of party politics.

Like other practitioners of state constitutionalism, Sequoyah's leaders avoided open violence as a tool of legal change. A preference for process, deliberation, and consent characterized the tactical orientation of the movement. Wishing to be taken seriously by political parties and average citizens, its leaders opted for republican forms of mobilization—conventions, campaigns, pamphlets, lobbying—to express displeasure with the political status quo.

The Sequoyah movement gained the support of Democrats, but its petition for statehood ran headlong into the contrary priorities of Congress and a Republican president. Rather than recognize the State of Sequoyah, Congress established the State of Oklahoma by merging Oklahoma Territory and Indian Territory into a single political unit. But because the Sequoyah Constitution had so perfectly navigated political pressures, it was treated as a template for Oklahoma's constitution during a successor convention. Once the narrative of constitutional creation had been rewritten, and the Indian claim to exclusive authorship repudiated, the dominant legal order absorbed the people of Indian Territory and their political ideas.

From Tribal Rule to State Constitutionalism

The origins of the Sequoyah movement lay in the troubled relations between an emerging American political order and the Indian nations. A January 9, 1809, letter from Thomas Jefferson to the deputies of the Cherokee Upper Towns typified the perspective of white officials toward American Indians. Jefferson explained that "the industrious pursuits of agriculture and civilized life" can be secured only by establishing the rule of law through democratic processes:

> In proceeding to the establishment of laws, you wish to adopt them from ours, and such only for the present as suit your present condition; chiefly indeed, those for the punishment of crimes and the protection of property. But who is to determine which of our laws suit your condition, and shall be in force with you? All of you being equally free, no one has a right to say what shall be law for the others. Our way is to put these questions to the vote, and to consider that as law for which the majority votes—the fool has as great a right to express his opinion by vote as the wise, because he is equally free, and equally master of himself.

According to Jefferson, white citizens served as teachers to native peoples, who freely weighed the benefits of adopting European rule of law mechanisms "as they think best." In making the transition to republican rule, Indians could count on "the counsel and assistance of the government of the United States." Despite a stated desire for dialogue, violence and legal sanctions also emerged as attractive instruments against tribal rule when government officials became impatient or suspicious. Over time, the 1787 Constitution's grant of authority to Congress to "regulate Commerce . . . with the Indian tribes" evolved into expansive power over tribal affairs once they were deemed as subjects internal to the legal order and subject to federal law through treaties. Faced with a mix of missionary activity, governmental aid, legal coercion, and military might, many of the tribes declared, "The hatchet shall be forever buried." Indians took up farming, leased land to ranchers, and began to see value in their children "learning to talk the language of the white people." As their social existence changed, their theory of self-governance, too, underwent major revision.[4]

For generations, the federal government executed treaties with tribal leaders, wringing concessions in exchange for a promise to be let alone or consulted over Indian affairs. Treaty provisions established U.S. jurisdiction over the tribes and periodically changed the size of tribal lands. When it no longer suited governmental interests or changed conditions could be cited, such deals were ignored, renegotiated, or abrogated. Once authorities stopped treating Indians as fully independent nations, they struggled with how to handle tribal claims of authority. Increasingly, representatives of conventional sovereignty perceived tribes in cultural terms, eyeing Indian efforts to preserve self-rule as a threat to the project of creating one American people and authoritative law.

As best they could, tribes resisted encroachments, with resistance sometimes taking the form of legal writing. Native peoples invoked natural law, American constitutional law, treaties, and ordinary laws in an effort to retain a measure of sovereignty. Letters, petitions, and memorials eventually gave way to instruments for alternative self-organization. Ironically, as Indians took up republican methods of protest, tribal governments increasingly resembled the conventional state governments from which they wished to remain independent.

The Civil War ushered in the next phase of domination and resistance. When hostilities between the North and South broke open, each of the Five Tribes decided to throw in its lot with the Confederacy—some tribes more grudgingly than others. A number of leading figures in Indian Territory had owned slaves, who made up nearly 14 percent of the population. Shared borders, kindred economic interests, aggressive courting by the Confederacy's Bureau of Indian Affairs, and distrust of the federal government pushed the tribes toward the South. These miscalculations gave the United States grounds to become more suspicious of Indian sovereignty and to reconsider the terms of its relationship with the native peoples after cessation of hostilities.

During the summer of 1866, representatives for each tribe negotiated peace treaties with the United States. These instruments preserved but sharply curtailed Indian self-rule. The 1866 treaties contained similar conditions: abolishing slavery and granting property rights to freedmen, ceding lands in the western part of Indian Territory to Kansas tribes, and exacting permission for the construction of railroads across Indian Territory. Each tribe acknowledged the supremacy of the U.S. Constitution and federal laws. The agreements created a General Council to make laws for Indian Territory at annual sessions called by the superintendent of Indian affairs or special sessions called by the secretary of the interior. The Council's legislative authority was limited to certain subjects, such as relations between tribes and freedmen, the administration of justice, and common defense and safety. In a brute reminder of federal oversight, the president of the United States reserved the authority to suspend any law enacted by the Council.[5]

More serious plans to fuse the various Indian republics into a single political unit would soon be formulated. In 1870, prominent tribal leaders met at Okmulgee and drafted a constitution for Indian Territory. Encouraged by federal authorities, the gatherings in fall and winter occurred under the auspices of existing treaties. The president of the General Council appointed a committee "to advise a permanent organization of the Indian Territory as contemplated in the treaties of 1866." A day or two later, the committee issued a report recommending the writing of a constitution, "republican in form, with due regard for the rights of each tribe under existing treaties."[6]

The Okmulgee Constitution produced by the committee envisioned a "confederacy" that preserved the integrity of "[e]ach of the nations" entering the union. At this point, tribal leaders still contemplated "a purely Indian Government" that would afford "better protection of their rights, the improvement of themselves, and the preservation of their race." One provision ensured that "no right of property or lands, or funds owned by any one nation shall be in any manner invaded by citizens of another nation; and . . . the rights of each of these nations to its lands, funds and all other property shall remain the sole and distinct property of such nation." Other features of the constitution established the principles of divided government and legislative representation based on tribal population. A governor would head the executive branch, and a thirteen-point Declaration of Rights afforded every citizen of an Indian nation rights resembling those of U.S. citizenship.

Though a dramatic exercise of popular sovereignty in its own right, the Okmulgee Constitution failed to secure the necessary support of two-thirds of the Indian population. The Chickasaws refused to assent to the Okmulgee Constitution because it did not guarantee equal representation of the tribes in the legislative branch. Even so, that deliberative exercise proved to be a catalyzing experience. It demonstrated that the system of separate Indian republics, each with its own laws (and overseen by U.S. law), remained unsatisfactory to many inhabitants.

Meanwhile, more vigorous efforts to reorganize the affairs of the region commenced in Washington. In his 1871 State of the Union address, President Ulysses S. Grant called for the formation of a territorial government in Indian Territory. President Grant urged territorial governance as a logical extension of existing Indian policy. Formal political integration would facilitate the federal goal of civilizing native peoples. Tribes had been "induced to settle upon reservations, to cultivate the soil, to perform productive labor of various kinds, and to partially accept civilization." He hoped that federal policy cared for the Indians sufficiently to "induce those still pursuing their old habits of life to embrace the only opportunity which is left them to avoid extermination."[7]

While President Grant insisted that "every right guaranteed to the Indian by treaty" ought to be observed, he hinted at a broader plan: "Such a course might in time be the means of collecting most of the Indians now between the Missouri and the Pacific and south of the British possessions into one Territory or one State." A year later, the president again justified the creation of a formal territory as a legal enclave to protect native interests, within the context of a broader policy of assimilation. He described the change as a transitional one, intended "to protect the Indians from the inroads of whites for a term of years, until they become sufficiently advanced in the arts and civilization to guard their own rights, and from the disposal of the lands held by them for the same period."[8]

Indian anxiety over the future increased with every federal plan to integrate them into the polity like ordinary citizens. In 1874, Congress created a commission to determine whether the inhabitants of Indian Territory were ready for full territorial status. When the commission recommended implementation of President Grant's proposal, "[t]his caused a greater outburst of oratory and memorials by the Indians than any succeeding act of Congress in relation to Indian Territory during the next twenty years." On January 20, 1875, a convention of Cherokees signed a memorial bearing 4,000 signatures protesting the commission's recommendation. The Osage Nation, too, charged the United States with bad faith.

Congressional plans to reorganize the region appeared to be another blow to Indian sovereignty. Some complained that the commission had acted at the behest of corporate railroad interests, exploiting treaty terms for profit. Others objected that the piecemeal dispossession of Indians served as the unstated motive. At all events, tribal leaders saw efforts in Washington to move toward territorial status as an exercise in domination. If Indians did not seize a more active role in governance, decisions about political reorganization would be made for them.

Additional factors multiplied Indian fears of legalized extinction. Enforcement of the federal law did little to deter white squatters, who asserted control over unassigned lands through "an elaborate choreography of invasion, expulsion, and reinvasion." Settlers saw themselves as asserting their natural rights to land and liberty. Designations of land for Indians on paper proved to be no impediment to practitioners of frontier sovereignty. Indian Territory, roughly the size of South Carolina or Indiana, contained arable land, open areas for grazing, timber, coal, and gold. These natural resources made the region a desirable destination. Once lawbreakers began to work the earth, the ceaseless logic of pioneer sovereignty often led authorities to ratify encroachments on Indian lands.[9]

The growing presence of slaves freed by the tribes, war refugees, and black settlers exacerbated the threat to Indian identity. Dreams of a black homeland, nurtured by the Freedmen's Oklahoma Immigration Association, helped to triple the region's black population between 1870 and 1890. Migrants founded twenty-nine all-black towns and one colony, with two of the largest towns—Boley and Clearwater—located in Indian Territory. These highly visible experiments in race-based sovereignty, fueled by public calls for black migration, enhanced native peoples' worries about black colonization.[10]

Changes in federal law played perhaps the largest role in fostering a fear of Indian extinction. National officials decided to move decisively against tribal rule in the name of civilizing native peoples and integrating them into American society. In 1887 Congress passed the Dawes Act, which directed the apportionment of estates held collectively by the Five Tribes. The federal law forced Indians to register for individual shares of the land and seek U.S. citizenship. Allotment promised to replace Indians' own property regimes with the Anglo-American system. Although the primary goal was to create farmer-citizens out of the Indians, the law also served other objectives. It opened Indian Territory to settlement by non-Indians in an effort to satisfy the clamor for frontier sovereignty. Some lawmakers also envisioned the relocation of former slaves in the region as a solution to the problem of wandering and dislocated freedmen. The Curtis Act of 1898 abolished tribal governments and tribal courts, effective March 4, 1906, and made all Indians subject to federal jurisdiction. The American legal order would tolerate Indian beliefs and ways of life, but now it moved more aggressively toward a single national law and conception of individual citizenship to bind all citizens and territorial inhabitants.[11]

It became painfully obvious that the form of government in Indian Territory had to change, but it remained uncertain what the place would become. Oklahoma Territory had been carved out of Indian Territory in 1870. By the turn of the century, the question was no longer whether Indian Territory would be admitted to the Union as a state, but whether there would be a single state or two-state solution.

The very structure of state constitutionalism assumed the validity and supremacy of the 1787 Constitution. Congress had been granted the power to admit new states to the Union. In practice, the process typically involved a groundswell of popular support in a territory, followed by an enabling act passed by Congress authorizing further lawmaking and ratification proceedings. State constitutionalism and pioneer sovereignty share origins, however, since the official acquisition and organization of lands often served as the impetus for frontier lawmaking. By the same token, state constitutionalism would be impossible without the migrants who, subscribing to their own theories of law, populated an underorganized region.[12]

Calls for "mass meetings" over the statehood question began to multiply. One such prominent call issued by leading citizens of Indian Territory on February 3, 1900, deplored, "Uncertainty prevails everywhere, and with reference to everything." Those who agitated for a change in political status painted a dire portrait of the breakdown of law:

> In the administration of the law, a very chaos prevails. Of the five Indian systems, some survive with powers abridged and without judicial functions, and some with fragmentary judicial functions whose existence adds to the general confusion. Monstrous incongruities are patent everywhere. The law provides how a man may acquire a fee simple title to property in

towns, yet, without a judicial hearing, he may be deprived of the right to
live upon it.[13]

Given this "most distressful state," citizens sought "recourse [in]
traditional American methods: to meet in convention assembled, there
to agree upon remedies for existing ills and concert lines of action and
perfect organization." They urged "the people of the Indian Territory,
without regard to race or political affiliations, to meet in mass meeting
at every place in the country . . . maturely to consider their interest in
the light of the present situation." Their call for political renewal was
guided by a confidence that "the history of our country teaches us that
demands, founded in justice and urged with moderation, but with
continuity of thought and action, have never yet failed of success."

Indian activists who worked for statehood parted ways from traditionalists willing to use all means at their disposal to protect tribal sovereignty. While dissatisfaction provoked some leading citizens to take
up republican methods, unrest among traditionalists led not to "moderation" but rather to open confrontation. Fiercely opposed to allotment, full-blood Indians gathered at the Hickory Ground to plot ways
of obstructing the work of the Dawes Commission, which had been
charged with dissolving tribal governments and carrying out the partition and redistribution of Indian land. Chitto Harjo, an eloquent Creek
known to whites as "Crazy Snake," emerged as a leader of a more aggressive instantiation of Indian sovereignty. Harjo would later testify
before Congress: "I am informed and believe it to be true that some citizens of the United States have title to land that was given to my fathers
and my people by the Government. If it was given to me, what right has
the United States to take it from me without first asking my consent?"
If "ancient agreements and treaties wherein you promised to take care
of me and my people" would not be kept, he warned, then more drastic
measures had to be taken to protect Indian authority.[14]

At its peak, the Snake movement counted some 5,000 adherents
among the Five Tribes, as well as sympathetic freedmen. Full-bloods,
who comprised Harjo's most loyal followers, proclaimed him heredi-
tary chief. Harjo convened the national council of the House of Kings
and House of Warriors, which announced the reestablishment of ancient laws and courts recognized in the Creek Treaty of 1832. The
Snakes passed laws prohibiting Creeks from hiring whites or leasing

land to them on pain of a fine and fifty lashes. Not only did members of the movement encourage Indians to refuse their individual allotments, they also threatened to whip supporters of allotment, seized property, and destroyed survey equipment. Tribal leaders, who sought a moderate path, had difficulty suppressing the Snakes without eroding their own support, so they turned to the federal government for help. Things came to a head in 1901, when troops arrested scores of Snakes during a bloodless "uprising." For his defense of tribal sovereignty, Harjo became remembered as the old Snake with the "courage to defy/ The powerful makers of his fate."[15]

Agitation for political transformation did not rest with the native population. The white populace in Indian Territory had exploded in a short period of time through legal and illegal settlement, and by 1900, whites vastly outnumbered Indians 6:1. White citizens chafed under the existing patchwork legal order in which they lacked representation in Congress. Courts open to non-Indians had come only recently to the Territory, and tribal governments could exercise no jurisdiction over non-Indians.

The Honorable Yancey Lewis, a Texas native appointed United States judge for Indian Territory, presided over a convention on February 22, 1900. Expressing the concerns of many white citizens, Judge Lewis described a political system in flux: "[T]he old order is changed, but the new order has not come about; and in that gulf between the old and new, the Indian and non-citizen suffer alike, and suffer grievously." Lewis called the gathering "spontaneous combustion."[16] He spoke of "more than four hundred thousand people, breathing the air of American institutions, trained in the history and knowledge of our liberty . . . [starting] a movement to meet the demands and needs of the situation." Though "desiring to obtain no jot of that to which the Indian is justly entitled," attendees deplored the multiple taxation regimes of the many tribes and urged representation in Congress like other American territories.

A breakthrough occurred when Green McCurtain, principal chief of the Choctaw Nation, called a meeting of the chief executives of the Five Civilized Tribes. The chief executives met in Eufaula from May 21 to 23, 1903, to discuss whether they should support a separate state and if so, on what terms. An ingenious strategy emerged to preserve Indian authorship of their future. According to this bifurcated approach,

Indians would design a constitution, but whites and nonwhites would have a shared role during the deliberation stage. Tribal leaders recommended that each nation send delegates to an international constitutional convention. There, native people would draft a constitution for a separate state to be formed from Indian country. Noncitizens of Indian Territory could, if they wished, hold a separate convention to ratify the constitution, and any disputes might be resolved through conference. Each tribe agreed to memorialize Congress and seek the aid of civic organizations in stopping annexation with Oklahoma Territory.[17]

A formal call to all "Loyal, Patriotic Citizens" came from W. C. Rogers and Green McCurtain, principal chiefs of the Cherokee and Choctaw Nations, on or about July 1, 1905. Among the urgent reasons for a gathering of the people was the federal government's lifting of restrictions on settlement in Indian Territory and the allotment of Indian land. Deriding awkward and unresponsive rule by Washington, they complained, "[I]t is not American or equitable, nor necessary to longer govern the aforesaid country, wholly by Federal Government." Only a robust form of local governance more sensitive to the interests of ordinary people could satisfy their grievances. They insisted that the time had come for the inhabitants of the territory to be "endowed with the dignities and privileges of an American State." They announced August 21, 1905, as the day delegates should gather for the purpose of "drafting and framing a grand and up to date constitution." Though organizers faced long odds, some of the best and brightest men in Indian Territory believed they had nothing to lose and possibly something to gain by taking fellow citizens through this deliberative exercise.[18]

The Sequoyah Constitution would serve multiple functions for the native population, even though it might never become law. Importantly, the document would collect long-standing grievances and address fears of cultural erosion. Furthermore, the process of writing and debating the constitution would constitute civic training, preparing the native population for civic responsibility and engagement while showing outsiders the inhabitants of Indian Territory were ready for self-governance as American citizens. Even if the Sequoyah movement failed, the people of Indian Territory could still set the terms of debate over the unresolved question of statehood. Finally, having mobilized the local population, the document could be leveraged for partisan advantage.

The Sequoyah Convention: Party Politics, Progressivism

The Sequoyah Convention was gaveled to order in Muskogee on August 21, 1905. Pleasant Porter, principal chief of the Creeks, presided over the convention, along with Charles N. Haskell, a white man considered a friend of the Indians. For Porter, who had long battled conservative elements in his tribe, a new state had to replace a traditional tribal system on the threshold of extinction. Of the full-bloods for whom political change "came too soon," he lamented their "want of hope," as "there is no life in the people that have lost their institutions." Porter had earlier urged his people to accept allotment. "The effort to resuscitate and reestablish a government administered by ourselves thus far has proved futile, and the outlook is extremely unfavorable to success in ever again recovering even the most limited form of tribal government," he diagnosed. "Assuming this to be true, it behooves us to cast about and find what is best for us to do." To save the people, leaders should not cling to the remnants of tribal governments "bound to perish," but had to create new institutions worthy of support in a "businesslike way." Gaining the full rights and immunities of U.S. citizenship constituted the last, best strategy to avoid extinction. Participation in state government would show that "[t]hough our tribal organization is fading away, we will be transformed as a potent factor, an element within the body of Christian civilization."[19]

Though Indian peoples elected some three hundred delegates and alternates at conventions in twenty-six districts, roughly a fifth attended sessions regularly. After two days of meetings and inspiring orations, the Sequoyah Convention adjourned to allow the Constitution Committee to commence its work. With W. W. Hastings of Tahlequah as chair, the Constitution Committee split up into eleven subcommittees to deal with different parts of the constitution. The committee added William Murray, a white lawyer for the Chickasaw nation.[20]

One of the talented politicians who worked on the Sequoyah Constitution was Robert Latham Owen, part Cherokee and raised in Virginia. Owen had relocated to Indian Territory with his mother and gained a reputation for populist politics in the Democratic Party. From 1885 to 1889, he filled the post of United States Indian agent for the Five Tribes. During Owen's tenure, he helped draft legislation conferring U.S. citizenship on every Indian residing in Indian Territory. Trained as a lawyer, he held a leadership role in the bar association in the territory and helped organize the first national bank in Muskogee. At the convention, Owen gave a resounding speech and threw himself into committee work.[21]

The Sequoyah Constitution emerged primarily through the work of Murray, Owen, Haskell, Hastings, and John R. Thomas. On August 29, the Constitution Committee discussed and approved the preamble, along with a name for the proposed state. After a "hot discussion" during which participants entertained suggestions to name the proposed state after Indianola or Tecumseh, the committee decided to honor the Cherokee who captured words. Members of the convention avoided the warlike symbolism of Tecumseh, who died on the battlefield against the federal government, in favor of the more placid connotations associated with Sequoyah, who developed a writing system and spent much of his life making cultural links among nations.[22]

On September 8, delegates adopted the draft constitution by unanimous vote. All told, the Sequoyah Convention lasted twenty-one days, producing a highly detailed constitution and a map dividing Indian Territory into forty-eight counties. To commemorate the occasion, Pleasant Porter issued a proclamation. In it, he described the proposed State of Sequoyah by turns as the fulfillment of an ancient promise made by the white man, the natural fruits of cultural and political assimilation, and the ultimate test of the good faith of the American people. "From time immemorial," Porter wrote, "the Indians as a heritage of the original inhabitants have been promised a state, an empire of their own." Driven west by successive invasions, the Indians were forced to settle in contested lands. They had "taken on the dress, the customs, and the religion of the white man and they welcome him as a brother." Now, "the national government must grant us separate statehood or make a confession."[23]

Though it was doubtful that the Sequoyah Constitution would ever become implemented, it nevertheless served a significant expressive function for Indian peoples. Not only did the document gather native rage against the dominant political order, but, like the Confederate Constitution, its authorship was motivated by a collective desire to preserve a fading lifestyle. Again and again the theme of cultural preservation had emerged at the convention. Haskell read a poem by a Delaware citizen into the record:

> Sweet the solemn intonation, sad the chimes so faint so low,
> Marking the time for dying nations once supreme, now fading so.
> . . .
> Ere we reach the sunset station, Hearts pure son of love proclaim.
> All glory to the dying nations to heaven and nature's own refrain.[24]

The framers of the Sequoyah Constitution believed that the anticipated destruction of tribal forms facilitated the creation of a conventional state. As Porter reminded those assembled before him: "[O]ur present governments shall not be annihilated but transformed into material for a nobly builded state. 'Thus shall we have life not death.'" The theme of statehood as a means of cultural preservation later reappeared in the framers' memorial to Congress, when proponents stressed that "the people of Sequoyah compose a community, separate and distinct from any other on earth, with a different history, different associations, and different sentiments, and with different ideals and hopes."

Observers, too, saw the deliberative process as a method of confronting irresistible political and social forces. The *Vinita Daily Chieftain* described "the spectacle of half-a-hundred old warriors, picked from the Five Nations, together with their followers," as "a last endeavor to save themselves from being lost in the onward roll of civilization." The Sequoyah Constitution would be a final Indian masterpiece, "worthy of the painter's brush or the poet's pen."[25]

Sequoyah's supporters drew on several sources of law justifying a new constitution. As "people of pure American stock," they insisted upon "the natural right which is inherent in every great body of human beings to govern themselves." They buttressed this claim by asserting "the character of our people, being educated, industrious, thrifty, law-abiding, and learned in the art of self government." In so doing, they drew on civic republicanism's emphasis on virtue and knowledge as capacities for self-governance. Advocates cited older treaties and laws that recognized the tribes' "unrestricted right of self-government." These legal sources included an American treaty with France, which contemplated the formation of states out of the land "as soon as possible," the post–Civil War treaties, and other agreements and laws promising Indians that their lands would not be incorporated into any territory or state without their "free and full consent."[26]

What the convention ultimately produced did not closely match leaders' calls for Indian independence and cultural survival. The distance between public rhetoric and constitutional architecture was jarring. In proposing a conventional state, albeit one designed by native peoples and primarily populated by them, participants gave up the possibility of an independent Indian nation based purely on tribal forms of organization. Instead, facing legal extinction, Sequoyah leaders dramatically downscaled their ambitions. Draftsmen engaged the potent language of self-determination, but the form of popular sovereignty the constitution actually created was subordinate to the U.S. Constitution and subject to approval by the federal government. They did not purport to reconstitute a national people. The constitution disclaimed any "purpose of setting up or organizing a State government until such time as the Congress of the United States shall enact a law for the admission of the Indian Territory as a State." Unlike Indian Stream or Icaria or even the Confederacy, Sequoyah would make no attempt at exercising sovereign power without the express approval of national leaders.

As a matter of form and substance, the government that emerged from this process resembled that of any other conventional state or territory. What, then, explains the disconnect between the people's motivations and their actual design? Part of it had to do with the fact that while indigenous populations faced bleak circumstances, they did not intend a new state to replace any tribal forms that survived. Another reason involved the intended audience. Indian authors crafted the instrument to appeal to white territorial citizens and authorities in Washington. Believing legislative approval already to be a tall task, supporters of the new state went to great pains to minimize opponents' ability to characterize their actions as reflecting racial chauvinism, tribal animosity, or traitorous designs.

Though portrayed as a cultural exercise to Indians, in fact, the constitution created no formal mechanisms to ensure Indian survival. Unlike the Okmulgee Constitution, the Sequoyah Constitution preserved no distinctly native organizations, institutions, or customs. In the place of tribal institutions, customs, and practices, the instrument created state and local forms of governance. Instead of relying on explicit guarantees of Indian sovereignty, Indian interests would have to be protected by governmental arrangements familiar to the general population. When it came to legislators and judges, the principle of tribal representation was exchanged for one based on geographic representation. Rather than promoting group rights, the constitution enumerated individual rights.

If the law served native peoples in the new state, it would be because they happened to populate the region and organized sufficiently to influence its politics, not because the law openly protected the Indian way of life. On this point, the Sequoyah Constitution differed from the Confederate Constitution, a leading model for cultural sovereignty. Without written safeguards of important institutions or customs, Indian influence might wane merely through a shift in demographics or due to party politics. But it was a risk that leaders of the movement were willing to take. As faith in tribal organizations became relocated to state forms of governance, civic republicanism's conception of freedom as a participatory ideal triumphed over the goals and technologies of cultural sovereignty. To a large extent, then, Sequoyah's leadership envisioned that tribal mindsets and affiliations would be traded for a new civic identity in which being Indian also meant embracing other sovereigns and broader notions of political community. Going through the process of writing and debating a constitution helped to prepare native people for these attitudes and habits of American citizenship.[27]

The people of Indian Territory may have lacked the Icarians' universalist ambitions, but they shared a willingness to operate within the established federal order. Indian leaders opposed more aggressive acts of defiance urged by traditionalists, believing them to be counterproductive. Instead, they embraced the vernacular of civic republicanism and adopted the tools of mainstream constitutionalism. Although tribal sovereignty and transplanted European forms of self-rule differed in genesis and substance, the Sequoyah leadership deliberately blurred these differences as they signaled their desire to be treated as part of a single "American people." With ambitions downscaled and tactics moderated, delegates pursued legal creativity within the parameters of regional demands and party politics.

Ordinary politics dictated the substance of the Sequoyah Constitution so much that its provisions tracked the spirit of Progressivism, the agenda of the Democratic Party, and a consensus over regional interests. The constitution reflected Progressivism's critique of laissez-faire economic policy, as well as reforms long sought by Populists. As it ascended, the Progressive Movement inherited many of Populism's causes when that agrarian movement dissipated. Like the Populists, Progressives wished to curb rampant corporate behavior, empower workers against abusive employment practices, and increase direct democracy. Progressives broadened their concerns to appeal more to urban centers by reforming education and the legal system, exposing political corruption, and protecting the vulnerable from the excesses of industrial democracy.[28]

On questions of sexual and racial equality, the constitution reflected the ambivalence and conservatism of many native people and, more generally, the Democratic Party. The political community envisioned by the constitution was inclusive of Indians, but less congenial toward blacks and women. As to women's rights, Owen actually pushed for a provision extending the right to vote to women. That measure failed, as Sequoyah hesitated to join the states of Wyoming, Colorado, Utah, and Idaho, all of which had recently granted women the franchise. The convention did pass a resolution deferring the matter to a duly elected legislature. The Sequoyah Constitution codified this compromise, directing the General Assembly, "at the first session thereof, [to] enact laws to extend the right of suffrage to women of rightful age, and otherwise qualified."

On the question of race, delegates preserved the status quo. Endorsing the logic of *Plessy v. Ferguson,* which approved Louisiana's policy of "separate but equal" rail cars, the Sequoyah Constitution segregated public schools on the basis of race. Ordinary laws in Oklahoma Territory already did so. Resistance to racial equality grew out of a legacy of slavery in Indian Territory and the cultural outlook of movement leaders, as well as strategic calculations in seeking broad support for Sequoyah. While the Creeks and Seminoles made strides in welcoming freedmen as equals, other tribes struggled mightily with discrimination and violence against freedmen.[29] Indians and freed slaves intermarried, but few territorial citizens hurried to make progress in the realm of civil rights.

Expressing a healthy skepticism of government, the Sequoyah Constitution began with a bill of rights. Chief among those was the right of the people to "alter and abolish their Constitution and form of government whenever they may deem it necessary to their safety and happiness" so long as doing so did not interfere with the U.S. Constitution. This language mirrored the Okmulgee Constitution, which spoke of the people's "inalienable right to alter, reform or abolish their form of government." It also resembled such state constitutions as Massachusetts and Virginia, which codified Americans' revolutionary legacy.[30]

If the convention charted a cautiously exclusionary course on matters dealing with sex and race, a number of institutional innovations and regulations would be seen as forward-looking for the time. Delegates perceived direct democracy to be the best defense of native ways and agrarian existence. All judges—from the highest court in the state to the lowliest justice of the peace—would be elected, a leftover tenet of Jacksonian Democracy. Each of the three members of the Sequoyah Supreme Court would have to represent a Grand Division within the state. The business of the courts, like that of the legislature, would be subject to regular political control.

In another departure from the federal experience, the Sequoyah Constitution guaranteed that "[t]he courts of justice shall be open to every person, and remedy offered for every injury to person, property, or reputation." In comparison, a right of access to the courts had not been explicitly mentioned in the U.S. Constitution, but would later be derived by judges from the First Amendment and Due Process Clause. In addition to familiar procedural protections, a criminal defendant would be entitled to "the names of the witnesses and an abstract of the evidence adduced against him" before the grand jury. Some trial rights reflected a concern for the working class and the poor. An accused was guaranteed bail except for capital offenses. Citizens could not be imprisoned for private debt.[31]

Not only did the drafters of the Sequoyah Constitution strive to preserve an agrarian ideal, they also tried to anticipate some of the social problems that had undermined democracy in other states. A number of Sequoyah's leaders also belonged to the Democratic Party, and they believed that a Progressive constitution would help the party to gain an advantage over its Republican counterpart. It could bolster Democrats' case that they were on the side of the common man, while casting Republicans as the lackeys of oil and big business. But this meant that any ethical impulse in the new constitution would have to be constrained by pragmatic considerations. Compromise rather than consistency would have to be the touchstone. Moreover, unlike stronger forms of ethical politics, Sequoyah's leadership did not cast their positions on political membership (e.g., race and sex equality) in stone, but instead understood them to be revisable on the basis of ordinary politics.

Buffeted by party politics, the Sequoyah Constitution comprised a hodgepodge of reforms. A number of the provisions defied the prevailing economic order—without going so far as to demand the public ownership and redistribution of goods. Drafters hoped to return moral considerations to economic affairs, not purge the polity of undesirables or restructure the economy. In responding to voters' wrath against big business, the document regulated corporations extensively. As the principal drafters later revealed, these provisions were "largely taken from the recent constitution of Virginia." Like the Commonwealth of Virginia's 1902 Constitution, the Sequoyah Constitution established a three-person State Corporation Commission appointed by the governor and confirmed by the Senate. The commission was charged with the additional duty of supervising and regulating "all transportation and transmission companies doing business in this State," and given the power to set charges and rates. To fulfill their functions, commissioners had "the powers and authority of a court of record," lending the entity a quasi-judicial character.[32]

Codifying a growing suspicion against monopolies and the avaricious behavior of corporations, another provision directed the General Assembly to "enact laws preventing all trusts, combinations and monopolies, inimical to the public welfare." Proponents of Sequoyah went further than Virginians by compelling corporations to "fix uniform maximum and minimum prices for said articles of commerce and common consumption and use, offered for sale in this State." They outlawed price discrimination, making it unlawful to "demand from the people of this State a greater or higher price for any article of commerce of common consumption" than that charged the inhabitants of any other state.[33]

Banks, too, found themselves a target of populist ire. Banks doing business in the state had to be approved under a general banking law and "cease all banking operations within twenty years from the time of its organization" unless the General Assembly extended the time. To deter rapacious lending practices, the constitution defined usury as a "greater rate of interest than ten per centum per annum." Usurious lenders faced a penalty of "double the amount of the entire interest so charged."[34]

Members of the Sequoyah convention deployed the higher-law tradition to empower workers against employers' exploitative practices. They banned employers from demanding that workers release them from liability for injuries as a condition of their employment. Such contracts or work conditions were deemed "null and void" as a matter of public policy. To protect workers against crushing debt, "[t]wo months of current wages, for personal service, shall not be subject to garnishment." To minimize corporate influence on access to justice, drafters disabled the legislature from "limit[ing] the amount to be recovered for injuries resulting in death, or for injuries to person or property" or extending special privileges, franchises, or immunities to corporations. A separate provision prevented the legislature from postponing, releasing, or "in any way diminish[ing]" any obligation or liability of a corporation.[35]

Codifying Progressive concerns about the exploitation of children, the Sequoyah Constitution forbade employers from using "the labor of children under twelve years of age in factories and workshops." More stringent provisions regulated the mining industry. Except to perform clerical duties, boys under the age of fourteen, and women or girls of any age were barred from being employed by companies extracting coal or iron, or working other mines.[36]

Education proved to be another area where Indian people's values accorded with that of the Progressive agenda. The constitution declared it the duty of the state to "provide for its citizens the best possible preparation for intelligent and virtuous citizenship." To cultivate the "general intelligence and virtue" necessary to self-governance, the state promised "free public education for all persons between the ages of six and twenty-one," and education for the deaf, dumb, and blind. It directed the general assembly to create "a university of the first class." Among the Indian population, a quality education had long been prized to "give our children the power and knowledge to act for our people, and make them able to defend . . . our rights and our heritage." Deliberations over the Okmulgee Constitution had earlier been marked by similar considerations.[37]

Drafters made clear that any ethical impulse arose from a consensus, a cross section of ideologies and faiths. The constitution did not draw inspiration from any particular religious tradition; it also went further than many jurisdictions in separating church from state. It ensured "the rights of conscience" and guaranteed that the state would not give "preference" to any religion. Joining states like Georgia, Florida, and Missouri—and going beyond the demands of the U.S. Constitution—the Sequoyah Constitution prohibited financial aid "directly or indirectly" to religious groups. Troubled by the possibility of religious control of public education, it unequivocally barred state and local authorities from allowing religious groups to "control any part of the school funds" or providing financial "support [to] any sectarian school."

Ratification: Deliberation, Discipline, Partisanship

Once delegates returned home, the Sequoyah Constitution was submitted for approval through initiative. According to ancient traditions, tribal government had to take account of the voice of the people in the resolution of the most serious affairs. Under Cherokee clan law, consensus was essential to tribal action. Some tribes, such as the Chickasaw, often referred serious matters directly to their people. This principle dovetailed with the Anglo-American higher-law tradition, incorporated in the protocols of the Five Tribes for altering their constitutions.[38]

Campaigning over Sequoyah began in earnest almost as soon as Porter gaveled the proceedings to a close. Framers of the constitution fanned out across the plains, giving speeches and urging residents to turn out at the polls. Proponents marshaled every argument at their disposal to bring territorial residents into the fold. To social conservatives worried about rampant vices in the territories, they claimed that a separate state would be best able to implement the federal policy of prohibition. In Democratic circles, pro-Sequoyah forces argued that partisan interests aligned in favor of independence. To reach individuals concerned about the plight of indigenous populations, they astutely appealed to America's international reputation "as a beach light to all the nations of the world," suggesting that approval of the state would be seen as an act of democratic justice "to three-fourths of a million of its children in Sequoyah." Fulfilling the government's promises to Indian people would bring "honor before all the world."

A pamphlet published by the Campaign Committee of the Constitutional Convention summarized key arguments in favor of separate statehood. All of the arguments were grounded in the fundamental right of the people to "control their own affairs and make laws for their own government" as "God given, inalienable, and indestructible." The brochure went on to rebut opponents' main arguments. In response to the concern that Sequoyah would have an "eccentric, strange and peculiar" boundary, proponents pointed out Maine, Maryland, and Rhode Island as states with even more irregular shapes. To the objection that a one-state solution would be more powerful and efficient, advocates noted that four senators were better than two and that "it would be more economical to conduct a conservative, economical administration of a smaller state than be joined with Oklahoma, which would rush into extravagance" for public institutions "already established." Any suggestions that a one-state solution would more speedily lead to statehood should not be entertained, for such proposals had already languished in Congress for years. Supporters of Sequoyah did not flinch from exploiting racial sentiments against the joint state movement. As Owen argued in the *Muskogee Phoenix,* the people should not unite with Oklahoma Territory in part because "Oklahomans are from Kansas where colored children attend school with the whites."[39]

Conventions sprang up to deliberate the merits of the Sequoyah Constitution. Tribal deliberations favored Sequoyah. In short order, the national councils of the Cherokee, Chickasaw, and Choctaw Nations passed resolutions endorsing the proposed state.[40] Tribal unanimity, however, fell just beyond the grasp of the movement. The Creek Nation did not approve separate statehood, but instead, after heated discussions, passed a resolution endorsing the idea of single statehood.

Opponents organized meetings to castigate the draft constitution and publicize the merits of a one-state solution. Some argued that the convention was unauthorized, implying that the U.S. Constitution foreclosed popular constitutionalism without preapproval. Others resented Indian efforts to "dictate" the terms of statehood, for "the white man has developed the territory, created the taxable values, and will have the greatest part of the burden of the expenses." Overlooking the actual substance of the constitution, the *Oklahoman* dismissed the Muskogee convention as evidence of "Indian supremacy." Its editors predicted that "Indians will get their opportunity to vote while the white brothers who are assisting will grab the offices." Those who favored joint statehood urged citizens to stay away from the polls or ignore the movement entirely.[41]

For their part, supporters of Sequoyah discredited these "mass meetings, called conventions" as poorly attended and unrepresentative. "[N]o citizens were invited," they pointed out, "and . . . no citizens were permitted to participate unless they were known to have the same peculiar views as the promoters of the joint State propaganda." When a territorial judge announced that statehood proponents were unwelcome in his courtroom and ordered a Marietta crowd to be driven from a meeting hall, Murray planted himself near the judge's quarters and flayed him verbally.[42]

Average residents of Indian Territory appeared to be more supportive of Sequoyah than elites. Murray later reported that the proposal had difficulty generating favor "among all the newspapers, and professional men generally, but it was intensely popular with the Indians and farmers." A number of white residents had migrated from Southern or border states, with many feeling a greater kinship to the native people of Indian Territory rather than to the denizens of Oklahoma Territory. The futures of the white yeoman farmer and the Native American, both facing extinction, had been successfully yoked together by the constitutional vernacular of the day.[43]

Proponents of Sequoyah had reasons to celebrate the results. With some 75 percent of eligible voters having cast ballots, 59,279 favored the Constitution, and by extension the idea of separate statehood, while 9,073 rejected it. The people had spoken. Yet it remained to be seen how federal authorities would interpret this attempt at state constitutionalism.[44]

The movement's leaders now calibrated their message for the ears of congressional leaders. In support of a two-state solution, Sequoyah's leaders tried to capitalize on whites' preference for the domesticated Indian. To illustrate their capacity for self-discipline, the Five Tribes emphasized their cultural and political differences with the "wild tribes" of Oklahoma Territory. These integrated Indians "object[ed] to being classified with the reservation Indians," who "have been slow to take part in political affairs." Because the Indians of Oklahoma Territory had no experience in matters of government, they "are possibly not qualified to assume the responsibilities of United States citizenship." In contrast, "[o]ur friends in Congress must not forget that, comparatively speaking, there are but few full bloods in Indian territory, and that a great majority of them are thoroughly capable of taking care of themselves and of their own affairs. The Indians of the Five Tribes have never been reservation Indians; they have always been self-sustaining."[45]

Fear of racial discrimination in a consolidated state dovetailed with these perceived social differences. Because the people of Oklahoma "have been in contact with the wild tribes only (necessarily extremely ignorant and unlearned in all of the refinements of life, and who have been degraded by the open saloons of Oklahoma), . . . [t]here would be a strong tendency to discriminate against the Indians of Indian Territory, both socially and as to their property and civil rights." Thus, a separate state of Sequoyah preserved the cultural ideal of the assimilated, industrious Indian even as it guaranteed the fair treatment of Indian people.[46]

Recognition of the proposed state would enhance citizens' ability to make laws, which they had already begun to do to deal with the many problems arising in Indian Territory. Among the complaints about territorial rule:

> Hundreds of thousands of our children are growing up without proper means of education, to become criminals, because of ignorance, when we are willing to pay for their schooling, if we only had legal means of providing for it. We have no way of caring for the insane. We have no way to care for the deaf, dumb, and blind. We have no way to care for the sick, the halt, the lame, or our pauper classes. We have no way to provide for the speedy hearing of criminal or civil cases. Our citizens accused languish in jail for long periods of time, waiting the administration of justice through the insufficient Federal courts, which exercise jurisdiction from small misdemeanors up to murder.

A delegation was appointed to present the people's petition for statehood to President Roosevelt. The president received the delegation but balked at the request for his support, citing the Republican Party's platform. Without his backing, the delegation turned to friends from neighboring states. In December 1905, Congressman Arthur Murphy of Missouri introduced House Resolution 79, "providing for the admission of the State of Sequoyah into the Union." Similar bills were introduced in the Senate. No action would ever be taken on these bills. Rather than endorse the Sequoyah movement's hard work, President Roosevelt announced his support for a one-state solution. Within weeks, Congress passed an enabling act authorizing a statehood convention.

Absorbing Tribal Sovereignty

A creature of conventional politics, the Sequoyah Constitution remained captive to majoritarian politics from beginning to end. In the final analysis, it would have been hard to expect a Republican president to act against the interests of his party, which feared that a two-state solution would produce two Democratic states. The territorial status quo facilitated Republican control through its patronage system. Republicans had dominated the early politics of the Twin Territories on the strength of its reputation as the party of Lincoln and by opening up the area to settlement through the Homestead Act. More recently, infighting between factions of the ruling party and local corruption eroded the party's historical advantages. Haskell, Murray, and Owen foresaw that inroads could be made with the electorate on behalf of the Democratic Party by assuming a leadership role in the statehood movement.[47]

Taking ownership of the Sequoyah Constitution, and later the Oklahoma Constitution, paid political dividends. Once the president staked out a position on the matter and Indian consent to some form of statehood had been secured, events rapidly aligned for Oklahoma's admission to the Union. But not before some partisan fireworks erupted over ratification. When the Oklahoma convention finished its work, President Roosevelt derided the length of the instrument as well as the corporate provisions carried over from the Sequoyah Constitution. Roosevelt was also reportedly incensed at the constitution's racial provisions, which defined the "negro race" as "all persons of African descent" and the "white race" to "include all other persons." Republicans urged him to work against ratification, predicting that the instrument would solidify the Democratic Party's hold on local politics.

The attorney general of the United States fired off a letter to the convention detailing the administration's objections to the constitution. Roosevelt also dispatched William Howard Taft to Oklahoma

City, where Taft assailed the Oklahoma Constitution as "Bourbanism and despotism, flavored with Socialism." "I would reject the constitution," Taft advised, "I would vote it down for it is no constitution at all." He called it "complicated beyond any constitution I have ever examined," especially compared to the U.S. Constitution, "a model of comprehensive diction and brevity." Taft pronounced the initiative and referendum provisions "more radical" than even Oregon's experiment allowing the people to make municipal policy. The corporate regulations appeared "so strict that they are likely to frighten foreign capital away."[48]

The constitution became a weapon against the Republican Party, one that Democrats brandished with delight. William Jennings Bryan, preparing for another run at the Oval Office, toured the area in support of the constitution. Speaking in the same hall where Taft delivered his remarks, Bryan called it "the best constitution in the United States," crafted by "wise" citizens. Because it contained improvements upon the federal Constitution along with "the corrections made necessary by the experience of other states," the Oklahoma Constitution embodied the considered judgment of the people.[49]

Haskell joined Bryan on some appearances. He excoriated Taft for appealing to "sectional prejudice" and for "his utter inability to appreciate the character of people to whom he was talking." Turning Taft's girth into a metaphor for the corrupt regime, Haskell declared, "I can tell the corpulent secretary that I would much prefer Bourbanism, populism and socialism to the regime of Africanism, carpetbagging and corporatism under which these territories have been laboring through the grace of the Republican party." All of the intolerable conditions of territorial life Haskell laid squarely at the feet of the party in power.

Republican machinations failed to derail the people's bid for statehood. Worse, opposition to the work of the convention further damaged the Republican brand in the eyes of voters. Having earlier attacked the Sequoyah proceedings, Republican resistance to the Oklahoma Constitution came off as self-interested obstruction of the people's right to self-determination. Going through another convention process scrubbed the Sequoyah Constitution of its connotations as the exclusive product of Indian authorship. The union of the two territories reduced lingering fears of Indian domination of state politics.

For these reasons, the Oklahoma convention process greatly improved the constitution's appeal to non-Indians in the territories and among members of Congress.

Oklahoma was admitted to the Union on November 16, 1907, completing a significant act of legal consolidation. Relatively unorganized lands now formally became an indispensable component of the constitutional order. Formerly ungovernable denizens of Indian and Oklahoma Territories had become integrated into the national community. For those who perceived tribal rule as a dangerous form of cultural sovereignty rather than a distinctive and legitimate form of politics in its own right, the creation of Oklahoma appeared to put to rest the Indian threat of political fragmentation. To a large extent, the demise of Sequoyah recalled the end of the Indian Stream Republic, where a democratic experiment at the edge of the legal order became absorbed by the logic and structure of conventional sovereignty. In both cases, the 1787 Constitution set the outer parameters for the formation of new civic identities, institutions, and influence. But in at least one respect, members of the Sequoyah movement could claim a victory that escaped the citizens of Indian Stream: they had an entire state to call their own.

A first set of elections that year ushered in rule by the Democratic Party, just as Republicans feared. The Democratic Party's combination of conservative positions on questions of race and sex, coupled with its identification with popular economic reforms, allowed the party to position itself as a reformist coalition of red and white men. Although the Indian people's hopes for Sequoyah may have been dashed, their labors had not been in vain. Through their constitution-writing efforts, native people and their white allies set the agenda on statehood. For years, national leaders had refused to alter the political status of Indian Territory until all the tribes gave their consent. Now, that had arguably occurred. From the start, participants portrayed the Sequoyah Constitution as an expression of Indian consent for legal reorganization consistent with the Atoka Agreement, with a strong preference for separate statehood. Porter, Haskell, and other leaders of the movement knew they faced almost certain failure, but they gambled that the writing exercise would generate sufficient attention to make regional concerns a congressional priority. They also hoped a productive political experience would calm Indians determined to resist any form of statehood. These two functions fulfilled by the Sequoyah Constitution—the first deliberative, and the second disciplinary—proved largely successful.[50]

More than just removing a roadblock to political development, the Indian independence movement shaped the legal and political institutions that displaced earlier forms of self-rule. While opponents hoped that the movement "has been almost forgotten," the Sequoyah Constitution proved to be so well considered and in synch with the prevailing sentiments of the region that it became incorporated into Oklahoma's original constitution when delegates met at Guthrie. As Haskell put it, "there were several differences, but very little of great consequence." This was as true of the regressive elements as it was of the progressive features. Despite the organized efforts of suffragists, the Oklahoma Constitution did not extend the franchise to women. Having received the imprimatur of national officials for the new state, the Oklahoma legislature also systematically extended Jim Crow, joining its Southern neighbors. Women and blacks replaced Indians as democratic projects. Murray voiced the sentiment shared by many who had advocated Indian equality: the negro "must be taught in the line of his own sphere, as porters, bootblacks and barbers and many lines of agriculture, horticulture and mechanics in which he is an adept, but it is an entirely false notion that the negro can rise to the equal of a white man in the professions or become an equal citizen to grapple with public questions."[51]

Of the Oklahoma Convention, an astute observer declared, "[Y]ou can take a pick and dig beneath the surface in this organization anywhere and you are bound to find a corner of that Sequoyah map buried." A majority of the delegates from Indian Territory had participated in the Muskogee Convention; the rest sympathized with its aims. Murray, who had an influential part in the drafting of the Sequoyah Constitution, played an equally pivotal role in the formation of Oklahoma's ruling instrument. He presided over the Oklahoma Constitution Convention in Guthrie. A ferocious champion of agrarian existence, he fought for many of the forward-looking elements to be carried over into the Oklahoma Constitution.

Partisan gains lasted well after Oklahoma joined the Union, trickling down to the authors of the Sequoyah Constitution. Leaders of the movement capitalized on their newfound reputation by taking influential roles in the new state. Riding the Democratic crescendo, Haskell became Oklahoma's first governor. Owen also saw his political fortunes climb with his energetic work on behalf of Indian Territory's future. Elected U.S. senator from Oklahoma in 1907, he served three terms. Oklahoma voters elected Murray to the first state legislature, and he later became Speaker of the House and governor. These figures believed in separate statehood to vindicate the principle of Indian consent, but above all, they were practitioners of practical politics and never inalterably opposed to single statehood. Once Sequoyah failed to secure congressional approval, as predicted, Democrats threw their support behind single statehood. With Oklahoma's admission to the Union came enhanced reputations, political careers, and financial rewards.

The partisan effects continued to redound to the Democratic Party's benefit. Policies originally charted in the Sequoyah Constitution became adopted as part of an invigorated Democratic Party's platform. With statehood imminent, local party conventions and assemblies of laborers and farmers broke out in anticipation of elections to the Oklahoma Convention. The various platforms and proposals that emerged continued what Haskell called the process of "harmonizing the Indian and white element of Indian Territory." Of the 112 delegates elected to the Convention, only 14 were Republicans. Later, aspiring Democratic candidates lined up to swear fealty to this agenda in advance of the 1907 election. In this sense, beyond its absorption in the Oklahoma Constitution, the Sequoyah Constitution lived on in the partisan texts and retail politics of the governing party.[52]

What of Indian survival? As debate over Oklahoma and Indian Territories came to a head, Congress enacted a joint resolution extending the life of tribal governments "until all property of such tribes, or the proceeds thereof, shall be distributed among the individual members of said tribes." This law had the effect of extending the deadline indefinitely and lifting Indians' sense of siege, as allocation would take years to complete. With the separate state movement dissipated by the early twentieth century, national leaders saw little need to go further in addressing Indian concerns. A conventional state had been formed from the Twin Territories, in response to citizens' agitation for local self-rule.[53]

Decades later, Congress would restore a measure of self-rule to the tribes. The 1934 Indian Reorganization Act ended the Dawes Act's

allotment policy and restored to each Indian tribe "the right to organize for its common welfare" and the power to "adopt an appropriate
constitution and bylaws." While Congress returned limited lawmaking power over remaining tribal lands, it did not reverse any land allotments already carried out. New Deal lawyers led by Felix Cohen
spearheaded a program to assist tribes to write constitutions. They
drafted memos outlining essential features of an American constitution
and shared model constitutions with tribes interested in recovering the
art of Indian self-governance. If Cohen's diagnosis can be credited, then
the destruction of tribal forms and enforced fidelity to conventional
sovereignty fostered a measure of political ignorance. "For many
years, . . . most of the Indian tribes have not only been denied the right
to manage their own affairs, but have even been denied a voice in those
affairs," he explained. "It thus happens that many Indians who are interested in the idea of self-government do not have very much practical
knowledge or experience in the tasks of government."[54]

To be sure, the Sequoyah movement failed to achieve its dreams of
a republic with the size and clout of any other state, dominated by
Indian leaders. Once the dust had settled, a lone county in Oklahoma
bore Sequoyah's name. Movement leaders convinced the native populace to put their faith in republican institutions familiar to the white
population and give up their dream of an independent Indian nation.
Nevertheless, the native peoples had, through mobilization and writings, expressed their dissatisfaction with prevailing political conditions. They had recovered their voice, gained a taste for politics, and
found a party they expected would pay attention to their concerns.
For a time, Indians had a simple method for ascertaining who had their
interests at heart: they simply asked political hopefuls where they
stood when the proposed State of Sequoyah was being debated.[55]

Not every Indian became politically energized by these developments. Some came away demoralized by the federal government's latest assault on native sovereignty. Even as more Indians took part in
Oklahoma's public affairs, others turned apathetic or withdrew. Beyond the tribes themselves that survived, small conservative orders such
as the Snakes or the Nighthawks (a Cherokee organization) persisted.
Members of these traditionalist communities lived in cabins near cer-
emonially important places such as the Hickory Ground. Occasionally, they would send letters to Washington telling national officials

that the law as expressed in older treaties will remain valid "[a]s long as the water runs" and reminding them that "[t]he home of Indians will be there forever."

The sun had not set on the Five Tribes; neither would they have "an empire of their own." Sequoyah's creation, defeat, and absorption all testified to the broader political transformation that took place, mediated by the American constitutional tradition. The boundaries of political community, too, had been redrawn and new civic identities acquired. White migrants to Indian lands traversed from "intruders" and "usurpers" to "sovereign citizens." In the eyes of public officials, recalcitrant native peoples—"weak tribe[s]" that were "ignorant of the language and laws of the white man"—had shown themselves capable of self-governance and thus deserving of citizenship. Yet full membership in the emerging liberal democratic order came on the strictest of terms: the abandonment of tribal sovereignty, undermining of group identity, and loss of lands.[56]

At a crucial moment in American history, Pleasant Porter's vision of the republican order remade became the one worth pursuing: "my people and the white man living side by side in a prosperous land on terms of perfect intellectual and political equality, and each doing his share toward the maintenance and support of that state." The two populations would be forever linked together through the new state's constitution and iconography. Perhaps the best evidence of the impact of the Sequoyah episode is the opinion of a former critic. The *Daily Oklahoman,* which had opposed Indian statehood, in hindsight acknowledged that "subsequent developments have proven that the result of its deliberations have been indelibly fixed in the history of the new state of Oklahoma."[57]

CHAPTER SIX

A Charter for the World
1947

Take your stand now before time has corrupted you.

—ROBERT MAYNARD HUTCHINS, "ADDRESS TO THE GRADUATING CLASS," UNIVERSITY OF
CHICAGO, 1935

The dawn of the twentieth century brought the closing of the American
frontier, and along with it, dwindling public tolerance of disruptive,
territorial versions of popular sovereignty. Major legal transformations
now occurred primarily through ordinary processes—partisan politics,
the courts, and on rare occasions, constitutional amendment. Defenders of conventional sovereignty welcomed the use of these orderly pathways for change. But crisis after crisis served to accelerate legal creativity, leading to the birth of what New Deal economist Rexford
Tugwell called an "emergent constitution." This happened through
generations of judicial interpretations and other "accumulative processes of law," treated as faithful to the 1787 Constitution but, in all
frankness, departing from the Framers' original intentions. For Tugwell, the crisis had reached a turning point because "all three branches
escaped the confines of the Constitution," and so removed from the
will of the people, the legal instrument "cannot create loyalty to institutions." Tugwell voiced some of the same complaints of judicial interpretation raised by dissidents of another age. Twentieth-century liberals, like their conservative counterparts, grew uneasy about whether
America's increasingly judge-made Constitution could continue to
generate the respect, predictability, and salience required by the rule
of law. Once again, pressure increased to write new constitutions to
reconnect legal text with the hopes and dreams of modern citizens.[1]

Many of the constitutional adaptations favored by liberals occurred as the country tried to recover from the economic collapse of the 1920s and 1930s. But military conflict also had its consolidating influence on the legal order. The dual quality of war's relationship to democratic constitutionalism came to fruition in the aftermath of the Second World War. On the one hand, the mobilization of society to defeat a common enemy profoundly reshaped domestic laws, institutions, and the economy—even what it meant to be an American. On the other hand, the fight against totalitarianism opened opportunities to critique the national legal order. By the mid-1940s, innovations in war-making technology, a thirst for a lasting peace, and an optimism about the rule of law gave rise to social movements that questioned the future of a distinctively American Constitution.[2]

As fighting came to a close, people revived ancient dreams of one world community. Their grievances multiplied, as did the scale of legal solutions. The most prominent manifestation of global sovereignty involved the creation of the fledgling United Nations and, along with it, the strengthening of principles of international and humanitarian law. But to the horror of certain observers, these enlightened developments left intact the sovereignty of each nation and the dangerous mix of tribalism, chauvinism, and imperialism. To such critics, the atomic bomb had irrevocably changed the equation. In the wake of the devastation of Hiroshima and Nagasaki, the nation-state system had to be dismantled once and for all and replaced by a true international legal order. Otherwise, it would only be a matter of time before democracies collapsed under nuclear devastation and authoritarianism returned with a vengeance. A stronger, more just political system had to be created to bring the people of the world together under a single constitution.

Robert Maynard Hutchins proved to be one of the most persistent critics of the emerging postwar order and an energetic proponent of the theory of global sovereignty. The son of a preacher, Hutchins had risen to become dean of Yale Law School at twenty-eight years of age. A few years later, the Board of Trustees of the University of Chicago appointed him university president. From that position, Hutchins threw himself into debates over academic freedom, embarked upon educational reforms, and lectured on matters of war and peace.[3]

Hutchins's most sustained challenge to the constitutional status quo took place from the fall of 1945 through the summer of 1947, when he presided over the Committee to Frame a World Constitution. Over a course of two years, the group produced a written instrument that rivaled the minimalist, patchwork international order embodied in the United Nations Charter. Proponents hoped that, in time, a charter for the world might erode and supplant the American legal order. The issue was now publicly joined: Which legal framework could best secure the survival of the human race in the atomic age? Was it a system that remained dependent on the blind hope that national self-interest would produce forbearance and intermittent cooperation, or one empowered to interdict the spread of nuclear arms and adjudicate disputes between countries? For Hutchins and members of the world government movement, the epoch characterized by "the competitive anarchy of the national states" had to be brought to an orderly and expeditious close.[4]

Uniting politically to abolish war had been a longtime Enlightenment dream, proposed by thinkers such as Bentham, Kant, and Rousseau. All the same, this mid-twentieth-century experience represented a significant turn in the people's ideas about politics, community, and the rule of law. The rise of global sovereignty entailed the harmonization of several projects: the development of nonterritorial citizenship, an abiding belief in universal law and human rights, and increased reliance on supranational institutions.

The Chicago Plan ultimately did not entail either an exercise of cultural power or ethical renewal. Rather, the World Constitution could be understood as American conventional sovereignty taken to its ultimate conclusion. Drafters ingeniously borrowed from several sources for its grand vision, drawing most copiously from American ideas of self-governance in order to repudiate long-standing features of that very tradition. They insisted that a single, heterogeneous republic could be formed out of the material of existing cities, states, and nations. Yet every step of the way, the architects of the World Constitution argued that the ends of their writing project were the same ones facing revolutionaries at America's founding: security, happiness, liberty, and virtue. The difference, they insisted, was primarily one of ambition and scale: these promises would finally be extended to the people of the world on terms they would have a role in making.[5]

Federalists for a Nuclear Age

In Hutchins, one discovered a penchant for idealism married to an impressive knowledge of classical republican and democratic ideas. Known as "a visionary and an iconoclast," he proved to be an outspoken internationalist as Europe erupted in warfare. Though he preached engagement with neighbors, until Pearl Harbor he extolled the virtues of the Democratic policy of "all aid short of war" for European allies.[6]

Hutchins initially attacked the wartime priorities of conventional authorities and eventually broadened his critique to the underlying basis of their legal authority. He became incensed by Franklin Delano Roosevelt's 1941 State of the Union address, in which the president proclaimed "The Four Freedoms"—freedom of speech, freedom of religion, freedom from fear, and freedom from want—as rationales for American participation in the war. Steamed that FDR had "appropriated all the idealism of the world for . . . the War Party," Hutchins gave a speech on January 23, 1941, titled "America and the War." He wished to counter the president's cheapening of enlightened ideals by urging greater progress toward them domestically. In his address carried by NBC radio, he argued: "We Americans have hardly begun to understand and practice the ideals that we are urged to force on others." America needed to demonstrate itself as "a nation which understands, values, and practices the four freedoms" before leaping into combat.[7]

Hutchins worried that total war would arrest democratic progress: "We shall think no more of justice, the moral order, and the supremacy of human rights. . . . When we remember what a short war did to the four freedoms, we must recognize that they face extermination in the total war to come." A few months later at the university chapel, Hutchins preached similar themes grounded in constitutional values: "The President cannot literally mean that we are to fight on till the four freedoms ring everywhere," for it would mean "a program of perpetual war" and a form of "new imperialism." War is "a false path to the four freedoms everywhere," he thundered. Although Hutchins emphasized strong themes of universal law and human rights, he initially prodded national leaders to reform the American constitutional order to better reflect its own aspirations.[8]

After Japan attacked Pearl Harbor, he made an agreement with the federal government to bring the Manhattan Project to the University of Chicago. The Project's research led to the explosion of the first atomic weapon. Hutchins later came to regret his role in ushering in the nuclear age. As the global conflict deepened, President Hutchins urged Americans to "try to establish the good society here and now. . . . We need a new order for America."[9]

Once hostilities ended, Hutchins—now the chancellor of the University of Chicago—felt freer to offer an alternative vision of the postwar order. Under the banner of world government, he began to give stronger legal prescriptions that would encompass not only the United States but rather all nation-states. His emerging theory of global governance was driven by an overriding fear of weapons of mass destruction and the frailty of the nation-state system. On August 12, 1945, he participated in a radio discussion on the topic, "Atomic Force: Its Meaning for Mankind." Hutchins warned that it was only a matter of time before America's nuclear advantage evaporated. He noted the disastrous incentives created by amassing these weapons:

> If a man has a chance to dominate the world through the control of atomic energy, that is a very large stake. And if he has, through the advances made by the scientists in his country, an opportunity to use this atomic force in such a way as to justify him thinking that he has the edge on his enemies, he will take advantage of the situation and start another international conflagration. . . . The only hope, therefore, of abolishing war is through the monopoly of atomic force by a world organization.[10]

Possession of this new technology encouraged a false sense of security, but even worse, it fostered an ethic of domination. "Instead of saying, 'Let us use our knowledge and our resources for the benefit of all mankind,' we say, 'Let us use our knowledge to make more terrifying weapons of destruction; and let us use our resources to usher in the American Century, in which we shall dominate the world." The people needed to save America from itself, as much as from rogue countries.[11]

President Hutchins's orations spurred colleagues at the University of Chicago and elsewhere to join the debate. G. A. Borgese, a professor of humanities and political science, and Richard P. McKeon, dean of the Humanities Division, wrote Hutchins in the fall of 1945, responding to his "call to action." They put the stakes in terms that average citizens could comprehend, saying that "world freedom . . . is the essence of the American dream." But that dream would be shattered in the absence of legal intervention because no country's nuclear advantage could endure forever: "America, degraded to serfdom or catapulted to autocratic power over all men, even if she won the world with all its ruins would lose itself." Thus, the "alternatives are world rule—with supreme authority vested in a global organism—or world ruin." There would be "one world or none."

"A world constitution is needed," Borgese and McKeon declared. Drafting such an instrument seemed like a "staggering" task, too much to expect from any bureaucratic or diplomatic bodies, which are "inhibited by statutory routines" and the "dogmatic wall of national sovereignty." Instead, the University of Chicago "should take the lead in constructive thought" on the design of a new legal order, given its position as an American institution of higher learning steeped "in the unparalleled opportunity and liberty of this country" and the "decisive role" played by the university "in ushering in the atomic age." Research on the topic of world order should be based in the humanities, the two insisted, for the problem demanded "systematic philosophy, not fragmentary empiricism."

Hutchins and other participants in this exercise would have to become federalists for a new age. Like the virtuous men of 1787, they faced "an apparently irreconcilable antithesis between the individual sovereignty of States and aggregate sovereignty, while the 'consolidation of the whole into one simple republic' seemed as inexpedient as unattainable." And just as the Virginia plan "contrived a way out of the impasse," so too an ingenious proposal for world governance could turn the unimaginable into a possibility. These advocates for global sovereignty believed that the odds of success would improve dramatically if a world constitution were based largely on "the uniqueness of [the American] experience." The people's "constitution and way of life were an evolutionary emergence controlled by the conscious intellect, in broad daylight." Through their own extensive democratic experimentation, Americans had become adept at employing historical knowledge to unite the "ideal" and the "real," the "intellectual" and the "practical."

Hutchins instantly warmed to the idea, organizing the Committee to Frame a World Constitution. Though Hutchins served as the president, McKeon presided over the proceedings as chair, with Borgese as secretary. Borgese, a fiery émigré from Fascist Italy, dominated debates and became known as "chief architect" of the World Constitution. From the ranks of the university they added Robert Redfield, dean of social sciences, Wilbur Katz, dean of the Law School, and Tugwell from the Institute of Planning. Rounding out the group were Erich Kahler of Princeton, Albert Guérard of Stanford, Charles McIlwain of Harvard, Harold Innis of Toronto, and Stringfellow Barr, who had recently established the Foundation for World Government. James Landis, dean of Harvard Law School, philosopher H. E. Hocking, and Beardsley Ruml of the Federal Reserve Board participated in some of the committee's activities, though none signed the final draft constitution. Elisabeth Mann Borgese, who would later earn the nickname "Mother of the Oceans" for her work on the Law of the Sea Convention, contributed several key memoranda as a staff member. The committee made some efforts to diversify its membership along racial lines— Ralph Bunche was mentioned as a possible candidate for "integrating the Committee"—but their recruitment did not bear fruit.[12]

As deliberations began in December 1945, Hutchins continued to bring public attention to the legal and human stakes involved. "The news of damnation," he explained, "tells us in dramatic, spectacular fashion, how extremely unpleasant it will be for us if we do not" succeed in building a new constitutional order. International agreements on arms control were "absolutely imperative" but also plainly inadequate because "they will merely guarantee, if they are effective, that the next war will end with atomic bombs instead of beginning with them." Only a "world federal government and real atomic control" could prevent the next nuclear war.[13]

A mixture of fear and idealism rather than anger and alienation propelled the committee's work. The group convened for two days each month, laboring for eight hours a day and churning out 4,000 pages of material. Its deliberations were animated by a desire for survival of the human race, democratic institutions, and an ethical existence. Members found themselves guided by the "basic belief . . . that World Government is the only alternative to world destruction." All internationalists during this time believed freedom and security had to be achieved on a global scale, but they worked along parallel tracks, and occasionally at cross-purposes, to attain their divergent political visions.

Philosophically, committee members found themselves pulled between two tendencies during debates. Some—who called themselves legal "minimalists"—preferred a supranational organization with only enough power to deal with matters of security, feeling that it had the best chance of being adopted. Others pressed for a "maximalist" vision of the law, "holding justice paramount and . . . centered on a Bill of Human Rights." Maximalists, led by Borgese, worried that the rhetoric of "security," far from making world government palatable, would instead prove divisive because atomic fear might be "a particularly American phenomenon," and talk of security "automatically provokes the query: 'Whose security?'" At the end of extensive conversations, they proposed that "the word security should be shunned" in favor of the language of "peace," which they believed would rally people to its idealism and inclusiveness. The World Constitution ultimately approved by the Chicago group embraced the maximalist goal of "justice," though it toggled between these visions in the particulars, embracing certain substantive ideals that might gain widespread approval while leaving other values somewhat less determined.[14]

Drafters had no illusions that their instrument would be adopted wholesale or immediately. Though expecting the constitution to be implemented in the near future would be unrealistic, the text could nevertheless serve powerful expressive and deliberative functions. More broadly, the existence of the document could help create a new democratic culture that might one day facilitate the establishment of comprehensive global governance. To defeat the outdated ideology of nationalism once and for all, the people's mind-sets, political beliefs, and even their vocabulary had to be changed.

Participants pressed on because they wished to create "a concrete picture to show what a Federal Republic of the World, under certain conceivable circumstances, might look like." Even as the committee began deliberations, the Soviet Union continued to spread its influence behind the banner of global socialism, with "a plan for world government, an army and an administrative machine to carry out the plan, and an underground." Borgese advised, "if we do not propose anything, Russia may win the consent of half of the world—her half."[15]

A draft constitution could also serve as an antidote to the most defeatist attitude: that world government was too utopian a project. If citizens of the world could assemble, deliberate, and deliver a cogent plan for governance on a small scale, then others might be inspired to join their efforts. While any constitution has force only to the extent of social approval, Hutchins believed that, as with the American experience, legal text could help to generate political and cultural bonds. Members of the committee framed the constitution for a world state "in the hope that the discussion leading to its institution and its existence thereafter will promote the formation of the community which can be its only durable foundation."

At the outset, the committee poured its energies into defining terminology and principles. A key decision was made to distinguish their project of outlining a "world union, federal in structure," from a "world state, unitary in structure." Despite unanimity in belief that the nation-state system had to be dramatically altered, they did not go so far as to create a system that immediately abolished the sovereignty of nations. Instead, at least for the foreseeable future, political authority would be divided between extant states and world government, each of which would have "limited sovereignty." The world government would not have power to change the character of member nations, with the constitution treating them not as "creatures of the world government" but as "units penultimate to the world government" with "constitutions which can be altered only by the will of their constituents." And yet, in an extension of America's own founding approach, the authority of world government would be "popularly derived" from "all the peoples of the world."[16]

The committee reshaped ideas of popular sovereignty to make its proposal palatable. But make no mistake—the essential sovereignty of nation-states that joined the Republic would be fundamentally altered. Component states would retain internal sovereignty over matters not delegated to the central authority, though "none of the federated states retains any vestige of external sovereignty." Going beyond the powers afforded the American Congress in 1787, the World Government would acquire the capacity to "legislate for the common good of the world community on any matter which is decisive for the common interest, even if this involves contravention or nullification of the laws of the several federated states." Such a sweeping transfer of legislative power could not be legitimate without explicit consent: a change in the character of states permitting "such intervention in the affairs of local communities must be provided for in the constitutions of local government."[17]

Seeking wisdom in close rereadings of *The Federalist,* drafters seized upon a basic principle of federalism: "the necessity of the central government acting directly upon individuals" when sustained by majority support of the people. Such authority was indispensable not only for enforcing federal law uniformly but also in its capacity to "build up" attachments to the federal government by "accustom[ing]" citizens to "the common occurrences of their political life." How necessary governmental power was to survival determined how far that power should reach. Although it would have been nice to have centralized power over foreign commerce, that control "is not essential to survival." By comparison, survival of the human race depended on "effective control of the war-making capacities of the individual states" and therefore "plenary authority made sense in that field." It followed from this realization that a traditional law-based system made sense to regulate war making and the building of armaments. A rule-of-law approach required sanctions and "the idea of world police and world judicial system" having jurisdiction over violations of laws promulgated by the central government.[18]

The Chicago group appreciated how their project differed from constitutions of the past and therefore faced fresh challenges. As Erich Kahler explained, unlike constitutions authored for nation-states, the text would not initially be grounded in a "historically given substratum" of culture, shared experience, and tradition. Moreover, a world constitution would have "no external counterpart to face," being "directed only inward." Finally, whereas "almost all historical constitutions . . . arose from an act of liberation or emancipation of the people," a world constitution "is motivated by the urge to secure peace in the face of growing international anarchy and the perilously increased destructiveness of warfare." The committee's work filled this gap by trying to create a new democratic culture, one that would eventually bind together antagonistic countries, unsettle existing alliances, and create new civic identities.[19]

Working from a set of basic principles, the Chicago group deliberated upon various proposals. In formulating ideas, members consulted plans for international organizations such as the League of Nations and the United Nations, as well as the constitutions of China, France, Spain, the United States, and the United Kingdom. Throughout, the American Constitution stood as "an important antecedent, if not the most important of all." Participants labored with pragmatic considerations in mind, aware that composing a constitution "is an act of faith and an act of will. . . . The draft of a constitution is a working hypothesis hovering between the desirable and the possible." At one pole, the UN represented the "possible that does not tend toward the desirable," while the other pole consisted of desirable but far-fetched ideals. The trick was to come up with first principles that had a chance of being implemented one day, if not right away. "The formula" they settled upon was hybridity of legal ideas. Success could then be measured by how well the worthy political designs from around the world were fused together. "[W]e can be headed for something that makes sense if Communism becomes democratic, and Democracy becomes Communistic," such that words so often hurled as epithets in an increasingly bipolar world gained deeper, synthetic meanings.[20]

Taming Nationalism

What the committee produced became known as the Chicago Plan, an exemplar of global constitutionalism for the nuclear age. Throughout the constitution, drafters employed what they believed to be "the common language of democracy being competitively spoken today by all peoples and rulers, tyrants included." In broad strokes, the document borrowed the main features of American conventional sovereignty: divided government, a preference for heterogeneity and compromise, a mix of expanded powers and individual rights, and political power distributed geographically. But even familiar concepts and institutions were entirely revamped; foundational principles had to be revised to suit a global project.

Perhaps the most visionary step of the constitution entailed the relocation of sovereignty from the people of independent nations to "the people of the world." Americans' conception of political community, grounded in sharing a bounded space, became completely unmoored from its territorial origins. In other words, the drafters took seriously the idea that the right to self-rule inhered in mobilized individuals rather than nation-states; and that the right was available even to those from Western, nondemocratic traditions. Although the implications of global sovereignty beyond authorizing a world government were not fully fleshed out, the constitution's federal structure strongly suggested the possibility of dual citizenship—in the world community as well as in each nation-state—until the day that boundaries between nations fell.

Theoretically, the very concept of world sovereignty attacked the foundations of American notions of law and community. If, in fact, popular sovereignty was a universal right, then it followed that a mobilized people of the world could overthrow a legal order that no longer served their needs. Accordingly, the Preamble of the Preliminary Draft of a World Constitution asserted on behalf of "the people of the earth" the right to create a new "covenant and fundamental law" to govern "the Federal Republic of the World." It did so with the "common goal of mankind" of achieving "spiritual excellence and physical welfare" in mind, which could be realized only within a legal order founded on "peace and justice." The end of world government, therefore, was the establishment of "universal peace."[21] Through this radical concept of the people, the framers tried to subvert the nationalistic underpinnings of the American legal order.

Another tenet of global sovereignty was a commitment to individual rights for all people. Capturing an ascendant belief in basic human rights, the constitution began with a concise Declaration of Duties and Rights. Despite Hutchins's soaring rhetoric of ethical reform, the committee's pragmatic instincts and collaborative decision making led it to shy away from comprehensive moral transformation. Instead, drafters seemed mostly satisfied with universalizing widely accepted negative rights. Here and there, the basis for positive rights could be discerned, but they were almost always mentioned at high levels of abstraction. Drawing both upon the "Law of Nature" and positive law, the constitution guaranteed "release from the bondage of poverty and from the servitude and exploitation of labor"; "freedom of peaceful assembly and of association, in any creed or party or craft"; and "protection of individuals and groups against subjugation and tyrannical rule, racial or national, doctrinal or cultural, with safeguards for the self-determination of minorities and dissenters." Although the constitution invoked the French Declaration of the Rights of Man and Citizen, some members of the Committee saw the World Constitution as also codifying, in a more detailed way, the modern liberties that President Roosevelt had urged on a worldwide basis. "The freedom from fear is the specific right to which a world state is directed," McKeon wrote, "and the constitution as a whole should be a declaration of that right." Several of the drafters believed that freedom from fear included economic security as well as more specific guarantees of the necessities of life. After poring over the rejection of a new bill of rights by French citizens on May 5, 1946, they doubted that any more substantive articulation of affirmative economic rights would survive debate among nations. As a result, they kept references to "human welfare" vague.[22]

The World Constitution imposed a handful of duties on individuals, something the 1787 American Constitution never attempted. New duties included each citizen's responsibility to engage in "productive labor according to his ability," abstain from violence except to "repulse violence," and "do unto others as he would like others to do unto him." Citizens of the World Republic were charged to work for the "spiritual and physical advancement of the living and of those to come." These provisions, fulfilling the Chicago group's goal of attacking nationalism as a source of selfishness and violence, amounted to a limited ethical intervention. These values can be seen as glosses on traditional liberal and republican values: self-control, equality, self-defense, virtue. Moreover, it is not apparent whether these duties were enforceable commands (as, say, John Brown's Christian-inflected edicts were enforced through trial and "suitable punishment") or merely aspirations. The drafters' overriding concern for broad consensus and the politics of ratification suggested the latter.[23]

Legislators and judges of the World Republic received explicit authorization to "express and specify" other "freedoms and franchises as are inherent in man's inalienable claims to life, liberty, and dignity of the human person." In this way, judge-made rights on the world stage would gain a modicum of democratic legitimacy that had often eluded judge-read, unenumerated rights in the American legal system. Individual rights could be enforced against the World Government as well as "any of its component units." These rights included freedom from discrimination on the basis of race, nationality, sex, caste, creed, or doctrine; freedom against slavery and forced labor; and "freedom of communication and information, of speech, of the press, and of expression by whatever means, . . . [and] of travel." The committee extended a number of criminal protections from the Anglo-Saxon tradition, including freedom from arbitrary search or seizure, the right to a fair trial, and the right to resist excessive penalties and ex post facto laws. In a compromise, capital punishment "shall not be inflicted under federal law," but the matter was otherwise left open for component states due to fears the question would stymie approval of the constitution.[24]

Hutchins had repeatedly argued that "since the great aim is a world community, the great task is education." A World State could not be sustained without "common understanding, a common tradition, common ideas, and common ideals." The constitution reflected the universalist aims of liberal education by guaranteeing the right of every child from age six to twelve be instructed at public expense. But unlike the 1787 Constitution, education would not be left to local control but rather made an imperative of the highest order. Education had to be "accessible to all without discrimination of age or sex or race or class or creed." Segregated or unequal education, like that dispensed in a number of American regions, violated international norms. A view shared by many liberal educators, as a legal principle it was nevertheless a conviction ahead of its time expressed in the decade before *Brown v. Board of Education*. These provisions demonstrated the drafters' commitment to equality, pluralism, and universal values while signaling antipathy toward lingering strains of racial and cultural sovereignty. The legal instrument deemed such theories of political power antithetical to the idea of one world community. In this way, the World Constitution extended the American project of battling alternative theories of popular sovereignty to a global enterprise.[25]

Like smaller-scale variants on conventional sovereignty, the World Constitution tried to inculcate greater respect for communal values in the economic sphere without destroying capitalism. It characterized "four elements of life—earth, water, air, energy" as "the common property of the human race." Though the management of such elements may be handled by the state or delegated to individuals or corporations, decisions must be "subordinated in each and all cases to the interest of the common good." A separate provision barred "preferential agreements or coalitions of vested interests" that interfered with equal access of any state to raw materials and sources of energy. Beyond these common elements, the constitution did little to interfere with economic relations. In this respect, the Chicago Plan distanced itself from more aggressive socialist reform projects.[26]

In other major respects, the World Constitution aggressively repudiated basic features of the international order. World federalists depended on pockets of liberal dissatisfaction with the United Nations while stoking belief in global sovereignty. As the UN Charter had taken shape, Hutchins condemned its incremental approach. The provision that allowed a single Security Council member to veto a measure typified the weakness of the system:

You can not have all the advantages of membership in a world organization and none of the disadvantages. You can not have all the attributes of sovereignty and give up some of them. . . . You can't, for example, have an effective world court if you are going to insist that the court can't judge your country without its consent. You can't have an effective world organization if the organization can act only when it is unanimous.[27]

Departing from the UN on first principles, the World Constitution would be organized according to the belief that "the 'nation-state' is by definition and nature the enemy and antagonist of the World States." Its signatories announced, "the age of nations must end, and the era of humanity begin."[28]

The UN Charter, too, aimed to "save succeeding generations from the scourge of war" and protect "fundamental human rights." Nevertheless, the "United Nations was not designed to put an end to the competing anarchy of sovereign states, but to perpetuate it," Hutchins observed. Enforcement of international law remained primarily in the hands of each country's legal and political processes unless agreement within the Security Council could be reached. The General Assembly possessed merely advisory authority, and a single Security Council member could veto resolutions. The Security Council had "primary responsibility for the maintenance of international peace and security," with Article 12 disempowering the General Assembly from deliberating or making recommendations while the Security Council exercises any of its powers regarding "any dispute or situation." Unequal participation and institutional gridlock characterized the UN.[29]

In comparison, the World Constitution traded faith in the self-interest and good judgment of each nation for a greater belief in supranational institutions to resolve conflicts. In the view of proponents, "war must and can be outlawed and peace can and must be universally enacted and enforced." Whereas the UN Charter confined lawmaking authority to a Security Council composed of five permanent and ten nonpermanent members, the Chicago Plan lodged full lawmaking power in a World Council that could claim to be representative of every region on earth.[30]

If it was a gargantuan task to destroy nationalism in a single stroke, it might nevertheless be possible to "defunctionalize" or "subdue" nationalism over time. To do so, the committee pursued a three-point strategy: representational mechanisms ensuring a minority voice in world policy making, substantive laws guaranteeing individual and group rights, and the establishment of courts and a Tribune of the People able to enforce minority rights. Drafters began with a creative scheme for representation. They began by carving up the world into nine Electoral Colleges or Regions, roughly corresponding to "nine Societies of kindred nations and cultures." These regions were selected based on several considerations, including geography, cultural and linguistic similarity, and historical alliances or enmities. The constitution did not grant these organizations formal powers because of the risk of "promot[ing] a new kind of supranational . . . pride, competition, and fear." Nevertheless, taking advantage of "the rise of the Region" by incorporating the phenomenon into the World Constitution "may well weaken, in due course of time, obliterate the nationalism of the nations" by pressuring existing states to merge.[31]

A World Council would be invested with lawmaking authority, drawn from nominees in the nine Electoral Colleges. The unicameral legislature was intended as an improvement upon the American system, where "frequent deadlocks between the two houses of Congress are likely to result in failure to enact much desirable legislation." Nine councilors would be elected from each region to compose the World Council. Turning the American Electoral College into a representative mechanism, architects designed a deliberative body "twice removed from national prejudices." Drafters hoped this system of representation would foster alternative cultural ties and promote cooperation without replicating destructive nationalistic tendencies. This design choice reflected the committee's repudiation of "the present assignment of representatives in UN," which was a "serious hindrance" to "an evolution which will eventually give all nations and all people an effective and appropriate voice in international deliberations."[32]

In diminishing the importance of national sovereignty, this basic organizing feature also underscored "the equality of man." If designers had blindly followed the principle of equality of states—"then a Chinaman would have far less rights than a Luxemburger or Panamian." By the same token, if they had embraced the pure democratic principle of "one man, one vote," world government could be easily dominated by large populations without strong democratic traditions. Instead, the Chicago Plan blazed a middle path, settling upon a republican formula in which "English-speaking peoples . . . would neither appropriate an artificial majority . . . nor become subject to groups with less experience in representative government."[33]

Although members of the committee perceived the UN to be flawed in concept, for pragmatic reasons they thought the international organization might serve as an interim legal order on the way to an integrated world government. It might serve the same historical function as the Articles of Confederation, which had been proven to be plainly inadequate but prepared the people for the need to have a more centralized and effective form of government. Perhaps the UN could itself, through amendment, be transformed into a world government, if such modifications operated as "entering wedges for more radical transformation." The drafters repeatedly cited the American founding as an example of dedicated citizens overcoming daunting odds to alter a legal system in a fundamental way. Then, too, critics had derided the Constitutional Convention's work as "utopian, a visionary project, an indigestible panacea." And yet the fledgling U.S. Constitution not only survived the ratification process but also flourished. Perhaps history would repeat itself on a grand scale.[34]

The Chicago group believed that "strong executive leadership" would be crucial to matters of security and justice—"a concession to the American point of view by the few European-trained members of the committee." Vigorous leadership from the Oval Office had happened in times of crisis, but "it is an unfortunate constitution indeed which demands war to rectify its defects." Surveying legal systems across space and time, drafters found a global trend toward a form of executive organization "strong and independent enough for efficient action, and responsible enough not to become dictatorial."[35]

They agreed that electing a world president who might be seen as "the symbol of the conscience and tradition of mankind" required a secret ballot based on nominations from the nine Electoral Colleges. "[N]o two successive Presidents shall originate from the same Region," ensuring that no single nation or region could dominate the leadership of the World Republic. To avoid the American problem of presidents preoccupied with reelection efforts, the world president would serve a single six-year term. Reinforcing drafters' preference for good order over order alone, the constitution described the president not as "Commander in Chief" but rather as "Protector of the Peace."

Tearing a leaf from the parliamentary tradition, the constitution provided that the world president should appoint a chancellor, who would help appoint a cabinet as well as serve as the president's representative before the World Council. At the same time, the text formalized some of the features that had accreted to the American vice president and ad hoc officials over the years "because of the urgent need for presidential leadership in legislation and in general policy framing." The chancellor and cabinet would serve at the president's pleasure, but a government could also be dissolved through a no-confidence vote in the World Council. Overall, these features would foster "a more intimate participation" in the legislative process.[36]

Apart from the Convention and World Council, national interests were relegated to the House, one of four special bodies. This Madisonian approach to the problem diffused nationalism's influence by using institutions to constrain and ultimately overcome tendencies to see issues in selfish ways. The constitution entrusted the House with the "safeguarding of local institutions and autonomies and the protection of minorities," whereas the Syndicalism (or Senate) would chiefly serve as a voice for unions, syndicates, and occupational associations. The idea that certain associations should be granted functional representation so as to "economize democracy" came from the European experience, notably Germany, France, and Russia. Creation of these bodies, invested with "paralegislative power," offset some of the disadvantages of a unicameral legislature. Such drawbacks included the risk of domination by majorities, the possibility of groupthink, and suppression of local or individualistic concerns. The Syndicalism would also serve as a forum for the "mediation or arbitration of non-justiciable issues among such syndicates or unions or other corporate interests." World government would benefit from the expertise of professional groups while "the economic and social pressure groups and lobbies, with the disturbances emerging therefrom, are absorbed and neutralized."[37]

Perhaps the most ingenious innovation was the Tribune of the People, who would act as "spokesman for the minorities." Inspired by the Roman tradition of plebeian tribunes, this officeholder had the responsibility to "defend the natural and civil rights of individuals and groups against violation or neglect by the World Government or any of its component units." The Tribune would be expected to "demand, as a World Attorney before the World Republic, the observance of the letter and spirit of this Constitution; and to promote . . . the attainment of the goals set to the progress of mankind by the efforts of the ages." A modern analogue could be found in Sweden's Parliamentary Attorney General of Justice. Some committee members envisioned the office to formalize the function of American public interest lawyers such as Louis Brandeis, who earned the moniker "Attorney of the People."[38]

Great care went into designing an office that could claim to represent minority sentiment among the people of the world, yet escape capture by the majority coalition. Once the president and Council had been selected, the candidate with the second-largest vote among eligible candidates during the secret ballot would assume the title of Tribune. Excluded from the pool would be anyone nominated for president, serving as acting president or alternate for the past nine years, or originating from the same Region as the president. The Tribune could not be removed except through impeachment. Unlike the chief lawyer in most countries, the Tribune would not be merely an extension of the ruling coalition, the national party, or a policy maker within a president's own administration. Ideally, the Tribune should represent "those that are depressed economically or snubbed racially or unexpressed politically."[39]

The idea of plural representation as a means of ensuring good order carried over to design choices concerning international courts. Under the Chicago Plan, the legal system would be made up of sixty justices constituting a Grand Tribunal, appointed by the president and subject to two-thirds veto of the Council. Unlike the American system, which grants justices life tenure, justices of the Tribunal would serve staggered fifteen-year terms, making them more responsive to the world community.[40]

The constitution created five separate benches, assigning twelve justices to each bench. Every region of the world would be represented in a bench. Unlike the International Court of Justice (ICJ) created by the UN Charter, which enjoys jurisdiction only when a party consents to the adjudication of a particular controversy, world courts would have standing jurisdiction over broad subject areas. Moreover, under UN rules, only nation-states could be parties to ICJ adjudication. By contrast, each bench of the World Republic would have its own jurisdiction over individuals as well as nations. The proper grounds for lawsuits in world courts ranged from conflicts between the world government and component units to controversies between world government and individuals involving federal law.[41]

A Supreme Court would be empowered to review the decisions of the benches. Drafters wished to improve popular control over the Supreme Court, one of the apparent lessons drawn from FDR's experience during the New Deal. Adopting an idea championed by Hutchins, the world president would wear two hats, serving as chairman of the Tribunal and as chief justice of the Supreme Court. In doing so, the executive would return to "play[ing] an active role as dispenser of justice," in the mold of Solomon or Justinian. The Council's chairman would serve on the Supreme Court as vice-chairman ex officio. Thus, the vice-chairman could offer a legislative perspective and check on presidential abuse, though the two officials could, in theory, cooperate to advance an agenda. Five additional justices representing each of the benches would join these two to make up the Supreme Court, somewhat diluting the impact of aggressive agenda setting over time.[42]

Here, as elsewhere, design choices reflected what Borgese called a rejection of the "Locke-Montesquieu trinitary orthodoxy," which holds that the branches of government should be separated "with extreme rationalistic rigor." Instead, while staying true to a mixed constitution, the committee searched for ways to encourage novel forms of interaction between the various components of government. Energy and overlap to foster "active democracy" proved to be the powerful guiding principle, rather the isolation of functions for fear of governmental abuse.[43]

A gradual monopoly on war making comprised the final element of the strategy to legalize peace. Though the preamble asserted that the people would "surrender their arms" to world government, the constitution itself assumed that the effort to outlaw war had to occur in stages and through a combination of techniques. After imposing a duty on citizens to abstain from violence, the committee created an institution called the Chamber of Guardians, which enjoyed "exclusive" power over the armed forces of the World Republic. Chaired by the president, the group would include six elected civilians from different Regions as well as one former president. Strict control of armament production formed a key component of peace strategy. The

Chamber of Guardians was to set "limits to the domestic militias of the single communities and states or unions thereof." The manufacture of armaments and armed forces beyond levels established by this institution would be "reserved to the World Government."[44]

Promoting the "Good World Community": Deliberation over Discipline

If all one cared about was the degree of institutionalization of the World Constitution, it should be seen as an abject failure. Because the framers actually pursued a broad range of deliberative goals, however, the constitution met with greater success on this front. At the level of agenda setting and development of democratic culture, the constitution did much to push forward the conversation about world government. Because the committee had no interest in creating an underground community, the constitution served no measurable disciplinary functions.

In terms of strategy, Hutchins and his colleagues eagerly developed revolutionary principles but showed little interest in revolutionary methods of state building. World community would be built through reason rather than force. Support for global sovereignty had to be cultivated through the media, among elites, and in public meetings, not in the streets or underground. The drafters agreed that ratification by "delegations of states and nations as represent two-thirds of the population of the earth" shall establish the Federal Republic of the World and cause the constitution to go into effect. Apart from recommending this threshold, they deliberately left the precise consent mechanisms open ended. They did dangle the tantalizing possibility that "plebiscites could do the job without the disheartening prospect of filibustering and dead-ends in the legislatures."[45]

After sharing their work with representatives of a handful of nations to gauge their reactions, the committee delivered the constitution to the University of Chicago Press for publication. The phases of study and consultation had ended, and the committee believed the time had come for the "intervention of public opinion." Its members understood the constitutional procedure for establishing world government to be a "never ceasing process of amendment and emendation."[46]

Though theirs was hardly the only plan for global sovereignty, it quickly gained a reputation as the most sophisticated. Public reaction came strongly and swiftly, with analysts proclaiming the fruits of the committee's work either heroic or outlandish. Some found the World Constitution "a work of great industry, devotion, and ingenuity" in the name of "a great cause." *Life* magazine hailed it as "the best-deliberated attempt yet to draft a one-world constitution," a plan both "detailed" and "imaginative." The *Chicago Daily Tribune* gave the World Constitution a cooler reception. Typifying the response from defenders of conventional sovereignty, the newspaper attacked the unauthorized quality of the proceedings and characterized world government as a foreign threat to the national legal order. Dismissing Hutchins's committee as "one of a rash of militant globalist organizations," a staff writer darkly underscored the "super-secret" proceedings that produced the document. Eyeing the bill of rights suspiciously, he pronounced it "a combination of Franklin D. Roosevelt and Karl Marx rather than anything taken from the United States Constitution." The world government structure had "many unusual bodies and officials with odd titles." Such a design amounted to a "plural marriage with other forms of government which are not only a great deal worse, but represent a great diversity of badness." Even more ominously, the draft "could grant to the world president dictatorial powers."[47]

The committee's work transpired as one piece of an international movement in favor of world government, but it was a movement that the group did not try to lead or control. Scientists voiced early opposition to the bomb, led by such luminaries as Albert Einstein, Eugene Rabinowitch, and Robert Oppenheimer. Starting with efforts to intercede in the use of atomic technology for warfare, many scientists got behind efforts for a world state. Oppenheimer endorsed Emery Reves's *Anatomy of Peace,* a best-selling book that criticized the UN as too weak to stop war and helped popularize the idea of "one law." In 1946, the Federation of Atomic Scientists produced *One World or None,* which sold more than 100,000 copies.[48]

Scientists soon discovered allies in elected officials, students, and religious leaders. Among the more high-profile supporters of world government was Owen Roberts, associate justice of the U.S. Supreme Court. In May 1943, while still on the bench, he gave a speech before assembled members of the American Society of International Law. Justice Roberts urged attendees "to rouse and enliven public sentiment in this country in support of an integration of our own and other nations in a world organization." Such a redesign contemplated that "[s]upra-national law must be law affecting and binding individual citizens of the nations belonging to supra-national Government, in the same sense that the law of the United States, consisting of the Constitution, and the statutes adopted pursuant to it, bind every citizen of the nation." Justice Willliam O. Douglas, who joined the board of the World Federalists, favored amending the UN Charter to create a world state, insisting that "greater security means greater freedom for the individual" in the atomic age. In particular, he called for the formation of both a representative assembly and an international court of justice.[49]

Members of the committee monitored the policies and activities of grassroots organizations devoted to the cause but most maintained a certain distance from their activities. Students made up a crucial component of the movement. Harris Wofford Jr., a student at the University of Chicago, founded the group Student Federalists, dedicated to "mak[ing] world citizenship in a world community a political fact." He would later go on to help establish the Peace Corps and serve as U.S. senator from Pennsylvania. Like the committee, students criticized the United Nations for having no authority over individuals and being "[in]capable of making, interpreting, and enforcing world law." To achieve a world state "in our time," young people pledged to educate their generation on the principles of world federalism and to train leaders for the cause.[50]

In February 1947, the Student Federalists merged with four other organizations to create the United World Federalists (UWF), an organization derided by the *Chicago Times* as "an outfit dedicated to the extinction of the American republic." Wofford authored a pamphlet in 1948 offering a friendly criticism of the UWF's proposal to establish a minimalist security government primarily dedicated to controlling weapons of mass destruction. In *Road to the World Republic*, Wofford objected that under the proposal "[d]ictatorships, forced labor, concentration camps would all be permitted. . . . New Hitlers could only be stopped if they started building weapons of mass destruction—if they caused mass destruction of their minorities there would be nothing that this World Government, or any national government, could do." That organization's proposed World Bill of Rights would offer liberties only to world criminals "instead of guaranteeing all men the minimum democratic rights of freedom of speech, association, conviction, and free elections for the world parliament." Drawing on America's federalist tradition, Wofford argued that a security-only proposal "failed the dual test the Federalists of 1787 set up: that any government formed must have the necessary means of enforcing its decisions on all its citizens, and that the citizens must have adequate means of controlling and altering the government." By contrast, he urged "[a]ll the progressive, idealistic, forward-looking segments of the population [to be] united around the maximal ideal of the Federal World Republic." Wofford described the idea of world citizenship as "the most progressive, if not revolutionary, proposal in American history. . . . the realization of the ideals of democracy and Christianity."[51]

Students may have endorsed the Chicago group's vision of good order, but Wofford pointedly critiqued a movement that had abstained from engaging actively and intelligently in the political arena. From this point on, he encouraged world federalists to "come down off their perch onto the plain of action." Beyond advocating a change in UWF policy, he proposed the creation of an educational division and broad efforts at field organizing. Activists in the United States needed to look toward the 1948 and 1950 elections as opportunities to seize control of a political party and secure the election of sympathetic congressmen. World government questions could be put on the ballot through the petition and initiative process in the several states or pressed in statehouses. People's conventions would educate and galvanize citizens.

Before long, religious organizations joined the efforts to legalize peace. Speaking to delegates to the World Federal Government Movement in Rome, Pope Pius XII endorsed world government as the most effective way to "end the armaments race" and promote the humane treatment of individuals within each nation. The House of Deputies of the Protestant Episcopal Church adopted a resolution stating that "peace between nations can be maintained only by law," urged the establishment of democratic and judicial institutions for doing so, and called on citizens to empower their representatives to discuss the formation of world government. In England, the Friends of Peace Committee insisted that "[t]he first political condition of the new peace will be the handing over of authority from nation-States to the world society." The United Nations could be "but a half-hearted step."[52]

Conventions broke out throughout the United States, as well as abroad. Participants believed world government to be inevitable due to technological advances or economic integration—the question was whether the political organization would be democratic or authoritarian in nature. Speakers stressed the need for a bill of rights to avoid an illiberal "state within a state," and cautioned against overcentralization to curb "revolt on the periphery and decay at the core." They demanded amendment of the UN Charter to "transform the United Nations organization into a world federal government" by increasing its authority and forming a true constituent assembly. A general convention of the Protestant Episcopal Church in September 1946 called on President Truman and Congress to work to strengthen the UN to "pursue the establishment of world law." Participants asked authorities to empower "representatives of the people" to discuss the organization of a world government with the representatives of other willing nations.[53]

Members of the Chicago group engaged in some outreach, but were hampered by their own preference for high-minded intellectual debate and the decision of elected officials to hold them at arm's length. They took to the airwaves, authored statements and essays, and participated in conversations on the 1947 Draft. For his part, Hutchins wrote and lectured tirelessly on behalf of a world state. In 1949 he turned in a speech at Marquette University arguing that the teachings of St. Thomas Aquinas "led irresistibly in our day to world law, world government, and a world state." Parsing the writings of Aquinas, Hutchins demonstrated that Aquinas's vision of the "perfect community" is characterized by peace, depends in part on positive law for its realization, and implies a community of international scope. He suggested that Catholic statements supporting a natural right to sovereignty might not be intended to "display any fondness for the modern state in its nationalistic manifestations" but rather may "mean that a people has the natural right to rule itself." Hutchins concluded by declaring that "Church and State—universal church and world state—must now work together for world peace founded on universal charity, which would realize the brotherhood of man, and universal democracy, which would bring justice to all mankind."[54]

Borgese finished *Foundations of the World Republic* before his death. Intended as "an explanation of the principles and purposes of the Preliminary Draft," the volume traced the history of world government, from Dante to Kant to Woodrow Wilson, to whom he paid homage as the world state's "first founding father." Having established the intellectual pedigree for the committee's project, he then called world government the "myth of our age"—not in a pejorative sense but rather as a desirable combination of "fable" and "power" to be translated into political reality. Despite its vague appearances in utopian and religious texts, Borgese insisted that the World Republic envisioned by the committee "is of this world." Borgese used his book to enumerate seven pillars of the Chicago Plan: democracy, virtue, justice, equality, representation, executive leadership, and peace.[55]

In a separate effort, Justice Roberts, along with John F. Schmidt and Clarence Streit, authored *The New Federalist*, which applied the principles of America's founding to the cause of world government. Recalling the original Federalist papers, they appeared serially under the nom de plume "Publius II," in the pages of *Freedom & Union* between October 1946 and February 1949. Roberts authored key papers on sovereignty, a federal judiciary, international trade, dual federal citizenship, and taxation. In *New Federalist No. 3*, he argued that "sovereignty in our political scheme rests in the citizen alone" rather than in the nation, which has "none to give up." Knowing the true source of power, "The people must abandon the false doctrine of national sovereignty if they are to unite in a world government of law. They must assert and exercise the sovereignty vested in each of them as human beings." In two other papers, he exposited on the nature of a federal judiciary. Roberts characterized the former World Court and the UN's ICJ as "not courts at all in the sense in which we speak of a court as one of the independent departments of government." Recounting America's own experience with the *Dred Scott* case denying citizenship to former slaves and the subsequent passage of the Fourteenth Amendment to rectify that situation, he advised that "some such provision should be embodied" in a world charter. Justice Roberts argued for dual citizenship in a federal union, though he confessed it might be desirable for immigration to remain temporarily subject to the power of constituent nations.[56]

Because the World Constitution was never authorized or implemented, it never grew beyond its embryonic stage. No bureaucracies were actually established, and the document apparently never served any disciplinary function for the Chicago group or immediate sup-

porters. Members of the committee had no desire to lead an underground community that rejected the legitimacy of nation-states; they
simply accepted their fate once the crusade ended. Yet written primarily to influence public debate, the constitution's deliberative functions
seemed to have been well served. By 1949, the world government
movement could point to measurable support of its vision. Newspapers and periodicals carried debates on a world state or world citizenship nearly every day. The World Federalists Association, which combined six separate groups, numbered some 50,000 members and 500
chapters. Fifty-six percent of Americans polled that year supported
reform of the United Nations to secure control of the armed forces of
all nations. The governors of nine states and the mayors of fifty cities
endorsed world government. Some twenty states legislatures in the
United States, including California, enacted resolutions approving
world federation. All told, nearly a hundred and fifty congressmen
and senators put their names to resolutions urging the creation of
world government.[57]

Social movements have sometimes had success shaping constitutional ideals, but this one, with its outsized ambitions, proved difficult
to sustain. The one world movement arose at a time when citizens
possessed an unusually strong faith in government, gained from avert-
ing economic collapse and defeating global totalitarianism. In Europe,
as in the Americas, people met and resolved to "give up the absolute
sovereignty of the State and unite in a single federal organization."
Finding the UN inadequate, Canada's prime minister declared "some
surrender of national sovereignty" necessary for the creation of world
government. In 1946, the first prime minister of an independent India
became a missionary for global sovereignty. "It is for this One World
that free India will work," Jawaharlal Nehru proclaimed. "We talk of
world government and One World and millions yearn for it." But beyond these notable declarations, the movement was simply too large,
was too diffuse, and lacked centralized leadership.[58]

The social conditions favoring global sovereignty came together
rapidly and just as suddenly dissipated. Even with significant support,
events rapidly overtook the people's audacious efforts at legal transformation. The movement for one government gained its initial impetus from widespread fear over atomic destruction. As the late 1940s
turned into the 1950s, that apocalyptic revelation lost its capacity to

generate broad-scale reform. Atomic testing and air raid drills occurred, but no nuclear conflagrations took place. Nations settled into the rhythms of the deepening Cold War, falling in line under the ideological banners of "democracy" or "communism," with some contending that agitation for a world state played into the hands of the Soviets. Nativists worried about loss of cultural identity and domination by other nations. Senator Tom Connally, who authored a reservation excluding the United States from the jurisdiction of the World Court, proclaimed the American people not ready "for the consolidation of our nation in the conglomerate masses of races and habits of other nations."[59] Voicing fears that representative government would diminish American influence abroad and reduce it to a posture of servility at home, the chair of the Foreign Relations Committee put it starkly: "In a world government we'd be outvoted. There are some 300,000,000 persons in India, 400,000,000 in China and 175,000,00 in Russia who would outweigh us in any world government."

Some opponents, including the Soviet Union, characterized global sovereignty as an "imperialist" project favored by "world capitalist monopolies." Defenders of the United Nations, for their part, claimed the mantle of realism, arguing that there is not even "the slightest possibility of setting up a world government in our time" because "none of the fifty-nine members is willing to go beyond the San Francisco Charter." They warned that movement leaders were "doing very serious harm" to their own aspirations by undermining the people's "faith in it." The *New York Times* chided one-worlders, predicting they had "honestly and sincerely assumed a responsibility which in the due course of time they will just as honestly and sincerely regret."[60]

Ultimately, world federalists in the United States failed to secure the support of conventional authorities. Early efforts at maintaining "informal" and "constructive" relations with reformers eventually turned into more aggressive efforts to deny the movement traction. Cordial meetings between proponents of world government and the Truman administration produced questions but never any public support. High officials had sworn to protect and uphold the American Constitution, and support for the United Nations was as far as any president was willing to go to advance ideas of global sovereignty. After the appearance of internal discussion, the U.S. State Department publicly rejected world government. In January 1946, Sumner

Welles called the idea "wholly impracticable," while Secretary of State George Marshall testified in Congress against proposals to strengthen the UN, asserting that the problems of war were not "solvable merely by new forms of organization." The ambassador to the UN also attacked the idea of world government to arrest momentum for broader legal transformations.[61]

The 1950s revealed a movement on its heels. In 1951, *Common Cause,* a journal created to publicize debates on world government, suspended operations. The 1953 Connecticut legislature rescinded a resolution favoring world government passed four years earlier. State legislators declared: "We favor neither the extreme of an international super-state to which our national sovereignty would be subject nor the extreme of nationalistic isolationism . . . the present best hope for a just and honorable peace lies in the United Nations." By the time President Eisenhower nominated John Marshall Harlan II to the U.S. Supreme Court, the "one world" movement had gained powerful adversaries. Anticommunists, in the name of protecting American law and the people's way of life, discredited supporters of global sovereignty. During this time, Senator Joseph McCarthy repeatedly assailed "One-Worlders." Pressed about his views at his 1955 confirmation hearings, Harlan denied being "an internationalist, or one-worlder or a unionist-now."[62]

Even as nuclear catastrophe faded as an impetus for political consolidation, more discrete international initiatives siphoned popular energy away from the more ambitious legal project. Sensing a shift in political fortunes, a number of world federalists themselves switched from advocating global government to pursuing the narrower, seemingly more plausible goals of disarmament, nonproliferation, and human rights. Hutchins himself turned his attention to domestic civil rights and liberties issues during the Red Scare, leaving the university for a post at the Ford Foundation and then later organizing the Fund for the Republic and the Center for the Study of Democratic Institutions.

Citizens hopeful for legal solutions to international problems watched as the dominant legal order gradually co-opted the concerns of the world federalist movement. Bilateral test bans began in the early 1960s, followed by multilateral agreements on testing and proliferation. Mechanisms for measuring compliance were developed—all within the existing international order that continued to privilege the nation-state.

Debates over a world state percolated into Congress over U.S. involvement in the United Nations. Though no world government proposals ever became federal law, these debates ventilated some of the passions citizens had for the issues.

As the United Nations gained acceptance and enlarged its jurisdiction, it was increasingly seen among reformers not merely as a transitional vehicle but as the best hope for limited world rule. In fact, the World Constitution made the UN Charter appear pragmatic and appropriately modest by comparison. A "burst of creative law-making without parallel in history" in the form of covenants and ICJ decisions buoyed piecemeal, incremental international lawmaking. In 1948, the United Nations adopted the Universal Declaration of Human Rights, taking away a major line of argument against the UN Charter, which mentioned but spelled out no particular human rights. For internationalists who might have wished for more, that authoritative document now came closest to spelling out the basis for world community. Two decades later when Rene Cassin, the principal draftsman of the UN Charter, won the Nobel Prize, organizers described his legacy as "the constitution of a world society. . . . It expresses our common ideals, and it embodies a goal which everyone can strive to attain." That statement revealed the extent to which the prevailing legal order had, in bits and pieces, accommodated the popular fears and aspirations of world federalists. By then, a number of the elements of the Declaration of Human Rights had been incorporated in treaties and the laws of individual countries.[63]

Prominent intellectuals and business leaders continued to urge the State Department to help develop "a system of world law" to end global conflict. Yet whatever reformist sentiment remained could easily be diverted into support for regional forms of cooperation. Instead of creating a pluralistic world republic, the regional alliances brought together kindred ideological partners for limited projects of mutual protection and economic development. In the view of Senator Arthur Vandenberg of Michigan, the Soviet Union's obstinance made universal world government unrealistic. If world government could not be achieved, then it "must become a defensive alliance (for war if necessary) against the recalcitrants." Regional compacts such as the North Atlantic Treaty should be exhausted "before we undertake a new international revolution."[64]

If anyone personified the fading fortunes for world governance, Justice Roberts fit the bill. He had been an early champion of one world, presiding over the Dublin, New Hampshire, Conference on World Peace in October 1945. Participants at that conference had resolved that "the only effective means to create ... a world order is to establish a world government." At that time, Roberts had urged the United States to "explore the possibility of forming a nuclear union with nations where individual liberty exists" as an interim measure. A year later, he attended the Episcopal Church as president of the House of Deputies, where he advocated the establishment of a "federal democracy among nations based on Christian principles." Like other internationalists of his generation, Roberts gradually shifted his support to regional alliances as the most practicable option in an increasingly bipolar world. In 1950 he became the first chairman of the Atlantic Union Committee. An outgrowth of Clarence K. Streit's Federal Union, Inc., this "citizen political action" group supported the consolidation of democracies to fight authoritarianism. Even with downscaled ambitions, the Atlantic Union Committee undertook to "transform the ideal of a Federal Union of the Free into living constitutional law and government, and thus deliver freedom and peace from the absolute national sovereignty and dictatorship that threaten both today."[65]

None of these regional measures or improvements to the UN system approached the sweep, coherence, or efficacy that might have come from a single sovereign regulating nuclear arms and promoting liberal democratic principles on a global scale. But in the absence of another nuclear catastrophe and altered political conditions, piecemeal legal improvements could be cited as progress rendering more drastic overhauls superfluous.

Hutchins and his allies failed to convince fellow Americans to give up their nation-based conception of sovereignty during their lifetime. Much of the failure of the World Constitution of 1947 can be explained by changes in social conditions, which became less congenial to radical political consolidation. When the Korean conflict escalated, observers concluded that world constitutionalism ran the same risk of totalitarianism feared in global communism. As for the strategic choices within their control, the Chicago group concentrated on building the intellectual infrastructure for a global constitutional movement. Members had neither the expertise for nor the interest in creating momentum for legal change on the ground. While the committee monitored the activities of like-minded groups, it eschewed efforts to seize the leadership of grassroots organizations. It shied away from making a strong claim to speak authoritatively for the people. When the conversation changed, members moved on.[66]

In the final analysis, the Chicago group may have underestimated the extent to which the world had changed since 1787. The success of the Founding generation in spreading a grammar of self-rule meant that opponents, too, had become adept at denying the claim that a popular consensus existed for legal change. No longer could large-scale transformations be implemented primarily through the efforts of elites. Mobilizing popular sentiment on a scale sufficient to generate domestic change, much less global reform, demanded sustained, perhaps even ruthless, direction. Wofford had been right—the Chicago group had neither the skill set nor the interest in providing grassroots leadership.

The committee's own ideas of how popular sovereignty might authorize a new constitution, too, had their shortcomings. These academics were hardly *sans-culotte,* and they stopped well short of proposing the use of extralegal measures to remake the legal order. Their ideas, like their actions, rendered them palatable to intellectuals: revolutionary in substance, yet grounded in classical ideas. In fact, proponents of the Chicago Plan proved to be proceduralists to a fault. In theory they argued that the natural right to self-rule encompassed the right to remake the U.S. Constitution, but in practice they accepted the legality of national form. Unlike the Confederates or even John Brown, the committee accepted existing national constitutions as legitimate until consent could be formally transferred to a supranational legal order. Global revolution had to be accomplished openly, through democratic means. Organizing themselves in the absence of broad-based approval, as some Americans had done, was unthinkable. Parochial forms of self-organization would also be counterproductive, given their universalist aspirations.

A high threshold established for ratification, coupled with the requirement that each member nation amend its own constitution to consent to global governance, certainly could be justified. Such a dramatic redesign of the international system surely required more than transient political support. Nevertheless, these procedures would haunt the movement when a powerful nation such as the Soviet Union opposed consolidation. Hutchins tried to surmount this difficulty by pointing out that "[t]wo-thirds of the earth's population may be counted in favor of world federation without including Russia and the United States." He then appealed to policy makers' pragmatic sensibility, claiming that the United States would be "better off" in such a form of government even if Russia persisted, since it would "have the support of numerous friends who cannot now be relied on." Still, resistance from the two most powerful postwar nations rendered a world republic a doubtful proposition.[67]

Because of the committee's decision to abide formal constraints on the perfection of popular sovereignty, the dream of world government remained shackled by each nation's protocols for making fundamental legal changes. When legal change stalled and political energy drifted elsewhere, so ended the prospects of one law for all. To this day, the 1947 World Constitution stands as a dissenting text in the story of the American Constitution's entrenchment. Far from being destroyed by agitation for transformation, conventional sovereignty emerged from the global crises of the twentieth century intact and revitalized. The law had become so enmeshed in Americans' sense of themselves as an exceptional people and theirs as a distinctive way of life that not even a movement of global dimension could alter the national Constitution's basic contours.

CHAPTER SEVEN

The Republic of New Afrika
1968

Whites in this country enjoy the fruits of 300 years of
White supremacy.

—IMARI A. OBADELE, "REPARATIONS NOW!," *New York Law School Journal
of Human Rights,* 1988

Despite constitutional amendments guaranteeing equality and the
right to vote, legal and economic progress for racial minorities and
women had occurred slowly within the conventional political system.
Explosive moments of legal creativity were followed by periods of
retrenchment, as the law settled into more predictable rhythms of
regular politics. The second half of the twentieth century brought
new opportunities to challenge the legal order through agitation and
litigation. Encouraged by the combustible optimism of decolonization and the spread of international human rights on the heels of two
world wars, social movements pressed their agendas more urgently
than ever. Yet as American law cautiously embraced racial egalitarianism, culminating in the Civil Rights Act of 1964 and Voting Rights
Act of 1965, some activists believed progress did not go far enough,
fast enough. To such critics, Freedom Rides and sit-ins failed to convey the depth of outrage at racial injustice; desegregated schools and
civil rights laws did not remotely begin to remedy generations of cruelty, disenfranchisement, and destruction of black culture. By the mid-
1960s, popular stress on the legal system was palpable. Max Stanford, founder of the Revolutionary Action Movement, described the
escalating racial tensions: "The year 1968 will be recorded as the year
when integration efforts proved a total failure," and "[i]t will be remembered as the year the Blackman realized *America is the Blackman's Battleground.*"[1]

Not only did an unprecedented degree of social activism emerge during this decade following *Brown v. Board of Education,* but the black community itself fractured over the people's orientation toward the American political tradition and the legitimate tactics for legal change. Martin Luther King Jr. and his allies may have pursued the politics of mass spectacle, but ultimately they sought reformation of conventional politics rather than its overthrow. Drawing upon American liberation texts, particularly the Emancipation Proclamation, King's vision of "the sons of former slaves and the sons of former slave owners . . . together at the table of brotherhood" conjured a pluralistic republic promised but not yet realized. Appealing to the conscience of white citizens to make changes to national and state laws served as the primary civil rights strategy.[2]

By contrast, Malcolm X (El-Hajj Malik El-Shabazz) became a prophet of black nationalism and armed self-defense. His brand of cultural sovereignty turned the American political tradition upside down. Separation, not integration, was presented as the key to black empowerment. Born Malcolm Little, he dropped his last name in favor of "X" in accordance with the Nation of Islam's teachings to signify that his identity had been lost due to American slavery. After becoming a minister for the Nation of Islam, Malcolm X boldly asserted, "[T]he masses of black people in America today don't go for what Martin Luther King is putting down." He ridiculed Martin Luther King Jr.'s philosophy of nonviolence as doing little more than "keeping negroes defenseless" and "lulling them to sleep and making them forget what whites have done to them."[3]

The assassinations of Malcolm X on February 21, 1965, and Martin Luther King Jr. on April 4, 1968, left groups jockeying to speak on behalf of black Americans. Debates over end goals and methods turned decisively in favor of militancy. Even the Congress of Racial Equality (CORE) and the Student Non-Violent Coordinating Committee (SNCC), two organizations crucial to activating citizens of all races to combat discrimination, careened toward ideas of black power. During this time, Robert Hutchins, from his perch at the Center for the Study of Democratic Institutions, estimated that 30 percent of the urban poor supported black separatism.[4]

Brothers Milton and Richard Henry, two close associates of Malcolm X, along with his widow, Betty Shabazz, wished to continue the fallen leader's work. In March 1968, just days before King would be gunned down in Memphis, the Henry brothers convened a people's convention in Detroit. Though interest in racial separatism had grown since the 1967 Newark Conference of Black Power, the Detroit convention went further than any other group in imagining how black sovereignty should appear. Denying that the 1787 Constitution ever legitimately claimed the allegiance of slaves or their descendants, delegates declared independence from the United States. In their view, American law had been infected by a theory of white power from the nation's earliest days, with the legal order designed to protect the influence, interests, and comfort of white citizens. Only a constitution blacks could call their own presented a comprehensive solution to generations of subjugation. Inspired by a wave of colonized peoples throwing off their chains, members of the Detroit convention vowed to establish a new political order from the wreckage of the old. They called it the Republic of New Afrika (RNA).

Attendees approved a blend of racial and ethical forms of popular self-rule. Though New Afrikans would have abhorred the comparison, at one level their legal vision resembled the Confederacy's model of racial power. Like their counterparts, they dreamed of a large-scale republic to save a people bound by skin color, history, and culture. Moreover, following the footsteps of past revolutionaries, New Afrikans did not seek permission from conventional authorities before engaging in political creativity but instead took it upon themselves to accelerate the conditions for secession. All options, including the armed defense of constitutional values, remained on the table.

Despite these crucial similarities, the followers of Malcolm X sought to subvert the Confederate model's legacy by gaining control over the fruits of white rule: land, resources, even the political imagination. New Afrikans designated the lands of the Deep South states, the site of enormous constitutional evil, as the site of a black homeland. There, they would finally seize the right to work and govern lands for themselves. Substantively, drafters envisioned authentically African institutions and laws while hewing to republican ideals of divided powers and popular governance. Indeed, New Africans went further than previous accounts of racial authority by incorporating a stronger ethical agenda. White power had failed to create peace and prosperity for all, but the exercise of black power might well lead to a more just society. The constitution fostered a new vision of citizenship based on a set of eclectic ideas: plural marriage, an emphasis on communal resources and social welfare rights, and a rehabilitative conception of justice.

But as New Afrikans would discover, the U.S. Constitution had become both remarkably resilient and culturally embedded. Defenders of conventional sovereignty could be found everywhere, even among the most aggrieved. A partial societal withdrawal from the political community might be accomplished, but a negotiated settlement involving a partition of land and power would be exceedingly difficult to achieve. Tactics that might have been treated as plausible forms of direct action in another time and place could now be more effectively discredited as extremism. Improved technologies allowed the government to monitor dissident groups to discourage violence, but with the effect of impairing efforts to implement unauthorized forms of popular sovereignty.

A Black Nation Ascendant

In developing their constitutional ideals, disciples of Malcolm X drew upon a rich tradition of black nationalism, which posited that African Americans comprised a distinctive people joined by a shared culture and historical injustice. Disgusted with the lack of racial progress in the wake of Reconstruction, black nationalists such as Henry McNeal Turner had earlier focused on efforts to repatriate slaves and freed persons to Africa. Turner had been enraged when the U.S. Supreme Court struck down the Civil Rights Act of 1875, "[f]or that decision alone authorized and now sustains all the unjust discriminations, proscriptions and robberies perpetrated by public carriers upon millions of the nation's most loyal defenders."

Subsequent figures, like Marcus Garvey or Huey Newton, spent their energies on revitalization or defense of the black community, usually within the interstices of the political order. All of these leaders built on memories of experiments in black self-rule in places such as Oklahoma, Florida, and the Sea Islands. No fewer than fifty all-black towns and settlements were formed in the Oklahoma and Indian Territories after the Civil War. At the turn of the twentieth century, E. P. McCabe nurtured hopes for a black homeland in the Midwest. Given

222 · AMERICA'S FORGOTTEN CONSTITUTIONS

these experiences the idea of a distinctive people, bound together by tragedy and survival, found purchase among black Americans.[5]

For proponents of black sovereignty, a nation existed before the state. "[It] is the people and their beliefs and their perspective (their way of looking at themselves and the world) and their way of life." Unlike some strains of ethnic nationalism, however, shared history and culture mattered more to black identity than a belief in genetic purity. America "began as a white nation, a new English nation, which grew up between 1607 and 1776 in a land away from England." White supremacy had always been a foundational principle of the constitutional order: "In America the Whites, led by the English, fought Indians and Afrikans for that in which they, the Whites believed: they believed in the superiority of Whites over Indians and Afrikans and the *right* of Whites to take all the land and oppress and exploit Afrikans and Indians." To black radicals, conventional politics, in its original form and as it developed over time, "help[ed] Whites better oppress and exploit Indians and Afrikans" and "protect the white nation." Thus, black sovereignty, along with a black civic identity, arose in opposition to historical hardships endured by the black community and a pervasive perception of white rule.[6]

Black sovereignty increasingly appealed to the Henry brothers, who grew frustrated with the glacial pace of legal change. They were born to a large, working-class family in South Philadelphia. Their father was a postal worker and their mother was a homemaker active in the church. Milton fought in World War II as one of the Tuskegee Airmen. While stationed in Alabama, he had an altercation with a bus driver who demanded that he sit in the back. In 1944, he was court-martialed and dishonorably discharged for protesting segregated bases and officers' clubs. After attending Lincoln University and Yale Law School, Milton relocated to Michigan, where he won a seat on the Pontiac City Commission. Richard, the younger of the two, studied journalism. He joined Milton in Detroit and edited a black newspaper. In 1961, the Henry brothers founded the Group on Advanced Leadership (GOAL), which initiated lawsuits and boycotts against businesses that refused to hire blacks.[7]

The 1960s saw the radicalization of the Henry brothers. Six years as city commissioner left Milton feeling that "in reality I had no power" and "couldn't make any changes in the things that were important." The Henry brothers became disenchanted with conventional law and politics, which focused on "the routine" instead of "a decent life" and "liberation." Despite efforts to solve these problems "within the American system," the New Deal, Fair Deal, and other major reform programs left unresolved "the same problems which have plagued us since the end of the Civil War." No longer seeing the point of enjoying an "integrated cup of coffee," Milton and Richard shed their "slave names" and renamed themselves Gaidi and Imari Obadele. Together they formed the Malcolm X Society, an "underground society designed to set up a group of quasi-military organizations in various cities throughout the United States for the purpose of defending black communities." Around this time, Gaidi met Malcolm X and became a confidante. The pair traveled to Liberia, Ghana, and Nigeria, where they observed African socialist experiments.[8]

Before long, the brothers agreed that the establishment of a black republic on American soil would be the best way to realize their martyred leader's vision. Their theory of popular consent began with the conviction that descendants of slaves were never parties to the original U.S. Constitution. Instead, Africans were kidnapped, brought to America in chains, and never consulted about the form of government they might wish to have. As Malcolm X put it during his *Message to the Grass Roots*: "You are nothing but a ex–slave. . . . You didn't come here on the 'Mayflower.' You came here on a slave ship—in chains, like a horse, or a cow, or a chicken. And you were brought here by the people who came here on the 'Mayflower.' You were brought here by the so–called Pilgrims, or Founding Fathers." Advocates of black sovereignty therefore took up the Garrisonian view of the U.S. Constitution as "the source and parent of all the other atrocities." In their updated critique, the government had long ago declared war against black people, "authorized by the United States constitution" through protection of the slave trade and "dehumanization of the Afrikan by relegating his/her status to that of three-fifths of a white man."[9]

Because of the U.S. Constitution's basic flaws relating to slaves and their descendants, basic questions of citizenship and the consent of the governed had never been properly resolved. Nor were the Reconstruction Amendments sufficient to generate consent from former slaves. The brothers seized on the gap between the passage of the

Thirteenth and the Fourteenth Amendments, after white people abolished slavery and before they ensured citizenship for "[a]ll persons born or naturalized in the United States." The Fourteenth Amendment's conferral of birthright citizenship upon former slaves was invalid because the law could only present a "sincere offer" of citizenship, not impose that status. Under Lockean principles and international law, freed slaves—and by extension their descendants—should have the chance to make an "informed, free choice" consistent with the right of self-determination. True consent, in turn, would involve choosing among four options: accepting U.S. citizenship, returning to Africa, emigrating to another country, or creating a new African nation-state on American soil.[10]

The Obadele brothers threw their efforts behind the option of establishing a breakaway nation-state called the Republic of New Afrika. They identified the states of Louisiana, Mississippi, Alabama, Georgia, and South Carolina for a black homeland. W. E. B. Du Bois had called this area, what remained of the "Egypt of the Confederacy," a "strange land of shadows." Not only did the region comprise contiguous territory containing many majority-black counties, but the land itself converged with the history of slavery. New Afrikans referred to the Deep South states as their "Kush District," after "the high civilization on the Southern Nile in ancient Africa called Ethiopia in the Bible." They considered their demand for territory modest because of their willingness to "give up [their] national claim to the land of the black ghettoes of the North" in exchange for land in the Deep South. Unlike other black separatists of the time, they refrained from making claims on other states such as Texas and Florida.[11]

The right to Southern territory as reparations sounded in two types of legal grievances. One involved the theory of unjust enrichment: "the taking of property from one man . . . and the giving of this property to another man." Returning to an older theory of pioneer sovereignty, New Afrikans argued that "the land of our nation is all the land in America where black people have lived a long time, and that we have built on or farmed or improved in some way, and that we have fought to stay on." Black people had "giv[en] to the land our blood and our sweat, our love and our hopes." America was a white empire built upon "stolen wealth." The time had come to see a return on generations of black investment, "labor which they stole from us during slavery."[12]

Alternatively, New Afrikans argued that handing over the land amounted to appropriate compensation for the injustices of slavery and postslavery apartheid. The acts of malfeasance included not only kidnapping, genocide, and theft, but also the deprivation of "a chance for a better life" due to racial discrimination, disenfranchisement, and forced assimilation. The wrongs perpetrated by the government cried out for recompense, just as reparations had been offered the Jews and Japanese Americans for their mistreatment during wartime. Because this theory emphasized redressing all reasonable harms from slavery and Jim Crow (not just lost labor), it was the farther-reaching of the two theories.[13]

New Afrikans demanded that a plebiscite be held for black Americans "as the descendants of kidnapped persons defrauded and held in America against their will." A plebiscite would determine which of the four options blacks preferred. Such a measure would comply with the demands of the American political tradition, "draw[ing] around us not only the protections of international law, not only the protections of the First Amendment—freedom of speech and the right of petition— but the protection of the Emancipation Proclamation, a legally important but neglected document, and the Thirteenth Amendment."[14]

Once the wishes of black people had been determined, a negotiated settlement could be achieved, just as the federal government had once reached peace accords with Indian nations. Alternatively, Congress might enact appropriate legislation to recognize black self-determination and award reparations under the Reconstruction Amendments. Although the republic's leaders believed the federal government already had the power to broker an agreement, they prepared an amendment to the U.S. Constitution explicitly authorizing reparations for victims of "the slave trade or other human rights violations against Afrikans, or their descendants."[15]

If peaceful means failed, New Afrikans girded themselves to use force. Their martyr had derided nonviolence as "the philosophy of the fool." Malcolm X proposed the formation of "rifle clubs" to defend black lives and property "[i]n areas where our people are the constant victims of brutality, and the government seems unable or unwilling to protect them." New Afrikans took the idea of self-defense further, embracing "revolutionary warfare as a nearly inevitable element in the struggle" for liberation. They cloaked themselves in the mystique of historical figures like John Brown, "who tried to set up a New Africa in Appalachia," as well as countless slave revolt leaders and revolutionaries "who struggled through blood and pain" to establish "free communities in the woods" or "slew the oppressor in order to seize land and power." Imari argued that "[i]n a people's war, people who believe the land is theirs resist the enemy with all means at their disposal."[16]

To these ends, leaders aspired to raise republican armed forces to accompany a black underground army. A People's Army had to be ready to take on "white civilian armies" bent on preserving white power at all costs, such as the Ku Klux Klan, but also render aid to black citizens if engagements with state police agencies escalated. An underground army, or guerilla force, "which the Republic neither directs, nor controls," would focus its efforts on "bring[ing] American industrial capacity close enough to destruction" so as to speed a negotiated settlement. Gaidi eschewed comparisons with the failed Confederacy, instead looking to Vietnam for inspiration that "[t]he United States can be destroyed" from within. But in fact—both in terms of embracing a large-scale model of cultural sovereignty and the tactics of armed secession—New Afrikans resembled the Confederates far more than they were willing to admit.[17]

New Afrikans were not the first to put ideas of black independence in writing. One of the earliest liberation texts authored by a black American can be found in an 1829 pamphlet by David Walker, born to a free mother and enslaved father. *Walker's Appeal* drew upon the Bible and Declaration of Independence in stating the case against slavery. In a call that instilled fear throughout slaveholding jurisdictions, Walker implored "the Coloured Citizens of the World" to shake off their "abject ignorance and wretchedness" and revolt against their masters.[18]

Appeals to America's canonical political texts continued to be a key strategy of black nationalists throughout the 1960s. James Forman's *Black Manifesto* appealed on behalf of "we the black people" to "white Christian churches and Jewish synagogues," demanding from such private institutions "15 dollars per nigger" for having "aided and abetted" the exploitation of black Americans. Other black power contemporaries focused more explicitly on political renewal. The Black Panther's Ten-Point Party Platform lifted copiously from the Declaration of Independence in demanding the "power to determine the destiny of our black community." Yet the document left the actual meaning of black self-governance open ended. It referred to material improvements in employment and wages, an end to police brutality and war, or increased access to housing and technology—without designing new institutions, practices, or rule-of-law mechanisms. Far from a complete plan for reorganization, then, such a document could simply be seen as a call for improved influence within conventional sovereignty.[19]

The Code of Umoja: Cultural Sovereignty and Ethical Authority

Under the leadership of Elijah Muhammad, the Nation of Islam called for "a home we can call our own." However, such statements about a black nation remained at the level of culture and history. The location of a black homeland and the means of achieving that goal often were left strategically ambiguous. Malcolm X pushed harder in the direction of legal separation. In November 1963, Malcolm X delivered a riveting message to a conference in Detroit. Expositing a theory of popular sovereignty in the vernacular, he distinguished between the "field negro" and the "house negro." He called prominent black leaders who preached patience and conventional politics "house negroes," nurtured by white elites in order to control black people. "The masses are the field negroes" like himself, who "hated the master." Truly independent self-governance had to be the end goal of popular agitation: "A revolutionary wants land so he can set up his own nation, an independent nation."[20]

Malcolm X returned to the topic of black revolution a few weeks later in New York. On December 4, he proclaimed that "America herself now stands before the bar of justice," subject to both divine and popular judgment. He tried to dispel the mirage of political power within the confines of the American Constitution. Whether initiated by white officials or black activists like King, conventional politics had produced no more than "a few crumbs of token recognition and token gains," with leaders engaging in a "false show with the Civil Rights Bill" and "false promises of integration." Malcolm X claimed that he and the Nation of Islam best represented the "downtrodden black masses," millions of citizens too demoralized to vote. Only "complete separation" from a "doomed white society" would save black Americans. Although he mentioned the possibility of repatriation as a solution, he also presented a black homeland in the United States as a fallback. If the "white government" opposed repatriation, "then America must set aside some separate territory here in the Western Hemisphere, where the two races can live apart from each other." On behalf of the black community, Malcolm X demanded "fertile, productive land on which we can farm and provide our own people with sufficient food, clothing, and shelter." The government must "supply us with the machinery and other tools needed to dig into the earth . . . until we can produce and supply our own needs."[21]

Beyond invoking the promise of pioneer governance and the goal of black self-subsistence, Malcolm X articulated two legal claims that would be honed by his followers. "If we are part of America, then part of what she is worth belongs to us," he reminded onlookers. He then thundered, "After four hundred years of slave labor, we have some back pay coming, a bill owed to us that must be collected."

Malcolm X's followers hoped to turn scattered references to a black homeland into a political reality. After his death, GOAL and the Malcolm X Society jointly sponsored a people's convention in Detroit on March 31, 1968—mere months after one of the deadliest urban riots. Letters invited recipients to attend a "historic conference" to "set up a separate Black government." Believing theirs would not be a lost generation but rather the first generation of black Americans to experience true self-governance, delegates adapted the words of the 1776 Declaration to the ends of black liberation. Citing 300 years of oppression that have "destroyed and broken and warped the bodies and minds and spirits," the New Afrikan Declaration of Independence announced the determination of "Black People in America" to "go a different way, to build a new and better world." Signatories declared themselves "forever free and independent of the jurisdiction of the United States of America" along with the obligations of citizenship foisted on them without their consent. Both individually and collectively, they engaged in political disaffiliation, foreswearing all rights attendant to American citizenship except those "belonging to human beings anywhere in the world," including "the right to damages, reparations due Us for the grievous injuries sustained by Our ancestors and Ourselves by reason of United States lawlessness." Situating their actions within international humanitarian law and global movements for self-determination, they called for a "world revolution" that would "free Black People in America from oppression" as well as ensure that "all people everywhere are so free."[22]

Early efforts at self-rule quickly followed political withdrawal. Participants at the Detroit convention authored a more comprehensive document, the Code of Umoja. This legal text, eventually ratified in conventions in 1975, served as the RNA constitution. Drafters hoped that a new legal text would help stave off the destruction of black families and save the black race. They feared that race relations and economic prospects for African Americans had so deteriorated by the late 1960s that "the ghettos are going to explode." Riots, protests, and other forms of civil unrest heightened concerns that authorities would soon begin a fresh round of repressions. Some believed that "black extermination units" trained by the U.S. military would carry out forced migrations, detentions, and even genocide as white solutions to the problem of urban decay. A plan to organize politically and teach blacks self-defense guarded "against the possibility of a Treblinka."[23]

Breaking from their own past, New Afrikans rejected messianic leadership in favor of rule-of-law solutions: bureaucracies, formal laws and rights, and a civic culture. Their constitution established black sovereignty in republican terms by assuring that "the first, foremost, and final source" of all law and power belongs to "the New Afrikan people." As precedent, the preamble invoked the practice of blacks in America who "since our arrival at Jamestown in 1619 fought for and established independent communities in the woods in the Afrikan tradition of self-government and state-building."[24]

A handful of rights would be guaranteed in this "New Society" built by descendants of slaves. Treasured rights carried over from the Anglo-American tradition included "protection of the individual's person and personal possessions," and "freedom of conscience, thought, speech, and association," though Gaidi indicated that free speech would not extend to the circulation of counterrevolutionary ideas. Once perfected, the legal order would brook no reversal of course. Nor would organized religion stand in the way of this constitutional vision: "no sect or religious creed subverts or impedes the building of the New Society," the government, or the aims of the black revolution.

The fruit of modern struggles included the right against "invidious discrimination based upon sex, color, natural or fortuitous disability, or creed," ending the "exploitation of man by man or his environment," and protecting "personal dignity and integrity." By codifying these rights, New Afrikans rode a crest of rights development worldwide, though in 1968 a right to dignity was barely on the horizon of American law, and a general right against exploitation would have been visionary.[25]

Characteristic of postwar accounts of cultural sovereignty, New Afrika's version of popular self-rule possessed a global dimension. Its founders may have lacked the pretension to rule people or territory beyond the lands of the Deep South, a necessary component of global sovereignty, yet they looked beyond the brute fact of national borders in much the same way as the Icarians. This disposition revealed itself in two areas: their great comfort with a transnational community and their law's permeability to foreign ideas. Though New Afrikans laid claim to a particular territory, the demands of governing a dispersed black nation required flexibility in their theory of political membership. Founders envisioned an "Afrikan people in North America" to be governed, though they also saw themselves as part of a larger community of "Afrikan people throughout the world." Adapting large-scale republicanism to the needs of diaspora governance kept the barriers to entry low. Regardless of "original place of birth or domicile in the world," every person of "Afrikan descent" enjoyed a right to seek RNA citizenship.[26]

Though the Code of Umoja was derived from a theory of black power, drafters stopped short of erecting racially exclusionary membership rules. Unlike the Confederate Constitution, the Code of Umoja embraced no institution or practices that kept another race subservient. Rather, they believed that the implementation of black governance would lead to true equality for all. A general respect for equality made it easier for New Afrikans to welcome nonblacks who accepted the core principles of cultural sovereignty. Commitment to revolutionary ideas, rather than skin color, would be the ultimate test of citizenship. "White people who feel they can live in the kind of society we are talking about can stay," Gaidi explained. "But they'll have to be cognizant of the fact that we'll have a new kind of law." One such figure was Yuri Kochiyama, a Japanese American woman active in Harlem's black power scene. She won New Afrikan citizenship under rules developed in 1969. Kochiyama, who had joined the Organization of Afro-American Unity (OAAU) after Malcolm X's split from the Nation of Islam, became integral to the New York consulate's communications and recruitment efforts.[27]

Formally, the constitution created a system of legislative supremacy. It empowered the People's Center Council to "make law and policy for the developing New Afrikan Nation-State." The People's Center Council consisted of elected representatives, the president, vice president, national ministers, and anyone else the Council deemed necessary to elect or appoint. Placing the legislative body above the judicial branch, the constitution provided that legal rulings bound all citizens and government officials "except the People's Center Council." Without waiting for formal recognition from outsiders, New Afrikans began to deliberate, enact laws, and discipline themselves. In their efforts to implement rule-of-law solutions straight away, they went beyond limits accepted by such groups as the Sequoyah leadership or world federalists. As practitioners of popular sovereignty, their closest analogues would have been the pioneers of old, John Brown and his men, or the Confederacy.[28]

The president was one among many members of the People's Center Council. Legislation of the People's Center Council "shall have precedence" over the acts, directives, or orders of "all officers and Governmental bodies." On a two-thirds vote, the People's Center Council could remove a member of the People's Revolutionary Leadership Council or other national officer. But, in a nod to the finality of popular sentiment, any official removed by the People's Center Council "may be duly re-elected by New Afrikan citizens." The people also had the right to recall their district judge or district representative.[29]

In practice, the People's Center Council met only twice a year unless specially convened. The People's Revolutionary Leadership Council, charged with "the power to interpret and execute the law" and implement Council policy when it was not in session, drove day-to-day legal and policy decisions for the republic. The Leadership Council was composed of the chair of the People's Center Council, the president, vice presidents, and every national minister. This body's decisions "shall be binding upon all citizens the same way as if they were decisions of the People's Center Council, until the People's Center

Council alters or abolishes such decisions." The Leadership Council not only made day-to-day decisions but also helped to ensure ideological consistency in New Afrikan policies and laws.[30]

The Code of Umoja infused its theory of racial politics with more potent ideas of ethical governance in order to distinguish it from the 1787 Constitution. Law as a legitimate force over individual lives had to be exercised in a morally justifiable fashion. Beyond the lack of influence over their political destiny, New Afrikans grappled with the problem of living in a decaying republic. Life in urban America for blacks was fraught with violence, drug dependency, failing schools, and "ever-increasing numbers" on welfare—all of it evidence that blacks had become "cyclic victims of a lack of self-respect and a lack of self-esteem." If such challenging conditions led the oppressed to construct a "nigger life-style" as a reaction to slave status and cultural deprivation, life in the New Communities instead would be "dictated by the finer cultural values" culled from the best moments of black history. To this end, the New Afrikan Creed required citizens, on pain of shame and banishment, to affirm "the spirituality, humanity, and genius of Black people" and endorse the value of community over individualism. New additions swore to "love my Brothers and Sisters as myself"; refrain from stealing, cheating, or misusing fellow citizens; and avoid gossip. The Creed extolled the virtues of patience, sacrifice, and keeping oneself "clean" in terms of body, dress, and speech. To protect the mind and body, the people outlawed marijuana.[31]

The Creed addressed one of the problems of maintaining low barriers to entry, namely, that the political community held itself open to Americans who did not yet appreciate black history and culture. To tackle this difficulty, the Code of Umoja described "conscious citizenship" as an ideal whose spread was essential to liberty. Becoming a conscious citizen meant taking the time to acquire knowledge about the history of "force and fraud" used by American governments against blacks, as well as the "human rights" basis of New Afrikan citizenship.[32]

In developing New Afrikan Ujamaa, leaders adapted proven African policies of economic self-reliance and cultural transformation for black people in America. The term ujamaa ("brotherhood" or "cooperative" in Swahili) was popularized through Julius Nyerere's economic policies after Tanzania gained independence from Great Britain. His 1967 Arusha Declaration established a democratic socialist government and sought to strengthen village cooperatives by stressing equality and hard work, with the major means of production owned by peasants and laborers. Adopting the idea of cooperative economics, the New Afrikan Declaration of Independence committed to "plac[ing] the major means of production and trade in the trust of the state to assure the benefits of this earth and man's genius and labor to society and all its members." In "pursu[ing] without cease the Aims of the Revolution," a government serving the people shall "ensure" the six Essentials of human life: "health, education, food, housing, clothing and defense for all."[33]

In the best of worlds, the implementation of socialist policies would spark the ethical transformation of the citizenry, with "purified social relationships" as the primary means of preserving good order by minimizing class conflict. If such an order could be formed, law itself might become less important over time. Ideally, once people "truly absorb" the Creed, the "individual New Afrikan thus becomes his own first-line policeman," with the family serving as "the community's second-line policeman." At that point, a formal police force would no longer be necessary. Police, prosecutors, and prisons, "necessary outgrowths of class struggle, instruments used to shield the ruling class," would be abolished in New Afrika. In the place of legal bureaucracies corrupted by white power, the Code of Umoja created novel institutions such as the People's Court, conciliators, and the Council of Judicial Elders. A judicial statute provided a list of crimes that would be handled in New Afrikan courts. These ranged from personal and property crimes to offenses against the state, such as espionage.[34]

The Code established a national People's Court, a district court for every population district, and as many other courts as the Council saw fit to create. Unlike the American system, the highest court could "exercise original jurisdiction at its discretion" as well as hear appeals. Instead of enjoying life tenure, justices on the twelve-member People's Court would be elected to six-year terms, overseen by a new chief justice every three years. These measures ensured that their highest law would be closely matched to popular concerns. In cases of "national importance," the People's Center Council had the power to hear an appeal from the People's Court, creating a direct legislative check on judicial overreaching.

New Afrikans unleashed a searing indictment of the American justice system, which had decimated the black population through draconian anticrime measures. Avoiding such a course of action, drafters structured the New Afrikan criminal justice system to emphasize community-based, rehabilitative resolutions whenever possible. In lieu of prosecutors, the People's Center Council appointed conciliators for every district. Conciliators, who served four-year terms, investigated crimes and initiated criminal actions. The accused had the right to be charged by the Council of Judicial Elders, a body of "wise men and women" that mirrored the grand jury. Many rights of the accused resembled those afforded in Anglo-American law, such as the right to trial by jury and the right against bearing witness against oneself. Beyond ascertaining the truth, the legal system aimed to "achieve justice and healing of the New Afrikan family." Among the sanctions a court could order in seeking "the healing of New Afrikan families and restoration of the victims": fines, imprisonment, publication, stripping of names, exclusion from the republic, and confiscation of property. The people outlawed capital punishment, long viewed as racially discriminatory and incompatible with the goal of reconciliation.[35]

National boundaries, local politics, and chauvinism would present no obstacle to substantive justice. To the contrary, the New Afrikan theory of law insisted on a permeable system of law to achieve political justice. The Code both authorized and encouraged the people's courts to borrow legal ideas from others nations' experiences. Judges "may adapt to our uses such procedures and precedents from other legal systems and the international law" to "serve the ends of healing and justice." The constitution itself explicitly incorporated rights established in the UN Convention on Civil and Political Rights.

New Afrikans later embraced polygyny, in which a man could have more than one wife, as a borrowed African practice. This law required considerable justification, given the black nation's formal commitment to sexual equality. Because black women outnumbered and outlived black men in America, Obadele explained, the community confronted a "statistical surplus" of black women. Allowing men to have multiple wives thus gave all women a chance at productive marriages. It could also reduce the risk of adultery, with men leading double lives and women serving as mistresses, as well as female homosexuality and out-of-wedlock children. "New marriage" would foster relationships "with love and without fear."[36]

With its canonical texts created, members of the Detroit convention set down to populate a provisional government. They selected Robert F. Williams, one-time head of the Monroe County (North Carolina) NAACP, as president of the provisional government. Williams, an outspoken proponent of armed black self-defense, had once insisted "[t]here [was] no Fourteenth Amendment, no equal protection under the law" in American towns where local authorities refused to enforce the law against the Klan and other white supremacists. At the time of Williams' election he was living in China, having fled charges arising from a riot.[37]

The convention elected Gaidi as first vice president and Betty Shabazz as second vice president. Imari accepted his designation as minister of information. Other high officials included Charles P. Howard, minister of state and foreign affairs; Raymond Willis, minister of finance; Obaba Oseijeman Adefumi, minister of culture and education; Obaboa Brady, treasurer; and Joan Franklin, minister of justice. The convention installed H. Rap Brown, a former chairman of SNCC who left for the Black Panthers, as RNA minister of defense. Delegates selected "Queen Mother" Audrey Moore, who had petitioned the United Nations in 1957 accusing the United States of genocide and demanding reparations for slavery, to be minister of health and welfare.[38]

With national officials in place, the provisional government moved on to recruitment. In the North, citizens would work under the mantra, "Prepare for the Exodus," while those on the Southern mission labored to "Prepare the Land." Literature played on popular dissatisfaction with the terrible conditions of urban life fostered by conventional politics. "Turn Toward Freedom," a New Afrika pamphlet urged. "Leave the struggle of the ghetto and make a better life." The nascent republic sought dedicated citizens with a skill or willing to learn one, who were "ready for clean air, a modern free home of your own, and a life without crime or want, a life where black people really live as brothers and sisters." Its platform included creating "a progressive, growing black economy," advancing the right of "black people to land, reparations, and independence," and establishing a national bank.

In addition to distributing the national newspaper and organizing meetings, the provisional government took advantage of the arts to spread its message. Recruits had to be taught principles of black power and the specific theory of New Afrikan self-governance, the history of "white atrocities against Black people in the modern era," international methods of revolution and nation building, and the techniques of self-defense. The Education Ministry sought to reverse the corrosive effects of urban existence created by the American constitutional order, through policies "designed to 'de-niggerize' Black people and to turn Black people into New Africans who can build and then maintain an independent, powerful, rich, progressive nation."[39]

The arts represented an effective means of disseminating the ideals of black sovereignty among average citizens. Imari authored the play, *The Malcolm Generation,* which reordered the pantheon of black leaders while trying to make black separatism palatable to former followers of Marcus Garvey and Martin Luther King. Garvey taught the Negro "to love blackness and think power." When his time came, King gave hope to "an unorganized and separate people" at a time when *Brown v. Board of Education* was widely defied by white folks. But King's moment ended when nonviolence revealed the nature of "violent, racist, unchanging whites." In an age of unrelenting violence, Malcolm X showed the black community how to defend itself and build a "new and better world." The tradition of black activism, Obadele's play taught, formed an unbroken path leading toward constitutional self-governance. Efforts to reform the American legal order once had a time and place, but conventional sovereignty itself could not be rescued from white domination.[40]

Another futuristic story, *The Killing,* opens after New Afrikans have brought "peace and power to the world." Securing "our freedom from the United States" had led to improved standing for blacks among the world of nations, technological advances, and economic justice. A "World Food Community," long a dream of reformers since at least the Second World War, had been realized. All of this had been achieved through a recalibration of political power throughout the international order. In a somewhat surprising revelation, readers are told that the rise of cultural sovereignty at some point ran headlong against the goals of global sovereignty, and in fact did a better job of meeting modern challenges. "The political power of the United Nations had grown but had been limited—like the power of national governments everywhere—by a pattern of strong local autonomy." New Afrika "had promoted this concept worldwide." As a result, "[t]oday there is considerable power—and responsibility—vested in local communities and the citizen." A character surmises that true governance by people where they lived might actually end warfare more effectively than supranational organizations and laws. Because of greater engagement and happiness, "this re-focusing of power in the local community, more than anything else, had prevented war."[41]

Such overtures brought an eclectic mix of people to New Afrika, which operated as an underground community spanning multiple cities. Many citizens were married, and nearly 60 percent had children. More than half had attended college. Half of the leaders held jobs in law, business, education, and journalism. Thus, at its height, the New Afrikan constitution successfully gathered members of the black middle and working class. Though no women served as president or in the military during the republic's most active years, nearly a third of its leadership, which included vice presidents and cabinet ministers, were women.[42]

The republic conducted itself as a small but active underground community governed by alternative rule-of-law mechanisms. Institution building was sporadic, but deliberative bodies, which are easiest to create, met and purported to make laws. The group's challenges in acquiring a base of operations or legal recognition hampered the further building of bureaucracies. RNA leaders occasionally convened ad hoc tribunals to enforce the Code of Umoja and New Afrikan Creed. Thus, the expressive, deliberative, and disciplinary functions of the constitution had the most success. The institution building ambitions of their enterprise, while certainly going further than John Brown's state-building project, never resembled anything like the settlements formed along America's frontier. To the extent founders intended the Code to sanctify extralegal tactics, it worked among a small, committed following but had difficulty penetrating mainstream opinion. These failures can be attributed to the aggressive posture of the New Afrikan theory of law, the militant tactics employed to shift public debate, and the reprisals that they incurred.

Freeing the Land

A major incident on March 29, 1969, made the Republic of New Afrika a household name and initiated a cycle of conflict from which the nascent legal order would never fully recover. Detroit police raided the New Bethel Baptist Church during the First New Afrikan Nation Day Celebration. A shootout ensued, leaving one officer dead and four citizens of New Afrika wounded. Police arrested all 142 occupants of the church. Later, all but twelve detainees were released for insufficient evidence. Judge George Crockett, an African American, ruled that nitrate tests conducted on the guns violated the defendants' right to be free from unreasonable search or seizure and their right to counsel. Newspapers accused him of "abuse of power" and racial favoritism. Outraged officers began a campaign to recall the judge from office. Both houses of the Michigan legislature passed resolutions denouncing the judge's ruling.[43]

Eventually, three people were tried for murder of the police officer and acquitted. As hostilities commenced between New Afrika and the legal system, the provisional government became embroiled in internal disputes over direction. A "constitutional crisis" erupted after Williams returned to Detroit from China, when he refused to assume responsibilities as RNA president so he could fight extradition to North Carolina. He resigned in the winter of 1969.[44]

A dispute between the Obadele brothers over tactics and a timetable for physical separation from the United States proved more momentous to the future of the political experiment. Imari wished to relocate New Afrika's base of operations to the South, whereas Gaidi believed such a provocation premature. Shaken by the New Bethel incident and an attempted coup by the minister of defense, Gaidi objected to "this madness that comes in with the military." He objected to the Cuban experience dominating New Afrikan policy and had come to the realization that precipitating revolution through violence "isn't the way [it] work[s] in this country really realistically, and the thing that could destroy the Republic."[45] Instead of forming a 100,000-member fighting force to deter white violence and gain leverage as Imari proposed, Gaidi counseled a more incremental approach to achieving a separate state. Since blacks outnumbered whites in key jurisdictions, he believed New Afrikans could alter power relations on a county-by-county basis:

If you bring in enough voters to take over a county, that gives you a sheriff. . . . Then we will have a legitimate military force, legitimate under U.S. law, made up of people who can be deputized and armed. . . . If we had only four sheriffs down there, with all that can be done with deputizing, we could change the state of Mississippi.[46]

In this way, the goals of black sovereignty might be met more subversively, with New Afrikans capturing formal offices, titles, resources, and powers on conventional sovereignty's own terms. Working within the existing power structure would also build the republic's loyal population without alienating "the average worker" afraid to be associated with "some military thing." This approach put Gaidi closer to CORE's revised tactics, even if disagreements remained over the institutions through which black sovereignty would be exercised.

Gaidi suspended Imari from office, while Hekima Ana temporarily assumed the presidency and called for elections. In March 1970, Imari emerged as the victor of an election in which Gaidi refused to run. For a time after the schism, each brother claimed to represent the Republic of New Afrika, one faction committed to political means of gaining independence and another emphasizing military might. Years later, Gaidi dropped his free name, along with his claim to leadership. He enrolled in Ashland Theological Seminary and became a preacher while continuing to practice law.[47]

With the leadership question resolved, Imari relocated operations to New Orleans, deep within the "occupied land of our nation." While their minds were now free, New Afrikans saw themselves as constituting a "captive nation." Their legal theory, which relied on modern developments to international law, fueled this attitude. Increasingly, they referred to Africans in America as a colonized people. They drew upon international law, especially the UN Covenant on Civil and Political Rights, which affirmed that "[a]ll peoples have the right to self-determination." New Afrikans proved well versed in the global vernacular of liberation, finding inspiration in Israel's founding in the midst of hostile nations and despite thousands of years of regional tumult. Officials dreamed of securing aid and perhaps recognition from China, "the only nation of color in the world who presently boast [sic] nuclear power."[48]

As free black people inhabiting land to which they did not yet hold title, "the main job of the Black government is to free the land." That declaration—"free the land"—became the group's rallying cry, underscoring the extent to which territorial control remained one of the attributes of self-governance that most eluded its grasp. Sovereign control of land would improve a people's claim to self-determination under international law and help their efforts to gain admission to the United Nations.[49]

Obadele began planning for a Land Celebration in the South that "would galvanize the minds of blacks in America" and build "financial and moral support, for the protection against reckless whites assaults which national, and therefore, world attention would bring." This desire to create a catalyzing event recalled John Brown's mentality born of desperation, but also the Confederates' overinflated hopes for external alliances. New Afrikans discovered Lofton Mason, a black farmer who agreed to sell them a twenty-acre farm in Hinds County, Mississippi. They planned to designate the property the capital of New Afrika.[50] This reflected an interim strategy in dealing with conventional jurisdictions until formal separation could be achieved:

> We planned to acquire a site, erect one or more buildings, and fly the flag. We would make plain in advance that this would not constitute a declaration of sovereignty. We might fence the land. We might have armed guards. But essentially the land would remain—until after the plebiscite—subject to the laws and sovereignty of Mississippi and the United States.

By opening a community center, the site might become "the hub of all RNA activities in Mississippi and the nation." Once New Afrika had a permanent base of operations, "the black nation would have a capital: subjugated still, unable to exercise full and unchallenged control over its citizens, but a capitol of the nation nonetheless." It "would create a 'frontier' for all black people. . . . And this frontier—like the American frontier, in the past, for white Americans—would lead to an outpouring of black genius and black creativity." Like the pioneers of old, New Afrikans would try to acquire territory, disrupt existing borders, and live under laws of their own creation. Yet they would turn the pioneer model on its head, rendering it an anticolonial device.[51]

Out of necessity, the New Afrikan theory of popular sovereignty was divided in two: legal principle and brute fact. Under legal principles, New Afrikans believed they were on their way to creating a de facto state. At the same time, conventional jurisdictions would still have power over its citizens as a matter of brute power, even if they lacked a sovereign claim over them as a matter of principle. In this way, New Afrikans' vision of local communities joined by higher principles resembled Icarianism. It also set New Afrika apart from other, more limited, approaches to black self-governance. Some black power groups tried to exploit federalism through community activism, economic programs, or ministries. For example, according to former CORE leader Floyd McKissick's vision of "Soul City," political clout could be gained in urban centers within a generation through black economic empowerment. McKissick's successor, Roy Innis, contended that a "nation within a nation" could be achieved through black control of schools, health care facilities, and local capital. Great variation in these empowerment programs could be discovered. But most groups worked within the federalist system without challenging the legitimacy of the basic political order. By contrast, New Afrikans denied the nation-state's very claim to their allegiance. They adopted localism, purely in temporary and tactical terms, as a transitional means of nation building until an independent country could be established.[52]

Even so, the group's leadership made strategic choices that rendered their efforts highly visible to the populace and, as it turned out, far more threatening to the American constitutional order. New Afrikans were attracted to the romance of pioneer sovereignty yet did not fully account for the historically contingent quality of its success. The American frontier had closed, economic and political consolidation was completed, and therefore the social conditions permitting pioneer governance to be a plausible approach no longer existed. Talk of repopulating the South sounded archaic and terrifying. Such a disruptive mode of politics now would be treated as utterly incompatible with political stability and the integrity of each state's laws.

Instead of obtaining the blessings of state authorities before embarking on their democratic experiment or pursuing quietly subversive tactics, members of the provisional government announced ahead of time which jurisdictions would be the focus of their takeover plan. The openness of their political ambitions, coupled with their endorsement of revolutionary violence, increased the odds of major confrontation with conventional authorities. If New Afrikans admired the blows of liberty struck by John Brown and black slave revolt leaders of the past, emulating some of their tactics would earn them a similarly forceful reaction.

Having left behind "the ruins of Harlem" for the "virgin expanses of Mississippi," New Afrikans sought to create a "zone of disputed sovereignty" in the Delta. Though bearing similarity to the Icarians' efforts to create a lacuna in the conventional legal order where experimental self-rule might take root, the New Afrikans refused to seek authorization for their actions. Taking the revolutionaries at their word, state officials perceived a major threat to the legal order and aggressively pushed back to deny the movement a foothold in the South. New Afrikans' indictment of white majority rule undermined the localist aspect of their vision, whose success depended greatly upon good relations or access to community resources. Clashes with state and local authorities began almost as soon as armed blacks flocked to Hinds County. The comings and goings of the group in Bolton, population 787, were observed by neighbors and monitored by law enforcement. Alarmed by the group's activities, local authorities soon joined forces with state and federal officials to track and disrupt the New Afrikans' state-building plans.[53]

On March 31, 1971, more than 150 people attended a ceremony consecrating the property in Bolton as the capital of the Republic of New Afrika. Leaders called the capital *El Malik* to honor Malcolm X. Though purely symbolic, the land dedication sent shockwaves throughout the region. As a reporter put it, "[t]he sight of the armed blacks on television enraged many whites in Mississippi in whom for years white demagogues have instilled the fear of an armed black uprising."

When newspaper headlines following the land dedication shouted "Black Nation Becomes a Reality," Mississippi attorney general P. F. Summer asked the U.S. Department of Justice to "clarify" the federal government's position regarding the black revolutionaries. Summer's letter, leaked to the press, called the New Afrikans' activities a "strike at both federal and state constitutional provisions and statutory authority, and portend grave implications for the continued domestic tranquility of our state and nation." He pronounced Mississippians "justifiably disturbed over the fact that a group of people can proclaim to the United States government and to the world that they have withdrawn from that government and are going to create a new nation carved out of our state." The attorney general vowed there could be "no separate nation set up on the soil of Mississippi." If the federal government "failed to exercise its constitutional duties" to stop the black "insurrection," Summer promised that Mississippi would take unilateral action to quash the separatist threat to public order and act "in defense of the United States."[54]

The New Afrikans' plan to control territory and subvert the constitutional order from within provoked efforts by agents of conventional sovereignty to reverse that triumphant image of black nationalism. Apparently, members had gone ahead with the consecration ceremony even before the land deal had been finalized. On May 3, Mason announced he was canceling the agreement to sell the land. Though the owner had accepted a partial down payment in good faith and allowed RNA members to begin making improvements on the land, he now had second thoughts.

It turns out Mason had some help changing his mind. State officials took the lead in direct actions against the group because no federal laws had yet been violated. Even so, behind the scenes, the FBI engaged in "counterintelligence efforts" through COINTELPRO, which monitored, infiltrated, or disrupted left-wing and right-wing activities during this era. COINTELPRO worked to prevent violence by black nationalists, discredit militant leaders, and curtail the popularity of the movement among young people. Obadele's name appeared on the FBI's national security emergency arrest list, known as the Administrative Index (ADEX). Advised by informants on the Hinds County situation, FBI agents approached Mason and implored him not to go through with the land deal.[55]

Initially sympathetic to the group, Mason's reversal gave the state another opening to move against New Afrika. On May 8, 1971, Attorney General Summer obtained a preliminary injunction forbidding the RNA from reentering Mason's property, operating in the state of Mississippi, or engaging in activities that threatened a breach of the peace. He also secured warrants to arrest members for trespass after RNA members had forcibly reentered the property. The attorney general, accompanied by the district attorney of Hinds County and more than a dozen sheriffs, visited the property to execute the warrants. They discovered that the group had already abandoned the premises.[56] Before law enforcement departed, they posted a court order on the padlocked gate, warning off trespassers. Citizens of the dissident republic had been ignominiously "evicted" from their capital.

In an attempt to resolve the community's dispute with the state, Obadele tried to meet with law enforcement officials. Summer refused, throwing New Afrikans' claim to be a sovereign nation back at them: "I have no power to conduct foreign relations." Instead, Summer declared victory in the press: "The RNA has now been enjoined from operating in Mississippi. They have been run out of the state." Incensed, Obadele fired off his own press release. "We shall return to El Malik at a moment of our own choosing," he said defiantly. "And anyone who gets in our way—the Mississippi National Guard or anyone else—will be utterly destroyed." Hinds County district attorney Jack Travis expressed no concerns about meeting with Obadele. Although Travis agreed not to enforce the trespass warrants against RNA members, he remained noncommittal about a global resolution.[57]

As New Afrikan efforts to acquire land became embroiled in a growing dispute with Mississippi, the group relocated to a house near Jackson State University. Taking the land matter into their own hands, leaders convened a People's Court at the Mount Calvary Baptist Church. Aware the court had no formal power to enforce any judgments, leaders nevertheless wished to show black people the "differences between 'their' law and 'our' law" and inculcate respect for New Afrikan law, which was "fundamental to nation-building." It would be a defiant performance of black autonomy and popular justice.[58]

RNA officials served papers on Mason, the landowner, and Summer, the attorney general of the "illegal Mississippi government," but none bothered to appear. Vice president Chokwe Lumumba conducted the proceedings, which began July 19. Before an overflowing auditorium, Lumumba explained that as a "captive nation" the people had to begin building independent institutions such as courts. Though lacking power in the conventional sense, black people would give their work the force of law through belief in their own decisions. Lumumba then presented the case on behalf of the provisional government, calling witnesses to the land transaction and introducing canceled checks as evidence. After deliberations, a three-judge panel determined that Mason had defrauded the people of New Afrika, a decision Obadele announced at a press conference on August 5. He then wrote to Mason and Summer to inform them of the decision of the People's Court. Obadele implored them to abide by the adverse verdict, since blacks had for so long obeyed the "white courts of this state in which We have had no voice."[59]

"A Government in Captivity": Shootout, Trial, Schism

The conflict reached a crescendo on August 18, 1971, ultimately crippling the Mississippi experiment. FBI agents, joined by local police officers, arrived at RNA headquarters in Jackson to serve a felony warrant against Sylee (Jerry Steiner), wanted for a murder in Detroit. An informant had alerted the FBI that Sylee had been seen in Mississippi working on the RNA's reparations campaign. The police also decided to act on a few outstanding misdemeanor warrants arising from an altercation between a reporter and citizens of New Afrika. At dawn, authorities demanded that all occupants of the house come out within sixty seconds, then waited another fifteen seconds. When no one appeared, officers fired tear gas through the windows of the home. A fierce shoot-out ensued.[60]

The firefight left one policeman dead and two other law enforcement officers, including an FBI agent, wounded. Sylee was not found on the premises but was arrested in Memphis days later. Police apprehended eleven New Afrikans for murder: seven involved in the shootout and four others, including Obadele, who were in a house down the road. Officers seized guns, ammunition, spent casings, materials that could be used to make Molotov cocktails, a live bomb, and various publications.[61]

A few days later, District Attorney Travis announced his decision to add charges under a law that barred armed insurrection against the state. Not to be outdone, Attorney General Summer blamed the federal government for failing to act against the "armed insurrectionists." The lieutenant governor of Mississippi called the shooting proof that New Afrikans posed "a clear and present danger to our people—white and black." U.S. Senator James Eastland "advocate[d] taking whatever steps are necessary to wipe out these hotbeds of revolutionaries" to protect policemen and "insure the survival of our country."[62]

From the perspective of New Afrikans and their allies, the authorities had instigated hostilities by bringing shotguns, a tank, tear gas, and an ambulance to the headquarters with the "purpose of forcing a 'shoot out' with the RNA." Being called into the streets early in the morning was merely the culmination of months of harassment and civil rights violations. Once police began firing their weapons with little warning or restraint, New Afrikans argued they had a right to protect themselves from politically motivated killings. A rallying cry went out on behalf of the "RNA-11," who were described as political prisoners.[63]

Like John Brown before them, Obadele and his fellow RNA officials entered a different phase of constitutional struggle once the legal process commenced. Behind the formal fact-finding process and adjudication of criminal wrongdoing lay a battle over the legitimacy of New Afrika's constitutional vision and its popular tactics for legal change. Representatives of the state saw their role as defending the integrity of conventional sovereignty, along with the associated values of order, law, peaceful relations between the races, and nonviolent methods. Prosecutors dramatized the mayhem caused by the New Afrikans' tactics. Conversely, the defendants seized the opportunity to present themselves as virtuous citizens dedicated to principles of natural law, constitutional law, and international law. Finding their options suddenly limited, they did their best to advance the cause of black sovereignty within a legal system whose authority they no longer recognized.

At the preliminary hearing, RNA Minister of Justice Bill Miller moved to dismiss the charges on the ground that the defendants were citizens of a foreign nation. The motion was denied. One RNA member pleaded guilty and another jumped bail. For their role in killing the police officer, the state tried three men separately for murder, and juries found each of them guilty. During trial, the district attorney repeatedly posed the question, "What were those people doing with all those guns in that house?" He answered his own question: "They were getting ready for a war."

The remaining defendants, including Obadele, faced federal charges of conspiracy to assault a police officer and possession of unregistered firearms. Ordered to stand trial in May 1973, he moved to dismiss all charges, raising all of the constitutional theories of citizenship and consent developed elsewhere. Obadele added a novel issue to his brief, arguing that only the U.S. Supreme Court had original jurisdiction over public ministers from a foreign country, so therefore the state court lacked authority to try him. He claimed that the Republic of New Afrika resembled the Cherokee tribe, recognized as a nation despite coincident sovereignty over land. If New Afrika were a foreign nation, then he ought to be treated as head of state and afforded immunity as a foreign dignitary.

Judge Walter Nixon Jr., who presided over the trial, allowed a hearing on this motion. Milton made an appearance in the case and led his brother through direct examination. After recounting the history of New Afrika, Imari proceeded to claim that the republic had received de facto recognition as a nation-state. Though the U.S. government never recognized New Afrika as a foreign nation, Imari claimed that he had met with State Department officials after notifying the Johnson administration of the republic's acts of independence. Moreover, he argued that Tanzania, Cuba, and China all had tacitly recognized the republic by conducting affairs of state with New Afrikan officials, notably through the announcement of Robert Williams as RNA president and negotiating his return to the United States.[64]

Judge Nixon rejected all of these arguments. He ruled that New Afrika was "not a sovereign nation in any sense of the word," and its members were entitled neither to diplomatic immunity nor to a hearing before the U.S. Supreme Court. Judge Nixon deemed Obadele "a citizen of the United States and subject to its laws," having no rights arising from any other constitution. Thus, he concluded that the Code of Umoja had no legal authority that American courts were bound to respect. It did not vest defendants with offices or a status that in any way disrupted the state's ability to enforce its laws against them. At the conclusion of the trial, the jury found the defendants guilty on all counts. At sentencing, one of the defendants shouted at the judge, "Despite you: black people will be free!" For his part, Obadele accused the judge of becoming a party to the destruction of the black independence movement: "You have permitted your court to be used in a controversy which should be settled by political processes."[65]

Federal courts upheld the convictions, deferring to the "violence prone" nature of the organization. This evidence of their activities, which included vivid descriptions of the New Afrikans' ideology and plans, supported the jury's decision that federal conspiracy laws had been violated. Although RNA members claimed to have armed themselves merely as "defensive precautions," the appellate tribunal saw something more behind the jury's verdict: "[T]here is no doubt that there was a common plan to defy, intimidate and shoot it out with any law enforcement officers when the opportunity presented itself."[66]

The court's application of the rule of law marginalized New Afrika's insurgent legal theories, with minimal involvement by high officials in the U.S. government. Hekima Ana, a vice president; Offogga Quddus, a regional interior minister; and Karim Njabafudi, a fifteen-year-old, received life sentences for murder. A fourth, Addis Ababa, was sentenced to two ten-year terms for assault. In the federal case, the judge imposed prison terms ranging from three to seventeen years. All told, Imari Obadele spent three years in federal prison before being paroled. Through the ordinary operation of criminal law, the authorities had protected the integrity of the conventional order and publicly rejected the New Afrikans' right to secede.[67]

With key members of the government-in-exile incarcerated, the republic's land acquisition plan "had been decimated." Outside of prison, a small cadre of committed citizens remained in the South to carry on the work of nation building. For a time, Alajo Adegbalola took over as acting president. Lumumba became minister of justice, and then assumed the role of acting president when Obadele reported to prison. But law enforcement actions ended any glimmer of hope for mass migration of African Americans to the region. The enterprise not only sounded dangerous, but it had also been legally discredited. As Obadele conceded, "No huge exodus to Mississippi . . . has resulted."[68]

During Obadele's time in prison, organizational fissures opened in the provisional government. Some felt that Milton had been proven right: they had been woefully unprepared to confront the South. Momentum began to build within the RNA leadership to restructure the constitution along the lines of "democratic centralism" to avoid such mistakes in the future. A constitutional crisis occurred as the 1978 elections approached. One faction of the provisional government, led by Lumumba, proposed a constitutional amendment that would restrict the vote to movement members or the provisional government. In the view of this faction, national elections were premature and unlikely to produce strong revolutionary leadership in dangerous times.[69]

Another faction, led by Obadele, opposed any change to the Code's guarantee of "direct popular election." This faction considered such a move to preserve ideological purity as "a major retreat—indeed, as a catastrophe" because the future of New Afrika "rested on how well people were able to involve themselves in governmental processes." To the imprisoned leader's dismay, the People's Center Council wished to make the change itself, in apparent violation of the fundamental law requiring a majority vote of New Afrikan citizens to ratify amendments to the Code of Umoja.

When the People's Center Council voted to restrict voting for the offices of president and vice president to a national convention, Obadele sprang to action. Obadele argued that Lumumba had never been properly installed as acting president and tried to remove him for failing to organize elections on a timely basis. In response, Lumumba, backed by the People's Center Council, argued that Obadele's imprisonment caused the line of succession to go into effect, without the Council needing to act further. He also claimed that while the first slate of national officers had been elected by popular vote, the Code itself left for the Council the power to determine "the method of national elections for Presidents and Vice Presidents."[70]

After unilaterally removing Lumumba from office, Obadele appointed the Central Committee of the Malcolm X Party to conduct national elections. In doing so, he was merely carrying out his constitutional duty as duly elected president to ensure that elections occur on schedule. After the tallying of votes in Washington D.C., Atlanta, and inside some prisons, Obadele reclaimed the presidency.

Meanwhile, the faction that opposed Obadele's power play met in New Orleans. It elected Dara Abubakari, an important figure in the Delta civil rights community, as New Afrikan president. Lumumba and two others were elected vice presidents. Each slate of revolutionary leaders then claimed to act as the duly elected provisional government and speak on behalf of black people. Once again, the black nation had been split asunder.

When Obadele was released from prison, he brokered negotiations to try to repair the schism. After a year and a half of discussions, an accord was finally reached. The two republics merged, led by Obadele and Abubakari as co-presidents. All national officers retained their posts, while the People's Center Councils became a single body. But nothing would ever be the same. Any momentum the group had within the black community had dissipated; the RNA's capacity to offer a plausible model of self-rule had long been lost. The group's repeated clashes with defenders of the legal order forced a downscaling of their political vision to survive. Despite repeated efforts to draw federal officials into negotiations, no presidential administration ever opened such discussions.

Nor did any foreign country or international body act on New Afrikan requests for humanitarian assistance. Just as Confederate hopes for foreign aid were dashed, so too New Afrikans' plea for intervention fell on deaf ears. But if the chance of foreign aid arising in the 1860s was in the realm of possibility, it became little more than a fantasy a century later. By this time, the consolidation of the national legal order had not only been completed, but America's status as a superpower gave it maximal control over domestic affairs. Given the country's influence abroad, other nations treated New Afrikans grievances as internal matters of the United States.[71]

New Afrikans never gave up the dream of black self-determination but rather became increasingly satisfied with more modest achievements. Having backed away from violence as a means of obtaining political power, they became participants once more in conventional politics. Upon his release to RNA politics, Obadele felt demoralized to discover that black people "in the short space of a half-decade had all but abandoned defiance and the struggle to preserve our New Afrikan personality." He lamented the civil rights–oriented "negro paradigm," which had retaken hold of the popular imagination. Conventional sovereignty had shown itself to be remarkably resilient and vigorous, satisfying just enough of the grievances made by blacks to prevent a successful independence movement. The technologies and resources available to preserve the U.S. Constitution had multiplied, making secession a near-impossible task.[72]

Obadele became a leading figure in the black reparations movement. By the mid-1970s, the RNA had largely returned to operating within the normal constitutional order. Officials now curiously denied ever urging that "conventional politics should be abandoned by black people." New Afrikans continued to work on their Anti-Depression Program, unveiled in 1972. Directed at Congress, the program sought approval of its independence proposals, direct reparations to descendants of slaves, and indirect reparations in the form of funds marked for building New Communities. New Afrikans also pursued an agenda that included reforming the tax code, vigorously enforcing antitrust laws, instituting price controls, and ending the Vietnam War.[73]

RNA leaders linked the formation of self-governing black communities to President Johnson's War on Poverty. Short of full reparations, they hoped to gain amendments to federal laws that would allow them to secure grants under programs created by the Housing and Urban Development Act of 1965 and the Urban Growth and New Community Act of 1970. Such changes would have to permit "cooperative development agencies created by blacks." With federal funds, they hoped to establish alternatives to "once vaunted, now dying American cities."[74]

After his prison experience, Imari's tactical orientation moved closer to his brother's. In the fall of 1976, Obadele proposed that black citizens in Jackson elect a counterpoint to the all-white municipal council. This black municipal council was "a strategic method used for the transformation of political and economic power to the Black community." It would not "at this juncture" try to seize full power but would instead fight for local authority. Once organized, such a countergovernment could file for control of federal development funds so expenditures would go to housing and industry "owned by the people." Even if no monies were actually disbursed, the campaign would nevertheless "habituate" demoralized Jackson citizens to elections "sanctioned" by black power.[75]

Little came of these plans in Mississippi. With state-building efforts in the South stalled, the New City campaign turned toward Philadelphia and Detroit, where RNA leaders hoped the existing base of New Afrikan citizens could form economic cooperatives using tax money. They looked for ways to accumulate capital, with an eye toward eventual control of radio, television, and banking. But no federal funds came, and the dream of "cooperatively owned industry and modern New communities" did not come to fruition.[76]

In the area of reparations, the movement achieved some success in mobilizing others and raising awareness. Obadele joined mainstream organizations such as the National Conference of Black Lawyers in forming N'COBRA (National Coalition of Blacks for Reparations in America). Acting on the N'COBRA proposal, John Conyers submitted a bill in the House to create a commission to study slavery and discrimination against African Americans and present recommendations to Congress as to "appropriate remedies."

Former RNA leaders, too, reverted to conventional methods of resistance. Imari Obadele earned a doctorate in political science and taught at Temple University, developing a black history curriculum. Lumumba, who had sworn allegiance to New Afrika as a law student and participated in many of its foundational moments, earned a reputation as the "people's lawyer" for his criminal defense and civil rights work. In June 2013, he was elected mayor of Jackson, Mississippi, winning 85 percent of the vote. After his departure from New Afrika, Milton Henry founded Christ Presbyterian, where he preached black nationalism from the pulpit. Black sovereignty remained integral to his sermons but assumed a mostly social, and less overtly political, incarnation.

Interest in black separatism waned in later decades, though conflict flared up from time to time. On October 20, 1981, radicals tried to rob a Brinks armored car in Nanuet, New York. Two police officers and a Brinks guard were slain during the bungled robbery. Police arrested several members of the Weather Underground and Black Liberation Army, along with Fulani Sunni Ali, chair of the New Afrikan People's Center Council.[77]

Ali later won her release after witnesses established her presence in New Orleans at the time of the robbery. A burst of popular resistance ensued. When federal officials subsequently opened a major investigation into groups committed to overthrowing the government, New Afrikans collectively refused to testify before a grand jury. Obadele boasted that his people had "'shut down' the grand jury by a stream of defiant witnesses, filling the jails." Even so, these moments of direct action were few and far between; state building in any significant fashion had stalled. For all practical purposes, the government-in-waiting had become like many other advocacy groups, marked by a broad agenda and organized according to superficial rule-of-law mechanisms.[78]

Ideological divisions, the loss of key personnel to prison, and exhaustion with racial issues after major civil rights successes diminished New Afrika's appeal. Liberal successes prevented broader coalitions from developing beyond existing pockets of despair. Through the processes of criminal law, theories of black sovereignty were discredited, legal claims rejected, and violent means repelled. Although popular sentiment gave birth to a dissident constitutional vision at a high point of black activism, the republic faced intense competition for resources and social support. Once isolated by the state through the rule of law, New Afrikans had little choice but to accept obsolescence or return to regular politics as a means of advocating for black interests.[79]

CHAPTER EIGHT

The Pacific Northwest Homeland
2006

Racial loyalties must always supersede geographical
and national boundaries.

—DAVID LANE, "88 PRECEPTS," KATJA LANE (ED.), *Deceived, Damned & Defiant: The
Revolutionary Writings of David Lane* (1999).

With the twentieth century in the rearview mirror, it became possible
to consider the project of legal and economic development nearly
finished. The political community had been enlarged and diversified
by gradually bringing marginalized populations into the fold. Little
now escaped the rule of law, which could be exercised over every controversy in which the nation had a plausible interest. High officials
and ordinary citizens alike could be counted on to protect the integrity of the legal order through persuasion and cunning.

America had transformed itself from a fledgling republic into a
modern liberal democratic nation, where individual rights were cherished and each citizen could pursue his conception of the good life. The
legal order tolerated dissent, but absorbed and dispersed it. Along
the way, its defenders laid waste to competing ideas of popular rule.
These ideological battles went well beyond conquering theories of
racial self-governance. Male-dominated approaches to governance,
once a staple of traditional civic republicanism, began to be dismantled. Not only did women win the franchise, but they also toppled
restrictions on sexual expression, policies prescribing traditional sex
roles, and laws criminalizing abortion and homosexuality. Acceptance of a heterogeneous population crystallized into pluralism as a
foundational tenet of the liberal order. In the place of a robust but
parochial basis for fundamental law, the system sought to create a

thin and inclusive civic culture. All of these adaptations took place under the auspices of the original Constitution, but that was a legal fiction. In actuality, the collective changes represented the latest iteration of conventional sovereignty.

While many Americans welcomed these shifts in constitutional interpretation, others found them disturbing in substance, and their inability to arrest such developments alienating. The law not only had become impotent in disciplining culture but also had become enslaved by it. For white citizens unwilling to reconcile themselves to the modern terms of civic membership, the answer might be to withdraw to isolated locales. In these oases, disillusioned individuals could elude the polluting forces of contemporary existence, champion the virtues of racial solidarity, and return to traditional family values. To the more ambitious handful, salvation lay in dreaming of a white homeland, where someday a more responsive brand of moral politics might reign supreme once more.

Ironically, then, the successful adaption of the 1787 Constitution to modern life produced a resurgence of ideas of cultural sovereignty. But the theory and practice of white rule itself had to evolve to remain relevant to the experiences of average Americans. Over the years, underground theories of white rule accumulated a myriad of disgruntled positions, from free speech and religious freedom, to concerns about the imperial presidency, to reducing taxes and the size of government, and to ensuring gun rights. Increasingly, the challenge for these nonconformists became how to make a theory of white sovereignty coherent.

Though loosely united by ideology, the Aryan community found itself divided by tactics. No central structure existed for deliberation. Some activists engaged in local forms of resistance while others worked to gain influence within the party system. Even underground figures willing to resort to terror, harkening back to how the Sons of Liberty fought British tax policies or the Klan resisted Reconstruction, could not agree on a desired outcome. Without an endgame, white power ideas would lack potency and remain easily ridiculed.[1]

Another shift involved the role of territory. Over the years, many proponents of white sovereignty gave up the dream of restoring Confederate rule. The nonwhite and immigrant population in the South had multiplied faster than in many other regions, leading to a rising black middle class and elected officials from all backgrounds. But even white politicians could no longer be counted on to fight the excesses of pluralistic democracy. At the same time, the Pacific Northwest emerged as a desirable locale for a white homeland. Despite its reputation as a source of high-tech jobs, the region's history, demographics, and ecology were attractive to dreamers. With the exception of urban centers, which are racially and ethnically diverse, the remaining areas were homogenous and sparsely populated. What is more, early laws expressed some of the most strident versions of racial sovereignty, deterring migration and settlement by nonwhites. Oregon's original constitution extended equal rights to "white foreigners" while barring "free negroes" from "com[ing], resid[ing], or be[ing] within this state," and denying the vote to blacks and the Chinese. Other Northwest states slowed demographic change by prohibiting aliens from owning land, obtaining public employment, voting, serving on juries, or holding office. To advocates of white power, the region contained a natural constituency.[2]

Beyond impressing visitors as an unspoiled corner of the world, the region's terrain formed natural boundaries. The symbolism of ecological purity also proved attractive for strategic reasons. An all-white nation in the Pacific Northwest could serve as a geographic counterpoint to Washington, D.C., forcing the population to choose sides when the North American continent inevitably fractured into a series of ethnic and race-based nations vying for supremacy. The only missing ingredients for white liberation were a mature political-racial consciousness, sufficient arms, and a plan of action.

After toiling at the margins of political relevance, practitioners of white sovereignty regained their interest in constitutional law. A handful of Aryans in 2006 drafted, deliberated, and approved a constitution for an all-white republic. Their brand of racial sovereignty improved upon the Confederate model along multiple dimensions. Where their predecessors assumed that preserving the institution of slavery would sufficiently protect white civilization, the end of slavery and Jim Crow ushered in an unsettling world based on radical equality and individualism. Preserving white families in the face of modern challenges now required formal law, special bureaucracies, and new technologies. As with the black nationalists before them, the onset of internationalism pushed Aryans to imagine a worldwide community without ceding control over the law to supranational organizations, other nation-states, or nonwhite populations. But they would demonstrate an even stronger commitment to ethical reformation than their forebears, proposing potent means of reeducating, stratifying, and disciplining white citizens after expelling nonwhites from their midst. These would-be founders would offer harsh and creative ideas for the restoration of white rule without remorse or pity, convinced they had one last opportunity to save the people from themselves.

Aryan Legalism: Rebranding Whiteness, Sanctifying Violence

Harold Covington, an Aryan activist, was born to a working-class family in North Carolina. Staunch Republicans, his parents were mainstream conservatives who opposed *Brown v. Board of Education* and, in the words of a family member, "the people who were least equipped to digest and accept the speed at which things changed." Even so, they kept their children in integrated public schools. For the younger Covington, this experience proved radicalizing. He described his racial awakening as a white child who suffered at the hands of faceless bureaucrats experimenting with desegregation. Covington proudly recounted a scuffle he had with three black boys from which he supposedly emerged victorious. Whether truthful or apocryphal, the story revealed his state of mind: the public sphere had long been a site of racial and legal strife.[3]

Around the time he enlisted in the U.S. Army, Covington became affiliated with a number of neo-Nazi and Aryan organizations. After his discharge from the Army in 1972, he spent time in Ireland, Britain, and Rhodesia making contact with fringe groups and militias. Eventually, Covington returned to the United States and assumed the leadership of the National Socialist Party of America. He vacated that position in the aftermath of a violent encounter in which Klansmen and Nazis opened fire on Communist demonstrators in Greensboro. In 1980, Covington unsuccessfully sought the Republican nomination for North Carolina attorney general, though he pointed to his 43 percent share of the vote as proof that conservatives secretly shared his views. Sensing few realistic opportunities to break into a political system that abhorred his values, he eventually gave up conventional means of political engagement. Instead, Covington began working to rebuild the ideological infrastructure of the Aryan movement.[4]

For Covington, a "turning point" in Aryan history occurred with a lawsuit brought by the Southern Poverty Law Center against Richard Girnt Butler. After breaking from his mentor Wesley Swift, who started the Church of Jesus Christ Christian, Butler served as the pastoral leader of the Aryan Nations Church in Hayden Lake, Idaho. Among other things, he preached that God had promised the Kingdom of Heaven to whites alone, the "descendants of Adam." Butler, like many practitioners of white sovereignty, pointed to *Brown* as a galvanizing moment: "And the '54 decision, I started saying, . . . there's something wrong, we're losing, you can't have two people be citizens of the same country at the same time, you know, two races." By the early 1980s, when Butler began convening the Aryan Nations World Congress and related "Freedom Festivals," the region had become known as an international center of white supremacy and Christian Identity.[5]

On July 1, 1998, Victoria Keenan and her son Patrick, who were of Native American heritage, drove near the compound in northern Idaho. The car apparently backfired, leading armed gunmen working for Butler to think they had been fired upon. Members of Butler's security force chased down the Keenans, held them at gunpoint, and threatened to kill them. The Southern Poverty Law Center represented the two in a high-profile lawsuit relying on common law causes of action such as assault, battery, negligence, and false imprisonment.[6]

At the conclusion of the trial, an Idaho jury awarded the plaintiffs $6.3 million. Butler's compound had to be sold to satisfy the judgment, with plans to rededicate the land. In 2005, advocates for equality celebrated the opening of the Human Rights Education Institute, erected in place of the compound. A granite monument was inscribed with the words of the Universal Declaration of Human Rights. The symbolism in the demolition of the Aryan Nations headquarters and chapel enraged the Aryan community. Covington marked September 2000 as the occasion "when the loathsome Morris Dees brutalized and despoiled Pastor Butler of his home of 30 years." That event led him to promise "two things to myself, to Pastor Butler, and to such posterity as may remain to our race." He would "devote the rest of my career to the creation of an independent and sovereign Aryan nation in the Pacific Northwest . . . [and] write a book that would serve as a kind of intellectual and literary launching pad for the Northwest Migration and for the new nation to come, a kind of Northwest Turner Diaries."[7]

According to Covington and fellow advocates of white sovereignty, American law had been perverted to oppress patriots and advance an anti-Christian, multiculturalist agenda. What is more, the seizure of the Hayden Lake compound demonstrated the foolishness of expecting peaceful coexistence with nonwhites inside the existing legal order; outsiders would pursue them until the alternative community was eradicated. Thus, the progressive use of the law spurred racially conscious whites to think more ambitiously and, eventually, seek to reclaim the law themselves. With the construction of a "peace park" in place of the compound, liberals celebrated the substitution of what they viewed as a totem of hate with a symbol of racial enlightenment. Covington and his allies tried to invert the symbolism by using the event to mobilize others to embrace the virtues of white rule.[8]

Like any dissident movement, the Aryan—or "racially conscious"—white community treasured a handful of canonical texts. One such legal text was the 1996 Aryan Nations Declaration of Independence. Lifting heavily from the 1776 original, this document replaced the "patient sufferance of these colonies" with "the patient suffering of the Aryan people in America." The main target of popular ire: "the present Zionist Occupied Government of the United States of America." Acting in league with nonwhites, the United States had pursued the "eradication of the White race and its culture," as well as "abrogat[ion] [of] the Constitution, the Bill of Rights, and the Common Law; instead adhering to Executive Order, Judicial Decree, and Martial Law."[9] Just as Confederates once feared an expanding abolitionist coalition, so too modern Aryans felt that a vast conspiracy had formed to deprive them of the rightful power to rule.

Among more specific complaints, the document revived the grievances of the "people and sovereign states of the South," dating back to Reconstruction. But Aryans updated their blistering assault on radical equality by folding in twentieth-century events, from desegregation to unchecked immigration and feminism. The liberal project of creating one nation through the expansion of individual rights had merely destroyed what was distinctive and valuable about the American way of life. Advancement of this agenda through constitutional law had thoroughly corrupted the conventional order, divided the white population and made them ashamed of their heritage, and accelerated the extinction of the white race. The Declaration accused the government of engaging in "systematic genocide of the races, with malice aforethought, through a rigorous system of forced integration/assimilation of Blacks, Indians, Latinos, Asians, and White Aryans." Fear of international law and the global economy exacerbated the sense that the white community had lost control over its own destiny. The people's far-ranging complaints included "subject[ing] us to a jurisdiction foreign to our Constitution," "allow[ing] unlimited immigration and drug traffic," and "allowing free trade to the detriment of our workers and families."

Invoking "the God of our folk" and "the sovereignty of our people," the "representatives of the Aryan people" reclaimed the rights of "a free and independent nation." Two practical consequences flowed from this assertion of popular self-rule. First, because Aryans believed the original Constitution to be a lost cause, white people "are absolved from all allegiance to the United States of America, and . . . all political connection between them and the federal government thereof, is and ought to be, totally dissolved." Second, the "free and independent nation" that replaced conventional sovereignty would enjoy "full power" to perform all acts "which independent nations may of right do." In disaffiliating from the political order and asserting full lawmaking power, the Aryan Nations' actions recalled approaches taken by other breakaway republics.

Another document set forth "Fundamental Principles of Northwest Migration" and had a twofold purpose: reversing the legal achievements that spurred racial diversity and creating the demographic conditions for restoring white self-rule. Its authors sought to accelerate white flight such that it became more focused as "mass migration" to the Pacific Northwest, with the ultimate goal of establishing an independent nation. Aryan leaders encouraged members of the white race to de-integrate the Northwest "with only the minimum delay necessary" to put family affairs in order.[10]

An organization started by Covington called the Northwest Front tried to fill the vacuum left by Butler's fall. Its "sacred" goal: establishing a Northwest American Republic (NAR) in which whites can rule themselves through a sanctified law. Describing themselves as "pioneers of a new age," members pledged to implement these principles with "honor, steadfastness, loyalty, courage, and purity." Their invocation of the frontier myth was accurate in one sense: they hoped to use the tools of ethnic cleansing to repopulate the land. Shared Aryan culture, however, rather than the happenstance of controlling territory, served as the legitimate foundation for the right to govern. Ethical reform proved central to their legal project, for they decried the "spiritual poison of 'modernization.'" To lay the foundations for a new state, they promoted the Butler Plan, named in honor of the man who had done so much to revive the white sovereignty movement through his spiritual emphasis. According to the plan, "The White racial nationalist movement has completely wasted the past fifty years." Because of the entrenchment of liberal constitutional values, white leaders now openly acknowledged that it was "now no longer possible for the Aryan race to recapture the North American continent in its entirety." The time had come to give up any imperial ambitions for white civilization that might linger through nostalgia for a glorious past. Desperate times called for desperate measures, and the "only remaining option to secure the existence of our people and a future for White children is for the remnant of the racially conscious population of North America to relocate to the Pacific Northwest and establish our own sovereign nation."[11]

Just as Confederates and black nationalists turned to written constitutionalism to preserve their populations from existential threats, so too Aryans found themselves driven to author legal texts out of a concern for cultural survival. Racially aware whites acted to reverse "destructive demographic trends" suggesting that "[w]hite people will be a minority in the United States and Canada by the year 2050, and . . . will have vanished completely from North America by 2100." According to Aryan calculations, "by the year 2020, the median age of the White population of North America will have become so high that we will no longer be capable of reproducing ourselves in sufficient numbers to overcome the tide of mud-colored Third World immigration." Only legal separation and a return to a blend of cultural and ethical sovereignty could save what remained of white civilization.

By paring down its goals to manageable proportions, Aryans hoped to not only stave off extinction but also "concentrate what few remaining resources we have into a smaller area." The Butler Plan identified the "core territory" of the proposed homeland to encompass the states of Idaho, Oregon, and Washington. These states had "an estimated population of 11.2 million, of which the overwhelming majority are (officially) White. Once the non-White population of the major metropolitan areas is subtracted, . . . we are for all practical purposes dealing with an all-White territory, one of the few remaining in the world."[12]

The plan described four phases toward the establishment of a sovereign nation-state. Phase One involved encouraging racially conscious members of the white community to migrate to the Pacific Northwest. "Incomers," or migrants to the region, represented the core of the Homeland's population. This met the goal of providing "a refuge for all the persecuted and endangered Aryan peoples of the world." The plan proposed the creation of a resettlement agency, an idea borrowed from Israel. Consistent with ideas of republican citizenship, the agency would be tasked with ensuring that migrants can be self-sufficient, housed, and gainfully employed.

Previous plans to resettle northern Idaho had been "fatally flawed" because they rendered racially conscious whites too concentrated, secluded, and visible—and therefore easy to identify, isolate, and eradicate. Instead, "[e]specially at the beginning, we need to be able to melt into the local population and become indistinguishable." Cities presented abundant teaching moments because "metropolitan areas contain more 'racial diversity' and it will be far easier to work with the local native born White population when there are minorities and the problems minorities bring to point out as examples." The realities of urban migration and political engagement required a major shift from the Confederate approach to cultural sovereignty. "We are not seeking to run away into the north woods and hide," Covington explained, "We are seeking to build a new nation." The "realities of 21st century life" dictated that the movement be based in the cities, where white people could be found. It may be important to become familiar with the rural Northwest, but "we will not make a revolution from a few cabins in the deep forest."

Phase Two entailed propaganda and missionary work among "native Northwesterners" as well as "organic migrants." The first segment of the populace grew up in an environment controlled by liberal institutions, which taught them to be ashamed of their white heritage. The second "base of converts" would consist of "newcomers [who] are essentially conservatives or simply apolitical White people . . . fleeing their own localities to get away from the problems caused by multiculturalism and Third World immigration, but who would never admit to their true motivations."[13]

Each source of recruits posed its own challenges. Organic migrants tended to be "liberal elitists who want to have their cake and eat it too," but whose rationalizations must be broken down so they understand that their desire for "a stable environment" and "a good place to raise kids" will be met only in a nation formally organized under Aryan principles. Many of these persons already fled the cities of California, which "became the first state that is officially majority non-White." Native Northwesterners, by comparison, required far more effort to convert because they "genuinely do not understand what multi-culturalism and diversity mean for them in the long run."

Phase Three entailed the creation of a movement whose "goal is to present the government of the United States with a situation whereby the struggle to retain the Northwest becomes politically and financially unsupportable, and letting the Homeland go is the lesser of two evils from their point of view." To generate favorable circumstances for secession and then capitalize on them, there must be a "radical Aryan independence party slim and trim and ready to break out at a moment's notice if needed." In addition to "the creation of a few basic policy documents and [the development of] a general consensus surrounding the idea of independence," three conditions had to be satisfied: creating an apparatus capable of wresting power away from the existing political structure, credibly withdrawing the consent of the governed, and fostering "the loss of credible monopoly of armed force by the state."

Phase Four came after the restoration of white rule. The plan prescribed targeted socialist policies to help working-class and dislocated whites to land on their own feet. Economic self-sufficiency among the population served as a cornerstone of the new order, after "vocational training for young White people." A stable infrastructure must be fashioned to lure to the Northwest "serious, adult men and women who are coming to build a new nation."

The plan traded on Butler's enormous popularity in Aryan circles, even as it sought to mobilize whites more broadly to seize their political destiny. Divisions over ideas and tactics always existed, but Covington now moved to capture the imagination of Aryans worldwide. In fact, his approach differed from Butler's in several respects. To begin, Butler had provided charismatic leadership to white people as a cultural entity ("the Folk") and their needs for self-defense, whereas Covington saw a need to develop a political program and the rule of law. Once this shift in ends and means occurred, Covington's plans necessarily turned from ministry and training toward institutional design and governance.[14]

Butler's constitutional theory had emphasized the small-scale strain of the republican tradition. He governed Hayden Lake through "common law," which amounted to immutable, religious principles of white governance. The common law, given a gloss from the beliefs of Christian Identity, encompassed rules established by Butler and followed as a matter of habit and custom by residents of his compound and followers. One document that expressed principles of white sovereignty was the Nehemiah Township Charter and Common Law Contract. On July 11, 1982, Butler joined fifty-eight other members of white supremacy organizations in Hayden Lake to draft a document sketching how "Aryan freemen" might govern themselves. David Lane, who would go on to form the secretive and violent organization called the Order, appeared among the signatories. The Charter sought to simultaneously invoke Anglo-American traditions and procedures while subverting them. Its authors not only signed the document, but also had it duly notarized and filed in Kootenai County, Idaho.[15]

The Charter invoked America's covenantal tradition, with signatories "combin[ing] ourselves together into a Civil Body Politic for our better ordering and preservation under and by GOD's law." Seeking a "return to the organic Life-Law of our Race," the Aryan freemen pledged to establish a "Theocratic and Republican" form of government. They explicitly forbade the creation of a legislature, for "GOD himself has already legislated the only laws necessary to our preservation and prosperity and He cannot be improved upon." The Charter purported to establish common law judges, court clerks, and the Posse Comitatus and Militia for "the preservation, protection and sustenance of our Aryan race." Envisioning government on a miniature scale, the Charter alternately referred to the white community as a "township," "racial nation," "county," "association," and "shire."

Beyond embracing "radical localism," the Charter rejected most other aspects of conventional sovereignty and created new institutions through which legal opposition could be effectuated. It freed members from obeying tax or conscription laws. After forming a mutual defense pact, the Charter gave members of "this Association or Guilds" the right to seek the protection of other members from "outside Authority." Aryan judges were forbidden from enforcing the laws of "any government outside the Association" unless previously certified as compliant with divine law, and "common law Judges shall have veto power over such outside statutes, ordinances, and usages with no right to appeal over veto." Several provisions extended "rights and benefits" to each signatory's family members and group members by reviving "the ancient ancestoral [sic] social order of our Race predicated upon Clans, Kith, Kin and Sept."[16]

Although the Charter envisioned a distinctive people in form and substance, it created a compact with a loose superstructure. As a practical matter, it left everyday authority to racially conscious leaders, organizations, and heads of families to interpret common law principles of racial freedom as they saw fit. By contrast, Covington's legal vision necessarily entailed a more systematic account of lawgiving and organizational development. He also decisively rejected local governance in favor of a large-scale republic. An Aryan republic would be a true competitor to the United States, with its system of laws a visible improvement upon the original. Covington's emphasis on constitutionalism brought him closer to William Potter Gale, whose United States Christian Posse Association sought to revive the Articles of Confederation. White separatists had always traced their political history through such texts as the Magna Carta, Declaration of Independence, and Confederate Constitution, but mostly they looked upon them as relics of their heritage rather than as forming coherent precepts. The Northwest Front now wished to try its hand at a more serious integration of Nazi beliefs and American law, with all of the tensions and compromises that forming an Aryan legal history and culture might entail. Though it might take years to acquire widespread support or validity, a draft constitution nevertheless served the immediate goals of rebranding and outreach. As the true heirs of the American experiment, the Northwest Front wanted to show "[t]he local people where we settle . . . that we are fellow Americans and people like themselves."[17]

Covington perceived a need to discipline whites for state-building purposes; it was not enough simply to bring them together. Where

Butler welcomed whites of all stripes to Hayden Lake, Covington became convinced that "[t]he shaven heads and the tattoos and the petty hooliganism of the Skinhead scene must henceforth be kept away from the Northwest." Through a more effective presentation and enforceable moral code, white citizens can be reborn in the image of the Aryan warrior. A constitution could also satisfy the need to sanitize unfashionable policy views and extreme tactics. Violence, authorized by popular sovereignty, had to be unleashed against two kinds of enemies: first, nonwhites, through techniques of ethnic cleansing; and second, insufficiently virtuous white citizens (i.e., those who failed to demonstrate racial consciousness or engaged in morally suspect behavior).

More generally, the Northwest Front's turn toward American constitutionalism caused members of the movement to rethink how to engage the public over the future of a white nation. Members favored a tricolor flag over the Aryan Nations' flag, which had evoked the swastika. A key to a shift in tactics, and hopefully changed perceptions, entailed subtle changes in terminology. During outreach, inclusive and familiar political rhetoric such as "republic" replaced words that had acquired unhelpful connotations. Even the term "Aryan" needed to be avoided "because it causes confusion among the uninitiated," conjuring an image of "tattooed, shaven headed punks who swill beer and wave assault rifles in the air and scream 'White Power.' " It was "bad propaganda" to "confront people, on their initial contact, with ideas, concepts, terms and symbols that require an immediate, long and abstruse explanation."[18]

Without repudiating the movement's genesis or history, it became increasingly important to revamp its presentation. Insider terms and Nazi imagery appealed to true believers but horrified or distracted countless others. Because Americans' memories of European Nazism remained overwhelmingly negative, reproducing their terminology and symbolism wholesale would stall, not advance, the cause of white sovereignty—a continued exercise in "wasted time."

The Aryan community's materials reflected concerted efforts to construct a political vocabulary accessible to working-class whites. Not only should activists bypass overladen terms, but also "Esoteric terms like 'Cascadia', 'Arya', etc. should be avoided as well . . . we are going to have trouble enough overcoming our image problem." In one of Covington's novels, a freedom fighter corrects a compatriot that the party governing the future republic "was not white supremacist but white separatist." White pride, cleansed of the desire for white domination, may prove easier to sell.[19]

From the start, the Northwest Front pioneered the use of technology to nurture racial solidarity. The Internet allowed like-minded persons to find each other, share ideas anonymously, keep political dreams alive, and foster a sense of community regardless of geographic distance. The movement could enjoy a presence, fostered by blogs, chat rooms, and a mixture of public and limited-access forums. Eventually, the medium would be employed not merely to create an electronic footprint but also to lay the foundations for a future state. Aryans published a raft of pamphlets, statements, plans, handbooks, and novels on the Web.

To a large extent, the Internet had fostered what might be called "leaderless resistance." But no movement can succeed without strong leadership, the systematic development of ideas, and careful planning. Aided by generous First Amendment protections, more deliberative interactions gradually emerged on the Internet. Drafting sessions could be held with minimal effort. Even an e-convention could be conducted when a face-to-face convention with the entire underground community might not be possible. The white resistance realized its members had to be prepared to strike, and then lead, when the opportunity for deliverance finally came.[20]

The Northwest Independence Trilogy: Restoring Political Faith

One of the more ingenious decisions was Covington's choice to spread the message of legal resistance through works of fiction, which he made available on the Internet. White separatists had to act with care, as defenders of conventional sovereignty possessed untold resources to monitor, infiltrate, and disrupt their efforts. Within the confines of the First Amendment of the U.S. Constitution, contrarian political and legal values—even justifications for violence—could be effectively disseminated through Aryan fiction without running afoul of authorities. "These books," as the author acknowledged, "are at the moment the primary items of propaganda the Northwest Front possesses." Covington intended for his books to construct a "revolutionary mythos" as well as to "predict and portray exactly how a White revolutionary movement of Northwest independence might succeed, based on the reality of what we have to work with today." He "wanted to convey to our people a sense of POSSIBILITY about the coming Northwest American Republic . . . for readers to see and internalize the POSSIBILITY of victory." That is, the fictional works helped to constitute a white community and tended to its identity and morale. Furthermore, Covington wished to "provide us all with some kind of vision of our own post-revolutionary future as a White nation." When studied carefully, the books presented a coherent legal program, along with a road map for achieving that alternative legal order.[21]

As the author admitted, if a book "does not answer its political and social purpose, then it can be as entertaining and as gripping and as literary as can be, . . . but it will still be a failure from my point of view." In turning to fiction, Covington recognized that revolution was a supreme act of imagination. The impossible had to become possible. Political traditions must be invented that seem at once fresh and familiar.

Beyond facilitating white separatists' escape from legal sanction, the genre helped to normalize the movement's aims and tactics. The books are filled with illustrations of the superiority of white culture and populated by freedom fighters with scruples, who dream of a brighter future, fall in love, and overcome tragedy in their own lives. The narrative form elicits emotional responses in the reader so as to promote receptivity to the movement's values and worldview, reaching those who might not otherwise be converted through a traditional manifesto or pamphlet. Even when things appear bleak for the Aryan agenda, these writings provide comfort and inspiration. The approach harnesses the power of fiction to give the return of white self-governance the air of inevitability.

When in an unguarded moment Covington said he aspired to author a corollary to *The Turner Diaries,* he revealed a desire to convince readers of the necessity of revolution through the power of the written word. That fictional work, which describes the violent overthrow of the U.S. government and the extermination of Jews and nonwhites, has inspired countless militia movements and nativists. The Order, whose members served prison sentences for acts of economic sabotage and assassination, had drawn on the novel for its organizational structure and tactics. The Northwest Independence Trilogy may have a regional focus and contain aesthetic differences, but political advocacy and organizational planning remained the underlying reasons for writing.[22]

Covington described *The Hill of the Ravens,* the novel that opens the series, as political creed in the guise of fantasy. "[It] is not primarily a work of fiction, the purpose of which is to entertain," he explained. "It is a political polemic that has been deliberately written, from the ground up, with a specific purpose in mind." He set the book in the twenty-first century, some forty years or so after the end of the War of Northwest Independence. A generation has grown up in the Republic. The war had long been won; stable, white rule fulfilled America's ancient promises of life, liberty, and happiness. Homes are affordable because of generous loan assistance programs. Crime is nonexistent, and the environment is much improved: "The air is clear without a single scent of pollution."[23]

Violence appears in the book sporadically because the revolutionaries succeeded, comforting readers that terror is a temporary strategy of the oppressed. Once the homeland has been secured, force becomes routinized and directed primarily against offenders of ordinary law and traitors in their midst—central features of the novel's plot. Sectarian differences among whites remain to be managed; the legal order must be guarded against whites who are lazy or hold counterrevolutionary ideas.

Throughout, one encounters efforts to undermine popular belief in the conventional legal order. American law, which has grown so complicated that it becomes emblematic of society's decline through loss of control to elites, must be simplified. A single bound volume containing the entire criminal code can then be distributed to citizens. Thus, Aryans shared with the Icarians a longing for a time when the law not only reflected the people's values but could be easily understood and internalized by them.

The books dramatize a violent reordering of the legal system. At one point, the author explains why the chief justice of the U.S. Supreme Court must be assassinated. Through its rulings, the Court had perverted the original Constitution by "destroy[ing] the last vestiges of democracy in the two-party system by declaring primary elections unconstitutional" and "enshrining forever in the Constitution . . . a woman's right to choose not only to murder her child, but to do so up until and including the very moment of natural birth." Murdering the highest-ranking judicial officer as punishment not only shows the audacity of the resistance but also signifies the ritual killing of the legal order. The sacrificial spilling of blood ends the corruption of the law by unelected judges and initiates the birth of a new political order. Once the Aryan revolution has dethroned lawyers and priests from their privileged place in the constitutional order, measures can be enacted to ensure that "the law served as a shield and not a sword."[24]

New connections among whites are forged after religion is put in its proper place. In a somewhat surprising twist, the history of religious liberty in America is seen as a hindrance to white rule. The critique is complicated: religious pluralism elevated faith-based difference over racial self-interest, while encouraging some religions to try to dominate others. Doing away with tax exemptions for religious groups "removed the problem of organized religion from the social and economic equation, and reduced religion to the purely theological level, which helped in maintaining the delicate social balance between peoples of conflicting faiths."[25]

Most of the events in the Northwest Trilogy take place in Western Washington. By allowing the revolution to unfold locally, the novels depict how macroprinciples of law can inspire regular people and shape events at the level of micropolitics. As Aryans have long foretold, the North American continent starts to fracture into racial and ethnic republics. Aztlan, a semiautonomous province of Mexico containing parts of states from the former Southwest, arises to challenge the United States and the new Aryan nation-state.

A Distant Thunder, the second in the trilogy, tells the story of the war from the perspective of a freedom fighter, a working-class American. Shane Ryan, the ninety-one-year-old hero, is interviewed by a woman conducting research on the revolution. In the course of their exchange, Ryan fondly recalls his racial awakening and participation in the war as a member of the Northwest Volunteer Army. The setup is disarming—what could be feared from such a grandfatherly figure? By putting a curious young woman at the feet of an elder statesman to learn a people's revolutionary history, the novel's structure invites readers to suspend disbelief and facilitates the transmission of political values. Developing racial consciousness requires seeing the world in a new way.

Once again, the book opens by reminding the reader that whites are destined to govern. The main character reminisces, "Sometimes I sit and I look at my grandchildren and I see the calm and safe, all-white world of peace and plenty they live in, this land of ours, and I swear I think I dreamed it all or imagined it, that my childhood and my young manhood was some kind of nightmare." The new political order is the reality; through a literary trick, the reader's present has been relegated to a bad dream. Manipulating time, the novel paints the revolution as a fait accompli—the alignment of contingencies for success replaced by factors within one's control. Moral purity, faith in the people, clever tactics, and hard work are presented as the keys to constitutional transformation. Racial disaffection figures largely in the world that must be overcome: "The United States into which I was born was all a lie. A cheap, shoddy, vicious, evil lie that deserved nothing but death at the point of a sword." The dislocation and disillusionment of white people simply exposes the need to create a new culture of consent.[26]

A Distant Thunder ends partway through Ryan's reminiscences of a white nation's political rebirth. Ryan, captured on the field and tortured by the U.S. government, is released as a gesture of good faith in advance of a peace conference at Longview, Washington. *A Mighty Fortress,* the final book in the trilogy, takes readers to the end of the War of Independence and the peace talks through the eyes of two young revolutionaries. The book concludes with the signing of a treaty, the lowering of the U.S. flag at Longview, and the raising of the Northwest American Republic's tricolor flag. With these symbolic acts, the guerilla movement's transformation is complete: a fringe community has become a self-governing people.

Aryan grievances are portrayed in the book but partly disguised within plot devices. At the outset, Aryans lay claim to the inheritance of the Founding generation. Recalling the theory of cultural sovereignty developed earlier by the Confederates, they insist that "the United States of America, in its original form as envisioned by the Founding Fathers, was a political entity created by and for white people" or "a national expression of . . . the Manifest Destiny of the white race." However, the American legal order as it exists today has "only the most remote and tenuous historical connection" with the basic principles of white rule: "The United States was never intended by the Founding Fathers to be multi-racial, or multi-cultural, or diverse."

Departures from the original design of the U.S. Constitution have led to a morally bankrupt society. The government has turned not only tyrannical but also "irredeemably corrupt, and its continuation in power is antithetical to the pursuit of life, liberty, and the pursuit of happiness." Its policies are "deeply repulsive to every concept of human decency." Showing signs of irreversible decay, America is "riddled with crime, corruption, poverty, sexual perversion, unemployment, ill health, mistreatment of the elderly, the destruction of the national infrastructure, a dysfunctional educational system, and national malaise and demoralization."

The leading cause of conventional sovereignty's demise is its embrace of pluralism. "Modifying the racial composition of America away from the dominant white society that it was as it rose to power, towards a mixed, racially diverse society, has been catastrophic, an unmitigated disaster." Diversity did not impart strength. On the contrary, "it creates weakness, division, chaos, corruption, and deep social sickness."

Aryan leaders resort to armed revolution because they have no choice. For the past century, "all peaceful attempts to alter and reverse the racial and social policies of the United States have failed." The electoral process is incapable of restoring just rule because it has been "turned into a weapon of genocide against America's white inhabitants." Nor can the judiciary be counted on to help white people because it has been honed into "an instrument of racial and social tyranny." Meanwhile, America is drawn into foreign wars that enrich Jewish bankers but drain the country of precious resources.

White revolutionaries call on "all Americans of European heritage to take up arms against the United States and apply such force and coercion as necessary to compel the government of the United States to change its wicked and destructive behavior, and to punish those who are responsible for such behavior." It soon becomes apparent that pluralism is not the only problem: rampant individualism, feminism, sexual libertinism, and legal doctrines such as equality and the so-called right to privacy have all hastened the republic's decline. The Aryan community demands that "decent men" rise up against "infanticide by abortion," homosexuality, and the "moral perversion known as feminism," which teaches "the false idea that men and women are somehow competitors and enemies and that the bearing and rearing of white children is somehow shameful." Rejecting these tenets of the modern liberal order would one day lead to the restoration of white civilization.[27]

The book mostly compiles and dramatizes complaints scattered throughout other Aryan texts, such as *The Northwest Migration Handbook*, the Aryan Nations Declaration of Independence, and the *88 Precepts* of David Lane (of the Order). In the hands of race-conscious whites, originalism—an interpretive methodology that strives to discern the subjective intentions of a founding generation or the apparent public meaning of their actions—was deployed to justify and recover a lost Aryan nation. The original U.S. Constitution represented a covenant binding man and God. According to Aryan legal history, that text unified race, culture, and power. White men would never have acted against their interests by endorsing absolute equality or radical individualism. The failure of that document to protect white sovereignty with greater clarity should be taken as simply too obvious to mention for Americans living at that time.[28]

The argument may seem appealing given that mention of slaves in the original Constitution obviously disadvantaged them. How did the Aryans resolve conflicting text, namely, the Reconstruction Amendments, which guaranteed equality in broad language? Like the black nationalists, they declared these amendments illegitimate due to their failure to satisfy the basic requirements of consent. On this point, one finds congruence in the beliefs of Aryans and black nationalists. Each wished to undermine the legitimacy of those legal achievements: the former for going too far in promoting equality; the latter for not going far enough. Black nationalists argued that the amendments imposed citizenship upon them, whereas Aryans insisted that these measures were forced on the South and therefore did not bind white Americans.

The Reconstruction Amendments, like other legal developments endorsing equality and pluralism, subverted the original design of the Constitution. Once these additions were voided, one must default to the original legal-cultural regime fashioned by statesmen with Americans' racial interests in mind. In this respect and others, the Aryan community embraced the history of the defeated Confederacy, which served as a crucial model in their theory of sovereignty. Ironically, this neo-Confederate perspective mirrored the legal critique of black nationalists. Two dissident communities holding disparate conceptions of law nevertheless shared a common understanding of the original Constitution as an expression of white sovereignty.

Over a hundred years had elapsed since the Confederacy had failed. Much had transpired, chipping away at what remained of white power. Indeed, federal efforts to desegregate the schools were remembered as a missed opportunity to reestablish white rule in the South. "When Eisenhower sent in the army to integrate the schools. . . . That's when the trouble really started," Covington stated. At that moment, "[t]he people of the South should have risen up again and re-formed the Confederate States of America and seceded again, and the rest of the country should have supported the South."[29]

That moment had come and gone. The legal order had survived the civil rights movement, limping on with grave wounds. Reduced to equal status with every other social group, whites became demoralized, dispossessed, and divided by class and religion. A healthy revolutionary state must successfully weld these elements back together into one Aryan people, "so long as there is a basic common ground of nationhood and racial welfare at the core of it all."[30]

The NAR Constitution: Cultivating White Consciousness

By early 2006, Covington had had enough of obscuring his legal theories in novels. He came around to the feeling that repopulation without a plan for governance may be incomplete. On June 2, 2006, Covington posted a draft of a proposed constitution on the Internet. He called it a "semi-final interim draft" and invited comments. This version contained Covington's own notes, offering insight into his thinking as it developed. By that point, the document had been five months in the making.

A few months earlier, Covington had announced to the online Aryan community that "[o]ne of the suggestions which has been made is that we draw up a draft Constitution for the Northwest American Republic and attach it to the Handbook as an appendix." While his "initial gut feeling was that this is way, way premature," he came around to the view that "this might be of some value as an exercise to get us into the habit of thinking about an all-White future and deciding exactly what it is we want and what we're fighting for." He then volunteered to coordinate such a discussion.[31]

Covington established certain ground rules to guide the drafting sessions. He prefaced his remarks with a mission statement. "The internet isn't exactly Liberty Hall in Philadelphia," he remarked, but then opened the floor "for ideas, discussions, suggestions, criticism, etc. on the preparation of a draft constitution for the Northwest American Republic . . . a Homeland for all White people." The online discussion proceeded according to several "grounds and assumptions." The breakup of the Soviet Union and Yugoslavia stood as reminders that ethnic nationalism remained alive and well, and it was only a matter of time before the United States fractured "into separate racial and ethnic and social enclaves." Although a draft constitution "has no legal force" at this stage, the very act of writing functioned as "practice for a 'dry run' towards re-shaping society" in anticipation of the impending crisis. History rewarded those who were prepared. The draft constitution would be like a "replacement part" on the shelf "ready to jam home into the mechanism of society if and when things fall apart a lot faster than we now expect." In crafting the document, they "should try to distinguish between a Constitution and law," taking care to focus on designing the "foundation of a society and state." The drafting sessions would be open to "[a]ny and every White person who's interested" and took the process seriously.[32]

During the ensuing debate, a few participants voiced concerns about the exercise itself. The deliberation seemed like an indulgence because, as one person put it, "we still have not had a dozen of us in the same room at the same time," much less seized territory to govern. Despite such reservations, the project moved forward. Chief among the reasons for writing was a desire to achieve ideological discipline. By conducting a debate over governing values through this legal framework, the group honed its agenda and belief system. The process would lend substance, coherence, and order to their constitutional ideas. Undergoing the process would develop a crisper sense of the common ground shared by white leaders.

Writing down certain values underscored the Aryan community's claim of continuity with American history and culture. In doing so, they helped to ensure vitality of those values and arrest further erosion. At the same time, inscription of their ethical commitments and preferred institutions also improved the organization's effort to distinguish itself from the other white supremacist groups clamoring for public attention. A constitution could help the Northwest Front gain a competitive advantage by helping to secure the support of disgruntled Americans. The mainstream media tarred all of these groups with a broad brush, treated as criminals or thugs without legal principles or a sense of history. Armed Aryan groups such as the Order demonstrated a commitment to violence so as to ignite a race war but gave little thought to what would replace conventional sovereignty once it had been destroyed. With a constitution in hand, the Northwest Front alone could say it had a vision for the future.

Employing the language of constitutional law, in turn, sanitized radical beliefs. The instrument aimed to reassure white Americans that the independence movement pursued constructive goals. Their audience no longer consisted only of already ideologically committed individuals gathered in underground hangouts, but now encompassed busy suburban families longing for a better life. Without giving up on the community's past, constitutional language scrubbed fringe religious and political beliefs of their more off-putting accoutrements. Unlike the juvenile Hitler-worship and racial bile that typified neo-Nazi writings, the tone of the NAR Constitution presented itself as high-minded and politically courageous. More than any other piece of work, the legal document could serve as a tool for recruiting disaffected mainstream citizens.

The drafting process took around nine months—"[l]ess time than the U.S. Constitution, to be sure" Covington noted, "but then we weren't restricted to saddle bags and the speed of a horse for communication." Covington served as principal drafter, assisted by a Constitutional Committee, "a group of about two dozen men who contributed ideas on content, language, etc." The committee included some of the Order prisoners, "specifically David Lane himself before his death, Richard Kemp, David Tate, Richard Scutari, and Bruce Pierce." The group received input from militia prisoners Steve Anderson and Walter Elijah Thody, Rick Cooper, and Louis Beam, as well as "Old Fighters" in the movement such as former Rockwell associates Carl Geharis and Scotty Earbend."[33]

Three or four drafts were circulated, "mostly sent to the men in prison" and made available on the Internet. Feedback could be given online in the form of "Constitutional Commentary," and through telephone calls and regular mail. Covington acknowledged that "many of our sharpest and most interested consultants were in prison," which affected the frequency and thoroughness of discussion. The entrenchment of conventional authority made quality deliberation and effective resistance challenging in the modern age. Because of constant surveillance, "the feds probably have more of a complete record of our new nation's first Constitutional debate than we do." He faulted the ascendance of the national security state for impeding the legitimate expression of popular sovereignty: "King George never had the Patriot Act, warrantless wiretapping, warrantless bugging, extraordinary rendition, or legalized torture." Although a number of white resistance leaders stayed in hiding or had been incarcerated, the drafters envisioned a full convention to be held in the future, when the time was right for a more public gathering. Until then, the NAR Constitution would be published as part of *The Northwest Migration Handbook* and on the Internet.[34]

The drafting committee turned out a sophisticated piece of work. Many provisions entailed rewrites of provisions in the 1787 Constitution, but a fair number can be understood as repudiations of major legal and political developments from the twentieth century. Like a number of postwar constitutions, the NAR Constitution took ideas from a wide array of sources. The committee members did not hesitate to look abroad for ideas from experiments in cultural sovereignty, choosing to borrow from Nazi Germany, Rhodesia, and South Africa's apartheid regime. All in all, the document proved to be a hybrid of American liberation texts, Christian Identity ethics, and Nazi forms of bureaucracy and control. The constitution blended cultural and ethical forms of popular sovereignty as a means of distancing itself from the failed American Constitution and cleansing the white populace of its corrupting power.[35]

Like their predecessors who founded the Confederacy, Aryans turned to written constitutionalism in order to preserve racial culture. They believed that white culture best fostered the virtues of hard work, capacity for wise rule, and stable family structures. If that nineteenth-century breakaway republic served as their domestic inspiration, then these men would go to greater lengths in using basic law to preserve race-based governance. Through the constitution they hoped to design a government that might "stand forever . . . as a bulwark and guardian of our race." De facto white rule depending on conventional forms of government such as states' rights had utterly collapsed, so the Northwest Front proposed bolder theories of power and bureaucracies capable of enforcing white sovereignty. Though Aryans traced their history through the vanquished South, much had changed in race relations since the end of slavery. With the plantation system destroyed, that institution no longer served as a plausible means of social control. Furthermore, generations of immigration and racial mixing had irrevocably altered the composition of the U.S. population. Years of liberal education had robbed white citizens of their racial consciousness. A desire for more aggressive technologies to recreate and maintain racial identity made national authority—and Nazi methods—exceedingly attractive.

The NAR Constitution made whiteness the explicit cornerstone of republican citizenship. Rather than adopting a cosmopolitan model recognizing group rights for whites or relying on localism to preserve white political power, the constitution envisioned an all-white republic. Trading forbearance for efficiency, the legal text authorized the forcible exclusion of nonwhites from the polity. On behalf of "the Aryan peoples of the earth," their self-appointed agents established a republican form of government to save the white race. They adapted the axiomatic Fourteen Words of David Lane—"We must secure the existence of our people and a future for White children"—to codify the overriding purpose of the political project. Lane himself had been inspired by Hitler's *Mein Kampf.*

The first article of the constitution, which concerned "nationhood and citizenship," repeated Lane's statement in its original form. After establishing the "prime directive" that white "civilization may be preserved and White children may be raised to responsible adulthood in safety, prosperity, and tranquility," the instrument created separate categories of belonging and a stratified citizenship structure. Drafters made residency a race-based but more inclusive legal concept than citizenship. "All White people, of any nationality or previous citizenship, shall have the right to live permanently in the Northwest American Republic as legal residents." The republic would hold itself out as a homeland "for the use and habitation of White people of all nationalities, cultures and creeds worldwide."[36]

At the same time, providing sanctuary did not mean that Aryans would relinquish control over public affairs to recent immigrants simply because of their shared race. Citizenship, which included "exercise of the franchise and participation in government and the political process," would be subject to more stringent requirements. Drafters did away with birthright citizenship, a feature that rewarded illegal immigration to the United States and facilitated white complacency. The legal status of citizen "shall not be automatically conferred at birth, or through racial identity alone." Instead, citizenship had to be "earned through responsibility fulfilled." In other words, the constitution erected a virtue threshold for the management of political and civil rights.[37]

These provisions, read together, paved the way for a layered conception of political membership. The first qualification of legal whiteness was explicitly racial, a condition that was necessary but not sufficient for full membership. One must be a person "of unmixed Caucasian racial descent from any one of the historic family of European nations, who shall have no known or identifiable non-White ancestry, and no visibly non-White element in their genetic makeup." A provision classified Jews as "an Asiatic people" and forbade them from entry to or residence in the Republic. The second requirement involved satisfying ethical and conduct-based standards for citizenship. By zealously guarding the formal terms of membership, the people ensured that only the most virtuous whites would rule. This entire approach repudiated long-standing features of the modern liberal order barring race-dependent policies, including racial gerrymandering, as well as legal rulings disfavoring excessive conditions on the right to vote.[38]

Even after a person gained citizenship, the status was further "divided into three classes" for purposes of electoral power, "with each class of citizenship holding one, two, and three votes respectively." A weighted franchise system had a precedent in the 1969 Rhodesian Constitution, which maintained separate voter rolls based on race, education, income, and property ownership to ensure power stayed in "responsible hands." Drafters kept the idea of tiered voting but used civic responsibility as the criteria for political power. They dispensed with the principle of one person, one vote—a linchpin of conventional sovereignty—because it rewarded ignorance and apathy. Instead, under the NAR Constitution, "[t]hose who demonstrate superior civic and political responsibility, and who display the greatest dedication to state service, . . . shall thereby have the greatest say in the political process." Through this hierarchy of citizenship, the drafters hoped to incentivize public service and ensure that power rests with the virtuous few. These provisions formalized the creation of a "new racial elite," rewarding a select class of citizens with greater clout and prestige. Purged of nonwhite, immoral, and antirepublican elements, the people could then proceed to govern themselves according to the highest standards.[39]

Given the nation-state's reliance on complex biological and behavioral metrics to ascertain a person's race, a new agency would be empowered to formulate "standards of race and citizenship." This department, called the Bureau of Race and Resettlement, "shall set all racial parameters and codes" and "establish scientific and cultural standards of racial identity." The same agency would help white migrants secure housing, find suitable employment, and assess their bona fides to participate in self-rule. Although the bureau would possess significant policy-making and enforcement authority, citizenship status "may be legally reduced or revoked" through not only agency decisions but also legislation, presidential decrees, and judicial decisions. A conflict over one's citizenship status presumably would be resolved by the standing Constitutional Committee established in another part of the constitution.[40]

The mechanisms for racial evaluation grew out of a broader philosophical position on matters of equality. Not only did drafters refuse to carry over the despised Reconstruction Amendments, but they also assiduously avoided the word "equality" throughout the instrument. Their reasons for excising the language of equality from the constitution went beyond racial distrust. Aryans opposed equality as a general principle on the ground that the idea inhibited evolutionary processes and, in leveling the social relationships between people, destroyed what is true and good in society. "The concept of 'equality' is declared a lie by every evidence of Nature," one Aryan manifesto put it. "It is a search for the lowest common denominator, and its pursuit will destroy every superior race, nation, or culture." The

NAR Constitution solved the problem of inculcating civic virtue that had bedeviled previous generations of white rulers. The document did so not by restricting equality to whites alone, as earlier republican theorists had done, but rather by creating new hierarchies among white citizens.[41]

If the idea of equality had infected the foundations of white republicanism, then the disinfecting power of the law had to reach into all domains where equality had taken hold. In no other place than the home had false constitutional principles wreaked more havoc. Abortion, miscegenation, feminism, and homosexuality all threatened future generations. Under the guise of liberty and equality, authorities had interpreted the U.S. Constitution to allow these practices to flourish. In response, the NAR Constitution rejected *Roe v. Wade* and all subsequent decisions affirming a woman's right to terminate her pregnancy. A provision declared "[t]he right to life of unborn children, beginning at conception." Repudiating the principles of individual autonomy and racial equality recognized in such Supreme Court decisions as *Loving v. Virginia,* "[a]ll residents and citizens shall refrain from the abomination of sexual congress or contact with non-Whites." Another provision prohibited citizens from engaging in homosexuality, rejecting such major rulings as *Romer v. Evans* and *Lawrence v. Texas,* which had extended principles of equality and autonomy to sexual minorities. Violation of any of these tenets—in particular, willful miscegenation or committing acts of homosexuality—could lead authorities to strip an offender of citizenship or reduce his citizenship class.[42]

In place of a hyperindividualist model of family life endorsed by conventional sovereignty, the NAR Constitution restored patriarchy. This emphasis recalled the ethical strategies utilized in the constitutions authored by John Brown and the followers of Malcolm X. For the Aryans, like those previous groups, a program of moral revival required restructuring the family to ensure any gains. Seeking to resuscitate older sex roles and subordinate the individual to both the state and family, the Aryan constitution acknowledged the traditional family unit and its values as "foundations of the state" and declared that "the protection of the family shall be and shall remain a primary goal and supporting pillar of the Republic, its laws and institutions."

The "traditional nuclear family" was "based on the institution of marriage, with the wife and mother as the heart and the gainfully employed father as the head." In defining the family unit this way, the instrument sought to revive a lost patriarchal order. But the constitution did not try to turn the clock all the way back to an earlier century. While traditional sex roles were expected in the home and the virtues of chastity and modesty had to be rigorously observed, women had permission to serve in the military during the revolutionary period. Additionally, women could become full voting members of the republic, work outside the home, and hold office.[43]

To make such changes comprehensively, the NAR Constitution favored bureaucracies and political arrangements that prized force and effectiveness. In terms of structure and substance, the text exemplified a rejection of the modern liberal democratic nation-state. Instead of being predicated upon a fear of tyranny by the majority, the charter sought to maintain the undiluted power of a cultural majority. A desire for enhanced technologies of control to foster racial solidarity and ensure ethical governance led the framers to favor a ruthless consolidation of authority. Federalism and separation of powers could no longer exist as Americans know it. Experience had shown that these institutional arrangements, based on the writings of Madison and Jefferson, rendered the basic law too unpredictable. Instead, there should be only a glorious national republic, suggesting an intention to replicate German Nazism's successful fusion of a decentralized Weimar Republic into a single centralized state. Reminiscent of the July 14, 1933, law promulgated by the Reich Cabinet providing that "[t]he National Socialist German Workers Party constitutes the only political party in Germany," the constitution declared the republic "a unitary or single-party state, with the Northwest Front serving as the official party of government." The party's "primacy" was "enshrined in this Constitution" because of its "historic role in . . . implementing the Revolution and securing the independence of the Republic." One-party rule best preserved the constituiton's ideological consistency over time. The NAR Constitution therefore approved efficiency over compromise, and monologue over dialogue.[44]

Although Aryans tactically exploited federalism in the short run to undermine the dominant constitutional order, they would close down the law's permissiveness toward dissent at the first opportunity. The moment that the NAR Constitution gained popular approval, "[a]ll state and local governments, offices and agencies thereof which existed under the previous rule of the United States of America" would be immediately "abolished." Local jurisdictions might still exist informally, but "shall be subordinate to the central government and laws of the Republic, and the authority of the National Convention and the State President." The constitution did not mention states at all, and the document contained no corollary to the Tenth Amendment to the U.S. Constitution or any other acknowledgement of the states' sovereignty. These structural changes accorded with the overall project of large-scale racial nationalism by disempowering any institutions that might pose obstacles to ideological purity. On this point, the Aryans split from the Confederate approach, which subsumed racial identity and culture within a federalist framework and plantation economy. Indeed, it could be said that Aryans learned a valuable historical lesson from the divisions that eventually tore apart the Confederacy. They would take no chances with states' rights this time around.[45]

Drastic changes to the judiciary also would ensure the success of the new racial-ethical order. In a departure from the original design of the American Constitution and Madisonian ideas of divided government, the NAR Constitution provided that "the government . . . shall consist of two branches, executive and legislative." Judicial review, a cherished power contemplated in the U.S. Constitution and recognized in the landmark ruling *Marbury v. Madison,* would be no more. Instead, the exclusive power to "enforce" and "interpret" the Constitution would be lodged in "a standing Constitutional Committee of the National Convention, to whom constitutional issues may be referred for determination by the Convention as a whole, by the executive branch, by state agencies, and by the courts." New Afrikans, too, had earlier made the legislature the final arbiter of their constitution's meaning, but Aryans went the extra step of stripping all courts of the power of judicial review. National courts would continue to exist but become a shell of their former selves, denied any "policy-making role whatsoever" and charged "solely to serve as bodies for the determination of fact in criminal cases or non-criminal matters such as property ownership, inheritance, etc."[46]

As the principal drafter's notes reveal, the framers neutered the judiciary in response to hated decisions on social questions as well as *Bush v. Gore*—"No Nine Old Swine on some Supreme Court appointing presidents or making and un-making laws at their whim." Covington explained that "[t]he idea is to excise the judicial branch completely from government" and deny judges the power to "create social trends or implement weird, anti-social policies." No longer could the courts subvert the original intentions of the people as mores shifted from one generation to the next.[47]

The chief executive would be called the "State President." Drafters likely lifted this title from the 1961 Constitution of South Africa in remembrance of the apartheid republic. The president would become the patriarch of the Aryan republic, a symbol of manhood. Only a "first-class citizen" who is a "military veteran" would be eligible to serve. Neither the "natural born" citizen clause nor the residency requirement was adopted—in all likelihood, because drafters wished to ensure a broad pool of eligible white candidates from around the world. Aryans envisioned a strong president who could claim support directly from the people. The Electoral College would not follow these individuals into the Northwest American Republic, as the state president would be "elected by direct popular vote of all citizens." Instead of a four-year term followed by the possibility of reelection, a state president would serve a single six-year term. The president would enjoy significant latitude to appoint ministers and "create or dissolve ministerial portfolios," but have no power to dissolve or neglect the Ministries of Defense, Interior, Finance, or Race and Resettlement.[48]

Aryan legal theory made the restoration of honor to civic life a priority, promoted from the top down. Moral standards bound the highest leaders as much as ordinary citizens. Aryan people would look to the state president, who was expected to "instill and maintain the highest standards of personal courtesy, deliberation, maturity, integrity and courage in the manhood of the republic." Ethical renewal also influenced the design of the justice system. The constitution directed the state president to "establish and supervise a National Honor Court." This court would develop and enforce protocols "for the resolution of personal differences between individual male residents and citizens of the Republic, up to and including private combat by mutual consent, in accordance with the ancient and historic traditions and practices of the European family of nations." Individuals who consented to trial by combat would be immunized from criminal or civil liability. However, members of the military and civil guard could be prohibited from "issuing or accepting a challenge, dueling, or participating in a legal duel." By reintroducing dueling as a method of dispute resolution, leaders hoped to usher in a new age of chivalry.[49]

As the head of the executive branch, commander in chief, commander of the Bureau of State Security, and chief magistrate, the state president would possess unprecedented authority. The state president could invoke extraordinary powers pursuant to "special executive order." In a time of "national emergency or legislative recess," special measures might be taken "to preserve life, liberty, and the existence of the Republic." The only check on the abuse of executive power lay in the Convention, which must confirm or reject the assertion of emergency authority within sixty days. A declaration of martial law by the state president must be ratified by the Convention within fourteen days, with the possibility of renewal "for such time as the Convention shall think fit."

A state president's authority in foreign affairs would be more circumscribed, consistent with the Aryan critique that American presidents have too easily committed troops in foreign lands. The constitution vested power to declare war solely in the Convention. It also prevented the president from ordering "military action of any kind outside the borders of the Republic or in any foreign country, except by a special executive order in cases of the strongest and most overriding necessity and national urgency," and for no longer than seven days. Codifying a far more restrictive version of the War Powers Act, a one-time extension of seven days might be granted, but after that point a "full session debate" must take place during which the state president would either report the success of the military action or request a formal declaration of war.[50]

After the National Convention passed legislation, the president could "veto all or part of any bill presented to him." In a major change from the U.S. Constitution, however, a veto may be overridden based on a simple majority vote. All treaties must be confirmed by the National Convention, and could be revoked or abrogated only by the Convention in full session. Members of the Convention would serve two-year terms, with their salary set by national referendum in order to end the self-interested practice of legislators fixing their own salaries.

The NAR Constitution retained a separate Bill of Rights enumerating "absolute and inalienable rights." In a notable departure, drafters reversed the priority of First and Second Amendment rights, giving pride of place to the right to bear arms. Symbolically, this change also underscored the preference for force over debate. Eschewing the elegant ambiguity of the Second Amendment, the Constitution gave detailed safeguards for gun rights. Drafters dropped the phrase "well-regulated militia" and added "and other personal arms for defense of the state and of their lives and property," establishing that the right to bear arms was both an individual and collective right. A clarifying clause prohibited any kind of regulation that "qualifie[d] or restrict[ed]" the right, including "licensing, registration, fee, taxation, restriction on transportation, or other such impediment." A separate provision forbade the restriction of "ammunition, powder, cartridge casings, and other ancillary equipment or supplies necessary to the exercise of the right to keep and bear arms." Together, these provisions fostered a well-armed society.[51]

Freedom of expression, so crucial to the success of the white resistance movement, was carried over to the new instrument. "All residents and citizens ... shall enjoy the right to complete freedom of speech, freedom of artistic and creative expression, and freedom of the press." As rewritten, the provision went beyond the original language of the First Amendment and incorporated the collective weight of judicial interpretations of that provision. For the sake of avoiding vice, the constitution excluded "obscenity and/or pornography" from an otherwise broad guarantee of individual expression.[52]

Drafters became convinced that religion had become a wedge issue used to distract and divide the white majority. Facing dwindling numbers, they shrewdly calculated that obstacles to the creation of affinity among whites had to be removed. Aryans cited the Irish Republican Army's experience as a lamentable instance where religion divided a white community, whereas Franco's Spain stood as an example of how to overcome "factions and tendencies and ideological divisions." Consequently, the framers omitted any statement separating church from state but they also refrained from "establish[ing] any kind of state religion." They hoped to straddle two objectives: encouraging "freedom of religion" while permitting some variance among religious practices. If race and religion are entwined tenets of Christian Identity, the constitution tried to untangle these threads, making racial identity central to the new legal order while fostering religious pluralism. At least one of the drafters, David Lane, reportedly practiced a racialized version of Asatru, which entailed worship of Norse gods.[53]

Drafters thus imagined a white republic, but not a Christian Identity state. They aspired to constitute "a community of blood, not faith." Leading practitioners of Christian Identity could be counted among the Republic's "founding fathers," but the constitution honored Christian Identity as a "predominant" religion rather than the official one. At the same time, refusing to endorse separationism, viewed by conservatives as an attack on religion itself, helped to retain the coalition's core. This compromise implemented the Northwest Front's promise "to lay aside all differences of religion between White people, now and forever." Freedom of religion folded within it "the right to raise children in the religion of family and cultural tradition," a right acknowledged in U.S. Supreme Court decisions but not to the degree that some members of the Aryan community would prefer. Other familiar provisions inveighed against "arbitrary search and seizure of goods and property" and demand respect for "due process of law."

As for protections in the criminal justice system, the constitution required a warrant for all ordinary arrests, but carved out a glaring category: no warrant would be required of "officers or agents of the Civil Guard or Bureau of State Security . . . in order to prevent immediate disorder or criminal behavior." Several rights reflected a concern for the working class. A citizen could initiate criminal proceedings without having to rely on a prosecutor. Every person charged with a crime shall have "the right to counsel and advocate of his choice," and legal expertise would have to be rendered free of charge. Once a person has been detained, the constitution prohibited magistrates from setting bond on terms "demonstrably outside the available resources of any defendant or accused person."[54]

Certain features of the NAR constitution codified the Aryan critique of unbridled capitalism. To be sure, they did not completely give up on the free market system, as the Icarians and many contemporary Communists had done. Instead of requiring government ownership of property and the means of production, the Aryans' brand of socialism supported targeted government programs to help citizens with the basic necessities of life. The NAR Constitution ensured citizens "the right to adequate and life-preserving medical care, free of charge." Another provision guaranteed "the right to adequate food, shelter, clothing and to a safe and stable home for children." Additionally, "all residents and citizens of the Republic shall have the right to gainful and productive employment." A related provision established a powerful right to education, notoriously absent in the U.S. Constitution: "All citizens and residents of the Republic shall enjoy the right, free of charge, to all such education, technical training, vocational training, and instruction."

Rights entailed responsibilities. Consistent with the Aryan vision of ethical citizenship, the constitution itemized a "Bill of Responsibilities." The republic required service in the "armed forces and a set term in the reserves" of all able-bodied male residents and citizens, reflecting dissatisfaction with how the American military was constituted: too diverse and overly dependent on the working class. Residents and citizens alike would have the duty to avoid sexual contact with nonwhites, refrain from homosexuality, and not engage in acts of "disloyalty, subversion, or counterrevolution." Several parts of the constitution reflected deep concern about the polluting effects of material existence, usurious loans, and the crushing nature of debt. One provision enjoined individuals, corporations, and government entities from "charg[ing] any form of interest, premium, or any other form of fee or bonus for any loan of money." Nothing of value could be accepted for performing religious functions. If a central theme connected these provisions preventing fees and excessive salaries, it was a conviction that an oligarchy of monied interests had seized control of the law. As Lane's *Precept 77* explained, "A nation with an aristocracy of money, lawyers or merchants will become a tyranny." Denying professionals unfettered liberty over fees returned power to working-class whites.

Of the various possible functions a constitution could serve, the NAR Constitution has been most successful in fulfilling its expressive, deliberative, and legitimating dimensions. In a single public document, unhappy white citizens can find most of the Aryan community's grievances catalogued, along with a plan for self-governance. No longer is inciting a race war the exclusive goal of the movement. Turning to written constitutionalism and popular sovereignty has led to something of greater value: the development of a distinctive Aryan legal theory, familiar to students of American history yet updated to reflect the modern white experience. Even so, any deliberative achievements have been limited by the failure to subject the draft constitution to further discussions or proceedings to ratify it. Insofar as the Aryan movement openly endorses violence as a means of political change, it has needed strong justifications from the legal tradition. It now has such arguments. Whether such efforts at sanitization through legal forms are accepted, as always, ultimately remains a question for the people as a whole.

Any intended disciplinary functions have, to date, been the least successful. The size of the Northwest Front's membership is unclear, and it does not appear that any lawlike mechanisms have arisen to back its moral injunctions with force. In fact, there is little evidence the organization tries to enforce the moral provisions of the constitution among its membership or the broader Aryan community. The NAR Constitution, for now, remains in the same realm occupied by the World Constitution—an ideological triumph, one template for governance, and an evocative call to arms.

What are the Aryans' prospects for success going forward? As a document of recent vintage, the NAR Constitution's prospects for success are bound up with its peculiar fusion of Christian fundamentalism, Nazi ideology, and policy positions. In the minds of its proponents, the American political tradition is capacious enough to incorporate all of these disparate ideas. Even so, one must ask whether it is possible to defy so many legal, cultural, and political developments of the twentieth century and still gain a sustainable following among disaffected whites. At some point, a group can accumulate so many defeated positions that it is impossible to generate the cohesiveness necessary to create an alternative legal community.

Beyond practical obstacles, ideological stumbling blocks lurk. One challenge is the tension between the document's professed respect for the rule of law and neo-Nazis' glorification of violence. The proposed constitution implies an end someday to randomized violence, terrorism, and pogroms, and a return to the virtuous state's monopolization of force. But related texts in the Aryan canon present a bloody vision that remains far from the average citizen's experience. The consistent, hard line taken by defenders of conventional sovereignty against secession has reduced public tolerance for extreme measures of constitutional change. By itself, widespread unhappiness does not translate into receptivity toward violence, and modern revolutionaries cite mostly a string of spectacular failures wrought by armed insurrection rather than crowning successes, at least on American soil.

Another major hurdle to internalization of the Aryan constitution is the movement's Nazi heritage. Although a few partisans recognized this as an impediment to coalition building, even they refused to break cleanly from this authoritarian tradition. Playing down overt references to Nazism may work in the short run, but adopting Nazi bureaucracies and other methods risks alienating whites who might otherwise sympathize with the substance of their agenda. In retaining their fondness for ideas that led to mass cruelty and genocide, movement leaders may have underestimated the power of World War II in reshaping the political imagination. Appeals to Nazi methods might not move the person who recalls the liberation of Europe as part of America's heroic past.

That history, perhaps more than any modern event, has fostered a hatred of totalitarianism and love of individual-centered liberty. In the same vein, by proposing a single national republic, the NAR Constitution rejected the Jeffersonian tradition of small-scale governance that many Americans find indispensable to ordered liberty. Just as black nationalists discovered it a supremely difficult task to recover the people's lost racial consciousness, so too Aryans encounter a liberal mind-set today that abhors discrimination and overweening state power. New Afrikans found the principle of equality so powerful that they left it intact. By comparison, the Aryan assault on equality is so strident it risks alienating whites. Whether discontent among whites can be fomented to the point of accepting such a radical re-education, more than anything else, may dictate the future of Aryan politics.

Lacking control over established means of altering the U.S. Constitution and finding little in the way of mainstream support for their values, racially conscious whites have turned sharply away from conventional sovereignty. They remain part of an underground community, biding their time while stoking disaffection among working-class Americans. Importantly, they also spend time revising popular theories of law and community. Until conditions favor a legal rupture, Aryans nurture dreams of white rule restored.

Epilogue

For over two centuries, the American political tradition demonstrated an astonishing suppleness and vigor. The U.S. Constitution, a fragile dream at its inception, grew into an enduring system of institutions and laws. One American people, a mere figment of select imaginations in the late eighteenth century, became impressively constituted through law, politics, education, and the arts. The rule of law's reach now extended from sea to sea. Above all, pluralism, equality, and individualism had seemingly prevailed over the forces of tribalism, hierarchy, and authoritarianism.

Triumphalistic explanations of the Constitution's longevity, which hold that intrinsically superior ideas inevitably won out, have obscured deeper ideological processes at work. In actuality, the development of American law has been marked by patterns of creation, entrenchment, resistance, revision, and consolidation. Together, the eight constitution-writing stories in this volume revealed the legal culture as a whole to be characterized by adaptation and reversal, innovation and regression, fragmentation and reorganization. Sifting through experiences left out of the legal canon has made it possible to recover two main socio-ideological dynamics after America's founding. One involved the relentless groundwork necessary to propagate a legal vision premised on the idea of one people. Employing a variety of techniques over time, agents of the dominant order defended a conventional theory of politics, even as they co-opted or disparaged competing ideas about popular sovereignty.

Another dynamic has been the unabated process of defiance through design. Despite securing the loyalty of most citizens and acquiring advanced technologies to police legal culture, authorities could never eradicate the people's impulse to write or the ideas expressed in their legal texts. Confronted by intolerable circumstances, Americans expressed their dissatisfaction by writing ever more constitutions and laws. Under the duress of historical usage, theories of popular sovereignty mutated and multiplied. These models of self-rule made the legal tradition a lived experience, useful not only for their makers but also for subsequent generations of Americans who believed they could perfect their plan of government the next time. Folk legal theorists learned to behave as scavengers, extracting what they wanted from others' experiences to assemble new histories, identities, worldviews, and rules to live by. They showed themselves to be tenacious innovators, artful builders—even spellbinding storytellers.

But there was far more to the story than the oppositional tendencies to preserve and reconstitute legal ideas and political community. If contradiction is the test of political truth, then the tradition has fostered a constant public evaluation of governing ideals. As founders labored to bring their legal worlds into existence, alternative forms of popular authority vied for influence against established forms of politics. A theory of conventional sovereignty, descended from the 1787 Constitution and initially carried out through pioneer experiments, blossomed into a vision of law based on pluralism, individualism, and incrementalism. At the same time, a wealth of other approaches to legal authority exploded, predicated on shared ethics, culture, or humanity. Ongoing engagement among the varied accounts of political power produced further iterations—some plausible, others fanatical.

Each form of popular sovereignty faced distinctive challenges. Certain theories of governance, such as a property-based conception of power founded on settlers working the land, turned out to be highly contingent upon historical circumstances. Once those conditions evaporated, so went any prospects for success, and it would be folly to expect congenial conditions to materialize again anytime soon. Cultural and ethical theories of constitutionalism fared better over time, as they did not depend on either shared territory or a formal recognition on the part of other sovereigns for their legitimacy. Such visions of political power and shared identity could generate the cohesiveness and sense of order critical for the rule of law to take root. Underground communities observing lawlike norms sounding in such approaches might not only survive but also prosper, especially if they operated on a modest scale. Only when cultural or ethical visions of law showed more ambition, and when supporters defended them through extralegal means, did the risk of destruction or assimilation became greatest.

Tribal forms of governance had non-European origins but resembled cultural theories of law. American law initially treated Indian tribes as foreign nations; then, as native peoples were swept up in the broader project to create a single legal order, they found themselves forced to fit existing categories of civic membership. Once federal law gained supremacy over Indian nations, the practice of native sovereignty careened between two possibilities: nonexistence or continuation as domesticated organizations with a special past.

As theories of law became more numerous and intricate, constitutional functionality fragmented. The ascendance of the U.S. Constitution exacerbated this dynamic, not only exerting a gravitational pull on legitimate approaches and tactics but also having a dispersal effect on what any new constitution could plausibly accomplish. An alternative constitution could fulfill a number of functions for a community, even if the text never achieved a desired level of legitimacy. Ironically, as constitutions became more plentiful, it became harder to unify all the functions one might ideally want from a constitution. Operating in less than ideal situations, would-be founders had to be willing to accept something short of total victory. Communities partially constituted by law became prevalent, as did constitutions that remained strictly in the realm of ideas and public discourse.

Of the constitutions in this volume, only two—those of Icaria and Sequoyah—secured a measure of recognition (the first by operation of state law, the second by operation of federal law). Yet all of the constitutions satisfied a variety of crucial objectives for their intended population. The functions actually served by dissenters' constitutions expanded over time as they struggled to survive in the shadow of the American legal order. As it became infinitely more difficult to displace a mercurial account of conventional sovereignty, the prospects of actually implementing new bureaucracies faded. The expressive features of a new constitution thus took on the greatest function for those who lacked resources or refused to compromise their principles. A constitution that fulfilled mostly an expressive function resembled the manifesto of old: allowing ordinary citizens to air grievances, declaring first principles, constituting a people, and asserting the right to rule.

In related fashion, the deliberative potential of a constitution assumed a higher profile. If dethroning a political regime became a nearly impossible task, an alternative legal text might still stimulate discourse or shape matters of law and policy. The possibility of altering the terms of debate increasingly emerged as reason enough for discontented Americans to write. The World Constitution, authored with full knowledge of the daunting task ahead, best illustrated this set of motivations. Members of the working group foresaw almost certain failure in the near term. When the already slim odds of such a project dissipated, the Chicago group did not repudiate their plan, but rather redoubled their efforts in the hope that the fruits of their labor would shape the conversations of future generations. The same could be said about the constitution for the proposed Northwest American Republic in that the document helped to recast the Aryan movement in more palatable terms and improve the standing of one organization vis-à-vis other groups in the competition to represent white citizens.

For a community already organized in some fashion and enjoying predictable relations, a written constitution could exert a mighty disciplinary force upon its members. It could be used not merely to encourage solidarity but also to enforce it. No external authorization was necessary for a constitution to be treated in lawlike terms; a normative community need only accept the text as authoritative. The world federalists may have shown reluctance to use their unauthorized constitution to impose behavioral norms, but many practitioners of ethical sovereignty did so with relish, from John Brown to Imari Obadele. The Icarians, too, almost certainly would have continued their legal project in the absence of state approval. Because moral reform constituted both a condition of self-rule and a desired end goal under such legal theories, there was little reason to wait to make the written principles a part of their daily lives. In fact, ethical theories of power virtually demanded that advocates elevate their level of virtue before they could credibly demand that others submit to a program of moral transformation.

A new constitution could be an invaluable recruitment tool. By definition, dissenters faced a numerical disadvantage. They had to navigate a central dilemma: success required deep and broad support, but waiting for consensus before embarking on the path of constitutional rediscovery might doom a project at its inception. A number of founders solved this problem by starting the planning at an early stage and promoting a draft constitution among natural constituencies. Of course, the drawing power of a legal text could vary widely. At the broadest level, a new constitution might help to loosen a sense of loyalty one might have for the dominant legal order and cultivate new allegiances. Proudly asserting the existence of an emerging political community encourages others to believe in its future. Beyond speaking to a sympathetic audience, a text could be used for more specific ends: bolstering allegiances by awarding titles and responsibilities, gaining key advisors, and securing resources for state building. Populating an entire government-in-waiting became possible with the diffusion of constitutional functionality.

As ideas of self-governance became more plentiful, and even outlandish, citizens found it tempting to reach for legal language to make their agendas more palatable. Civic republicanism and written constitutionalism no longer constituted theories containing consistent classical meanings but now served as multipurpose conduits for repackaging substantive ideas. Many advocates did so in part to sanitize controversial principles, end goals, and tactics. To be sure, the mere act of wrapping radical ideas in the language and rituals of popular sovereignty and written constitutionalism does not make them mainstream. But undergoing the writing exercise itself can send positive signals about the seriousness of a rule-of-law project, the maturity of a political community, and the intentions of a marginalized group. These signals can go some way toward altering public perceptions of an unpopular social group or political movement.

Taking a panoramic view of the American political tradition has made it possible to see how ordinary citizens could remake basic ideas of power and community and the challenges they confronted. Iconoclasts subverted the dominant legal order from within the political tradition, using the very language and tools that have been crucial to its creation and maintenance. Through it all, Americans drew on their experience in self-governance to advance their conception of the good

life. Each constitution revealed places of sympathy and irritation between contending theories of law. Many of the groups emphasized
responsibilities and duties to others, suggesting a lingering dissatisfaction with rights-based liberalism. Yet, despite the diversity of legal
visions, agreement could still be found over the broad contours of
ideal government. Even the authors of the most radical constitutions
embraced the principles of popular decision making, divided powers,
and enumerated rights. They might have chafed at efforts to curtail
the people's natural right to re-create their government, but they uniformly accepted the idea that a legitimate claim to rule according to
the will of the people must conform to a protocol.

A shared commitment to legality should come as welcome news to
anyone concerned about stable government. Even as founders engaged the political tradition instrumentally, they were also shaped by
the tradition and the principle of legality in important ways. Each set
of drafters tried to appeal to Americans who did not already share
their views in lock-step fashion. To communicate with such strangers
and bring them over to their side of things, they took up the idioms of
democratic constitutionalism. That even the most aggrieved can still
muster faith in the political tradition suggests that constitution writing can serve as a crucial outlet for otherwise destructive energies.
The collective desire to be heard and to be treated as sovereign decision
makers worthy of respect can be satisfied to some degree through the
publication of a constitution.

All of this leaves a glimmer of hope that differences can be bridged—if
not with the authors themselves, then perhaps with other members of
their normative community. The points of ideological contact can be
exploited: critiques may be accommodated, support siphoned away,
and the disaffected reintegrated. Critics who labor within the higher-
law tradition prove they possess political energy, imagination, and
love for the rule of law—qualities every healthy legal order needs in
abundance. With some luck, such energies might be redirected back
into conventional politics.

Where unrest cannot be so easily absorbed, the political tradition
exerts pressure on dissidents to tame their tactics or defend them,
even if it does not always moderate their beliefs or objectives. Extralegal defiance of constitutional law might be overlooked if modest in
nature and serving virtuous goals. Open violence, however, closely

associated with covenantal and French influences, has been consistently treated as incompatible with rule by reason. A group willing to use force in defense of an insurgent constitutional vision may alienate allies and will almost certainly trigger an overwhelming response from defenders of deliberative democracy.

Over the long run, the tradition has encouraged dissidents to subscribe to time-honored principles, though they can no longer abide the authorities acting in their name. Proponents of popular sovereignty cannot be seen to stand for lawlessness, so they must articulate where legal boundaries should lie. Bold thinkers willing to cast their grievances in Americans' common tongue and abide legal limits may win self-respect, influence, and glory. Those who forgo the tradition entirely risk not only an inability to rouse fellow citizens but also political irrelevance.

For policy makers who are attentive, the constitutions in this book laid bare the sources of unrest. Continued doubts about a capitalist economy fueled experiments with philosophies that restructured the ownership of goods and labor relations, while opening up economic opportunities. The ascendance of a pluralistic society left some detractors convinced that the legal order threatened unfashionable but worthy cultural beliefs and practices. A good number of citizens worried that a liberal democracy lacks the moral aspirations of a good society. And the rise of courts to a central place in public affairs stimulated disgruntled citizens to try to reorganize the criminal justice system or restrict the power of judges to interpret a constitution. How well authorities confront these bubbling concerns will go a long way in discouraging the most destructive efforts to reshape the political order.

For the discontented, the lessons are more sobering. With a little planning, it is always possible to develop a coherent political alternative. It is a relatively easy task to publicize grievances—indeed, under the terms of conventional sovereignty today, dissenting views must be tolerated. Authoring a constitution can galvanize discontent and draw newcomers to one's cause. A committed group can even begin to behave in lawlike ways and make inroads with disaffected populations. Yet establishing a legal order that outlives its birth moment is infinitely more challenging. It takes a rare union of astute political design, tactical ingenuity, and amenable social conditions. Even when a measure of internal cohesiveness is secured for a community, the recognition of neighbors may remain elusive.

The demise of the constitutions in this volume underscores a number of these obstacles. For some, internal disarray proved to be their undoing. The Icarian Constitution, which offered a utopian socialist order, withstood enormous social upheavals. In the end, irreconcilable differences between a charismatic founder and citizens left the community's social compact in tatters. The Icarians' enclave-style republic shielded citizens from outside influences as best it could, but heightened expectations from years of self-governance could not be quashed by one man's edicts. In many small legal orders, loyalty to individual personalities can war with democratic control. That destructive dynamic played out in Icaria's political experiment. Cycles of infighting led to demoralization and defections, until at last the political order collapsed from within.

For other founders, shifts in social conditions beyond their community largely dictated the outcome. The Sequoyah movement could not surmount the party politics arrayed against its proposed state. No matter how united the movement became, its plans were held captive by existing power arrangements. An eerily familiar story unfolded with world federalists. Initially buoyed by fear of nuclear technology and searing memories of global war, public conditions rapidly turned inhospitable to the Chicago group's message of peace through one law. Despite enjoying measurable popular support, world federalists struggled to gain traction against defenders of the nation-state system or reformers who preferred more modest forms of international cooperation. The Cold War made fundamental reform of this sort untenable, as the world experienced a resurgence of national sovereignty.

Other people's dreams of self-governance were dashed mostly through their own tactical choices. John Brown's assault on a remote town in Virginia, Imari Obadele's plan to establish a black capital in Mississippi to great fanfare, and Indian Stream leaders' armed resistance of New Hampshire all count as decisions that generated a forceful response from the authorities. In each episode, dissidents capitalized on political sentiment shared by fellow Americans. But their extreme measures raised the stakes of legal conflict exponentially, rendering supporters at once visible and vulnerable. Their actions threatened conventional sovereignty's dual mission to create a single people and facilitate orderly legal change, and did so in ways that could no longer be ignored.

The demise of these constitutions tells us something more about a constitution as a system of ideas: even an imperfect legal order can have a tenacious hold on the people's imagination. The most successful among democratic experiments exploited widespread concerns, while trying unusual, often localized, modes of organization. Withdrawal and self-rule could work under carefully tended circumstances. To the extent citizens cloaked their true ambitions and avoided open conflict, they enjoyed the capacity to create an alternative world in the interstices of the law. Conversely, large-scale constitutional visions usually elicited strong condemnation, especially when paired with violent tactics. The more ambitious the scale of a project, the more difficult it became to generate social support for an alternative legal order.

As the events of 1787 became a distant memory, audacious forms of political resistance encountered ever-longer odds. The closing of the American frontier ended pioneer lawmaking for all practical purposes. But it remained useful as a model for working out one's own theory of popular sovereignty. That spectacular, bloody failure of Southern secession reduced many Americans' appetite for armed separatism. At the same time, the rise of the nonviolent social movement as a regular participant in ordinary lawmaking meant disfavoring, more than ever, extreme methods of legal resistance.

As conventional sovereignty became an entrenched and layered practice, ordinary law became an effective instrument to deprive radicals of their claim to speak for the people. The regular enforcement of the laws could be used not only to disparage alternative constitutional theories but also to discourage certain popular tactics of legal change. The legal order's means of protecting itself and its citizens became more sophisticated, as new agencies acquired expanded powers and deployed advanced technologies to monitor, infiltrate, and undermine radicals. All of these developments reduced the chances that new visions of constitutional law might completely overtake the existing institutions of government.

None of this is to say that the revolutionary spirit could be crushed entirely or funneled exclusively into regular politics. Americans kept writing constitutions, almost as if their lives depended on it. But folk statesmen found the task of moving fellow citizens to action harder over time, despite order-shattering changes around the world and unsolved problems on the home front. Twentieth-century revolutionaries discovered the prospects for legal transformation hampered by not only political obstacles but also cultural attitudes. Each statesman, in his own era, lamented the mind-set of Americans who should make up their natural constituencies but who were not more receptive to their theories. Beyond battling complacency and a willingness to settle for flawed solutions, they found it enormously difficult to dislodge deeply held legal beliefs.

That, in the end, may have been the hardest lesson to learn. A brilliant design was necessary but not sufficient for long-term success. Building an alternative legal culture proved to be an infinitely complex endeavor. Theories of power and community had to resonate as well as stand up to scrutiny. How to harness the social conditions of the day and persuade unhappy citizens to action mattered far more than sublime words on paper.

Notes

Prologue

1. James Wilson, Speech at a Public Meeting, Philadelphia, Oct. 6, 1787.
2. James Wilson, Speech in Convention, Philadelphia, Nov. 26, 1787, in James DeWitt Andrews, ed., *The Works of James Wilson* (Chicago, 1896), 525–545; Bernard Bailyn, *The Ideological Origins of the American Republic* (Cambridge, MA, 1967); Gordon S. Wood, *The Creation of the American Republic, 1776–1789* (New York, 1969); Pauline Maier, *Ratification: The People Debate the Constitution, 1787–1788* (New York, 2011).
3. Works that exemplify the single tradition approach include Akhil R. Amar, *America's Constitution: A Biography* (New York, 2006); Edward S. Corwin, *The "Higher Law" Background of American Constitutional Law* (Ithaca, NY, 1967); Larry D. Kramer, *The People Themselves: Popular Constitutionalism and Judicial Review* (New York, 2004); Leonard W. Levy, *Original Intent and the Framers' Constitution* (New York, 1988). The dualistic approach to studying the constitutional tradition is best illustrated by Christian Fritz, whose historical work pits the principle of unmediated sovereignty against a growing tendency to restrain the people's revolutionary authority, *American Sovereigns: The People and America's Constitutional Tradition Before the Civil War* (New York, 2009), and Bruce Ackerman, whose constitutional theory focuses on ordinary politics punctuated by rare moments of intensive higher lawmaking, *We the People: Foundations* (Cambridge, MA, 1993). My approach differs from theirs by emphasizing the divergent forms of popular sovereignty, tactics, and functions.
4. Many studies of popular constitutionalism focus on social movements or elites who co-opt the institutions of conventional government for legally transformative agendas. Bruce Ackerman, *We the People: Transformations*

(Cambridge, MA, 1998); Barry Friedman, *The Will of the People: How Public Opinion Has Influenced the Supreme Court and Shaped the Meaning of the Constitution* (New York, 2009); Steven M. Teles, *The Rise of the Conservative Legal Movement: The Battle for Control of the Law* (Princeton, 2008); Ann Southworth, *Lawyers for the Right: Professionalizing the Conservative Coalition* (Chicago, 2008); Stuart A. Scheingold, *The Politics of Rights: Lawyers, Public Policy, and Political Change* (New Haven, 1974). For pivotal work on backlash politics during the civil rights era, see Gerald Rosenberg, *The Hollow Hope: Can Courts Bring about Social Change?* (Chicago, 1991); Michael Klarman, *From Jim Crow to Civil Rights: The Supreme Court and the Struggle for Racial Equality* (New York, 2004).

5. Zachary Elkins et al., *The Endurance of National Constitutions* (New York, 2009), 1.

6. Walter Murphy urges us to locate all constitutions along a "spectrum of authority." See "Constitutions, Constitutionalism, and Democracy," in *Constitutionalism and Democracy*, ed. Douglas Greenberg et al. (New York, 1993); see also Beau Breslin, *From Words to Worlds: Exploring Constitutional Functionality* (Baltimore, 2009), 25–29.

7. John Locke, *Second Treatise on Civil Government* (1690), ch. 13, § 149; The Federalist No. 1 (Alexander Hamilton), *Independent Journal,* Oct. 27, 1787.

1. The Republic of Indian Stream, 1832–1835

1. Gordon S. Wood, *The Radicalism of the American Revolution* (New York, 1991), 308; Bernard Bailyn, *The Ideological Origins of the American Revolution* (Cambridge, MA, 1967); William E. Nelson, "The Utopian Legal Order of the Massachusetts Bay Colony, 1630–1686," *American Journal of Legal History* 47(2) (2005): 183–230.

2. Daniel Doan, *Indian Stream Republic: Settling a New England Frontier, 1785–1842* (Hanover, NH, 1997), 1–5, 12–18.

3. The Paris Peace Treaty of September 30, 1783, art. 2.

4. Alexis de Tocqueville, *Democracy in America* (New York, 1992), 298. Tocqueville goes on to observe: "The citizen of the United States does not acquire his practical science and his positive notions from books; the instruction he has acquired may have prepared him for receiving those ideas, but it did not furnish them. The American learns to know the laws by participating in the act of legislation; and he takes a lesson in the forms of government, from governing. The great work of society is ever going on beneath his eyes, and, as it were, under his hands." Ibid., 299.

5. Eduardo Moisés Peñalver and Sonia K. Katyal, *Property Outlaws: How Squatters, Pirates, and Protesters Improve the Law of Ownership* (New Haven, 2010), 55–63; Paul W. Gates, *History of Public Land Law Development* (Washington, DC, 1979).

6. Lisa Ford, *Settler Sovereignty: Jurisdiction and Indigenous People in America and Australia, 1788–1836* (Cambridge, MA, 2010), 55–64, 85–107.

7. The minutes show that a special meeting on June 11, 1832, appointed David Mitchell, Luther Parker, Phineas Willard, Hermau Bechalder, and Nathan Judd to draft a constitution and commence the state-building process.

8. A handful produced constitutions, including Vermonters who declared independence from New York in 1777 and the three counties that seceded from North Carolina to establish the Republic of Franklin in 1784. Other efforts to fashion governments from settlements or existing states occurred along contested boundaries of Kentucky, North Carolina, Tennessee, Virginia, and West Virginia. Christian G. Fritz, *American Sovereigns: The People and America's Constitutional Tradition Before the Civil War* (New York, 2007), 44–79, 246–276. The violent reaction of backcountry farmers over a whiskey tax in 1794 presented another, early challenge to how authorities would perceive direct acts of resistance. William Hogeland, *The Whiskey Rebellion: George Washington, Alexander Hamilton, and the Frontier Rebels Who Challenged America's Newfound Sovereignty* (New York, 2006); Thomas P. Slaughter, *The Whiskey Rebellion: Frontier Epilogue to the American Revolution* (New York, 1986); Steven R. Boyd, ed., *The Whiskey Rebellion: Past and Present Perspectives* (Westport, CT, 1985).

9. Edward A. Channing, *A History of the United States* 3 (New York, 1926), 373.

10. Doan, *Indian Stream Republic,* 14; Roger Hamilton Brown, *The Struggle for the Indian Stream Territory* (Cleveland, 1955), 3–4. The "Proprietors of Philip's Grant" became known as the Eastman Company after Eastman bought into the group, while the Bedel Company charter described itself as the "Proprietors of Bedel's grant." Doan, *Indian Stream Republic*, 10–18. Brown reports that after 1825, the Eastman Company's petitions were considered for seven years straight, but action was tabled in the House each time. Brown, *Struggle*, 29.

11. Doan, *Indian Stream Republic,* 96–98.

12. Brown, *Struggle,* 27–29; Grant Showerman, *The Indian Stream Republic and Luther Parker* (Concord, NH, 1915), 35–37. The 1824 action by New Hampshire allowed two individuals—Nathaniel Perkins and Jeremiah Tabor—to retain title to 700 acres each.

13. The rise of this political conscience explains why 1829 is identified as part of Indian Stream's founding lore, though some commentators have missed this point. Showerman, *Luther Parker,* 56 n.10.

14. Doan, *Indian Stream Republic,* 128.

15. Ibid., 143; Brown, *Struggle,* 46–47. Letter from Reuben Sawyer to Eastman Company, May 18, 1829, Philip's Grant Papers, 68, in Brown, 47.

16. Minutes of June 11, 1832, in Showerman, *Luther Parker,* 55.

17. Indian Stream Constitution (1832), Part Second—Form of Government, in ibid., 60. The vote was 59–3 for approving the constitution.

18. Indian Stream Constitution, preamble.

19. François Joseph Audet, "La République d'Indian Stream," *Proceedings and Transactions, Royal Society of Canada* (2d series, 1906), 119–127; Showerman, *Luther Parker,* 97.

20. Indian Stream Constitution, Part Second—Form of Government.
21. New Hampshire Constitution of 1776.
22. Such a statement appeared in the preamble of a contract between residents of Indian Stream. Showerman, *Luther Parker*, 51.
23. Indian Stream Constitution, Part First—Bill of Rights, arts. 1, 12, 13.
24. An Act to Exempt Certain Property from Attachment, July 9, 1832, in Showerman, *Luther Parker*, 73.
25. Ibid., arts. 5, 6, 7, 8, 10. The New Hampshire Constitution of 1784 separates the proportionality principle and cruel and unusual punishment ideas into two provisions. These two sentences were not copied by the drafters of the Indian Stream document: "Where the same undistinguishing severity is exerted against all offenses, the people are led to forget the real distinction in the crimes themselves, and to commit the most flagrant with as little compunction as they do the lightest offenses. For the same reason a multitude of sanguinary laws is both impolitic and unjust."
26. Indian Stream Constitution, Part Second—Form of Government, The Council; Doan, *Indian Stream Republic*, 118–119, 125.
27. Indian Stream Constitution, Part Second—Form of Government. Article 37 of the New Hampshire Constitution articulates the principle of separation of powers: "In the government of this state, the three essential powers thereof, to wit, the legislative, executive, and judicial, ought to be kept as separate from, and independent of, each other, as the nature of a free government will admit, or as is consistent with that chain of connection that binds the whole fabric of the constitution in one indissoluble bond of union and amity."
28. Tocqueville, *Democracy in America*, 62–63; Albert Bushnell Hart, *Practical Essays on American Government* (New York, 1893), 135–136; Richard Middleton, *Colonial America: A History, 1565–1776* (Oxford, UK, 1992), 345; The Federalist No. 70 (Alexander Hamilton), *New York Packet*, Mar. 18, 1788.
29. According to An Act Regulating Marriages, Mar. 10, 1834, the republic recognized marriages performed by "every ordained Elder or minister of the gospel and every Justice of the peace who are commissioned in this place." Showerman, *Luther Parker*, 81. A couple's intention to wed had to be published for at three public meetings or three Sabbath days to be valid. Indian Stream Constitution, Part Second—Form of Government, Encouragement of Literature and Moral Virtue.
30. An Act for Organizing the Militia, July 9, 1832, in Showerman, *Luther Parker*, 73–74.
31. An Act to Establish Courts of Justice, July 9, 1832, in Showerman, *Luther Parker*, 69–70; An Act to Provide for Forming Juries, July 9, 1832, ibid., 71–72.
32. The Assembly of Indian Stream, Mar. 11, 1833, in Showerman, *Luther Parker*, 75–76; An Act to Prevent Vexatious Suits at Law, Mar. 15, 1834, ibid., 81–82; An Act for the Punishment of Assault and Battery and Murder, Mar. 15, 1834, ibid., 82; An Act Making Provision for Confinement of Criminals, Mar. 15, 1834, ibid., 84–85; An Act to Compel Witnesses to Attend When Summoned, ibid., 90. Throughout the 1830s, New Hampshire

rejected abolition of the death penalty, but narrowed the punishment's application to murder and treason by, among other things, barring it for the crimes of "theft, forgery, and the like." New Hampshire Const., part I, art. XVIII; Stuart Banner, *The Death Penalty* (Cambridge, MA, 2002), 131–133; Doan, *Indian Stream Republic,* 121–122.

33. Minutes of March 5, 1832, in Showerman, *Luther Parker,* 48–50; Indian Stream Constitution, The Assembly, sec. 5; An Act in Case of Perjury, Apr. 18, 1835, in Showerman, *Luther Parker,* 89–90.

34. Brown, *Struggle,* 52–59; Doan, *Indian Stream Republic,* 154–160; Showerman, *Luther Parker,* 50–55.

35. Doan, *Indian Stream Republic,* 153; Showerman, *Luther Parker,* 94–95.

36. Edwin R. Keedy, "The Constitutions of the State of Franklin, the Indian Stream Republic and the State of Deseret," *University of Pennsylvania Law Review* 101 (1953): 516–528. Showerman, *Luther Parker,* 97.

37. Fritz, *American Sovereigns,* 76.

38. Brown, *Struggle,* 62–64.

39. Showerman, *Luther Parker,* 95.

40. Attorney General Sullivan had earlier instituted trespass actions in state court against two settlers, Ebenezer Fletcher and Abner Hyland, in an effort to establish New Hampshire's claim over the territory. In 1823, a verdict against Hyland was secured, as the superior court ruled that the land belonged to the state and that it could take appropriate action "against the intruders." Doan, *Indian Stream Republic,* 96–99. A judgment adverse to Fletcher was rendered in 1827. The legislative acts of 1824 prevented enforcement of these judgments against the settlers.

41. An Act Regulating the Fees of the Sheriff, and Defining His Duty, in Showerman, *Luther Parker,* July 9, 1832, 71–72; An Act to Prevent Unlawful Services, Apr. 18, 1835, ibid., 88–89.

42. White to Secretary of State of New Hampshire, Mar. 30, 1835, *Adjutant-General's Report for 1868,* 276, in Brown, *Struggle,* 66–67.

43. Doan, *Indian Stream Republic,* 174–175, 200–202; Showerman, *Luther Parker,* 98–100.

44. Brown, *Struggle,* 77–79; Showerman, *Luther Parker,* 102–103.

45. Doan, *Indian Stream Republic,* 209–210.

46. Deposition of Richard I. Blanchard, Aug. 11, 1836, in Showerman, *Luther Parker,* 224–225.

47. Doan, *Indian Stream Republic,* 220–221.

48. *N.H. Patriot,* Nov. 23, 1835, in Showerman, *Luther Parker,* 107; Deposition of Benjamin Applebee, Aug. 11, 1836, in Showerman, *Luther Parker,* 250; Doan, *Indian Stream Republic,* 246.

49. Doan, *Indian Stream Republic,* 242–243.

50. Showerman, *Luther Parker,* 110–111.

51. Brown, *Struggle,* 93–94.

52. Doan, *Indian Stream Republic,* 174–175.

2. The Icarian Nation, 1848–1895

1. Arthur E. Bestor, *Backwoods Utopias: The Sectarian Origins and the Owenite Phase of Communitarian Socialism in America: 1663–1829* (Philadelphia, 1970), 1–19.
2. Carol Weisbrod, *The Boundaries of Utopia* (New York, 1980), xii, 78–79; The Federalist No. 56 (Madison), *New York Packet,* Feb. 19, 1788; New State Ice Co. v. Liebmann, 285 U.S. 262, 386–387 (1932) (Brandeis, J., dissenting); James Bryce, *The American Commonwealth* (New York, 1888), 468.
3. Etienne Cabet, *Travels in Icaria,* trans. Leslie J. Roberts (Syracuse, NY, 2003), 4.
4. Ibid., 8, 12, 18, 25.
5. *Popular Tribune,* Feb. 3, 1851, 4.
6. Cabet, 32–33.
7. Ibid., 41.
8. Ibid., 108.
9. Ibid., 110.
10. Christopher H. Johnson, *Utopian Communism in France: Cabet and the Icarians, 1839–1851* (Ithaca, 1974), 156–157. Johnson estimates that Cabet's writings drew more supporters from among poorer artisans, such as shoemakers and tailors, than from aristocratic craftspeople, such as jewelers and printers. Needless to say, European Icarianism did poorly among the bourgeois.
11. Mark Holloway, *Heavens on Earth: Utopian Communities in America 1680–1880* (New York, 1966), 200–201.
12. President of the Community, Cabet, "Appeal to Icarians of Europe and America and to Philanthropists," in Etienne Cabet, *History and Constitution of the Icarian Community,* trans. Thomas Teakle (New York, 1917), 285. The Icarian Committee put it thus: "[W]e intend going where there is not anything to destroy, and where we may build up our City and our Nation in Love and in Peace." *Address of the Icarien Committee to Those Who Desire to Ameliorate the Condition of the People.*
13. Cabet, *Travels in Icaria,* xxvii.
14. Etienne Cabet, *The History of the Colony or Republic of Icaria in the United States of America* (Nauvoo, IL, 1855); Cabet, *History and Constitution,* 214.
15. Ibid., 244–245.
16. Shaw describes the social contract—part writing, part oral affirmation—as a "provisional constitution, providing for the organization of a communistic society, arranging for its management while in the early formative stages." Albert Shaw, *Icaria: A Chapter in the History of Communism* (New York, 1884), 24–25. Johnson points out that some objections were raised to the preliminary social contract, which depended heavily on Cabet's charisma rather than elections. According to Johnson, as Icarianism became an export to the New World, it faded as a movement in Europe. Johnson, *Utopian Communism,* 250–251, 288.

17. An Act to Incorporate the Icarian Community, Feb. 1, 1851, in Jules Prud-hommeaux, *Icarie et Son Fondateur, Etienne Cabet: Contribution à létude du Socialisme Expérimental* (Philadelphia, 1972), 618–619.

18. Cabet, *History and Constitution,* 215.

19. Robert P. Sutton, *Les Icariens: The Utopian Dream in Europe and America* (Urbana, IL, 1994), 67.

20. R. V. Hine, *California's Utopian Colonies* (New Haven, 1966), 73. A woman who grew up in the colony noted: "The Icarians always celebrated the 4th of July. . . . Up went the flag of red, white and blue, to the applause and cheers of the crowd, to the roar of guns and the sound of trumpets. All joined in singing the 'Star Spangled Banner,' 'America,' and other American patriotic hymns." Marie Marchand Ross, *Child of Icaria* (Westport, CT, 1938), 34.

21. Shaw, *History of Communism,* 54.

22. Icarian Constitution (1850), arts. 7–9.

23. By contrast, the community at Aurora had no constitution and few bylaws. William Alfred Hinds, *American Communities* (New York, 1847), 47.

24. Regulations for the General Assembly, A Statement of Motives, Mar. 3, 1855.

25. Icarian Constitution, ch. II, § III, art. 28.

26. Ibid., arts. 29–30.

27. Ibid., ch. I, Preliminary Considerations; ch. II, § VI, arts. 49, 50.

28. The Law Concerning the General Assembly of the Icarians, art. 5, Jan. 30, 1850, reported in *Popular Tribune,* Feb. 8, 1851, 7; Icarian Constitution, ch. IV, § V, arts. 173–174.

29. Icarian Constitution, ch. IV, § V, art. 169.

30. Ibid., ch. IV, § I, arts. 110–111.

31. Ibid., ch. IV, § IV, arts. 125, 129–130, 136–149, 152.

32. Ibid., ch. IV, § IV, arts. 132, 151(1), 153–155.

33. The Law Concerning the General Assembly of the Icarians, art. 20, Jan. 30, 1850, reported in *Popular Tribune,* Feb. 8, 1851. Free discussion could only be reopened upon five votes in the General Assembly after six months elapsed. Ibid., art. 21.

34. Lloyd W. Gundy, "Liberty, Equality and Fraternity in Butter Rights: Icarian Rules Can't Govern Everything," in *Culture and Colony Life of the Icarians, Proceedings of the 1994–97 Cours Icarien Symposia* (Sunnyvale, CA, 1998), 11.

35. Icarian Constitution, art. 59.

36. Ibid., 12.

37. In the July 26, 1846, issue of *Le Populaire,* Cabet wrote: "Our *Communisme* wants the *affranchisement* (liberation) of Woman, the recognition of her natural rights, equality and education for her. Our *Communisme* requests just everywhere for all women, respect and filial love for all elderly women, fraternal friendship for all young women . . . our *Communisme* wants the first duty of the *Communauté* and men in general to assure the happiness of Women in general, and consider marriage, rendered perfect, as the best means to guarantee the happiness of Women which would result in the happiness of Men, Society and Humanity." Ibid., 5–6; Icarian Constitution ch. 1,

Preliminary Considerations; ch. 2, § III, art. 26; ch. III, § V, arts. 70–71. On the division of labor, see Robert P. Sutton, "The Icarians of Corning Iowa," in Robert P. Sutton, ed., *Adaptation of the Icarians to America* (Sunnyvale, 1993), 3, 9.

38. Charles Nordhoff, *The Communistic Societies of the United States* (New York, 1965), 117, 166, 271–276. According to the principles of "complex marriage," the Oneida Community permitted any man and woman to freely cohabit so long as they did so on the basis of consent. Ibid., 276; Icarian Constitution, ch. III, § XI, arts. 95–104.

39. Diana M. Garno, *Citoyennes and Icaria* (Lanham, MD, 2005), 23.

40. Sutton, *Les Icariens*, 81–84. On Amana's laws and practices, see Nordhoff, *Communistic Societies*, 43–59; Diane L. Barthel, *Amana: From Pietist Sect to American Community* (Lincoln, NE, 1984). On the resistance of Icarian women to Cabet's proposals to regulate family life, see Garno, *Citoyennes and Icaria*, 88–90.

41. Garno, *Citoyennes and Icaria*, 127. Cabet blamed some of the discord in the community on the women. In a document titled *Icarian Community Conditions of Admission*, and later published in *Le Populaire*, Cabet stated: "There are stronger reasons for making woman comply with the conditions than man; for when she is not imbued with the spirit of Icarianism, she can draw her husband away and bring to the Community more trouble and disorder. We have had sad experiences of this in 1849; there were some women who called themselves Icarians but who were not, who by no means understood our doctrines, who had only egotism and vainty [*sic*] with ignorance, without social qualities and without judgment, and who left France only to screen their husbands from persecution which their revolutionary conduct had drawn upon them; these women, we say, have been the principal cause of desertions and withdrawals, by their influence upon feeble and blind husbands." Conditions for Admission, Jan. 22, 1850, published June 12, 1850, Paris, in Garno, *Citoyennes and Icaria*, 250.

42. Sutton, *Les Icariens*, 68.

43. Ibid., 88–89.

44. Undated letter from Widow Favart, Mrs. Cabet to Pierr Roine [est. date Mar. 29, 1856].

45. Shaw, *History of Communism*, 57–58.

46. *Memorial Setting Forth the Reasons Why 72 Voting Members of the Icarian Community Petition for the Repeal of the Act of Incorporation of this Body*, Oct. 20, 1856.

47. Sutton, *Les Icariens*, 96–97.

48. Ibid., 97–98.

49. Shaw, *History of Communism*, 91–97.

50. Ibid., 98; Sutton, *Les Icariens*, 130–131.

51. Emile Péron, *Brief History of Icaria. Constitution, Laws and Regulations of the Icarian Community* (Corning, IA, 1880), 11, reprinted in Garno, *Citoyennes and Icaria*, 183–184.

52. Leroux's influence is discussed by Garno, *Citoyennes and Icaria*, 190–196.

53. Ibid., 103.

54. Complaint, Dec. 14, 1877, *State of Iowa v. Icarian Community* (Circuit Court, Adams County, IA, Jan. Term 1878); Plaintiff's Amendment to Information, Mar. 20, 1878, *State of Iowa v. Icarian Community* (Circuit Court, Adams County, IA, Jan. Term 1878).

55. Answer of Defendants, Aug. 9, 1878, *State of Iowa v. Icarian Community* (Circuit Court, Adams County, IA, Jan. Term 1878).

56. Shaw, *History of Communism,* 189, 192. Contract of the New Icarian Community of Adams County, Iowa (1879), arts. 11, 23.

57. Shaw, *History of Communism,* 128–131.

58. Lloyd W. Gundy, "Glimpses of the Immigration of French Icarians to America," in Lillian M. Snyder and Robert P. Sutton, eds., *Immigration of the Icarians to Illinois* (Macomb, IL, 1987), 23, 24; Sutton, *Les Icariens.* 142–143. At its largest, Icaria numbered around four hundred in the several American colonies.

59. Icarian Constitution, ch. 2, § V, art. 43.

3. John Brown's America, 1856–1859

1. U.S. Constitution (1787), art. I, § 2(3); art. I, § 9(1); art. IV, § 2(3).

2. Dred Scott v. Sandford, 60 U.S. (19 How.) 393 (1857); Mark Graber, Dred Scott *and the Problem of Constitutional Evil* (New York, 2006); Don E. Ferhrenbacher, *The* Dred Scott *Case: Its Significance in American Law and Politics* (New York, 1978).

3. Letter from Charles L. Remond, Esq., John Brown, *et al.,* Apr. 29, 1858; David N. Utter, "John Brown of Osawatomie," *North American Review* 137.324 (Nov. 1883): 435–446.

4. W. E. B. Du Bois, *John Brown* (New York, 2001), 154; Richard J. Hinton, *John Brown and His Men: With Some Account of the Roads They Traveled to Reach Harper's Ferry* (New York, 1894), 171; Truman Nelson, *The Old Man: John Brown and Harpers Ferry* (New York, 1973), 52, 59.

5. "Journal of the Provisional Constitution Held on Saturday, May 8th, 1858, Chatham, Canada West, Saturday, May 8th, 1858," in The John Brown Insurrection, Brown Papers, *Calendar of Virginia State Papers and Other Manuscripts from January 1, 1836, to April 15, 1869,* H. W. Flournoy, Secretary of the Commonwealth and State Librarian, ed. (Richmond, 1893), 269, 271–273; Hannah Geffert, "They Heard His Call: The Local Black Community's Involvement in the Raid on Harpers Ferry," in *Terrible Swift Sword: The Legacy of John Brown,* Peggy A. Russo and Paul Finkelman, eds. (Athens, OH, 2005), 23; Fred Landon, "Canadian Negroes and the John Brown Raid," *Journal of Negro History* 6.2 (1921): 174–182; Provisional Constitution and Ordinances for the People of the United States, arts. IV, XXX, reprinted in Flournoy, *Virginia State Papers,* 279, 280, 285; *The Life, Trial and Execution of John Brown,* Robert M. De Witt, ed. (New York, 1859), 51–52. The Provisional Constitution created two separate offices of president and commander in chief, the former elected and the latter appointed. The minutes

of the Chatham convention show that on May 10, 1858, Thomas M. Kinnard was nominated for president, but declined the nomination. J. W. Loguen's name was then tendered, but "[t]he nomination was afterwards withdrawn, Mr. Loguen not being present, and it being announced that he would not serve if elected." Osborne P. Anderson, *A Voice from Harpers Ferry* (Boston, 1861), 12.

6. Letter from John Brown to Henry L. Stearns, July 15, 1857, in F. B. Sanborn, *The Life and Letters of John Brown, Liberator of Kansas, and Martyr of Virginia* (Boston, 1891), 12–17; *A Declaration of Liberty By the Representatives of the Slave Population of the United States of America* (1859).

7. John Brown's Covenant for the Enlistment of His Volunteer-Regular Company, Aug. 1856, in Oswald Garrison Villard, *John Brown, 1800–1859* (Boston, 1910), 661–664 (app. B).

8. John Brown's Covenant, art. 4.

9. John Brown's Covenant, arts. 2–4.

10. David S. Reynolds, *John Brown, Abolitionist* (New York, 2005), 301–303.

11. Hinton, *John Brown and His Men*, 424; *A Declaration of Liberty.*

12. On the unconventional aspects of founding moments, see Bruce Ackerman, *We the People: Transformations* (Cambridge, MA, 1998); Bruce Ackerman and Neal Katyal, "Our Unconventional Founding," *University of Chicago Law Review* 62 (1995): 475–573; Akhil Reed Amar, "The Consent of the Governed: Constitutional Amendment Outside Article V," *Columbia Law Review* 94 (1994): 457–508.

13. The Christian example of maintaining an underground legal-ethical order within a hostile Roman Empire serves as a historical precedent. Augustine's account of two cities—a heavenly city constituted by the faithful that co-exists with an earthly city weakened by sinfulness—encourages the dissident to see himself as a stranger to ordinary law and the ways of the majority. Saint Augustine, *City of God* (New York, 1994), 413–427.

14. Nelson, *The Old Man,* 52, 59 (quoting Frederick Douglass).

15. Provisional Constitution and Ordinances for the people of the United States, preamble (1858).

16. Reynolds, *John Brown, Abolitionist,* 114.

17. Provisional Constitution, art. XVI.

18. Du Bois, *John Brown,* 99; Provisional Constitution, art. XXXIX. By all accounts, Brown was raised with Calvinist values and conducted himself in ways that prompted the descriptions "austere," "stern," "unyielding," and "devoted." Du Bois, *John Brown,* 20–21.

19. Provisional Constitution, art. XL.

20. District of Columbia v. Heller, 554 U.S. 570 (2008).

21. Provisional Constitution, art. XLII.

22. Constitution of Haiti, title IV, arts. 9–10 (1801). Article 10 declared: "Divorce will not take place in the colony"; C. L. R. James, *The Black Jacobins: Toussaint L'Ouverture and the San Domingo Revolution* (New York, 1989). John Brown bragged about his wide reading of the history and practices of insurrections, including that of L'Ouverture. Hinton, *John Brown and His*

Men, 182–183; Constitution of Haiti, ¶¶ 50–51 (1805); Benjamin Quarles, *Allies for Freedom: Blacks and John Brown* (New York, 1974), 46, 64, 111.

23. Provisional Constitution, arts. III-IV.
24. Compare Provisional Constitution, art. V with U.S. Constitution, art. III (1787).
25. There are only three death-eligible crimes: rape of a female prisoner, desertion or treason, and taking up arms against the community after "having been set at liberty on parole of honor." Provisional Constitution, arts. XXXVII, XXX-VIII, XLI; ibid., art. XXII.
26. "Head Quarters War Department Provisional Army, Harpers Ferry, Oct. 10th, 1859," in Flournoy, *Virginia State Papers,* 274–275, 322.
27. Letter to Editor of *Summit Beacon,* Dec. 20, 1855 (describing proslavery forces as "invaders" and stating that "[w]hat remains for the Free State men of Kansas, and their friends in the State, and the world to do, is to hold the ground they now possess, and Kansas is free"), in Louis Ruchames, ed., *A John Brown Reader* (London, 1959), 88–93; Advertisement, "To the Friends of Freedom," *New York Tribune,* Mar. 4, 1857, ibid., 102; "Old Brown's Parallels," *New York Tribune,* Jan. 3, 1859, ibid., 114–115 (arguing that excursion into Osage settlement to free slaves "forcibly restored [them] to their 'natural and inalienable rights,' with but one man killed").
28. Letter from Brown to Douglass, Jan. 9, 1854, in Ruchames, *John Brown Reader,* 84–85.
29. Jeffery Rossbach, *Ambivalent Conspirators: John Brown, The Secret Six, and a Theory of Slave Violence* (Philadelphia, 1982), 141–145.
30. Ibid., 140–141, 183, 193–195; Howe to Charles Sumner, Mar. 12, 1859, Howe Collection, Houghton Library, cited in ibid., 194.
31. Quarles, *Allies for Freedom,* 75–80; Nelson, *The Old Man,* 51–52.
32. Kate Clifford Larson, *Bound for the Promised Land: Harriet Tubman, Portrait of an American Hero* (New York, 2004), 158–162; Quarles, *Allies for Freedom,* 41–42, 79–80.
33. Robert Trueman, *Fragments to the Flames: John Brown, Harpers Ferry and the Canadian Connection* (North York, Ontario, 1996), 13.
34. Hinton, *John Brown and His Men,* 250; Nelson, *The Old Man,* 91.
35. Anderson, *Voice from Harpers Ferry,* 20, 24–25; Rev. Samuel Vanderlip Leech, *The Raid of John Brown at Harpers Ferry As I Saw It* (Washington DC, 1909), 5.
36. Leech, *Raid of John Brown,* 5; Nelson, *The Old Man,* 90.
37. Brian McGinty, *John Brown's Trial* (Cambridge, MA, 2009), 48–62.
38. Ibid., 55–58.
39. Ibid., 71–85.
40. Ibid., 136, 161–162, 203–204; De Witt, *Life, Trial,* 86–90; Robert L. Tsai, "John Brown's Constitution," *Boston College Law Review* 51 (2010): 151, 152–153, 163, 184–185.
41. The importance of a virtuous portrayal of the gathering at Chatham convention and the subsequent raid was not lost on Brown's supporters. Consider this description of the men solemnly gathered to ratify the Provisional Constitution: "So many intellectual looking men are seldom seen in one party, and at the

same time, such utter disregard of prevailing custom, or style, in dress and other little conventionalities. Hour after hour they would sit in council, thoughtful, ready; some of them eloquent, all fearless, patient of the fatigues of business; anon, here and there over the 'track,' and again in the assembly; . . ." Anderson, *Voice from Harpers Ferry*, 14.

42. Brown's charge to the group before it set off for Harpers Ferry included this one: "And now, gentlemen, let me impress this one thing upon your minds. You all know how dear life is to you, and how dear your life is to your friends. And in remembering that, consider that the lives of others are as dear to them as yours are to you. Do not, therefore, take the life of any one, if you can possibly avoid it; but if it is necessary to take life in order to save your own, then make sure work of it." Ibid., 28–29. Hinton, *John Brown and His Men*, 183 (quoting Richard Realf's testimony before the U.S. Senate).

43. *Brown's Interview with Mason, Vallandigham, and Others,* in Ruchames, *John Brown Reader*, 119. Vallandigham asked: "Did you expect a general rising of the slaves in case of your success?" Brown answered: "No, sir; nor did I wish it. I expected to gather them up from time to time and set them free," ibid., 123. Brown's lawyers, in arguing that he lacked the specific intent to commit the legal offenses, similarly said of the insurrection charge: "There is a manifest distinction between the effort made to run away with slaves, or inducing them to run away, and attempt to excite them to rebellion and insurrection."

44. Sentencing Statement of Judge Richard Parker, in McGinty, *John Brown's Trial*, 232–233.

45. De Witt, *Life, Trial*, 94; "Old Brown's Parallels," *N.Y. Tribune*; Sanborn, *Life and Letters*, 122.

46. A document found among John Brown's possession, titled "Vindication of the Invasion," argued that the attack had been planned and conducted "in accordance with my settled policy." Reynolds, *John Brown, Abolitionist*, 303.

47. Ruchames, *John Brown Reader*, 42–43.

48. Quarles, *Allies for Freedom,* 25–27; United States League of Gileadites, "Words of Advice and Agreement," Jan. 15, 1851.

49. Lysander Spooner, *A Plan for the Abolition of Slavery and to the Non-Slaveholders of the South* (New York, 1858); Randy E. Barnett, "Was Slavery Unconstitutional Before the 13th Amendment? Lysander Spooner's Theory of Interpretation," *Pacific Law Journal* 28 (1997): 977–1014.

50. Lysander Spooner, *The Unconstitutionality of Slavery* (New York, 1848); William M. Wiecek, *The Sources of Antislavery Constitutionalism in America, 1760–1848* (Ithaca, 1977); *The Collected Works of Lysander Spooner*, Charles Shivley, ed. (Weston, MA, 1971), 37–38.

51. Scott John Hammond, "John Brown as Founder: America's Violent Confrontation with its First Principles," in Russo and Finkelman, *Terrible Swift Sword*, 61.

52. Brown was described as "another Moses," and, after his execution, in increasingly Christ-like terms. Anderson, *Voice from Harpers Ferry*, 2.

53. Ibid., 8. Anderson went on to claim, "Insurrection has its progressive side, and has been elevated by John Brown from the skulking, fearing cabal, when in the hands of a brave but despairing few, to the highly organized, formidable, and to very many, indispensable institution for the security of freedom, when guided by intelligence."

54. DuBois, *John Brown*, 58.

55. Ibid., 59.

56. Nelson, *The Old Man*, 52–53.

57. Anderson, *Voice from Harpers Ferry*, 48; Nelson, *The Old Man*, 54.

58. Anderson, *Voice from Harpers Ferry*, 38.

59. Hinton, *John Brown and His Men*, 30–31, 35–36, quoting Frederick Douglass, *Life and Times of Frederick Douglass* (Boston, 1892), 386–387. Anderson's account of his own harrowing escape confirms these suspicions about tactical advantages the group hoped to gain from the local topography. Anderson, *Voice from Harpers Ferry*, 48, 52–54.

60. Provisional Constitution, arts. XLIII, XLVI.

61. Flournoy, *Virginia State Papers*, 279.

4. Confederate Anxieties, 1860–1865

1. Abraham Lincoln, "House Divided" Speech, Republican state convention, Springfield, IL, June 16, 1858.

2. Eric H. Walther, *The Fire-Eaters* (Baton Rouge, 1992), 282. On the conditions on the eve of secession, see Eric Foner, *Free Soil, Free Labor, Free Men: The Ideology of the Republican Party Before the Civil War* (New York, 1995); William W. Freehling, *The Road to Disunion*, vol. 2: *Secessionists Triumphant, 1854–1861* (New York, 2007); Mark A. Graber, Dred Scott *and the Problem of Constitutional Evil* (New York, 2006).

3. *Charleston Mercury*, Oct. 19, 1830, in Walther, *Fire-Eaters*, 123; Laura A. White, *Robert Barnwell Rhett: Father of Secession* (Gloucester, MA, 1965).

4. Walther, *Fire-Eaters*, 123–125; *Charleston Mercury*, Mar. 26, 1833.

5. Historians have consistently found the planter class to be a vocal but important minority in slaveholding states, though a larger bloc in some states such as South Carolina than others. James Oakes, *The Ruling Race: A History of American Slaveholders* (New York, 1982); Otto H. Olsen, "Historians and the Extent of Slave Ownership in the Southern United States," *Civil War History* 50(4) (2004): 401–417. On the literary production of "cultural nationalism" see Michael T. Bernath, *Confederate Minds: The Struggle for Intellectual Independence in the Civil War South* (Chapel Hill, 2010).

6. John C. Calhoun, Speech, Jan. 10, 1838, in Eric L. McKitrick, ed., *Slavery Defended: The Views of the Old South* (Englewood Cliffs, NJ, 1963), 19.

7. Jefferson Davis, inaugural address as elected president, Richmond, VA, Feb. 22, 1862; Georgia's Declaration of Causes of Secession, Jan. 29, 1861; Walther, *Fire-Eaters*, 63–64.

8. Hon. Alexander H. Stephens, Speech, Richmond, VA, Apr. 22, 1861; John Witherspoon DuBose, *The Life and Times of William Lowndes Yancey*

(Birmingham, AL, 1892), 387–389; George Fitzhugh, *Cannibals All! Or, Slaves Without Masters* (Cambridge, MA, 1960), 16.

9. Alexander H. Stephens, "Cornerstone Address," Savannah, GA, Mar. 22, 1861, in Jon L. Wakelyn, ed., *Southern Pamphlets on Secession, November 1860–April 1861* (Chapel Hill, 1996), 405–406; Letter from William Lowndes Yancey to James D. Meadows, Esq., June 6, 1859, in DuBose, *Yancey,* 383–384. On the role of slavery in colonial times, see Don E. Ferhenbacher and Ward McAfee, *The Slaveholding Republic: An Account of the United States Government's Relations to Slavery* (New York, 2001); Edward McPherson, *A Political History of the United States During the Period of Reconstruction* (New York, 1972); George William Van Cleve, *A Slaveholders' Union* (Chicago, 2010).

10. R. K. Crallé, ed., *The Works of John C. Calhoun,* vol. I (New York, 1854), 52–59.

11. Richard Keith Call, *Letter to John S. Littell* (Philadelphia, 1861), reprinted in Wakelyn, *Southern Pamphlets,* 179–194; Fitzhugh, *Cannibals All!,* 13, 71–82.

12. James Oakes, *The Ruling Race: A History of American Slaveholders* (New York, 1982), 123–150.

13. Jefferson Davis, Speech, U.S. Senate, Feb. 29, 1860, in William F. Cooper, Jr., ed., *Jefferson Davis: The Essential Writings* (New York, 2003), 166, 171; Robert Barnwell Rhett, Grahamville, July 4, 1859, in William C. Davis, ed., *A Fire-Eater Remembers: The Confederate Memoir of Robert Barnwell Rhett* (Columbia, SC, 2000), 6–9.

14. Sen. John C. Calhoun, Speech, Feb. 6, 1837.

15. George Fitzhugh, *Slavery Justified* (Fredericksburg, MD, 1850), 9; Fitzhugh, *Cannibals All!,* 213–214.

16. Jefferson Davis, Speech, U.S. Senate, Mar. 2, 1859, in Cooper, *Jefferson Davis,* 160; Edmund Ruffin, *Address to the Virginia State Agricultural Society, on the Effects of Domestic Slavery on the Manners, Habits, and Welfare of the Southern States; and the Slavery of Class to Class in the Northern States* (Richmond, 1853), 5–8, 12–16; Edmund Ruffin, *Slavery and Free Labor Described and Compared* (Washington, DC, 1860).

17. Jabez Lamar Monroe Curry, *The Perils and Duty of the South* (Washington, DC, 1860), reprinted in Wakelyn, *Southern Pamphlets,* 35, 45; Robert S. Tharin, *Arbitrary Arrests in the South; or, Scenes from the Experience of an Alabama Unionist* (New York, 1863), 62, quoted in William C. Davis, *A Government of Our Own* (New York, 1994), 6; Letter from S. F. Hale, Commissioner of Alabama, to Gov. Beriah Magoffin of Kentucky, Dec. 27, 1860.

18. Yancey, Speech, New Orleans, Oct. 29, 1860, in DuBose, *Yancey,* 533; Jefferson Davis, Speech, U.S. Senate, Jan. 21, 1861; Stephens, Speech, Apr. 22, 1861; Akhil Reed Amar, "Of Sovereignty and Federalism," *Yale Law Journal* 96 (1987): 1425–1520; Cass Sunstein, "Constitutionalism and Secession," *University of Chicago Law Review* 58 (1991): 633–670.

19. Howell Cobb, Speech, Atlanta, GA, May 22, 1861; National Republican Platform, Chicago, IL, May 17, 1860; Abraham Lincoln, "House Divided" Speech, Springfield, IL, June 16, 1858; Declaration of the Immediate Causes

Which Induce and Justify the Secession of South Carolina from the Federal Union, Dec. 24, 1860.

20. South Carolina Ordinance of Citizenship, Jan. 1, 1861, reprinted in *Charleston Mercury,* Jan. 3, 1861.

21. Robert Barnwell Rhett, The Address of South Carolina to the Slaveholding States of the United States, Dec. 25, 1860. When Virginia took up secession, the *Richmond Dispatch* saw the question as "whether she shall destroy or preserve her slave system of labor—the grandest and most efficient agency of wealth ever enjoyed by any community on the globe." *Richmond Dispatch,* Mar. 23, 1861, reprinted in Robert F. Durden, *The Gray and the Black: The Confederate Debate on Emancipation* (Baton Rouge, 1972), 11–14.

22. Jefferson Davis, *The Rise and Fall of the Confederate Government* (New York, 1961), 106–107.

23. A Declaration of the Immediate Causes Which Induce and Justify the Secession of the State of Mississippi from the Federal Union, Jan. 9, 1861; A Declaration of the Causes Which Impel the State of Texas to Secede from the Federal Union, Feb. 2, 1861; South Carolina Ordinance of Secession, Dec. 2, 1860; Mississippi Ordinance of Secession, Jan. 9, 1861; Alabama Ordinance of Secession, Jan. 11, 1861; Florida Ordinance of Secession, Jan. 11, 1861; Georgia Ordinance of Secession, Jan. 19, 1861; Louisiana Ordinance of Secession, Jan. 26, 1861; Texas Ordinance of Secession, Feb. 1, 1861; Virginia Ordinance of Secession, Apr. 17, 1861; Tennessee Ordinance of Secession, May 6, 1861; North Carolina Ordinance of Secession, May 20, 1861; Arkansas Ordinance of Secession, May 6, 1861.

24. Georgia Declaration of the Causes of Secession, Jan. 29, 1861.

25. Charles B. Dew, *Apostles of Disunion* (Charlottesville, 2001), 31.

26. Thomas R. Dew, *Review of the Debate in the Virginia Legislature of 1831 and 1832* (Richmond, 1832), 46–130; Hale to Gov. Magoffin, Dec. 27, 1860.

27. William Henry Trescot, *The Position and Course of the South* (Charleston, 1850), excerpted in Wakelyn, *Southern Pamphlets,* 14–32.

28. William C. Davis, *"A Government of Our Own": The Making of the Confederacy* (New York, 1994).

29. Journal of the Congress of the Confederate States of America, 1861–1865, vol. I, 25–39 (Washington DC, 1904); "The Confederate States of North America: Southern Confederacy Organized," *Alexandria Gazette,* Feb. 11, 1861. For profiles on delegates to the Montgomery Convention, see Charles Robert Lee, *The Confederate Constitutions* (Chapel Hill, 1963), 21–59; Davis, *"A Government of Our Own,"* 151.

30. Journal of the Congress of the Confederate States of America, vol. I, Mar. 11, 1861, 896. Rhett found himself joined by such figures as Thomas R. R. Cobb and Robert Toombs of Georgia, James Chesnut of South Carolina, and Wiley Harris of Mississippi.

31. Journal of the Congress of the Confederate States of America, vol. I, 101–102.

32. "Secret Sessions of the South Carolina Convention; The Federal Constitution," Correspondence of the *Columbia South Carolinian,* reprinted in *New York Times,* Dec. 31, 1860; Robert Barnwell Rhett, "The Confederate

Constitution," *DeBow's Review* 6 (Nov. 8, 1869), 929–934; Rhett, in Davis, *A Fire-Eater Remembers*, 26.

33. Jefferson Davis, inaugural address, Montgomery, AL, Feb. 18, 1861; Emory M. Thomas, *The Confederate Nation, 1861–1865* (New York, 1979), 37–66; Stephanie McCurry, *Confederate Reckoning: Power and Politics in the Civil War South* (Cambridge, MA, 2010).

34. Stephens, "Cornerstone Address," Wakelyn, *Southern Pamphlets*, 405–406. Stephens later clarified his remarks to conform them more closely to the prevailing theory of constitutional usurpation. He did not question the "patriotism" of the Founding Fathers or their "ability or wisdom." The mistaken assumption of racial equality was laid at the foot of "Jefferson, Madison, Washington" rather than the original Constitution itself, which "recogniz[ed] existing slavery and guarantee[d] its continuance." Myrta Lockett Avary, ed., *Recollections of Alexander H. Stephens* (Baton Rouge, 1998), 173–175.

35. Davis, *"A Government of Our Own,"* 294.

36. Journal of the Congress of the Confederate States of America, Mar. 6, 1861, 874; ibid., vol. I, Mar. 7, 1861, 883; ibid., Mar. 8, 1861, 855; White, *Rhett*, 197–205; *Charleston Mercury*, Mar. 25, Apr. 1, 1861, reprinted in White, *Rhett*, 203. A proposal by William Barry to prevent any state from abolishing slavery "without the consent of all the slaveholdings States" was tabled when the convention adopted the committee's report. Journal of the Congress of the Confederate States of America, vol. I, Mar. 9, 1861, 893–894.

37. Davis, *"A Government of Our Own,"* 252–253.

38. McCurry, *Confederate Reckoning*, 78–79. Hon. Robert H. Smith, *An Address to the Citizens of Alabama on the Constitution and Laws of the Confederate States of America* (Mobile, AL, 1861), 19; Letter of Yancey to Meadows, June 16, 1859, in DuBose, *Yancey*, 382–392. Proposals by Memminger, John Gregg, and Thomas R. R. Cobb to limit citizenship to "free white persons" or persons having less than "one-eighth . . . African blood" were voted down. Journal of the Congress of the Confederate States of America, Feb. 28 and Mar. 1, 1861, 859–861.

39. McCulloch v. Maryland, 17 U.S. 316 (1819); Gibbons v. Ogden, 22 U.S. 1 (1824); Permanent Confederate Constitution, art. I, § 8, par. 3; art. I, § 9 (Mar. 11, 1861); Rhett, "Confederate Constitution," 931–932.

40. Lee, *Confederate Constitutions*, 104–105; Rhett, "Confederate Constitution," 933; Confederate Constitution, art. II, § 2.

41. Stephens, "Cornerstone Address"; Confederate Constitution, art. I, § 6; art. II, § 2, ¶ 3.

42. Lee, *Confederate Constitutions*, 107–110; Confederate Constitution, art. III, § 2, ¶ 1; Hans v. Louisiana, 134 U.S. 1 (1890); White, *Rhett*, 198–199.

43. Rhett, "Confederate Constitution," 934.

44. Confederate Constitution, art. 7, § 1; Lee, *Confederate Constitutions*, 124–125.

45. Lee, *Confederate Constitutions*, 125–134.

46. Ibid., 134–137.

47. "A Rebel Manifesto," *New York Times,* Feb. 25, 1864; Proclamation by President Jefferson Davis Granting Letters of Marque, Apr. 17, 1861; M. Mason, Speech, Richmond, VA, June 8, 1861, in Edward A. Pollard, ed., *Echoes from the South* (New York, 1866), 166–173; Jefferson Davis, *The Rise and Fall of the Confederate Government,* vol. 2 (New York, 1958), 764; Henry A. Wise, Speech, in Pollard, *Echoes,* 150–153.
48. Abraham Lincoln, inaugural address, Mar. 4, 1861; Abraham Lincoln, First Annual Message, Dec. 3, 1861.
49. Davis, *The Rise and Fall,* vol. 1, 167.
50. Eric Foner, *The Fiery Trial: Abraham Lincoln and American Slavery* (New York, 2010), 238–247; Paul Finkelman, "Lincoln, Emancipation, and the Limits of Constitutional Change," *Supreme Court Review* 9 (2008): 349–387; Sanford Levinson, "Was the Emancipation Proclamation Constitutional? Do We/Should We Care?," *University of Illinois Law Review* (2001): 1135–1158; James Welling, "The Emancipation Proclamation," *North American Review* 130 (1880): 163–185; Richard Dana, "Nullity of the Emancipation Edict," *North American Review* 131 (1880): 128–134; Aaron Ferris, "The Validity of the Emancipation Edict," *North American Review* 131 (1880): 551–576. Lincoln announced his plan to free the slaves on September 22, 1862. He signed the final Emancipation Proclamation on Jan. 1, 1863. Jefferson Davis, Annual Message to Confederate Congress, excerpted in *Harper's Weekly,* Jan. 31, 1863, 67; Davis, *Rise and Fall,* vol. 2, 187–193.
51. David P. Currie, "Through the Looking-Glass: The Confederate Constitution in Congress, 1861–1865," *Virginia Law Review* 90 (2004): 1257–1399; Senate Proceedings, Mar. 18, 1863, reprinted in *Southern Historical Society Papers,* 48: 321–325.
52. McCurry, *Confederate Reckoning,* 124–132, 136–169,182–191.
53. Ibid., 218–269.
54. Message from President Davis to the Senate and House of Representatives of the Confederate States of America, Mar. 13, 1865; Letter from Jefferson Davis to Col. J. F. Marshall, July 11, 1862, reprinted in Cooper, *Jefferson Davis,* 254–255; Letter from Jefferson Davis to Georgia governor Joseph E. Brown, May 29, 1862; David Williams, *A People's History of the Civil War: Struggles for the Meaning of Freedom* (New York, 2005), 70–81, 90–91; Burton J. Hendrick, *Statesmen of the Lost Cause: Jefferson Davis and His Cabinet* (Boston, 1939), 352–362.
55. *Charleston Mercury,* Aug–Oct. 1863, in White, *Rhett,* 232; Thomas, *Confederate Nation,* 136–144.
56. Message from Jefferson Davis to the Second Session of the Congress of the Confederate States of America, Nov. 7, 1864; Message from Jefferson Davis to the Congress of the Confederate States of America, Mar. 13, 1865; *Charleston Mercury,* Nov. 19, 1864, Jan. 13, 1865; Thomas R. Hay, "The South and the Arming of the Slaves," *Mississippi Valley Historical Review* 6 (1919): 34–73; N. W. Stephenson, "The Question of Arming the Slaves," *American History Review* 18 (1913): 295–308; House Proceedings, Jan. 27, 1865

(statement of Rep. Leach), reprinted in Frank E. Vandiver, ed., *Southern Historical Society Papers: Proceedings of the Second Confederate Congress, Second Session* 52 (Richmond, 1992), 283–242; Act of Mar. 18, 1865, No. 148, 2d Cong., 2d Sess., in Charles W. Ramsdell, ed., *Laws and Joint Resolutions of the Last Session of the Confederate Congress (Nov. 7, 1864–Mar. 18, 1865) Together with the Secret Acts of Previous Congresses* (Durham, 1941), 118; General Order No. 14, Mar. 23, 1865, in *The War of the Rebellion: A Compilation of the Official Records of the Union and Confederate Armies*, vol. 3.4 (Washington, DC, 1880–1900), 1161–1162. The original plan to arm the slaves originated with Major General Patrick Cleburne. Durden, *The Gray and the Black*, 53–67, 93, 176–177, 252–253; *Charleston Mercury*, Nov. 3, 1864, reprinted in Durden, 97–99.

57. Page Smith, *A People's History of the Civil War and Reconstruction* (New York, 1982), 330.

58. Last Manifesto of the Confederate Congress, June 15, 1864.

59. William C. Davis, *An Honorable Defeat: The Last Days of the Confederate Government* (New York, 2001), 107–121.

60. U.S. Const., amends. 13–15; Davis, *Rise and Fall*, vol. 2, 561; Bruce Ackerman, *We the People: Transformations* (Cambridge, MA, 1998); Georges Clemenceau, *American Reconstruction* (New York, 1969); Garrett Epps, *Democracy Reborn* (New York, 2006); Eric Foner, *Reconstruction: America's Unfinished Revolution* (New York, 1988); Joseph James, *The Ratification of the Fourteenth Amendment* (Macon, GA, 1984); Eric McKitrick, *Andrew Johnson and Reconstruction* (Chicago, 1960).

61. Lincoln initially described the seceding states as "combinations" that opposed the laws of the United States and were "too powerful to be suppressed by the ordinary course of judicial proceedings, or by the powers vested in the Marshals by law." Abraham Lincoln, Proclamation Calling Militia and Convening Congress, Apr. 15, 1861. A few days later, he declared a state of "insurrection against the Government of the United States." Abraham Lincoln, Proclamation 81—Declaring a Blockade of Ports in Rebellious States, Apr. 19, 1861; Abraham Lincoln, Proclamation 83—Increasing the Size of the Army and Navy, May 3, 1861; Abraham Lincoln, Proclamation 84—Declaring Martial Law, and Suspending the Writ of Habeas Corpus in the Islands of Key West, May 10, 1861. Abraham Lincoln, Fourth Annual Message, Dec. 6, 1864. Abraham Lincoln, A Declaration of Amnesty and Reconstruction, Dec. 8, 1863. Peace terms negotiated between Sherman and Breckinridge initially did not require Southern acceptance of emancipation. Davis, *An Honorable Defeat*, 160–168. On the idea of the Civil War as trial by combat, see G. Edward White, "Recovering the Legal History of the Confederacy," *Washington and Lee Law Review* 68 (2011): 467–554; Cynthia Nicoletti, "The American Civil War as a Trial by Battle," *Law and History Review* 28 (2010): 71–110.

62. Rhett, *A Fire-Eater Remembers*, 96–102.

5. The Sequoyah Convention, 1905

1. Angie Debo, *And Still the Waters Run: The Betrayal of the Five Civilized Tribes* (Princeton, 1972), 7–12; Clara Sue Kidwell, *The Choctaws in Oklahoma: From Tribe to Nation, 1855–1970* (Norman, OK, 2007), 43–44; J. Swanton, "Introductory Note" to Grant Foreman, *The Five Civilized Tribes* (Norman, OK, 1934), xii; Duane Champagne, *Social Order and Political Change: Constitutional Governments among the Cherokee, the Choctaw, the Chickasaw, and the Creek* (Stanford, 1992), 13–123, 176–207.

2. Cherokee Constitution, July 24, 1827; Rennard Strickland, *Fire and the Spirits: Cherokee Law from Clan to Court* (Norman, OK, 1975), 65–66.

3. Grant Foreman, *Indian Removal: The Emigration of the Five Civilized Tribes of Indians* (Norman, OK, 1953); Annie Heloise Abel, *The American Indian as Slaveholder and Secessionist* (Cleveland, 1992).

4. Frank Pommersheim, *Broken Landscape: Indians, Indian Tribes, and the Constitution* (New York, 2009), 38–85; Treaty with the Cherokee, art. XIII (Nov. 28, 1785); Statement of Chestadadessa of the Wichitas, May 10, 1875, *Journal of the Sixth Annual Session of the General Council of the Indian Territory* (May 3–15, 1875), 30.

5. C. M. Allen, *The "Sequoyah" Movement* (Oklahoma City, 1925), 7–9.

6. "Okmulgee Constitution," *Chronicles of Oklahoma*, 3(3) (Sept. 1925): 216–228; Report of Special Committee, May 10, 1875, Journal of the Sixth Annual Session of the General Council of the Indian Territory (May 3–15, 1875), 39–40.

7. Ulysses S. Grant, State of the Union address, Dec. 4, 1871.

8. Ulysses S. Grant, State of the Union address, Dec. 2, 1872.

9. Danney Goble, *Progressive Oklahoma: The Making of a New Kind of State* (Norman, OK, 1980), 5–8; Carl C. Rister, *Land Hunger: David L. Payne and the Oklahoma Boomers* (Norman, OK, 1942); Annie Heloise Abel, *The American Indian under Reconstruction* (Cleveland, 1925); Minnie Thomas Bailey, *Reconstruction in Indian Territory: A Story of Avarice, Discrimination, and Opportunism* (Port Washington, NY, 1972); Donald A. Grinde and Quintard Taylor, "Red vs. Black: Conflict and Accommodation in the Post Civil War Indian Territory," *American Indian Quarterly* (Summer 1984); Thomas F. Andrews, "Freedmen in Indian Territory: A Post Civil War Dilemma," *Journal of the West* 4 (July 1965): 367–376.

10. Grinde and Taylor, "Red vs Black," 217–220; Arthur L. Tolson, *The Black Oklahomans: A History, 1541–1972* (New Orleans, 1974), 41, 81–88; Norman L. Crockett, *The Black Towns* (Lawrence, KS, 1979), 24–26, 40; Edwin S. Redkey, *Black Exodus: Black Nationalist and Back-to-Africa Movements, 1840–1910* (New Haven, 1969), 101; Melissa Boley, *"All Men Up": Race, Rights, and Power in the All-Black Town of Boley, 1903–1939* (PhD diss., Yale University, 2010).

11. Stuart Banner, *How the Indians Lost Their Land: Law and Power on the Frontier* (Cambridge, MA, 2005), 265–266.

12. U.S. Const., art. IV, § 3.

13. "The Call to the People of the Indian Territory," Feb. 3, 1900.
14. Daniel F. Littlefield, Jr. and Lonnie E. Underhill, "The 'Crazy Snake Uprising' of 1909: A Red, Black, or White Affair?," *Arizona and the West* 20 (Winter 1978): 307–324.
15. Debo, *Still the Waters Run*, 154–158; "Chitto Harjo," *Chronicles of Oklahoma* 13(2) (June 1935): 139–145; Alexander Posey, "On the Capture and Imprisonment of Crazy Snake," in Minnie H. Posey, ed., *The Poems of Alexander Lawrence Posey* (Topeka, KS, 1910), 88.
16. Amos Maxwell, "The Sequoyah Convention, Part I," *Chronicles of Oklahoma* 28(2) (1950), 161–192, 169; Address of Hon. Yancey Lewis, Feb. 22, 1900; Address of Hon. H. M. Furman, Feb. 22, 1900.
17. Maxwell, "The Sequoyah Convention, Part I," 161, 173–174.
18. Amos Maxwell, "The Sequoyah Convention, Part II," *Chronicles of Oklahoma* 28(3) (1950): 299–340; Allen, *The "Sequoyah" Movement*, 28, 34 (quoting the *Muskogee Phoenix*).
19. Debo, *Still the Waters Run*, 121–132; Porter speech before Creek Council at Okmulgee, Oct. 2, 1899, in John Bartlett Meserve, "Chief Pleasant Porter," *Chronicles of Oklahoma* 9(3) (Sept. 1931): 318–334.
20. Goble, *Progressive Oklahoma*, 190–192.
21. Wyatt W. Belcher, "Political Leadership of Robert L. Owen," *Chronicles of Oklahoma* 31 (Winter 1953–1954): 361, 363.
22. Ibid., 192–193; Maxwell, "The Sequoyah Convention, Part II," 305–306; Allen, *The "Sequoyah" Movement*, 34–53.
23. Scott L. Malcolmson, *One Drop of Blood: The American Misadventure of Race* (New York, 2000), 105.
24. Maxwell, "The Sequoyah Convention, Part II," 309–310.
25. Allen, *The "Sequoyah" Movement*, 56–57.
26. The 1835 treaty with the Cherokee contemplated the creation of a "permanent home for themselves and their posterity . . . where they can establish and enjoy a government of their choice and perpetuate such a state of society as may be most consonant with their views, habits, and condition." Not only did the treaty recognize the lawmaking authority of the Cherokee national councils, the United States further "covenant[ed] and agree[d] that the lands ceded to the Cherokee nation . . . shall, in no future time without their consent, be included within the territorial limits or jurisdiction of any State or Territory." Ibid., art. 5; Treaty with the Choctaw, art. IV (1830); Treaty with the Creeks, art. XIV (1832); *A Memorial to the Congress of the United States on Behalf of the State of Sequoyah* (1905).
27. Rennard Strickland, "Sequoyah Statehood, the Oklahoma Centennial and Sovereignty Envy: A Personal Narrative and a Public Proposal," *American Indian Law Review* 30(2) (2005): 365–371; Stacy L. Leeds, "Defeat or Mixed Blessing? Tribal Sovereignty and the State of Sequoyah," *Tulsa Law Review* 43 (2007): 5–16.
28. William E. Forbath, *Law and the Shaping of the Labor Movement* (Cambridge, MA, 1989); Richard Hofstadter, *The Age of Reform* (New York, 1955).
29. Plessy v. Ferguson, 163 U.S. 537 (1896). On the tribes' reactions to former slaves in their midst, see Bailey, *Reconstruction in Indian Territory*, 41–54;

Grinde and Taylor, "Red vs. Black," 213–217; Linda W. Reese, "Cherokee Freedwomen in Indian Territory, 1863–1890," *Western Historical Quarterly* 33(3) (Autumn 2002), 273–296.

30. Constitution of the Indian Territory, Declaration of Rights § 1 (1870) (Okmulgee). Virginia's constitution contained a similar provision. Constitution of Virginia, art. I, § 3 (1902). By contrast, Maryland and New Hampshire erected preconditions to popular sovereignty by requiring the perversion of the ends of government, liberty to be endangered, and available remedies to be exhausted. Constitution of Maryland, Declaration of Rights, § 4 (1776); Constitution of New Hampshire, Bill of Rights, art. 10 (1784); Christian G. Fritz, *American Sovereigns: The People and America's Constitutional Tradition Before the Civil War* (New York, 2008).

31. Sequoyah Constitution, art. I, §§ 9–15 (1905).

32. Reply of J. A. Norman to C. M. Allen, in Allen, *The "Sequoyah" Movement,* 97, 100, app. G. On the push to rewrite the Virginia Constitution, see Allen W. Moger, *Virginia: Bourbonism to Byrd, 1870–1925* (Charlottesville, 1968), 181–202; Sequoyah Constitution, art. IX, §§ 3–4.

33. Sequoyah Constitution, art. IX, § 12.

34. Ibid., art. X, §§ 3, 4.

35. Ibid., art. III, §§ 22–23.

36. Ibid., art. 8, § 9; art. XVI, § 11.

37. Statement of Running Chief of the Pawnees, May 8, 1875, Journal of the Sixth Annual Session of the General Council of the Indian Territory (May 3–15, 1875), 25–26.

38. Strickland, *Fire and the Spirits,* 22. Similarly, the Iroquois required any "specially important matter or a great emergency" to be submitted to "the decision of their people." The Constitution of the Iroquois Nations or The Great Binding Law (Gayanashagoma), ¶ 93.

39. Robert L. Owen, "Reasons For Not Wishing to Unite With Oklahoma," *Muskogee Phoenix,* Aug. 9, 1905, in Allen, 79 (app. D).

40. Resolution Endorsing the Action of the Principal Chief Relative to the Constitutional Convention and in Relation Thereto (Choctaw Nation General Council, Nov. 11, 1905), reprinted as Exh. D, Proposed State of Sequoyah, 44; Res. and Memorial (Chicasaw Nation Legislature, Oct. 18, 1905), reprinted as Exh. E, Proposed State of Sequoyah, 44–46; Joint Res. No. 11 (National Council Cherokee Nation, Sept. 30, 1905), reprinted as Exh. F, Proposed State of Sequoyah, 46.

41. "Takes a Puncture at Sequoyah Bubble," *Daily Oklahoman,* Nov. 5, 1905, 23; "The Democratic Future," *Daily Oklahoman,* Sept. 6, 1905, 4.

42. Gordon Hines, *Alfalfa Bill: An Intimate Biography* (Oklahoma City, 1932), 183–184.

43. William H. Murray, *Memoirs of Governor Murray and True History of Oklahoma,* vol. I (Boston, 1945), 317.

44. Opponents questioned the veracity of these figures. "The Sequoyah Vote," *Daily Oklahoman,* Nov. 21, 1905.

45. Green McCurtain, Principal Chief of Choctaw Nation, to Hon. Edward L. Hamilton, Chairman of Committee on Territories, S.D., 59–1, vol. 4–21,

reprinted as part of *Proposed State of Sequoyah,* 59th Congress, 1st Session, Senate Doc. 143, Jan. 16, 1906.

46. *A Memorial to the Congress of the United States on Behalf of the State of Sequoyah,* 7.

47. Goble, 92–104.

48. Constitution of the State of Oklahoma, art. XXXIII, § 445 (1907); Aaron Bachhofer II, "Strange Bedfellows: Progressivism, Radicalism, and the Oklahoma Constitution in Historical Perspective," *Chronicles of Oklahoma* 77(3) (1999): 244–271; "'No Constitution at All,' Declares War Secretary," *Daily Oklahoman,* Aug. 25, 1907, 1, 4, 17; "Constitution is Denounced by Taft, Before Big Crowd," *Daily Oklahoman,* Aug. 25, 1907, 1–2.

49. "Bryan Shows Republican Error," *Daily Oklahoman,* Aug. 27, 1907, 1–2; "Insulted the Intelligence of the People," *Daily Oklahoman,* Sept. 1, 1907, 1–2; "Bryan Speaks to Fully 10,000 Persons Here," *Daily Oklahoman,* Sept. 6, 1907, 1, 3; "Special to the Oklahoman—Tulsa," *Daily Oklahoman,* Sept. 6, 1907, 3; "'Short Grass' Precincts Visited," *Daily Oklahoman,* Sept. 7, 1907, 1–2.

50. James R. Scales and Danney Goble, *Oklahoma Politics: A History* (Norman, OK, 1982), 15–17; Lynn Musslewhite and Suzanne Jones Crawford, *One Woman's Political Journey: Kate Barnard and Social Reform, 1875–1930* (Norman, OK, 2003), 30–54; Letter from C. N. Haskell to C. M. Allen, Apr. 18, 1911, in Allen, *The "Sequoyah" Movement,* 84 (app. G), 88–89, 95. Urging all Chickasaw districts to elect delegates to the Sequoyah Convention, Murray acknowledged early on, "I do not think that a constitution framed by that convention will be accepted by Congress, but it will be the beginning of an organization for the Indian Territory around which every citizen, both Indian and White, must rally in the future affairs of Indian Territory." *St. Louis Republic,* Aug. 15, 1905, in Keith L. Bryant, *Alfalfa Bill Murray* (Norman, OK, 1968), 39.

51. Rennard J. Strickland and James C. Thomas, "Most Sensibly Conservative and Safely Radical: Oklahoma's Constitutional Regulation of Economic Power, Land Ownership, and Corporate Monopoly," *Tulsa Law Journal* 9 (1973): 167, 175–177; "Forget It," *Daily Oklahoman,* Nov. 24, 1906, 4; Letter from Haskell to Allen, in Allen, *The "Sequoyah" Movement,* 94; *Proceedings of the Oklahoma Constitutional Convention* (Guthrie, OK, 1907), 33, quoted in Goble, *Progressive Oklahoma,* 144.

52. Letter from Haskell to Allen, in Allen, *The "Sequoyah" Movement,* 95; Musslewhite and Crawford, *One Woman's Political Journey,* 30–33.

53. Joint Resolution Extending the Tribal Existence and Government of the Five Civilized Tribes of Indians in the Indian Territory, 59th Congress, 1st Sess., 34 Stat. 822 (Mar. 2, 1906).

54. Indian Reorganization Act, § 16, 48 Stat. 984, 25 U.S.C.A. § 461 et seq. (June 18, 1934); Felix S. Cohen, "Basic Memorandum on Drafting of Tribal Constitutions," Nov. 19, 1934, in David E. Wilkins, ed., *On the Drafting of Tribal Constitutions* (Norman, OK, 2006), 3–4.

55. "Sequoyahs Conduct Grass Root Campaign," *Daily Oklahoman,* July 22, 1906, 11.

56. Cherokee Papers, Report of S. W. Gray, Roach Young, and J. F. Thompson to Hon. S. H. Mays, 1895, in Debo, *Still the Waters Run*, 27–30; Pleasant Porter before *Select Committee*, vol. I, 623–629, in Debo, *Still the Waters Run*, 147; Treaty with the Chickasaw, art. 3 (1830); Treaty with the Chickasaw (1832).

57. "Review of Oklahoma's Long Struggle to Secure Statehood," *Daily Oklahoman*, Nov. 17, 1907, 2.

6. A Charter for the World, 1947

1. Rexford Guy Tugwell, *The Emerging Constitution* (New York, 1974), 529; Rexford Guy Tugwell, *A Model Constitution for a United Republics of America* (Palo Alto, 1970), 19, 21.

2. William E. Forbath, *Law and the Shaping of the American Labor Movement* (Cambridge, MA, 1991); Morton J. Horwitz, *The Transformation of American Law, 1870–1960* (New York, 1992); G. Edward White, *The Constitution and the New Deal* (Cambridge, MA, 2002). On the impact of war upon legal development, see Christopher Capozzola, *Uncle Sam Wants You: World War I and the Making of the Modern Citizen* (New York, 2008); Mary L. Dudziak, *Cold War Civil Rights: Race and the Image of American Democracy* (Princeton, 2002); Philip A. Klinkner and Rogers M. Smith, *The Unsteady March: The Rise and Decline of Racial Equality in America* (Chicago, 2002).

3. Milton Mayer, *Robert Maynard Hutchins: A Memoir* (Berkeley, 1993).

4. Robert M. Hutchins et al., *Preliminary Draft of a World Constitution* (Chicago, 1948), World Constitution, preamble.

5. Immanuel Kant, *Perpetual Peace: A Philosophical Sketch* (1795); Jeremy Bentham, *A Plan for an Universal and Perpetual Peace* (1789); Jean-Jacques Rousseau, *A Lasting Peace Through the Federation of Europe*, ed. C. E. Vaughan (London, 1917).

6. John W. Boyer, "Drafting Salvation," *University of Chicago Magazine* (Dec. 1995), accessed Sept. 22, 2013, http://magazine.uchicago.edu/9512/9512 Salvation.html.

7. Robert Hutchins, "America and the War," NBC radio address, Jan. 23, 1941, reprinted in *University of Chicago Magazine* (Feb. 1941): 7–12. Franklin D. Roosevelt, Annual Address to Congress, Jan. 6, 1941; Robert L. Tsai, *Eloquence and Reason: Creating a First Amendment Culture* (New Haven, 2008), ch. 5; Robert L. Tsai, "Reconsidering *Gobitis*," *Washington University Law Review* 86 (2008): 363–443.

8. Robert Maynard Hutchins, Speech, "The Proposition Is Peace," Rockefeller Memorial Chapel, University of Chicago, Mar. 30, 1941.

9. Robert Maynard Hutchins, *The Constitutional Foundations for World Order* (Denver, 1947), 21–22. Mayer, *Hutchins: A Memoir*, 252–253.

10. Robert Hutchins (with R. Gustavson and W. Ogburn), Radio Address, "Atomic Force: Its Meaning for Mankind," Aug. 12, 1945; "Hutchins Urges World State Now," *New York Times*, Aug. 13, 1945, 8.

11. Hutchins, *Constitutional Foundations*, 6.

12. Robert Redfield, "Introduction," in G. A. Borgese, *Foundations of the World Republic* (Chicago, 1953), viii; Mayer, *Hutchins: A Memoir,* 279; Stenotyped Proceedings of the Ninth Meeting of the Committee (Doc. 91), New York, Aug. 16–17, 1946, 104; Stenotyped Proceedings of the Tenth Meeting of the Committee (Doc. 107), Chicago, Oct. 24–25, 1946, 2.

13. Robert Maynard Hutchins, Speech, "The Good News of Damnation," Speech, Publicity Club of Chicago, Jan. 8, 1947.

14. "Press Release 1" (Doc. 71), Office of Press Relations, University of Chicago, July 18, 1946, 4; G. A. Borgese, "Of Atomic Fear and Two 'Utopias,' with a Definite Proposal for the June and Subsequent Meetings" (Doc. 58), June 11, 1946, 3; Stenotyped Proceedings of the Tenth Meeting of the Committee (Doc. 107), 58–72; Albert Guérard, "On the Hierarchy of Values" (Doc. 115), Dec. 30, 1946, 2.

15. "Structure of a Constitution," *Preliminary Draft,* 41; ibid., vi; Robert M. Hutchins, *The Atomic Bomb versus Civilization* (Chicago, 1945), 12; George T. Peck, "Some Comments on Problems and Trends as Emerging from Documents # 1 to 98" (Doc. 99), 1; Stenotyped Proceedings of the Seventh Meeting of the Committee (Doc. 67), Chicago, June 18, 1946, 12; Bernard Guillemin, "Russia and World Federalism: Russia and the Idea of Political Legality" (Doc. 108), Dec. 9, 1946; Stenotyped Proceedings of the Ninth Meeting, (Doc. 91), 193.

16. Mortimer J. Adler and R. P. McKeon, "Considerations Relevant to the Definition of World Federal Government" (Doc. 4), Dec. 1945, 3–4.

17. Ibid., 6; J. M. Landis, "Memorandum on the Minimum Amount of Power That Must Be Delegated to a Central Government" (Doc. 5), Dec. 1945, 2.

18. Landis, Memorandum, 3; Albert Guérard, "Contribution to (Borgese's) Draft of a Draft and Commentaries on Contribution to the Draft of a Draft With Special Reference to a Senate on a Territorial (Regional) Basis and an Assembly Elected on a (Weighted?) Population Basis" (Doc. 17), Feb. 20, 1946, 3.

19. Erich Kahler, "Some Remarks Concerning the Question of a 'Minimum Constitution'" (Doc. 45), Apr. 1946, 1.

20. Stenotyped Proceedings of the Tenth Meeting (Doc. 107), Oct. 24–25, 1946, 40 (remarks of Borgese).

21. G. A. Borgese, "Envoy of the Foregoing Explanatory of the Method and Purpose of Constitution One Hundred Eleven" (Doc. 112), Jan. 3, 1947, 5; World Constitution, preamble; Richard P. McKeon, "Notes in Reply to Questions Raised in Document # 64" (Doc. 75), July 15, 1946, 2.

22. Richard P. McKeon, "Federation and World Democracy," (Doc. 87), Aug. 10, 1946, 6. Other memoranda referred to certain rights as reflecting "Freedom from Fear and Freedom from Want" or the Assembly of Peoples as a bulwark "preserving freedom from fear." Elisabeth Mann Borgese, "Concordances Between the Constitutions of the U.S.S.R., the United States, and Drafts II and V" (Doc. 70), July 12, 1946, 17; Richard P. McKeon, "Draft V" (Docs. 76A and B), July 15, 1946, 2.

23. John Brown's Provisional Constitution, art. XXXIX (1858).

24. World Constitution, §§ 28–33.

25. World Constitution, § 31. Hutchins, *Atomic Bomb,* 12; Robert M. Hutchins, *The Education We Need* (Chicago, 1947); Robert M. Hutchins, *The Conflict in Education in a Democratic Society* (Westport, CT, 1953); Robert M. Hutchins, *The University of Utopia* (Chicago, 1953); Brown v. Board of Education, 347 U.S. 483 (1954). Plans for a world university, proposed in an early draft circulated by Borgese, were scrapped before the document was finalized.
26. World Constitution, § 28(2). These features of the Chicago Plan were popularly described as part of a "bill of economic rights." "Set-Up Is Outlined for a World State," *New York Times,* Mar. 21, 1948, 14.
27. Robert Hutchins, Speech, "What Shall We Defend?," June 11, 1940, reprinted in *Vital Speeches of the Day,* vol. 6, 547–549; "Toward a World Parliament," *New York Times,* Dec. 1, 1947, 20; Dimitris Bourantonis, *The History and Politics of U.N. Security Council Reform* (London, 2005); "Security Council," *Washington Post,* Jan. 14, 1946, 8; "The Veto Problem," *New York Times,* June 28, 1946, 20.
28. "Summary Report," *Preliminary Draft,* 43; World Constitution, preamble.
29. Hutchins, *Constitutional Foundations,* 16. UN Charter preamble (1945), arts. 12, 23, 24; "Dr. Urey Deplores 'Inadequacy of U.N.," *New York Times,* Feb. 22, 1948, 12; Townsend Hoopes and Douglas Brinkley, *FDR and the Creation of the U.N.* (New Haven, 1997); Stephen Ryan, *The United Nations and International Politics* (New York, 2000); Stanley Mesler, *The United Nations: The First Fifty Years* (New York, 1995); Geoff Simons, *The United Nations* (New York, 1994).
30. The U.N. Charter allows the General Assembly to "make recommendations" to members of the United Nations or the Security Council on matters within the scope of the Charter. U.N. Charter, ch. 4, art. 10 (1945).
31. These Regions consisted of *Europa* (continent and islands of Europe, along with United Kingdom and any "overseas English- or French- or Cape Dutch-speaking communities" as decide to associate); *Atlantis* (United States of America along with the U.K. if it prefers and "such kindred communities of British, or Franco-British, or Dutch-British, or Irish civilization and lineage as decide to associate"); *Eurasia* (Russia and "East-Baltic or Slavic or South-Danubian nations as associate with Russia"); *Afrasia* (Near and Middle East); *Africa* (sub-Saharan Africa and Pakistan if it so decided); *India* (with Pakistan if it preferred); *Asia Major* (China, Korea, Japan, along with archipelagoes of North- and Mid-Pacific); *Austrasia* (Indochina and Indonesia, along with Pakistan if it preferred and other Mid- and South-Pacific islands); and *Columbia* (Western Hemisphere south of United States). See World Constitution, arts. 4–6; G. A. Borgese, "Fifteen Cursory Remarks on Views A and B of a World Constitution" (Doc. 38), Apr. 1946, 1, 6; G. A. Borgese, "Envoy of the Foregoing Explanatory of the Method and Purpose of Constitution One Hundred Eleven" (Doc. 112), Jan. 3, 1947, 9.
32. World Constitution, arts. 6–7; Dieter Dux, "The 'Parliament of Man': The Problem of a World Legislature," in Elisabeth Mann Borgese, ed., *A Constitution for the World* (Santa Barbara, 1965), 63–78; Elisabeth Mann Borgese, "Introduction," *A Constitution for the World,* 12.

33. R. P. McKeon, "Federation and World Democracy," Aug. 10, 1946, 2. Albert Guérard, "Notes on Drafting a World Constitution" (Doc. 6), Dec. 1945, 33; "G. A. Borgese, "One World and Seven Problems," *A Constitution for the World*, 57–58.

34. Adler and McKeon, "Considerations Relevant to the Definition of World Federal Government" (Doc. 4), 8; Hutchins, *Constitutional Foundations*, 10; "Federalists Would Revise U.N. Charter," *New York Times*, Aug. 6, 1948, 7; "World Government Seen in a Few Years," *New York Times*, May 16, 1948, 20; "World Union Disciples Would Build Upon UNO," *New York Times*, Feb. 17, 1946, 69; Joseph Preston Barrata, *The Politics of World Federation*, vol. 1 (Westport, CT, 2004), 105–123; "World Constitution and United Nations," Hutchins, *Preliminary Draft*, 81.

35. John K. Jessup, "World Government," *Life*, June 21, 1948, 49, 53; World Constitution, arts. 5, 10, 35; Gertrude S. Hooker, "The Executive Power: The Problem of the World Presidency," in *A Constitution for the World*, 79–90; Dieter Dux, "Of Democracies and Autocracies in the World Today with Particular Regard to the Problem of the Executive" (Doc. 102), Oct. 24, 1946, 10; Elisabeth Mann Borgese, "Synopsis of Agreements and Disagreements on the Executive During the October Meeting" (Doc. 109), Dec. 16, 1946, 5.

36. World Constitution, art. 11; Dux, "Of Democracies."

37. Elisabeth Mann Borgese, "Functional Representation and Syndical Chamber" (Doc. 117), Jan. 21, 1947, 19; World Constitution, arts. 8–9; Erich Kahler, "Of Active and Passive Democracy, of 'Volk' and 'Publikum,' of a Syndical Chamber and Other Constitutional Problems" (Doc. 94), Sept. 18, 1946, 5; Erich Kahler, "Statement of Views on Some Topics of the August Meeting" (Doc. 98), Oct. 14, 1946, 1–2.

38. World Constitution, arts. 26–27; Elisabeth Mann Borgese, "The Tribune of the People: The Spokesman for Minorities," *A Constitution for the World*, 95–98; G. A. Borgese, "Envoy of the Foregoing Explanatory of the Method and Purpose of Constitution One Hundred Eleven" (Doc. 112), 7.

39. Elisabeth Mann Borgese, "The Tribune of the People," 98.

40. World Constitution, arts. 18–20.

41. World Constitution, art. 18; UN Charter, art. 14; Statute of the International Court of Justice, arts. 34, 36 (1945).

42. Hooker, "Executive Power," 88.

43. G. A. Borgese, "Borgese's Answers to Adler's Questionaire" (Doc. 68), July 10, 1946, 1; Elisabeth Mann Borgese, "Synopsis of Agreements and Disagreements in the Meetings of July and August" (Doc. 95), Nov. 18, 1946, 2; G. A. Borgese, "Envoy of the Foregoing Explanatory," 5.

44. World Constitution, arts. 35, 41. When the committee completed its work, eleven members signed the draft World Constitution: Adler, Barr, Borgese, Guérard, Hutchins, Innis, Kahler, Wilber G. Katz, McIlwain, Redfield, and Tugwell. McKeon, who found himself on the losing end of a number of debates, ultimately withheld his name.

45. "Topical Problems," *Preliminary Draft*, 54.

46. "On Further Stages of Study and Action," *Preliminary Draft,* 66; "Einstein Decries U.S. Rearmament," *New York Times,* Apr. 28, 1948, 2; "Dr. Einstein Hits Soviet Scientists for Opposing 'World Government,'" *New York Times,* Jan. 30, 1948, 1; "Einstein Urges World Government for Atomic Control to Avoid War," *New York Times,* Oct. 27, 1945, 15.

47. "17 Writers Frame a World Law Plan," *New York Times,* July 4, 1949, 2; "Urey Urges West Unite for Peace," *New York Times,* Jan. 27, 1948, 6; Grenville Clark, "A New World Order—The American Lawyer's Role," *Indiana Law Journal* 19 (July 1944): 289–300; Walter Lippmann, *The Stakes of Diplomacy* (New York, 1917), 141–145; Grenville Clark and Louis B. Sohn, *World Peace Through World Law* (Cambridge, MA, 1966); Clarence Streit, *Union Now* (New York, 1939); Lawrence S. Wittner, *Resisting the Bomb: A History of the Nuclear Disarmament Movement, 1954–1970* (Stanford, 1997). As for reactions to the Chicago Plan, see Jessup, "World Government," 49–55; Julian Cornell, *New World Primer* (New York, 1947); Fremont Rider, *The Great Dilemma of World Organization* (New York, 1946). Percy Bordwell, Book Review, *University of Chicago Law Review* 16(2) (Winter 1949): 386–388; Frank Hughes, "World State's Super-Secret Constitution!," *Chicago Daily Tribune,* Nov. 17, 1947, 1, 14–17; "Federation with What?," *Chicago Daily Tribune,* Feb. 6, 1948, 14; Frank Hughes, "World State Plan Is Given a Revamping," *Chicago Daily Tribune,* Mar. 21, 1948, 1.

48. Lawrence S. Wittner, *One World or None: A History of the World Nuclear Disarmament Movement Through 1953* (Stanford, 1993), 45, 59–79; "For a World Government; Einstein Says This is Only Way to Save Mankind," *New York Times,* Sept. 15, 1945, 11; "Einstein Asks U.N. Act in Spite of All," *New York Times,* Sept. 23, 1947, 16; "Urges World Rule Over Atom Power," *New York Times,* May 17, 1946, 14.

49. Compare Bruce Ackerman, *We the People: Foundations* (Cambridge, MA, 1993); William E. Leuchtenburg, *The Supreme Court Reborn: The Constitutional Revolution in the Age of Roosevelt* (New York, 1995) with Barry Cushman, *Rethinking the New Deal Court: The Structure of a Constitutional Revolution* (New York, 1998). Justice Owen Roberts, "Address at the Thirty-Seventh Annual Meeting of ASIL," in Christopher J. Borgen, ed., *"A Decent Respect to the Opinions of Mankind . . ." Selected Speeches by Justices of the U.S. Supreme Court on Foreign and International Law* (Washington, DC: American Society of International Law, 2007), 17; "Roberts Pictures Post-War Grouping," *New York Times,* May 2, 1943, 25; "Roberts Says U.N. Can't Keep Peace, Asks World Union," *New York Times,* Apr. 23, 1946, 1; "Douglas Endorses a World Regime," *New York Times,* Mar. 14, 1946, 12.

50. Revised Concord Charter of Student Federalists, in Gertrude S. Hooker, "First List of Parallel Organizations" (Doc. 28), Oct. 24, 1946, 8.

51. "Extinction of America," *Chicago Daily Tribune,* Nov. 9, 1949, 24; Harris Wofford Jr., *Road to the World Republic: Policy and Strategy for Federalists* (Chicago, 1948), 5–11, 26, 64–65.

52. "Pope Backs Plan for World Government; Sees It as a Means to Establish Peace," *New York Times,* Apr. 7, 1951, 3; Resolution of House of Deputies of

Protestant Episcopal Church, Sept. 16, 1946, reprinted in Hooker, "Parallel Organizations" (Doc. 28), 15; Statement of Friends Peace Committee, Dec. 1945, in Hooker, ibid.; "World Government Plea of Harrington," *New York Times,* Apr. 28, 1952, 15; "World Government Based on Baruch Plan Proposed Here by Rabbi Liebman, Author," *New York Times,* July 2, 1947, 4.

53. "Regime for World Called Inevitable," *New York Times,* Nov. 23, 1947, 42; "1950 Session Asked for World Regime; Briton Describes Plan to Draft Charter for a Government to Avert World War III," *New York Times,* Sept. 28, 1947, 53; "World Government Seen in a Few Years," *New York Times,* May 16, 1948, 20; "Federalists Propose Stronger U.N. to Rule," *New York Times,* Sept. 4, 1947, 6; "16 Groups Map World Federation As Conference Opens in Asheville," *New York Times,* Feb. 22, 1947, 7; "Episcopalians Ask World Union in U.N.," *New York Times,* Sept. 20, 1946, 6; "World Union Groups Adopt a Declaration," *New York Times,* Sept. 12, 1948, 25.

54. Robert M. Hutchins, Speech, "St. Thomas and the World State," Milwaukee, 1949; "World Government Is Urged by Hutchins," *New York Times,* Jan. 27, 1949, 6; "World Federation Held Survival Key," *New York Times,* Aug. 25, 1947, 8.

55. G. A. Borgese, *Foundations of the World Republic,* 15, 18, 21, 27–28, 66, 298–300.

56. Justice Owen J. Roberts et al., *The New Federalist* (New York, 1950), 12–13, 66–74, 93–97.

57. "One World or War Called Our Choice," *New York Times,* May 23, 1948, 59; Letter to the Editor, "Peace Through World Law," *New York Times,* Apr. 23, 1948; Letter to the Editor, "To Create World Government," *New York Times,* June 9, 1948, 28; Letter to the Editor, "World Government; Movement Queried as Untimely, Impairing Confidence in U.N.," *New York Times,* Feb. 9, 1947, E8; "World Government Plea," *New York Times,* Nov. 19, 1946, 33; "World Federalist Group Marks 30th Year and Tries to Put It All Together," *New York Times,* Aug. 1, 1977, 10; Wesley T. Wooley, "Finding a Usable Past: The Success of World Federalism in the 1940s," *Peace & Change* 24 (1999): 329, 330; Wittner, *One World or None,* 44–45; "Premier King Asks a World Regime," *New York Times,* Dec. 18, 1945, 8; "World Federation Vital, Nehru Says," *New York Times,* Aug. 15, 1948, 24; "Asks World Government," *New York Times,* Aug. 2, 1948, 22; "Catholic Groups Picket as Laski Calls for End of State Sovereignty," *New York Times,* Dec. 4, 1945, 1.

58. Wittner, *One World or None,* 307.

59. "UNO Bill in Senate Sparks a Debate," *New York Times,* Nov. 27, 1945, 8.

60. "Dr. Einstein Hits Soviet Scientists for Opposing 'World Government,'" *N.Y. Times,* Jan. 30, 1, 12; "Russians Attack Einstein," *New York Times,* Nov. 26, 1947, 4; "World Government Opposed by Russian," *New York Times,* Dec. 1, 1946, 33; Thomas J. Hamilton, "World Government and U.N.—A Debate," *New York Times,* Feb. 26, 1950, SM6, 18; "UNO Under Fire," *New York Times,* Oct. 18, 1945, 17.

61. Wittner, *One World or None,* 269–273.

62. "United Nations Backed; Connecticut Resolution Alters Stand on World Government," *New York Times,* Mar. 28, 1953, 9. "Harlan Disavows 'One World' Aims," *New York Times,* Feb. 26, 1955, 1.

63. Universal Declaration of Human Rights, G.A. res. 217A (III), U.N. Doc. A/810 at 71 (1948); Roger Norman and Sarah Zaidi, *Human Rights at the U.N.: The Political History of Universal Justice* (Bloomington, 2008); A. H. Feller, "We Move, Slowly, Toward World Law," *New York Times,* June 5, 1949, SM10; Presentation Speech of Aase Lionaese, Nobel Peace Prize, 1968; Stephen M. Schwebel, United Nations Council of Harvard, Letter to the Editor, "Road to World Government," *New York Times,* June 17, 1948, 24.

64. "World Body Urged to Prevent Wars," *New York Times,* Apr. 13, 1949, 7; "Atlantic Union Committee Formed!," *Freedom and Union,* Apr. 1949; *Declaration of the Dublin, N.H., Conference,* Oct. 16, 1945; "'Federal' World Urged by Roberts," *New York Times,* Sept. 17, 1946, 1.

65. "World Government Is Urged to Bar Ruin in Atomic War," *New York Times,* Oct. 17, 1945, 1.

66. "World Government Is Opposed by D.A.R.," *New York Times,* Apr. 23, 1948, 26.

67. Frank Hughes, "Dr. Hutchins Reveals Doubt of World Pact," *Chicago Daily Tribune,* July 25, 1948, 16.

7. The Republic of New Afrika, 1968

1. "Max Stanford Calls for Independent Black Nation," press release, Afro-American News Service, Apr. 17, 1968, in John H. Bracey Jr. et al., eds., *Black Nationalism in America* (Indianapolis, 1970), 513–517; Susan D. Carle, *Defining the Struggle: National Organizing for Racial Justice, 1880–1915* (New York, 2013); Clayborne Carson, *In Struggle: SNCC and the Black Awakening of the 1960s* (Cambridge, MA, 1981); Philip A. Klinkner and Rogers M. Smith, *The Unsteady March: The Rise and Decline of Racial Equality in America* (Chicago, 1999); Desmond S. King, *Separate and Unequal: Black Americans and the U.S. Federal Government* (New York, 1995).

2. Martin Luther King Jr., Speech, "I Have a Dream," Washington, DC, Aug. 28, 1963; Taylor Branch, *Parting the Waters: America in the King Years, 1954–63* (New York, 1989).

3. Louis Lomax interview of Malcolm X, June 1963, accessed Oct. 25, 2013, http://teachingamericanhistory.org/library/document/a-summing-up-louis -lomax-interviews-malcolm-x/; Alex Haley, *The Autobiography of Malcolm X* (New York, 1965); Manning Marable, *Malcolm X: A Life of Reinvention* (New York, 2011).

4. Robert Sherrill, ". . . We Also Want Four Hundred Billion Dollars Back Pay," *Esquire* 71(1) (1969): 72–75, 146–148.

5. Bracey, *Black Nationalism,* 513–517; Wilson Jeremiah Moses, *The Golden Age of Black Nationalism, 1850–1925* (Hamden, CT, 1978); Susan Carle, "Debunking the Myth of Civil Rights Liberalism: Visions of Racial Justice in

the Thought of T. Thomas Fortune, 1880–1890," *Fordham Law Review* 77 (2009): 1479–1533.

6. Imari Abubakari Obadele, "Reparations Yes! A Suggestion Toward the Framework of a Reparations Demand and a Set of Legal Underpinnings," in Chokwe Lumumba, Imari Abubakari Obadele, and Nkechi Taifa, (eds.), *Reparations Yes!* 4th ed. (Baton Rouge, 1995), 23, 57–58, quoting Imari A. Obadele, *A Beginner's Outline of the History of the Afrikan People* (Washington, DC, 1987), 19–20; Imari Abubakari Obadele, *Revolution and Nation-Building* (Detroit, 1970), 16–17; Imari Obadele, "The Struggle Is for Land," *Black Scholar* 3 (Feb. 1972): 24–32.

7. Francis Wilkinson, "The Lives They Lived; Segregationist Dreamer: Milton Henry b. 1919," *New York Times,* Dec. 31, 2006, 1; J. Todd Moye, *Freedom Flyers: The Tuskegee Airmen of World War II* (New York, 2010), 9–12, 107–108, 180; Hank Kilbanoff, "Vera Robinson Henry, 92, Mother of the Family of the Year in 1966," *Philadelphia Inquirer,* Oct. 30, 1988.

8. James Mosby interview of Milton Henry, July 11, 1970, Civil Rights Documentation Project, Ralph J. Bunche Oral History Collection, Moorland-Spingarn Research Center Manuscript Division, Howard University, Washington, DC, 699-1 to 699-645; Imari Abubakari Obadele I, "The Republic of New Africa—An Independent Black Nation," *Black World* 20 (May 1971): 81–89.

9. Malcolm X, "Message to the Grassroots," Northern Negro Grass Roots Leadership Conference, Detroit, MI, Nov. 10, 1963; Nkechi Taifa, "Reparations and Self-Determination," in Lumumba et al., *Reparations Yes!,* 1–12; Imari Abubakari Obadele, "Reparations Yes!," 23–66.

10. Imari Abubakari Obadele, *Foundations of the Black Nation* (Detroit, 1975), 5–9.

11. Obadele, "Struggle Is for Land," 31; Undated letter from Chokwe Lumumba, Detroit Consul Republic of New Africa, to Brothers and Sisters; Imari Obadele, *Freedom: The Eight Strategic Elements Necessary for Success of a Black Nation in America* (1968); W. E. B. Du Bois, *The Souls of Black Folk* (Chicago, 1903), ch. 7.

12. Obadele, "Struggle Is for Land," 24–32; Obadele, "Reparations Yes!," 60–61; Obadele, *Foundations,* 9–10.

13. Unlike some advocates for reparations, New Afrikans opposed efforts to limit the compensable period of injury. Compare Obadele, "Reparations Yes!," 23–24, with Boris Bittker, *The Case for Black Reparations* (New York, 1973).

14. Imari Abubakari Obadele, *Free the Land!: The True Story of the Trials of the RNA-11 in Mississippi and the Continuing Struggle to Establish an Independent Black Nation in Five States of the Deep South* (Washington, DC, 1984), 9, 27; Obadele, *Foundations,* 16.

15. Chokwe Lumumba, "Notes on Reparations for New Afrikans in America," in Lumumba et al., *Reparations Yes!,* 21–22.

16. Malcolm X, "A Declaration of Independence," Mar. 12, 1964 (press conference).

17. Obadele, *Foundations of the Black Nation,* XI, 13–16; Obadele, *Free the Land!,* 8; Obadele, "Republic of New Afrika," 89; Sherrill, "Four Hundred Billion Dollars," 75.

18. David Walker, *Appeal in Four Articles, Together with a Preamble to the Coloured Citizens of the World, But in Particular, and Very Expressly, to Those of the United States of America,* 3rd ed. (Boston, 1830), 4, 30.

19. *Black Manifesto,* Black National Economic Conference, Apr. 26, 1969; *Black Panther Platform and Program,* Oct. 1966; Mark S. Weiner, *Black Trials: Citizenship from the Beginnings of Slavery to the End of Caste* (New York, 2004), 307–310; Hugh Pearson, *In the Shadow of the Panther, Huey Newton and the Price of Black Power in America* (Cambridge, MA, 1996); Elijah Muhammad, *The Genesis Years: Unpublished and Rare Writings of Elijah Muhammad* (Phoenix, 2003), 446.

20. Malcolm X, "Message to the Grassroots."

21. Malcolm X, Speech, "God's Judgment of White America," New York, NY, Dec. 4, 1963.

22. Form letter from Brother Milton R. Henry, Mar. 3, 1968, quoted in "National Conference of the Malcolm X Society to be Held in Detroit on March 30–31, 1968, at the Central United Church of Christ, (CUCC), 7625 Linwood," Confidential Detroit Police Department Memorandum, Mar. 27, 1968; New Afrikan Declaration of Independence, Mar. 31, 1968.

23. Mosby interview of Milton Henry, 699-638; "Max Stanford Calls for Independent Black Nation," in Bracey, *Black Nationalism,* 516; Sherrill, "Four Hundred Billion Dollars," 75.

24. Mosby interview of Milton Henry, 699--30; Code of Umoja, preamble; art. I, §§ 1–6; art. III, § 1 (as amended, May 1999).

25. Code of Umoja, preamble; Sherrill, "Four Hundred Billion Dollars," 148.

26. Amendment to Code of Umoja, preamble, art. I, § 6, Mar. 28, 1997.

27. Sherrill, "Four Hundred Billion Dollars," 73–75; Diane C. Fujino, *Heartbeat of Struggle: The Revolutionary Life of Yuri Kochiyama* (Minneapolis, 2005), 177–185.

28. Code of Umoja, art. IV, § 1.

29. Ibid., art. III, § 2.

30. Ibid., art. IV, §§ 1–3; art. V, § 1.

31. Obadele, *Foundations,* 29, 56; Obadele, *Free the Land!,* 110–111; *The New Afrikan Creed* (as amended, 1993).

32. Code of Umoja, art. I, § 7.

33. Obadele, *Free the Land!,* 126; *New African Ujamaa: The Economics of the Republic of New Africa* (San Francisco, 1970), preamble.

34. Obadele, *Foundations,* 37–38; Obadele, *Free the Land!,* 22; Judicial Statute, § 12 (as amended, Nov. 30, 1985).

35. Judicial Statute, §§ 8, ¶ 4; 10; 13; Code of Umoja, arts. III, § 2; VI, §§ 1–4; Judicial Statute, §§ 2, 5, 6–9.

36. Obadele, *Foundations,* 42–48; Obadele, *Free the Land!,* 110–111.

37. Robert F. Williams, "Can Negroes Afford to Be Pacifists?," *Liberation* 4 (1959): 4–7; Robert F. Williams, *Negroes with Guns* (New York, 1962), 54–55;

Timothy B. Tyson, *Radio Free Dixie: Robert F. Williams and the Roots of Black Power* (Chapel Hill, 1999), 297–298.

38. Administrative Handbook, ch. III.
39. *Government Administration, Republic of New Africa*, 17–18, 23.
40. Imari Abubakari Obadele, "The Malcolm Generation," in Obadele, *The Malcolm Generation & Other Stories* (Baton Rouge, 1982), 26–56.
41. Imari Abubakari Obadele, "The Killing," in Obadele, *The Malcolm Generation & Other Stories*, 1–12.
42. Assata-Nicole Richards, "A Profile of the Leaders of the Provisional Government of the Republic of New Afrika 1968–1980: Employing Intelligence and Counterintelligence Information from State Authorities as Data Sources to Study Social Movement Activists" (M.A. Thesis, Penn State University, 2005), 78–81.
43. George W. Crockett Jr., "A Black Judge Speaks," *Judicature* 53 (1969–1970): 360–365.
44. "RNA President Henry Says Shooting 'Was a Set Up'," *Jet,* Apr. 17, 1969, 29–30; "Williams Resigns as Head of Black Separatist Group," *New York Times,* Dec. 4, 1969, 60; Russell J. Rickford, *Betty Shabazz: A Remarkable Story of Survival and Faith Before and After Malcolm X* (Naperville, IL, 2003), 327–328.
45. Mosby Interview of Milton Henry, 699-619 to 699-623, 699-627 to 699-628.
46. Sherrill, "Four Hundred Billion Dollars," 73–75.
47. Raymond L. Hall, *Black Separatism in the United States* (Hanover, NH, 1978), 220–222; Mosby interview of Milton Henry, 699-635.
48. UN International Covenant on Civil and Political Rights, Dec. 16, 1966; Obadele, "Struggle Is for Land," 26–27; Deborah Denard, "The Republic of New Africa: International Legal Implications," *Texas Southern University Law Review* 6 (1979–1980): 161–180.
49. Obadele, *Free the Land!*, 23; Malcolm X Society, "Proposed Provisional Government" (undated), 10; Obadele, "Reparations Yes!," 43.
50. Obadele, *Free the Land!*, 28–29.
51. "The Southern Development Project # 1: Establishment of the Capital" (undated); Obadele, "Proposals for the Black Agenda," in Obadele, *Foundations,* 64.
52. William L. Van Deburg, *New Day in Babylon: The Black Power Movement and American Culture, 1965–1975* (Chicago, 1992), 132–140.
53. Obadele, "Republic of New Afrika," 89; Obadele, *Foundations,* 26.
54. Jon Nordheimer, "Black 'Nation' Vexes Mississippi," *New York Times,* Apr. 10, 1971; Obadele, *Free the Land!*, 74–75.
55. Nelson Blackstock, *COINTELPRO: The FBI's Secret War on Political Freedom* (New York, 1975); Memorandum from SAC Detroit to FBI Director, "Counterintelligence Program Black Nationalist—Hate Groups Racial Intelligence (Republic of New Afrika)," Nov. 22, 1968, reprinted in Ward Churchill and Jim Vander Wall, *The COINTELPRO Papers: Documents from the FBI's Secret Wars Against Dissent in the United States* (Cambridge,

MA, 2002), 18–22; Excerpt from Dec. 2, 1970 Memorandum, in Churchill and Vander Wall, 122; Obadele, *Free the Land!*, 264–271.

56. "Mississippi Seeks to Arrest Leaders of Black 'Republic,'" *New York Times,* May 9, 1971; Obadele, *Free the Land!*, 74–75.

57. Obadele, *Free the Land!*, 74–75, 80–85.

58. Ibid., 84–87; Lewis Hugh Wilson, "The Hawkish Doves: A History of the Republic of New Afrika" (M.A. thesis, Mississippi College, 1986).

59. Obadele, *Free the Land!*, 109–115.

60. Imari Abubakari Obadele I, "The Struggle of the Republic of New Africa," *Black Scholar* (June 1974): 34.

61. United States v. James, 408 F. Supp. 527 (D. Miss. 1973).

62. "Policeman Dies; Separatists Charged," *New York Times,* Aug. 20, 1971, 15; "Grand Jury Set for 11 Separatists in Mississippi," *New York Times,* Aug. 24, 1971, 24; "3 Police Shot in Dixie Raid on Black Separatist Colony," *Detroit Free Press,* Aug. 19, 1971, 1A; "4 Black Separatists Freed, Leader Is Held for Inquiry," *New York Times,* Oct. 12, 1971, 18; Obadele, *Free the Land!*, 147.

63. "Black Jacksonians for Justice" (undated flyer).

64. Obadele, *Free the Land!*, 173, 191–195, 208, 220–222; *Jackson Daily News,* May 31, 1973, A1; *Jackson Clarion-Ledger,* June 1, 1973, B1; *Jackson Daily News,* June 18, 1973, A1.

65. Ron Harrist, "Judge Rules RNA Not Sovereign," *Jackson Clarion-Ledger,* June 28, 1973, 1A, 4A; Wilson, "The Hawkish Doves," 58–79. Officials of the Republic of New Afrika continued to make arguments of diplomatic and sovereign immunity, to no avail. United States v. Lumumba, 741 F.2d 12 (2d Cir. 1984).

66. United States v. James, 528 F.2d 999 (5th Cir. 1976); Wilson, "The Hawkish Doves," 80–85.

67. Obadele, "Struggle of the Republic," 32–41; Robert Deleon, "Plight of Ex-Air Force Vet, Pregnant Wife in Mississippi Told to Jet," *Jet,* Sept. 23, 1971, 6–8.

68. Imari Abubakari Obadele I, "Staying and Winning: The Struggle for Land and Independence in Mississippi," *Black World,* Feb. 1974, 90–91.

69. Obadele, *Free the Land!*, 145, 167–168, 276–282; Code of Umoja, art. VIII, § 2(B).

70. Obadele, *Free the Land!*, 281.

71. *Excerpts from An Appeal for United Nations Action to End a Threat to World Peace and Preserve the Human Rights of the New African People in America,* Sept. 1972.

72. Obadele, *Free the Land!*, 317.

73. Obadele, "Proposals for the Black Agenda to the National Black Political Convention in Gary, Indiana," in Obadele, *Foundations,* 62; Adjoa A. Aiyetoro and Adrienne D. Davis, "Historic and Modern Social Movements for Reparations: The National Coalition of Blacks for Reparations in America (N'COBRA) and Its Antecedents," *Texas Wesleyan Law Review* 17 (2010): 687–766.

74. Imari Obadele, "A Request for Definitive Action at the Democratic National Convention: A Statement to the Mississippi Loyalty Delegation," June 1972,

in Obadele, *Foundations*, 66–71; Imari Obadele, "Address to National Black Political Assembly, Chicago, Illinois (From Hinds County Jail)," Oct. 21, 1972, in Obadele, *Foundations*, 136–140; Obadele, "Solzhenitsyn, Kristol, and a Black Nation on the Gulf Coast," in Obadele, *Foundations*, 141–148.

75. Obadele, *Free the Land!*, 242–245; *New Afrikan Brief*, Mar. 1976, 2.
76. Obadele, *Free the Land!*, 325–327; Obadele, "Struggle of the Republic," 40.
77. Chokwe Lumumba, *Position Paper of the Provisional Government of the Republic of New Afrika on the Arrest of People Center Council Chairperson Fulani Sunni Ali (Cynthia Boston)*, Nov. 2, 1981, reprinted in *Black World*, Nov. 18, 1981, 3, 10–11, 14; Obadele, *Free the Land!*, 333–337; Arnold H. Lubasch, "Brink's Suspect Released After F.B.I. Checks Alibi," *New York Times*, Nov. 6, 1981, A1, B4; Colin Campbell, "Suspect Freed in Brink's Case Charges Persecution," *New York Times*, Nov. 7, 1981, 26.
78. Robert McFadden, "Brink's Holdup Spurs U.S. Inquiry on Links among Terrorist Groups," *New York Times*, Oct. 25, 1981, 1, 40; Obadele, *Free the Land!*, 336–337; "Brink's Figure Wins Her Release," *New York Times*, Oct. 20, 1983, B4.
79. Hall, *Black Separatism in the United States*, 216–217; Donald Cunnigen, "The Republic of New Africa in Mississippi," in Judson L. Jeffries, *Black Power: In the Belly of the Beast* (Urbana, IL, 2006), 93–115; Darren Hutchinson, "Racial Exhaustion," *Washington University Law Review* 86 (2009): 917–974.

8. The Pacific Northwest Homeland, 2006

1. David C. Rapoport, "Before the Bombs There Were the Mobs: American Experiences with Terror," *Terrorism and Political Violence* 20(2) (2008): 167–194.
2. Oregon Constitution, art. I, §§ 31, 34, 35 (1857); Idaho Constitution, art. 6, § 3; art. 13, § 5 (1890).
3. Sonia Scherr and Laurie Wood, "Little Big Man: Brother Discusses Neo-Nazi Harold Covington," *Intelligence Report* (Southern Poverty Law Center, Winter 2008), 2–3; Nicholas Goodrick-Clarke, *Black Sun: Aryan Cults, Esoteric Nazism, and the Politics of Identity* (New York, 2002), 7.

   For studies of political and legal backlash against *Brown v. Board of Education*, see Michael Klarman, *From Jim Crow to Civil Rights: The Supreme Court and the Struggle for Racial Equality* (New York, 2004); Gerald N. Rosenberg, *The Hollow Hope: Can Courts Bring About Social Change?* (Chicago, 1991). For a study of the legal strategy to overthrow racial apartheid in America, see Mark Tushnet, *The NAACP's Legal Strategy against Segregated Education, 1925–1950* (Chapel Hill, 2005).

4. Leonard Zeskind, *Blood and Politics: The History of the White Nationalist Movement from the Margins to the Mainstream* (New York, 2009), 47; Elizabeth Wheaton, *Codename GREENKIL: The 1979 Greensboro Killings* (Athens, GA, 1987), 73–76, 209–210.
5. Raphael S. Ezekiel, *The Racist Mind: Portraits of Neo-Nazis and Klansmen* (New York, 1995), 132; Goodrick-Clarke, *Black Sun*, 232–256; Betty A. Do-

bratz and Stephanie L. Shanks-Meile, *"White Power, White Pride!" The White Separatist Movement in the United States* (New York, 1997), 89–162.

6. Amended Complaint for Damages and Injunctive Relief and Demand for a Jury Trial, Keenan v. Aryan Nations et al. (District Court of Idaho, Kootenai County), Case No. CV 99-441, May 24, 1999.

7. "Human Rights Center Opens in Idaho Five Years After SPLC Lawsuit," Dec. 13, 2005, www.splcenter.org; Harold Covington, Oct. 16, 2003 entry, *Northwest Homeland,* accessed Sept. 30, 2011, www.nwhomeland.blogspot .com.

8. Nicholas K. Geranios, "Aryan Nations' Compound, Name Sold," *Asian-Week,* Feb. 23–Mar. 1, 2001.

9. Aryan Nations Declaration of Independence, Mar. 12, 1996. The Aryan Nations' *Twelve Foundation Stones for the Redemption of Our Racial Nation* affirmed a handful of principles expressed elsewhere: human law must reflect the values of the "racial nation," there could be no "separation of the 'spiritual' worship state and the political state," and government must be based on racial identity. Mattias Gardell, *Gods of the Blood: The Pagan Revival and White Separatism* (Durham, NC, 2003), 113–114.

10. "Fundamental Principles of Northwest Migration," in *The Northwest Migration Handbook,* 11.

11. "The Butler Plan," in *The Northwest Migration Handbook* (2003), 12–21.

12. The Butler Plan, "The Homeland."

13. *The Northwest Migration Handbook,* 2 (Introduction).

14. The plan was "[r]espectfully dedicated to the Reverend Richard Girnt Butler—a gallant Christian gentleman."

15. Nehemiah Township Charter and Common Law Contract, July 11, 1982. Filed with the Clerk of Kootenai County, Idaho, the document has been cited in actions challenging tax and licensing laws. See Michael Barkun, *Religion and the Racist Right: The Origins of the Christian Identity Movement* (Chapel Hill, 1997), 218–223; Zeskind, *Blood and Politics,* 69–77, 96–106; Allen D. Sapp, "The Nehemiah Township Charter: Applied Right Wing Ideology," Center for Criminal Justice Research, Central Missouri State University, Mar. 1986. In the 1980s Pete Peters undertook a project to file the "Remnant Resolves," a series of policy and legal positions composing a Christian covenant, in every one of the 3,049 courthouses in America. Barkun, *Religion and the Racist Right,* 220.

16. Nehemiah Charter Preamble, §§ 11–13, 22, 26, 31 (1982); Michael Barkun, "Violence in the Name of Democracy: Justifications for Separation on the Radical Right," *Terrorism and Political Violence* 12(3) (2000): 193–208.

17. Barkun, *Religion and the Racist Right,* 206–209; The Butler Plan, Phase Two.

18. The Butler Plan.

19. Ibid.; H. A. Covington, *A Distant Thunder* (2004), 59.

20. Brian Levin, "Cyberhate: A Legal and Historical Analysis of Extremists' Use of Computer Networks in America," *American Behavioral Scientist* 45(6) (2002): 958–988; ACLU v. Reno, 521 U.S. 844 (1997).

21. Northwest Homeland Blog, accessed Aug. 6, 2009, nwhomeland.blogspot.com /2003_10_16_archive.html.
22. T. R. Reid, "'Neo-Nazis' Inspire White Supremacists: Wave of Crime, Terrorism Tied to Novel," *Washington Post,* Dec. 26, 1984, A3, 8; Laura Parker, "U.S. Alleges Overthrow Plot," *Washington Post,* Dec. 12, 1984, A-3, 7–8; Sam Meddis, "Neo-Nazis Weakened, FBI says," *USA Today,* Feb. 18, 1985, 3A; "10 Guilty in Neo-Nazi Plot," *Los Angeles Times,* Dec. 30, 1985.
23. H. A. Covington, *The Hill of the Ravens* (2003), 13.
24. Ibid., 9.
25. Ibid., 100–101.
26. Covington, *A Distant Thunder,* 20.
27. H. A. Covington, *A Mighty Fortress* (2005), 87–88.
28. Memorandum to Director of FBI re: Christian Identity Movement, Right-Wing Terrorism Matters, Apr. 23, 1989, 4–5 ("Identity and the U.S. Constitution").
29. Covington, *A Mighty Fortress,* 19.
30. Ibid., 31–32.
31. Harold Covington, Feb. 15, 2006, in *Thoughtcrime,* accessed Sept. 30, 2011, http:downwithjugears.blogspot.com/2006_02_01_archive.html.
32. Harold Covington, Feb. 19, 2006, in *Thoughtcrime,* accessed Sept. 30, 2011, http://downwithjugears.blogspot.com/2006_02_01_archive.html.
33. Carl Sipton e-mail interview of Harold Covington, June 2009, Answer to Question 2; Answer to Question 13.
34. The Northwest American Republic Constitution has been published on the Northwest Front's website since the summer of 2009. Accessed Sept. 29, 2011, http://northwestfront.org/about/nar-constitution/.
35. Northwest American Republic Constitution, June 2006 Draft Outline, HAC Notes, June 2, 2006, http: http://groups.yahoo.com/group/UnitedAryan-Front/message/938 (last visited Sept. 14, 2011). Covington explained: "That October 2006 draft will probably stand for the NF for a long time. Everyone seems to like it, and I see no reason at present to re-open the subject." Sipton Interview of Covington, Answer to Question 8.
36. David Lane, *14 Words;* Northwest American Republic Constitution, § 1, arts. I, II.
37. Ibid., § 1, art. III.
38. Ibid., § 1, arts. IV, V; Gomillion v. Lightfoot, 364 U.S. 339 (1960); Harper v. Virginia State Board of Elections, 383 U.S. 663 (1966).
39. Northwest American Republic Constitution, § 1, art. VI; *The Northwest Migration Handbook,* 39–43 ("Building a New Racial Elite"); Rhodesia Constitution (1969); *Proposals for a New Constitution of Rhodesia* (Salisbury, 1969), 1; Richard Hodder Williams, "Rhodesia's Search for a Constitution: Or, Whatever Happened to Whaley?," *African Affairs* 69(276) (1970): 217–235; Reynolds v. Sims, 377 U.S. 533 (1964).
40. Northwest American Republic Constitution, § 1, arts. VII–VIII; § 2, art. III.
41. David Lane, *88 Precepts,* No. 29.
42. The group's position on abortion may be less absolutist than it appeared. Elsewhere, the Northwest Front voiced its policy preference for a system

requiring abortion to be performed only based on a court order and medical certification that a fetus is deformed or mentally retarded. The Program of the Northwest Front, § 4, accessed Aug. 20, 2009, http://northwestfront.org/nfprogram.html; Northwest American Republic Constitution § 5, arts. III, IV. The constitution established five grounds for revocation or reduction of citizenship: felony conviction; mental defect or insanity; "proven non-White racial descent to include Jewish ancestry"; willful miscegenation with non-whites; and proof of acts of homosexuality. On the history of antimiscegenation laws and their demise, see Ariela J. Gross, *What Blood Won't Tell: A History of Race on Trial in America* (Cambridge, MA, 2010); Peggy Pascoe, *What Comes Naturally: Miscegenation and the Making of Race in America* (New York, 2009).

43. Northwest American Republic Constitution, § 1, art. IX.

44. Law Against the Establishment of Parties, July 14, 1933, in R. E. Murphy et al., *National Socialism* (Washington, DC, 1943); Northwest American Republic Constitution, § 2, arts. I, VI.

45. Northwest American Republic Constitution, § 2, art. II(1).

46. Ibid., § 3, art. II.

47. Covington added this commentary to the draft of § 3, art. II: "Law-making resides in the people, not some tyrant in a black robe." Sipton Interview of Covington, Answer to Question 6 ("We all know the terrible, terrible destruction of our social fabric which has been inflicted by activist judges and the Supreme Court over the last 50 years who no longer merely interpret or enforce the law, but who create it through such egregious horse shit as finding a nonexistent "right to privacy" in the Constitution to justify infanticide.").

48. Act to Constitute the Republic of South Africa and to Provide for Matters Incidental Thereto, Part III, Apr. 24, 1961; Northwest American Republic Constitution, § 2, arts. VII, IX.

49. Northwest American Republic Constitution, § 3, art. IX.

50. Liberals, too, have called for the codification of emergency power mechanisms. Bruce Ackerman, *Before the Next Attack: Preserving Civil Liberties in an Age of Terrorism* (New Haven, 2006); John Hart Ely, *War and Responsibility: Constitutional Lessons of Vietnam and Its Aftermath* (Princeton, 1995).

51. Northwest American Republic Constitution, § 4, art. I. For a comparison, see U.S. Constitution, amend. II.

52. Northwest American Republic Constitution, § 4, art. II.

53. Harold Covington, blog entry, Feb. 19, 2006; Northwest Front Seven Points, Point V; Covington, *Hill of Ravens*, vii (describing Christian Identity as the "very backbone of the Northwest nation" despite its "tenuous . . . historical and theological basis").

54. Northwest American Republic Constitution, § 3, arts. VI, VIII.

Index